HELLENISM
in the
LAND
of
ISRAEL

Christianity and Judaism in Antiquity Series

Gregory E. Sterling, *Series Editor*

VOLUME 13

The University of Notre Dame Press gratefully acknowledges the generous support of Jack and Joan Conroy of Naples, Florida, in the publication of titles in this series.

HELLENISM

IN THE
LAND
OF
ISRAEL

John J. Collins · *Gregory E. Sterling*

EDITORS

UNIVERSITY OF NOTRE DAME PRESS

Notre Dame, Indiana

Designed by Wendy McMillen
Set in 10.8/13.2 Minion by Stanton Publication Services, Inc.
Printed in the USA by Edwards Brothers, Inc.

Manufactured in the United States of America

Library of Congress Cataloging-in-Publication Data
Hellenism in the land of Israel / John J. Collins and Gregory E. Sterling, editors.
    p. cm. — (Christianity and Judaism in antiquity ; v. 13)
    Includes bibliographical references (p.) and index.
    ISBN 0-268-03051-0 (cloth : alk. paper) — ISBN 0-268-03052-9 (pbk. : alk. paper)
    1. Judaism—Relations—Greek. 2. Greece—Religion. 3. Jews—Civilization—
Greek influences. 4. Hellenism. 5. Jews—History—586 B.C.–70 A.D.
6. Judaism—History—Post-exilic period, 586 B.C.–210 A.D. I. Collins, John J.
    II. Sterling, Gregory. III. Series.

BM536.G7H45 2000
296'.0933'09014—dc21

00-055988

∞ *This book is printed on acid-free paper.*

Christianity and Judaism in Antiquity Series (CJAS)

The Christianity and Judaism in Antiquity Program at the University of Notre Dame came into existence during the afterglow of the Second Vatican Council. The doctoral program combines the distinct academic disciplines of the Hebrew Bible, Judaism, the New Testament, and the Early Church in an effort to explore the religion of the ancient Hebrews, the diverse forms of Second Temple Judaism, and its offspring into religions of Rabbinic Judaism and the multiple incarnations of early Christianity. While the scope of the program thus extends from the late Bronze and Early Iron Ages to the late antique world, the fulcrum lies in the Second Temple and Early Christian periods. Each religion is explored in its own right, although the program cultivates a History-of-Religions approach that examines their reciprocally illuminating interrelationships and their place in the larger context of the ancient world.

During the 1970s a monograph series was launched to reflect and promote the orientation of the program. Initially known as Studies in Judaism and Christianity in Antiquity, the series was published under the auspices of the Center of the Study of Judaism and Christianity in Antiquity. Six volumes appeared from 1975 to 1986. In 1988 the series name became Christianity and Judaism in Antiquity as the editorship passed to Charles Kannengiesser, who oversaw the release of nine volumes. Professor Kannengiesser's departure from Notre Dame necessitated the appointment of a new editor. At the same time, the historic connection between the series and the CJA doctoral program was strengthened by the appointment of all CJA faculty to the editorial board. Throughout these institutional permutations, the purpose of the series has continued to be the promotion of research into the origins of Judaism and Christianity with the hope that a better grasp of the common ancestry and relationship of the two world's religions will illuminate not only the ancient world but the modern world as well.

Gregory Sterling, *Series Editor*

Contents

Abbreviations

Abbreviations of journals, reference works, and other secondary sources generally conform to Patrick Alexander et al., eds., *The SBL Handbook of Style* (Peabody, Mass.: Hendrickson, 1999). For abbreviations not listed in *The SBL Handbook of Style*, consult the following list.

ASORDS   American Schools of Oriental Research Dissertation Series
BS 2   *Beth She'arim II.* Edited by M. Schwabe and B. Lifshitz. New Brunswick, 1974
BTAVO   Beihefte zum Tübinger Atlas des Vorderen Orients
CPR   Corpus Papyrorum Raineri
ESI   Excavations and Surveys in Israel
GELS   *A Greek-English Lexicon of the Septuagint.* Edited by J. Lust, E. Eynikel, K. Hauspie. 2 vols. Stuttgart, 1992–96
GLAJJ   *Greek and Latin Authors on Jews and Judaism.* Edited by M. Stern. 3 vols. Jerusalem, 1974–84
JRA   Journal of Roman Archaeology
IAA   Israeli Antiquities Authority
INJ   Israel Numismatic Journal
JANES   Journal of the Ancient Near Eastern Society
SFSHJ   South Florida Studies in the History of Judaism
SPhA   The Studia Philonica Annual

Introduction

JOHN J. COLLINS
GREGORY E. STERLING

The conquests of Alexander the Great rank—on any reckoning—among the most momentous events of world history. Others before Alexander had established empires in the Near East, but there was no precedent for the blending of cultures from East and West that followed in the succeeding centuries. Alexander laid the foundation on which the Romans would build the cosmopolitan edifice of Western civilization. Of the various encounters between Greeks and oriental peoples, none was more momentous than the engagement with the Jews. Alexander, to be sure, wasted no time in Judea, and the story of his visit to Jerusalem is patent legend.[1] But when the powers of the East, Egyptian, Babylonian, and Persian, were buried by the sands of history, the Jews would continue to play a vital role in Western culture. Their historical significance was augmented by the rise of Christianity, which had originated as a Jewish sect, to a position of dominance in the West, but it did not depend on the success of this offshoot. While Christianity was still in its infancy, the Roman philosopher Seneca, who was no philo-Semite, acknowledged bitterly that "the customs of this accursed race have gained such influence that they are now received throughout all the world. The vanquished have given their laws to the victors."[2] In fact, while Greek philosophy, art and literature would become canonical in Western culture, Jewish traditions, largely mediated through Christianity, would have a decisive impact on Western religion. Much of Christian theology can be described fairly as the attempt to appropriate Jewish traditions in the categories of Greek thought.

Since the work of J. G. Droysen in the nineteenth century, the blending of cultures that followed the conquests of Alexander has been labeled "Hellenism."[3] The Greek verb ἑλληνίζειν was used by Aristotle to refer to the mastery of the Greek language.[4] The nominal form ἑλληνισμός, in the same sense, is credited to his pupil Theophrastes.[5] The broader use of the term to refer to Greek culture and customs first occurs in 2 Maccabees, where the building of a gymnasium in Jerusalem in the time of Antiochus IV Epiphanes is said to have led to ἀκμή τις ἑλληνισμοῦ, an extreme of Hellenism.[6] The usage in 2 Maccabees regards Hellenism as specifically Greek culture, something foreign to Judaism (a term which also first appears in 2 Maccabees). This is what Hellenism continued to mean until the work of Droysen, and it remains a common connotation of the term. Droysen altered the usage when he took "Hellenism to mean specifically the way of thinking of Jews under the influence of Greek language and thought, but generally the language and way of thinking of all the population which had been conquered by Alexander and subjected to Greek influence."[7] There is then some confusion as to whether Hellenism refers to the mixture of Greek and Oriental cultures or only to the Greek component in that mixture. Droysen has been criticized for creating too synthetic a picture of Hellenism. In the words of Yaacov Shavit: "This picture painted by Droysen ignored the heterogeneous character of Hellenism in various Eastern lands, and the difference in character and content of the Hellenistic component from one syncretistic culture to another." He continues: "It also ignored the continued existence of age-old autochthonous cultures with their own traditions; the manner in which these cultures came to terms with universal (and imperialistic) Hellenism; and the influence of those very cultures upon Greek immigrant settlers and their descendants."[8]

In modern scholarship, "Hellenistic Judaism" has traditionally meant the Judaism of the Diaspora, where the dominant, and often the only language, was Greek. The Judaism of Hellenistic Egypt, in particular, has left a rich literary legacy.[9] In writings such as those of the philosophically minded Philo, the pervasive influence of Greek philosophy and rhetoric is beyond dispute, although there remains a streak of stubborn particularism in Philo's Jewish identity.[10] The impact of Hellenism in the land of Israel, however, has been much more controversial.

Recent discussion of this issue has centered mainly on the great work of Martin Hengel, *Judaism and Hellenism*.[11] Hengel argued vigorously that Judaism in the land of Israel was also Hellenistic Judaism.

Even Jews who expressed themselves in Hebrew and Aramaic were influenced by Hellenistic culture in various ways. This was true even of people who consciously rejected Hellenistic culture, like the Essenes of Qumran. Hengel's thesis has not gone unopposed,[12] but it has been buttressed by several subsequent studies, both by Hengel himself[13] and by others.[14] If the word "Hellenistic" is understood in Droysen's sense as the blending of Greek and Near Eastern cultures, then there can be little dispute that Hengel is right. All the essays in this volume, in their various ways, provide corroborating evidence of the influence of Greek culture in Judea and Galilee, from before the Maccabean revolt on into the rabbinic period. There remains, however, the question of the limits of that influence, the persistence of Semitic languages and thought patterns and especially the exclusiveness of Jewish religion. Judaism in the land of Israel was decisively altered by its encounter with the Greeks, and in that sense it is properly described as Hellenistic Judaism. But Judaism remained nonetheless distinctive in the Greco-Roman world, and the Hebrew and Aramaic-speaking Judaism of the homeland remained distinct from the Hellenistic Judaism of the Diaspora. Hellenistic Judaism was heterogeneous, and its relation to Greek culture was never simply one of either assimilation or repudiation. The variety of ways in which Jews in Israel responded to and appropriated Greek culture is the subject of the essays in this volume.

Martin Hengel opens the volume with a vigorous restatement of the thesis of his classic *Judaism and Hellenism,* which is revisited in light of many new discoveries, but not revised. Hengel reviews the ideological conflict prior to the Maccabean revolt, and goes on to review the Hellenism of the Samaritans and the Hasmoneans. It should be noted that a supplementary article on Hellenism and Qumran is published separately in a volume on religion in the Dead Sea Scrolls.[15] John Collins probes the limits of hellenization in Judea, taking the conflict that culminated in the Maccabean revolt as a test case. Erich Gruen casts his net widely in a review of Jewish attitudes to Greek culture, which is broadly supportive of Hengel's thesis. Robert Doran adds further critical reflections on this era in his study of Jason's gymnasium and its portrayal in 2 Maccabees. Jan Willem van Henten and Edgar Krentz analyze a specific illustration of the Hellenism of the Hasmoneans, the honorary decree for Simon Maccabee in 1 Maccabees 14. Piet van der Horst reviews the use of Greek language and Hellenistic conventions in Jewish inscriptions. His review is supplemented by James VanderKam's account of the Greek materials in the Dead Sea Scrolls. Sean Freyne provides a study of regional variety by examining the evidence for Galileans, Phoenicians, and Itureans in the Hellenistic and Roman periods. Shaye Cohen extends the chronological range of the volume into the rabbinic period by examining some of the more subtle forms of Hellenistic influence. Tessa Rajak explores Josephus' understanding of those whom he considered barbarians, Greeks, and Jews. Gregory E. Sterling compares and contrasts the "Hellenistic Judaism" of Judea with that of Alexandria. Martin Goodman closes the volume in an epilogue that offers some reflections on the basic issues raised by the contributions.

The essays in this volume originated as papers at a conference on Hellenism in the Land of Israel, co-sponsored by the University of Chicago and the University of Notre Dame, April 18–20, 1999. The conference fell into two parts: the first addressed the Jewish encounter with Hellenism during the second century BCE and was held at the University of Chicago; the second part explored the encounter after the Romans entered the picture and was conducted at the University of Notre Dame. The discussion was enriched by the contributions of several scholars who participated in the conference in various ways but are not represented in this volume: Harold Attridge (Yale), Mary Rose D'Angelo (University of Notre Dame), Hanan Eshel (Bar Ilan University), Margaret Mitchell (University of Chicago), and Thomas H. Tobin (Loyola University, Chicago). We would like to acknowledge the support of the Divinity School and the Committee on Jewish Studies at the University of Chicago and the support of the Department of Theology and the Paul M. and Barbara Henkels Visiting Scholars Series at the University of Notre Dame, which made this conference possible.

Notes

1. Josephus, *Ant.* 11.329–39; E. S. Gruen, *Heritage and Hellenism: The Reinvention of Jewish Tradition* (Berkeley: University of California, 1998) 189–99.

2. Seneca, *De Superstitione*, apud Augustine, *City of God* 6.11; M. Stern, *Greek and Latin Authors on Jews and Judaism* (3 vols.; Jerusalem: Israel Academy of Arts and Sciences, 1976) 1.431.

3. J. G. Droysen, *Geschichte des Hellenismus* (ed. E. Bayer; 3 vols.; Tübingen: Mohr, 1952–53). Volume 1 was originally published in 1836.

4. *Rhet.* 3.5.1 (1407a 19).

5. Cicero, *Orat.* 79. See R. Bichler, *Hellenismus. Geschichte und Problematik eines Epochenbegriffs* (Darmstadt: Wissenschaftliche Buchgesellschaft, 1983) 7–8.

6. 2 Macc 4:13.

7. A. Momigliano, "J. G. Droysen between Greeks and Jews," in idem, *Essays in Ancient and Modern Historiography* (Oxford: Clarendon, 1987) 310.

8. Y. Shavit, *Athens in Jerusalem: Classical Antiquity and Hellenism in the Making of the Modern Secular Jew* (The Littman Library of Jewish Civilization; London: Vallentine Mitchell, 1997) 283.

9. G. E. Sterling, "'Thus are Israel': Jewish Self-Definition in Alexandria," *The Studia Philonica Annual* 7 (1995) 1–18; J. M. G. Barclay, *Jews in the Mediterranean Diaspora* (Edinburgh: Clark, 1996); Gruen, *Heritage and Hellenism;* J. J. Collins, *Between Athens and Jerusalem: Jewish Identity in the Hellenistic Diaspora* (revised ed.; Grand Rapids, Mich.: Eerdmans, 2000). See also the review essay of J. J. Collins, "Varieties of Judaism in the Hellenistic and Roman Periods," *Journal of Religion* 77 (1997) 605–11 and the classic work of V. Tcherikover, *Hellenistic Civilization and the Jews* (reprint with an introduction by J. J. Collins; Peabody, Mass.: Hendrickson, 1999).

10. See A. Mendelson, *Philo's Jewish Identity* (BJS 161; Atlanta: Scholars Press, 1988); E. Birnbaum, *The Place of Judaism in Philo's Thought: Israel, Jews and Proselytes* (BJS 290; Atlanta: Scholars Press, 1996).

11. M. Hengel, *Hellenism and Judaism: Studies in Their Encounter in Palestine during the Early Hellenistic Period* (2 vols.; Philadelphia: Fortress, 1974).

12. F. Millar, "The Background to the Maccabean Revolution: Reflections on Martin Hengel's *Judaism and Hellenism*," *JJS* 22 (1978) 1–21; L. H. Feldman, "Hengel's Judaism and Hellenism in Retrospect," *JBL* 96 (1977) 371–82; idem, "How Much Hellenism in Jewish Palestine?" *HUCA* 57 (1986) 83–111; idem, *Jew and Gentile in the Ancient World* (Princeton: Princeton University Press, 1992) 1–44.

13. Especially, *The 'Hellenization' of Judaea in the First Century after Christ* (Philadelphia: Trinity Press International, 1989); "Jerusalem als jüdische und hellenistische Stadt," in his *Judaica, Hellenistica et Christiana. Kleine Schriften II* (WUNT 109; Tübingen: Mohr, 1999) 115–56.

14. See especially L. I. Levine, *Judaism and Hellenism in Antiquity: Conflict or Confluence?* (Seattle: University of Washington Press, 1998).

15. J. J. Collins and R. Kugler, eds., *Aspects of Religion in the Dead Sea Scrolls* (Grand Rapids, Mich.: Eerdmans, 2000) 46–56.

Judaism and Hellenism Revisited

MARTIN HENGEL

Some Biographical Remarks

May I make a small addition to the title of my article: "Judaism and Hellenism Revisited"—*yes, but not revised.* I submitted my Habilitationsschrift in autumn 1966 to the Tübingen Faculty of Protestant Theology under the title: "Judentum und Hellenismus. Studien zu ihrer Begegnung unter besonderer Berücksichtigung Palästinas bis zur Mitte des 2. Jahrhunderts v. Chr." The English subtitle sounds (thanks to the ingenuity of the translator John Bowden) much better than the long-winded academic German one: "Studies in their Encounter in Palestine during the Early Hellenistic Period." I had written it in a bit less than two years and submitted it to the faculty with some hesitation and anxiety, because—like my dissertation about the Zealots—it was a Jewish and not a New Testament subject and I wanted to habilitate myself in the New Testament. On my fortieth birthday on December 14, 1966, Prof. Kurt Galling, the most competent expert in this field on our faculty and a very severe scholar, phoned and told me that he had read the work in three days and that he was very content: it was the greatest birthday present I ever had in my life.[1] The book appeared just thirty years ago in early summer 1969. Its subject, expressed in the title, has remained an important part of my research, but—as far as I can see—I do not have to revise its essential results. In the details of course there is much to supplement, to improve, and sometimes to correct: Research has in the last thirty years proceeded considerably. But the fundamental tendencies of my book have been confirmed, indeed strengthened, by new archeological discoveries, excavations, inscriptions, coins, and also by new texts, for example from Qumran. So I dare to maintain the main thesis without hesitation: Not only the Jews of the Greek-speaking Diaspora but also Judaism in the Palestinian mother-land since the Ptolemaic rule in the third century BCE may be called "Hellenistic Judaism," and this is even more true for the Roman era since Herod, a period which I treated twenty years later in 1989 in a smaller book of a hundred pages: *The 'Hellenization' of Judaea in the First Century after Christ.*[2] Therefore it is misleading to distinguish fun-damentally between a "Palestinian Judaism" in the motherland and "Hellenistic Judaism" in the Diaspora as is still usual. Scholars here dis-tinguish between a geographical and a cultural term. It would be more appropriate to make a distinction between languages, Greek- and Aramaic-speaking Jews, *and* between geographical regions, Babylonia, Syria, Palestine, Egypt, Asia Minor or Rome, because the Jewish Dias-pora was very differentiated, even more than Judaism in the motherland, which was not unified either. And we should not forget, especially in Jerusalem but also in Galilee or Syria and Babylonia, the bilingual Jews, who are so important for the beginnings of Christianity. This is—in a few words—one important result of my scholarly work dur-ing the last thirty years.

The comprehensive second volume, which I promised a bit too rashly in the introduction, remained unwritten. After ten years of *opera aliena* in business I had to recover lost ground in my proper field, the New Testament and the early Church, with lectures, seminars and ex-aminations, and in 1968 in Germany the student revolution began with its deep aversion to all sober historical work: Hellenism seemed to be an uninteresting theme; it smacked too much of colonialism. The Zealots got more approval. They became the subject of my inaugural lecture in Erlangen in 1969: *Was Jesus a revolutionary?* No good time for another big book about the cultural and religious problems of Hellenization and the Jews. But smaller investigations followed: *Between Jesus and Paul* about the Hellenists of Acts 6, in 1975,[3] and *Jews, Greeks and Barbarians,* in 1976, or *The Pre-Christian Paul,* in 1991, and *Paul between Damascus and Antioch,* in 1997, enlarged in German in 1998. In 1974, just twenty-five years ago, the English version of *Judaism and Hellenism* appeared in the masterly translation by John Bowden. He got the Schlegel-Tieck prize for it because of the quality of his translation. It brought a break-through in the English-speaking world.

But what was the reason that I chose this subject thirty-five years ago, when I began to write a Habilitationsschrift? It has a theological, a New Testament background. When I returned in 1954 from business (my biography is a little bit complicated) to the Tübingen Stift as a Stiftsrepetent (this means a tutor), nearly all my colleagues at the high table in the Stift seemed to be intoxicated by the sweet wine from Marburg. In the field of the New Testament in Germany during the fifties and sixties some sort of theological or historical-critical correctness predominated, which followed the *'religionsgeschichtliche Schule'* and saw in early Christianity predominantly a syncretistic Hellenistic religion, with its center, christology and soteriology, strongly influenced by mystery religions and a pre-Christian Gnosis. Even in the Gospels with their miracle stories one discovered a hellenistic *Theios-Anēr-* Christology and their authors were supposed to be anonymous pagan Christians. Especially the fourth Gospel became a half-gnostic work written by a converted Gnostic (so Bultmann), or by an Antiochean Greek (so E. Hirsch). As late as 1966, J. M. Robinson underlined "that the theological work of R. Bultmann and that of his pupils remains unchanged in the center of discussion."[4]

For the newcomer in the Tübingen Stift all these suppositions seemed to be strange and improbable. Jesus was a Galilean Jew, Paul even a Pharisee, and early Christianity had its origin in Jewish Palestine. Therefore he began to study Palestinian Judaism and wrote his dissertation about the Zealots, while cooperating in the Josephus translation of Michel/Bauernfeind. But on the other hand Paul from Tarsus was a native Greek speaker and the whole early Christian literature was written in Greek. So the catchword "Hellenism," or more exactly "Jewish Hellenism," was fundamental. But it was not—at least not in the first place—the platonizing "Jewish Hellenism" of Alexandria represented by Philo and his predecessors. Alexandria was apparently rather unimportant for the earliest Church. I had to look for "Jewish Hellenism" in the Palestinian motherland itself, because in the first twelve or fifteen years the new Messianic Jewish sect grew—as far as we know—only there and in Syria and Cilicia. If we want to clear up the beginnings of Christianity, we have to investigate first the impact of "Hellenistic civilization" in these regions.

Very quickly I recognized that it was not the *'religionsgeschichtliche Schule'* from Bousset to Reitzenstein that was the reliable guide through the labyrinth of the Hellenistic world and its religious thought but much more Rostovtzeff, Nilsson, Festugière, and A. D. Nock. For early Judaism I got decisive stimuli from Adolf Schlatter, the founder (a hundred years ago) of my later Tübingen chair, but even more from Tcherikover and especially from Elias Bickerman. His masterpiece *Der Gott der Makkabäer,* together with his essays, gave me the most important impulse for my own work. He is the scholar from whose publications I learned historical method. I could later thank him by helping him to publish his *Studies in Jewish and Christian History* in three volumes. His posthumously edited work *The Jews in the Greek Age* is by far the best later treatment of the subject, brilliantly written with unsurpassed authority. That according to the decision of the author the book was published without its "copious notes" and that "the typescript of the notes seems to have been destroyed"[5] is a sad loss for scholarship.

But what does the term "Hellenism" so popular today really mean? Elias Bickerman deliberately chose the title: "The Jews in the *Greek* Age," although he begins with a chapter "Alexander and Jerusalem." The Greek Age for him is the era of Greek-Macedonian domination in the Near East with the increasing influence of the "superior" Greek civilization, which after Alexander was most intensively felt in Syria and Egypt and—between both—in Palestine. As I wrote in my introduction to *Judaism and Hellenism,* this influence—we may call it "hellenization"—is "a complex phenomenon which cannot be limited to purely political, socio-economic, cultural or religious aspects, but embraces them all."[6] That is, it cannot be restricted to Greek *paideia,* philosophy and rhetoric, even less to syncretism and mystery religions. The modern catchword "syncretism," for example, is not very helpful to characterize the encounter between Jewish and Greek religious thought because from its very beginning the Israelitic-Jewish religion was always more or less influenced by 'alien' ideas, Egyptian, Canaanite, Assyrian, Phoenician, Persian, and of course later by Greek ones.[7]

Therefore the whole Israelitic-Jewish religious history of all times could be labeled with the woolly term "syncretism." Theocrasy or the *interpretatio graeca* of Semitic Gods must not be simply "syncretism." Such an interpretation is a typical Greek custom since Herodotus. I would restrict this often misused term to the conscious mixture of different religions, thus in the artificial foundation of the Sarapis cult by the first Ptolemy, later Gnostic texts like the Naassene hymn or magical papyri. On this point I really have to criticize myself. I had used the term 'syncretism' or 'syncretistic' in *Judaism and Hellenism* a bit too easily, still too much influenced by the spirit of the *'religionsgeschichtliche Schule'*, which I wanted to refute. *The real problem is how Jewish identity could develop and grow among the different influences* from the fourth century BCE up to the second century CE and become even stronger than it had been before.

For Elias Bickerman, therefore, the "theme" of his book was not Jewish syncretism—the term does not appear in the index at all—but "stability and change in Jewish society during the first centuries of the Greek Age" and I think that, in spite of enormous political and cultural changes during the time of Greek-Macedonian (and Roman) domination, the stability of Jewish society at the end of the second or first century BCE was more consolidated than in the fourth, and notwithstanding all political catastrophes this is even more true at the end of the second century CE, the time of Jehuda Ha-Nasi, the redactor of the Mishna. I could therefore change my theme again a bit and call it: *'Greek civilization and Jewish identity'*. This strong consciousness of the—religious—identity of Judaism was taken over by its heretical messianic-universalistic offspring, early Christianity.

Hellenism before Alexander and the Invention of Proselytism

You can also see from these reflections that the chronological limitation of our theme is difficult. In some way it is a story without end, as can be seen in the provocative book of Yaacov Shavit, *Athens in Jerusalem*,[8] which discusses the problems of "hellenizing the Jews" from antiquity to our present time. But of course we should be more modest. Bickerman's "Jews in the Greek Age" goes up to the beginning of the Hellenistic Reform in 175, my own work till the middle or the end of the second century BCE. The usual era goes till 31 BCE, thus the title of Peter Green's *Alexander to Actium: The Hellenistic Age*,[9] but in Syria and Palestine 'hellenization' reaches its climax only in the second and third centuries, under Roman rule.

But its beginning is even more difficult. Surely the triumphant advance of Alexander to India brought a deep shock for the whole Near East, with fundamental changes which also found expression in many Jewish sources, but these changes in administration and economy didn't come all at once. For the time being the old Persian system of satrapies remained. This can be seen from the Jehud coins which were used from the end of the fifth century till the time of the first Ptolemy and from the new-found Idumean ostraca of the late Persian and early Hellenistic period, where only the name of the ruler changed from "King Artaxerxes," to "King Philip" (Arridaios) and "Antigonos" (Monophthalmos).[10] On the other hand, contacts with "Greek culture" were present in Phoenicia and Palestine long before Alexander. We see this not only from the omnipresence of genuine and imitated Greek coins and Attic vases and other Greek products of art in Palestine but also from the presence of Jews and Samaritans as slaves in Greece and of Greek mercenary troops and merchants in Palestine. It was easier to travel during summertime from there by ship to the Aegean Sea and Greece than to Babylonia. That this influence was not only economic is shown by the well-known report of Clearchus of Soli about the meeting, already before Alexander ca. 347–345 BCE, in western Asia Minor between Aristotle and a cultivated Jew from Jerusalem who "not only spoke Greek, but had the soul of a Greek." This is hardly pure invention: it shows at least what a pupil of Aristotle thought to be possible at that time.[11]

In the work of the Chronicler from the late Persian or earliest Hellenistic time we find clear allusions to Hellenistic warfare, arming, tactics, war machines and fortifications, but also to Greek money and large-estate economy. Bickerman even compared it with early Greek historiography, which—in contrast to "strictly traditional" "oriental historiography," such as we find, according to Bickerman, in the books of Kings—had emancipated itself "from the authority of tradition." "The Chronicler, like Hecataeus of Miletus or Herodotus, gives such information concerning the past as appears to him most probable, and corrects the sources in conformity with his own historical standards." His "clue" to history is the idea of divine "retribution" and "personal responsibility," "a conception which appears about the same time in Greece too."[12]

I myself have described the work as a quite new timely interpretation of Israel's holy history. It is "pervaded by a rationalistic thinking which systematizes the historical events, typical for the *Zeitgeist* of early Hellenism."[13]

But this 'modern' work, which created a new genre of Palestinian rewriting of the sacred history of Israel—as we find it later in Jubilees, the Genesis Apocryphon, Eupolemos, Josephus' *Antiquities,* Justus of Tiberias and the *Liber antiquitatum biblicarum*—did not weaken Jewish identity but on the contrary strengthened it and therefore remained very influential for all later interpretations of the history of the chosen people.

Even when, understandably, our theme 'Judaism and Hellenism' begins with Alexander, it has a long and complicated prehistory. May I again quote Elias Bickerman: Already "in the fifth and fourth centuries BCE, Palestine belonged to the belt of an eclectic Greco-Egyptian-Asiatic culture, which extended from the Nile Delta to Cilicia."[14] We could add: The relations of this eastern Mediterranean belt to the Aegean were nearly as old and as strong as its relations to Babylonia, and go back to the Minoan culture of the second millennium BCE. Already the prophets remember that the Philistines came from Crete and the western islands. From Walter Burkert we can learn how up to the eighth century the oriental influence on the Greeks was stronger,[15] whereas during the seventh and sixth centuries the Greeks gained their superiority.

It is therefore necessary for the Old Testament scholar also to know the Greek literature between Homer or Hesiod and Polybius, as well as the Egyptian and Akkadian ancient Near Eastern texts. The knowledge about this "belt of an eclectic Greco-Egyptian-Asiatic culture" is a fundamental presupposition for our understanding of 'Hellenism' and 'hellenization' in Jewish Palestine after Alexander. It is also no accident that precisely within this 'belt' between Tarsus and Alexandria, Greek civilization flowered for nearly a thousand years until the Arab conquest. Just in this belt Christianity developed during its first twenty years.

At this point I have to make a slight correction. I spoke of the influence of the superior Greek civilization. But this is not enough to understand the phenomenon of 'hellenization.' On the side of the Western Semites, the Phoenicians since ancient times but also the Arameans and Jews, there was a strong inclination for convergence, partially prepared by the existence of the worldwide Persian Empire. For the Jews in their tiny temple state around Jerusalem it promoted the idea of the universal history and unity of mankind in combination with the one God of Heaven, creator of the world and master of human history, who was identical with the ancestral YHWH of Zion. The Greek counterpart was philosophical cosmopolitism and mono- or pantheism. For the Jews this implied a conflict between the global claim of their religious truth and the rigorous restrictions of ritual law between 'Israelites' and 'goyim', which could be compared with the Greek distinction between "Hellenes" and "Barbaroi" established by birth and *paideia,* i.e., education. This tension already becomes evident in Persian times from the contrast of biblical books like Ezra/Nehemiah on the one side and Jonah or Ruth on the other, and was also connected with a deep social conflict described by Morton Smith's study, *Palestinian Parties and Politics That Shaped the Old Testament,* which appeared in 1971.[16] This brilliant study was written quite independently of my book. There was already a deep social and religious cleavage in Palestinian Judaism during the Persian domination which was aggravated after Alexander under Ptolemaic rule in the third century. The more 'liberal' aristocracy stood against the minor clergy of the Levites and pious peasantry. Nevertheless, the universalistic claim of truth in Jewish religion and the particularistic claim of the election of Israel through God's covenant and the gift of the law could be united by an institution which was new in ancient religion and opened unexpected possibilities for Judaism at the beginning of the Hellenistic era: *proselytism.*

Already in the priestly codex of early Persian times we find a semantic change of the word גר "sojourner," i.e., the stranger who lives in the land:[17] it becomes a technical term for those strangers who join the exclusive Jewish religion and cultic practice. The translators of the Pentateuch in the time of Ptolemy II therefore used the neologism προσηλυτός, which we do not find in pagan Greek literature, for גר fifty-four times. In this way they reconciled the universal and particular claim of their own faith as it was confessed in the Shᵉma Yisrael: The stranger who—by an individual decision, a conversion—joined the אדוני אחד, the κύριος εἷς and his law, and consequently was circumcised, became a member of the elect people of God and so became a Jew. Both the universal claim of religious truth revealed in the divine law given to Moses and the possibility of individual conversion prepared Judaism better for the Hellenistic age than other nations. No wonder that the Jewish worship in the prayer houses of the Diaspora, independent from the temple in Jerusalem, with its pure 'Wortgottesdienst' (service of word), prayers, scripture readings, and homily, but without sacrifice, which was also quite new in ancient religion, became rather attractive even for Greeks, because it had more affinity to the teaching in philosophical schools [18] than to the local pagan cults everywhere. Aristobulus calls Judaism "our (philosophical) school" (αἵρεσις), and Philo considers the Torah as "the ancestral philosophy." So the Jews are "philosophizing" on the sabbath in their prayer houses.[19]

When Nicholas of Damascus, the most learned scholar of his time and peripatetic philosopher who for many years was counselor of Herod in Jerusalem, tells us that he "philosophized" together with the king during a sea trip from Caesarea to Rome, he surely spoke with him about practical philosophy, including Jewish wisdom and religion.[20] Since the Persian period Jewish wisdom in its international garb had been prepared for an encounter with (and reception of) Greek philosophical thought. It is sufficient to mention here Job, Proverbs 1–10, Qoheleth, and Ben Sira. An extremely fruitful synthesis in the field of intellectual history began here which shaped the development of thought worldwide up to the present day.

After these more introductory and basic remarks I want to pick up a few specific questions from this vast field of problems: the Samaritans, the Hellenistic "Reform" of 175–164, and the special "Hellenistic culture" in Hasmonaean and Herodian Jerusalem. The Qumran Essenes and Hellenism are the subject of a separate essay.[21]

Some Remarks about the Samaritans and Hellenism

A visible proof for the above-mentioned "Greco-Asiatic culture" is provided by the recently published Samaritan seals impressions of the Death-Cave in Wadi Daliyeh and the new Samaria Coins, which are often similar. Both, bullae and coins, belong to the time before Alexander, for Samaria was destroyed by him in 331 BCE and replaced by a Macedonian military colony.[22] Besides Persian and Phoenician motifs, these coins show an astonishing degree of Greek influence, some coins even having some Greek letters, because they imitated Greek models, especially from Athens. One, showing a Persian king upon his throne, probably has the name "Zeus" and on the reverse a galloping rider with a sword and the name "Yehoʿanah."[23] The bullae show several Greek heroes[24] and a few gods and they are even more Graecizing than the coins, in which the Persian patterns are stronger[25] because they were minted by the Persian governor. The Samaritan aristocracy seemed to be a bit more inclined to Greek fashion than their religious relatives in

Jerusalem,[26] but I doubt if we should speak of real religious syncretism. Probably the upper class there simply enjoyed the motifs of modern Greek artistical style more than the old-fashioned oriental ones. According to Josephus, now also confirmed by the Wadi Daliyeh Papyri, Sanballat, the leader of the Samaritans, had a daughter with the Greek name Nikaso. Sanballat came spontaneously to help Alexander at the siege of Tyre.[27] Probably before its destruction Samaria was much more important and wealthier than Jerusalem. Mrs. Winn Leith, the editor of the bullae, speaks rightly of "an internationalist atmosphere" in the town and supposes "that Phoenicia was the cultural mediator between Samaria and the outside world." It would be an interesting archaeological task to look under the following Macedonian and later Herodian military settlements for the remains of Persian Samaria. That Andromachos, the new Macedonian Satrap of Coele Syria (or of a part of it) was burnt alive by the Samaritans in their capital demonstrates the significance of their town. The revenge of Alexander led to its destruction and later to the foundation of Hellenistic Shechem (Sikima) as the new Samaritan center between Ebal and Garizim, with its temple upon the holy mountain Garizim.[28]

The names in the documents of Wadi Daliyeh are mainly Yahwehphoric. This suggests that the Samaritan patricians who fled after their rebellion to the cave in Wadi Daliyeh (I quote the editor) "may have worshipped YHWH, the God of ancient Israel. As in Jerusalem, seals and coins were not under the obligation of the Second Commandment."[29] In later centuries the Samaritans were no more inclined to 'syncretism' than the Jews in Judaea. The Hebrew inscriptions from the new templetown on Garizim in the second century were as 'orthodox' as later Samaritan synagogue inscriptions, with the Decalogue or the text of the Shema'.[30]

The same can be said of the small fragments of Greek Samaritan literature. The Samaritan Anonymus, who identifies Enoch with Atlas the brother of Prometheus, demonstrates a self-consciousness as strong as what we find in related Jewish texts and makes Abraham the first inventor of all wisdom, Egyptian and Greek, especially of astrology. In the poem of Theodotus the Canaanite town Shechem (Sikima), which is conquered and punished by the sons of Jakob, was founded by Hermes (an *interpretatio graeca* from Ḥamor). Here we find the usual Euhemeristic critique of the pagan Gods as in Jewish texts such as the third Sibyl.[31]

The Samaritans were no less 'monotheistic' than the Jews. During the threat under Antiochus IV they showed more national religious consciousness than the Jewish Hellenists in Jerusalem. The unnamed highest God whom they worshipped as Ζεὺς ξένιος, the 'hospitable Zeus' (2 Macc 6:2), was the universal God to whom Abraham paid tribute, according to Genesis 14 and was received with hospitality.[32] The Sabbath, the traditional cult in the temple of the 'most great'[33] or 'most high[34] God' and the other prescriptions of the Mosaic law were further observed unchanged there. It is no chance, that in two early Samaritan inscriptions from Delos (one ca. 250–175, the other ca. 150–50 BCE) the Samaritan Diaspora community upon this island calls itself "Israelites of Delos who offer (their gifts) to the holy (or to the sanctuary of) Hargarizim" (cf. 1 Macc 11:34). The name of the holy mountain [ים]הרגרי even appears in a fragment of a Samaritan liturgical text at Masada.[35]

It remains to consider Simon Magus from Samaritan Gittha and his alleged pupil Menander from Kapparetaia.[36] But both left Samaria. Simon probably worked last in Rome and previously in Antioch or Caesarea, imitating and provoking earliest Christianity; Menander lived about 100 CE in Antioch. Surely Simon was not the father of Gnosticism and all other heresies, as Irenaeus and the later Church Fathers relate. Luke makes him a 'magician' with the claim to be the power, i.e., the representative of the one, highest God. It is strange that scholars who are extremely critical of the 'historical Jesus' know an astonishing amount about the 'historical Simon Magus'.[37] When Justin writes that nearly all Samaritans worship Simon as the 'first (and highest) God' he exaggerates strongly and probably confuses him with Dositheos, who gained many adherents in first-century Samaria à la Deuteronomy 18 as a prophetic-messianic figure.[38] Neither is Simon Magus a proof for a special inclination of the Samaritans to 'Hellenistic' paganizing 'syncretism' nor does Gnosticism come from there. With very few individual exceptions the 'Hellenization' of Samaritans and Jews cannot be precipitately identified with crude syncretism, assimilation to a pagan environment, or open apostasy. This is as true for the motherland as for the diaspora.

The Hellenistic Reform after 175

There is one really dramatic and much disputed alleged exception: the 'Hellenistic Reform' in Jerusalem 175–164 BCE.

This event, which brought the deepest shock in Palestinian Judaism during the history of the Second Temple is still best explained by the hypothesis of Elias Bickerman in his ingenious book *The God of the Maccabees*. Those mainly responsible are the Jewish Hellenists, who wanted to convert Jerusalem to a 'Greek' city. After their splitting and the consequent internal strife, it was especially the leader of the radical wing, the high priest Menelaus and his friends, the Tobiads, who incited the king Antiochus IV to issue his decrees against the traditional temple cult and the observance of the Mosaic law. These religious decrees against an old and generally acknowledged ethnic religion were unusual for Greek thinking and moreover for a king who was said to be an Epicurean, but they have some relationship with the intransigence of the Torah in religious matters, with Ezra and Nehemiah, or the later Hasmonean politics of conquest with its forced circumcision,[39] only of course with reversed premises. They look nearly like an inverted Zealotism. We therefore hear nothing about a persecution of the Jews in other parts of the Seleucid empire.[40] The radical "Hellenistic reform" and its persecution were not caused by a purely political and economic power struggle between the leading families, the priestly Oniads and Tobiads and their adherents, which led to an intervention of the king and royal punitive measures, as Bringmann supposes,[41] but also had a religious background. The so-called "Hellenistic Reform" which began as early as 175 after the usurpation of the Seleucid throne by Antiochus IV and the displacement of Onias III from priesthood by his brother Jason can also not be separated sharply from the later escalation under the leadership of Menelaus, his ambitious successor, which led to civil war in Jerusalem and the royal decrees. The question of Bringmann: "Was the motive political or religious-reformational?" is a misleading alternative. It was both, because in ancient Judaism you never can strictly separate religion and policy.[42] The answer of Bringmann is in accordance with the widespread inclination today to play down the religious motives in ancient Judaism and to replace them with social or political ones. This is a fashionable tendency in modern historiography: an understanding for specific religious phenomena is decreasing. We find this tendency visible in current opinion about later Jewish groups like the Zealots and Sicarii and even the Pharisees, but also in the negation of a specific Jewish interest in proselytism.[43] Not only did Jacob Burckhardt in his *Weltgeschichtliche Betrachtungen* give the Jews the first place among "the greatest, historically most important and the most powerful theocracies,"[44] but he also regarded this as an essential characterstic of their history: "One sees the Jews again and again striving towards theocracy throughout all the changes that took place in their history." We should not forget that the Greek word formation θεοκρατία is only once used in ancient literature by Josephus in his *Against Apion*, to describe the constitution of the Jewish state.[45] The 'radical hellenistic reform' is the failed experiment of an 'antitheocracy'.

This reform and its later radical disastrous consequences had its own 'ideology' intimated in texts like 1 Maccabees 1:11 or 2 Maccabees 4:11–20. It began with a strong propensity for assimilation in the upper class and ended with the total apostasy of a smaller but still powerful faction under the leadership of Menelaus.[46] Probably there was no deep fundamental difference between the latitudinarism of the high priest Jason and his successor Menelaus. 2 Maccabees 5:8 calls Jason an "apostate from the laws"[47] who fled via the Nabateans and Egypt to Sparta "in the hope of finding refuge there as a member of a kindred people" (5:9): a strange end for a Jewish high priest of the famous family of the Oniads and of Zadokite descent.

Jason and his rival and successor, Menelaus, the protegé of the Tobiads, probably had similar 'progressive' religious opinions. This is suggested already by Jason's "delegation, representing the Antiochenes from Jerusalem bearing three hundred drachmas to pay for the sacrifice to Hercules" at the "quinquennial games . . . celebrated at Tyre."[48] The God of Zion with his hidden name was like the one "highest God" (θεὸς ὕψιστος), the "God (or Lord) of Heaven" (or of the universe)[49] identical with the Greek Olympic Zeus and the Semitic Baal Shamen. As has been supposed since E. Nestle, the שקוץ שמם in Daniel[50] is a scornful pun related to the new forced cult of this universal God on Zion who could be identified with Baal Shamen and Zeus Olympios. The Peshitta of 2 Maccabees 6:2 translates 'Zeus Olympios' with *b'l šmyn 'lwmpyws;* the Vulgate with Iovis Olympii. The meaning is always the same: the highest God. The enigmatic formulation Daniel 9:27a may be translated with Plöger: "and upon wing(s) of the detested idols comes one devastating" (ועל כנף שקוצים משמם). He is also reflecting Eissfeldt's proposal of a possible original text בעל כנף שקוצים (instead of ועל): "and a proprietor of wings, devastating, shall cause to cease sacrifice and oblation."[51] This could be a further mention of the Syrian-Phoenician God of heaven in connection with his widespread symbol, the winged sun of feathered heaven.

The ending of the Tamid offering, the building of a superstructure upon the altar, probably as Bickerman supposed a Semitic stone idol, a betyl, and the desecration of the sanctuary by unclean sacrifices, as for instance a swine, marked the introduction of a new really syncretistic cult for the assimilating Jews, the Syrian military colonists of the Akra and the Macedonian and Greek officials and officers in the town. These cultic details of the royal decrees together with the prohibition against practicing the Jewish ritual law, even against the possession of a Torah scroll, was surely not the invention of a king uninterested in questions of the religious and cultic law of a small people in his great kingdom, but a cunning move by Menelaus and his party, the radical Hellenists, who believed that the resistance of the majority of the Jewish population could only be overcome by a violent break with ancestral law. I can here quote Elias Bickerman answering his critics by an analogy: "The important royal decisions were more often than not instigated by ministers and courtiers. There was a Haman or a Mordechai behind the king and his edict. But his role remained secret. . . . Thus the monarch alone was praised (or blamed) for his decision. We may, thus, ask who was Haman in 167 BCE." The problem is that *this* Haman was a Jewish high priest.[52] Antiochus was blamed in Jewish tradition but praised in Greco-Roman sources.[53] For the Jews it was much more impressive to paint Antiochus as a megalomaniac enemy of God and to suppress the disastrous role of the two last high priests, thus already in Daniel and later in 1 Maccabees. This was a real *damnatio memoriae*. We see their ambitious characters and disastrous role all the more distinctly in Jason from Cyrene, a nearly contemporary work, epitomized in 2 Maccabees.

According to 2 Maccabees 13:4 Menelaus was killed because "he was the one responsible for all disasters" τοῦτον αἴτιον τῶν κακῶν εἶναι πάντων. But even in 1 Maccabees the collective responsibility and influence of the "Hellenists" is emphasized. The tragedy begins with the proposal of "lawless men in Israel" "to make a covenant with the gentiles around us." These "persuaded many" and "so got a favorable reception" in (the upper class of) the people (1 Macc 1:11ff.). The same is indicated several times in Daniel, where from the beginning the wicked king easily finds willing Jewish collaborators.[54] Even Josephus, who had as a Jewish source only 1 Maccabees, knows from an inaccurate Greek source, probably Nicholas of Damascus, the fatal role of Menelaus, who is for him (and his source) a brother of Jason.[55] He gives the information that Menelaus' acts of violence caused a split in the people, the rich Tobiads being on the side of Menelaus, while a majority supported Jason. Another important piece of information is that "Menelaus and the Tobiads withdrew to Antiochus and informed him that they wished to abandon their country's laws and the way of life prescribed by these, and to follow the king's laws and adopt the Greek way of life."[56] Josephus is here combining his Greek source and 1 Maccabees 1:14ff., probably because both had a similar content.

In reality Menelaus, whose relation with the Tobiads is also indirectly suggested in 2 Maccabees, came from the priestly order Bilga.[57] The mishnaic tradition that the members of this order were excluded from offering sacrifices for all time and the anecdote about Miriam from this priestly order, who apostasized, married a Seleucid officer and insulted the altar because it wasted the riches of Israel without helping them, are reminiscent of the fateful role of Menahem and his clan. The exclusion was the perennial punishment for their sacrilege. The fact that a Jewish high priest became the initiator of the desecration of the sanctuary and of the abolition of the law was such a scandal that it was consciously repressed in Daniel and 1 Maccabees, and in Talmudic tradition the apostate high priest was replaced by a woman belonging to his priestly order.[58]

Again I can quote Elias Bickerman in his answer to his critics: "The pagans never doubted the existence and power of foreign gods and for this reason were afraid to interfere with the cults in which they were not initiated. . . . Accordingly, we must postulate that Antiochus' intervention in the religious affairs was inspired by Jewish authorities." Or with a historical comparison in one sentence: "Menelaus was an anti-Ezra and Epiphanes his Artaxerxes."[59]

That the "Hellenistic reformers" had their own religious "ideology" can hardly be doubted. That a considerable part, even the majority, of the Jewish upper class including the ruling priest in Jerusalem did not engage in religious reflection at all is unthinkable. There were in a Greek way "enlightened" Jews even in the upper class of Jerusalem. A skeptical sage in the Ptolemaic period with international experience like Qoheleth spoke only about the one universal God of mankind. He never uses the tetragrammaton and the meaning of the term God

(אלהים) comes near to inexplicable fate.[60] Aristobulus, a contemporary of the events in Judaea and a Jewish peripatetic scholar at the Museion, writing for the Ptolemy VI Philometor, compares the universal God of Israel with the religious opinions of the Greek philosophers and postulates that Pythagoras, Socrates, and Plato have learned from Moses,[61] whose law contains the universal law and wisdom of mankind and must be interpreted allegorically to exclude improper anthropomorphisms. Using the Greek method of comparative religion[62] he quotes approvingly the famous opening of Aratos' *Phainomena*, only replacing Zeus by θεός, because "all philosophers agree that it is necessary to hold devout convictions about God, something our (Jewish) school prescribes particularly well."[63] Maybe he was already influenced in this slight criticism by the negative experiences in Jerusalem. Some decades later an unknown Jewish author, who attributes the letter of Aristeas to a Greek sympathizer, has less scruples. Here Demetrius of Phaleron informs king Ptolemy about the God of the Jews. "He is the overseer and creator of all, whom all men worship including ourselves . . . except that we have a different name, Zeus." It was all the more difficult later for the Jewish high priest Eleazar in Jerusalem to explain to the Greek ambassadors of the king all the ritual laws which separate his people from all others. These "iron walls" are necessary to keep Israel "pure in body and soul," preserving it "from false beliefs," worshipping "the only God omnipotent over all creation." This sounds rather unnatural and accordingly the explanation of these laws in detail is possible only by forced allegory.[64] Nevertheless all seventy-two translators from Jerusalem are said to be well-trained in Greek education.

Here also the consequences of earlier debates in Jerusalem become visible. The radical Hellenistic reformers in Jerusalem previously had a quite opposite experience expressed in 1 Maccabees 1:11: "because ever since we have kept ourselves separated from the nations around us we have suffered many evils." A Palestinian writer, the so-called Samaritan Anonymous, knows that the wisest man of the world, Abraham, brought the highest wisdom, astrology, to the nations of the West, first to the Phoenicians, then to the Egyptians and—this could be concluded—indirectly later to the Greeks. The law of Moses brought separation from the nations, but the enlightened, wise Abraham before him united them by wisdom he received from God. Again I quote the question of Bickerman against his critics: "Why should an enlightened Jew, ca. 170, follow the laws of Moses which seemed to the Greeks abstruse and inhuman and not the example of the pre-Mosaic patriarchs? Did not Jacob call a cult-stone God's dwelling (Gen 28:22)?"[65]

The argument that we have no texts about the religious self-consciousness of the radical "Hellenists" in Jerusalem does not mean much because as a rule the defeated or unsuccessful party in ancient Judaism has seldom left its own testimonies. This is true of the enemies of Nehemiah as well as of the Sadducees, the Zealots, or the Jewish Baptist Movement. We may call it a rule of history.

The New "Hellenistic" Culture in Jerusalem under the Hasmoneans and Herod

The rejection of "Greek manners" (ἑλληνισμός)[66] was only a temporary one. The Jewish resistance movement was from the beginning no real cultural unity but, rather, multifarious. Orthodox Chasidim later fought side by side with former followers of the high priest Jason or the Tobiad Hyrcanus from the Ammanitis. Eupolemus,[67] the priest and early Hasmonean ambassador to Rome, had a Hellenistic education and tried to rewrite biblical history in Greek language with a strong national, but at the same time rather liberal, religious tendency. The dilemma of the new Maccabean high priests and later kings was that they could only exist politically as Hellenistic states, with an army trained and equipped in the Greek manner, with Greek fortress- and palace-building, with an efficacious economy and tax-collecting in Greek style and the use of Greek language at least in all foreign affairs with other city-states and kingdoms, but also in all contacts with the Western Diaspora: Greek civilization had become a vital necessity.

One point typical of the "Hellenization" of the Hasmonean state was the use of pagan mercenary troops, beginning with John Hyrcanus. The successful politics of military expansion was possible only by Hellenistic warfare. Such heavily fortified towns as Samaria, Scythopolis, Gadara, Gaza or Dor could only be conquered by modern Hellenistic military technique. The continuous wars with only short interruptions since the beginning of the Maccabean revolt had exhausted Jewish manpower, therefore John Hyrcanus was already compelled to enroll pagan mercenaries.[68] Later, Alexander Jannaeus used troops from Cilicia and Pamphylia and perhaps also Thracians,[69] but no Syrians "because of their innate hatred against his nation."[70]

It is a strange thing. The radical Hellenists collaborated with the Syrian mercenaries in the Akra till it was forced by Simon Maccabee to capitulate in June 141 BCE. Hardly ten years later, again pagan mercenaries were present in Judaea, now as auxiliaries of the victorious Hasmonaeans and not only against external enemies but later also against their own pious Jewish opposition. Josephus, following Nicholas of Damascus, writes that Alexander Jannaeus would "never have quelled their rebellion, had not his mercenaries come to his aid."[71] In connection with the invasion of Demetrios Eukairos, whom the Pharisaic opposition summoned against Alexander Jannaeus in 88 BCE, the Seleucid king attempted in vain to cause Alexander's mercenaries to desert because they were Greeks.[72] Obviously these pagan soldiers from southern Asia Minor understood themselves as Greeks, speaking Greek as their colloquial language. According to *The Jewish War*[73] there were 8,000, but in *Antiquities* only 6,200, mercenaries who fought loyally on the side of the Jewish high priest and king[74] against the Seleucid invader. In comparison with the 6,000 Pharisees and the more than 4,000 Essenes, the latter number seems to be realistic.[75]

Later Salome Alexandra, the pious widow of Jannaeus, and Aristobulus II, her son, also employed pagan mercenaries. Surely they were not only placed at the frontiers and in a few fortresses but also in Jerusalem, for instance as a part of the royal guard, like the Krethi and Plethi under David and again later under Herod. The royal guard is first explicitly mentioned in connection with Aristobulus I,[76] who added the title King to that of High Priest.[77] The deep mistrust and acts of cruelty among the members of the Hasmonaean family as also the growing opposition of the Jewish 'pietists' against them made it probable that they preferred foreign—Greek—bodyguards. Aristobulus also conferred on himself the surname "Philhellene," very unusual for a Hasmonaean ruler but popular among other oriental kings and high officials as a sign of their civilized behavior and their policy favorable to the Greeks. According to the Alexandrian historian Timagenes in the first century, "he was a kind person"—we may add: to the Greek officers and advisers at his court, not to his family, whom he threw in prison or killed, or to the subjugated Ituraeans in Galilee, whom he forcibly circumcised and converted to Judaism. The officers of these 'Greek' mercenaries had contacts not only with the royal court but also with the Jewish aristocracy. Some of them may have converted to Judaism in the interest of their personal career and stayed in the country. Comparable advisers were the converted Idumean aristocrat Antipas, the grandfather of Herod, appointed as governor of Idumaea by Alexander Jannaeus and his son Antipater, who became the leading man under Hyrcanus II,[78] or later, without 'conversion,' Nicholas of Damascus and his staff in the time of Herod. Possibly Diogenes, "a distinguished man who had been a friend of Alexander (Jannaeus)," who was killed after the death of the king because he had advised him to crucify the 800 Pharisees,[79] was such an original Greek. Diogenes was a rather unusual name for a Jew from Palestine.[80] The greater part of these 'Greek' soldiers returned after their service to their homeland in southern Asia Minor, probably influenced and impressed by Jewish monotheism and ritual practice. This may be the reason why we nowhere find so much evidence for Judaizing 'Greeks' as in Asia Minor, from the Sabbatistai in Cilica in the time of Augustus up to the Hypsistarii in the fourth century CE.[81]

So in the time between about 130 and the conquest of the temple-mount in 63 by Pompey there were hardly fewer 'Greek' soldiers in Judaea than in the dark time of the Akra between 167 and 141, and surely their sometimes long stay did not leave the country totally unaffected. But in contrast to the time of the Maccabean rebellion, we find in Jewish Palestine no threatening Jewish assimilation to pagan beliefs and practices. This problem belonged to the past. As the *Psalms of Solomon* show, there was the loud protest of the pious against the Hasmonean rule and sometimes even civil war, but the authority of the Torah and the necessity of the Temple-cult were never called in question again, rather the existence of foreigners in the country allowed for successful proselytism among them. After the Maccabean revolution, עבדה זרה, the apostasy to paganism was no more a danger in Jewish Palestine; political-religious identity had become stronger in spite of the steady new progress of "Hellenization." We find one small indication of this development by a comparison between the Yehud and Samaria coins of the fourth century, which imitate Greek religious pictures and symbols and the new Jewish coins from the Hasmonaeans through Herod up to the procurators. Beginning with Alexander Jannaeus these coins have a Greek legend but now always without improper images.

During the long reign of Herod under the protection of the *pax Romana*, 37–4 BCE, the presence of foreign mercenaries, also Galatians and even Teutonics, and Greek advisers, teachers of rhetoric, artists, or simple fortune hunters in Jerusalem increased, but much more important was the steadily growing influx of pilgrims, especially to the great religious festivals, from the Jews of the Greek-speaking towns of Palestine itself but also from the Diaspora between Egypt and Spain. Some of them remained in the Holy City. Jerusalem—again—more and more transformed itself into a "Hellenistic City" but with a new, quite independent character in comparison with other Hellenistic towns in Palestine, Phoenicia, or Syria, without pagan sanctuaries, statues, or a gymnasium but with bright public buildings in Greek-oriental style, at its center the marvelous yet unique temple, beautifully rebuilt by Herod, which made Jerusalem one of the most famous places of pilgrimage in the Roman Empire before the catastrophe in 70 CE: *longe clarissima urbium Orientis non Iudaeae modo,* "by far the most famous city of the East and not of Judaea only," says Pliny the Elder.[82] May I quote M. Stern's comment on this text: "Nothing expresses the well-known growth of Jerusalem's fame from the Hellenistic age to the Julio-Claudian period more clearly than a comparison of the ways in which Polybius and Pliny referred to it. Polybius mentions Jerusalem only in relation to the temple. However, Pliny's characterization seems to surpass in some respects that of the Jew Philo."[83] This development of the Holy City from a rather provincial temple-town in Coele Syria to an internationally renowned metropolis in the Roman and Parthian Orient is a result of the Hasmonaean and, even more, Herodian policy of attracting Jews, Judaizing sympathizers and curious pagans as pilgrims from all over the civilized world.

Already the Hasmonaeans were interested in gaining influence in the Western Diaspora and in attracting pilgrims, visitors, and money from there. The annual temple tax of a half shekel or two drachmai, paid by each Jew over twenty years not only in the motherland but also in the Diaspora, was a custom probably introduced by the Hasmonaeans as a universal bond to link up the whole Diaspora with the metropolis and its sanctuary.[84]

The export of currency in precious metal to Jerusalem from abroad was at first not without difficulties. It was the influence of Herod and the relative legal security in the empire since Augustus which secured this inflow, which made the temple attractive and the priestly aristocracy of the town rich. The same is true of pilgrimage, because there is a close coherence between the transfer of the temple tax and pilgrimage. In the first third of the first century BCE there was a permanent insecurity in the eastern Mediterranean which only ended after Pompey's victory over the pirates and the Roman conquest of the East. A real stabilization was brought by the end of the Roman civil war. Formerly it was always possible that a pilgrimage could end at the slave market. Augustus created peace and security. The praise which Alexandrian sailors and passengers addressed to him shortly before his death ("it was through him they lived, through him they sailed the seas, and through him they enjoyed their liberty and fortunes")[85] was no exaggeration. Herod's foundation of Caesarea, the most important seaport between Alexandria and Seleucia, was a benefit to whole Judaea and corresponded with the benefits of the emperor.[86] Herod followed in Augustus' footsteps. His long reign brought peace for his country and—at least for its capital—growing prosperity, and this meant simultaneously more "Hellenistic civilization" on several levels, the economic and political, the artistic and architectural, the linguistic and literary, but also in the field of philosophical and religious thought. His sons, especially Antipas and Philippus, his grandson Agrippa I and his great-grandson Agrippa II received a solid Greek education and pursued a similar hellenizing and harmonizing policy.[87] I have not the time here to display this in detail. I will only give some indications. There is the new high priest Simon, son of Boethos from Alexandria, father-in-law of the king, whose family still remained powerful and influential after the death of Herod and founded its own 'party', the Boethusians. Another important development was the introduction of the synagogue into Jewish Palestine with its new service of the word without sacrifice, an invention of Ptolemaic Egypt and a revolutionary institution in antiquity, probably an import from the Greek-speaking Diaspora and supported by the Pharisees.[88] In Jerusalem the first synagogues were presumably introduced by Greek-speaking Jews from the Diaspora. The best example is known from the famous Theodotus inscription and had a Roman founder.

Another possibility was the production of religious literature in Jerusalem and its export to the Diaspora, and beyond that the critical revision of Septuagint translations that were deemed to be too liberal. One example is the Greek Minor Prophets Scroll from Naḥal Ḥever.[89]

We have quite a lot of Greek inscriptions from Jerusalem, especially on ossuaries. Here the great edition of Rahmani gives overwhelming evidence which should be studied by all these New Testament scholars who doubt that Jerusalem was not only a Jewish but also a 'Hellenistic' capital—surely *sui generis*—with its own Jewish-

Hellenistic culture.[90] Ossuaries from a second burial of the bones were introduced in Jerusalem ca. 20–15 BCE at the climax of Herod's reign. They are connected with the Pharisaic expectation of individual physical resurrection, a presupposition of the real eschatological restitution of all Israel. This apocalyptic hope is also a fruit of the 'Hellenistic Zeitgeist' in a typical Jewish Palestinian garb.[91] The introduction of these often highly artificially decorated limestone ossuaries again demonstrates the individualization of Jewish piety. Of the 897 ossuaries in the catalogue, about 233 are inscribed, nearly all coming from Jerusalem and the time between Herod and CE 70. One hundred forty-three of them bear Jewish and 73 Greek script, 14 or 15 have both, 2 are Latin and 1 Palmyrene.[92] This means that about 40 percent of the inscriptions were Greek or bilingual. The relation of the names is similar: of 147 names, nicknames, or probable names about 80 are Jewish, 52 Greek, and 7 Latin. This means that around Jerusalem there was a remarkable number of Greek native speakers and bilingual Jews and beyond that—I quote the editor Rahmani—"it can be concluded that in and around Jerusalem . . . even the lower classes of the Jewish population knew some Greek."[93]

An impressive newer discovery which confirms this picture is the Akeldama tombs[94] excavated in 1989. Of 23 ossuaries, 13 have only Greek and 5 only Hebrew inscriptions, 5 are bilingual. The most interesting, number 19, mentions an Ariston from Apamea in Syria, a proselyte with the Hebrew name Juda, who is probably mentioned in the Mishna Halla 4:11 bringing first fruits from Apamea, which was accepted by the priests "for they said: He that owns [land] in Syria is as one that owns [land] in the outskirts of Jerusalem." This special geographical feature of Syria explains why in the first ten years the mission of the Christian Hellenists from Jerusalem was restricted to Syria and Cilicia. The proselyte Ariston from Apamea is also an interesting parallel to the proselyte Nikolaos from Antioch at the end of the list of the Seven, Acts 6:5. Probably Syria was supposed to become a part of the enlarged Eretz Israel in the coming messianic time in relation with the restitution of the ideal Davidic kingdom and its borders.[95]

'Hellenistic culture' in Jerusalem since Herod and in the time of the procurators till 70 is briefly and precisely described by Luke in Acts 6; 12; 21–27, probably the most important source besides Josephus' *The Jewish War*, Book 2, and *Antiquities*, Books 18–20, for the history of Judaism and especially Jerusalem in the time of the procurators.

This special Jewish-Hellenistic milieu in Jerusalem and its environment was formed by the Jewish pilgrims, returning emigrants and students of the law from the Greek-speaking Diaspora, by the members of the Herodian court, Herod's family and their clientele, by some aristocratic priestly families like the Boethusians, by merchants, physicians, architects and other technical specialists, teachers of Greek language and rhetoric, skilled artisans and also slaves from abroad. In this Jewish-Hellenistic milieu the message of the new messianic-apocalyptic sect very soon found resonance and formed, as Luke describes it, a nucleus which, expelled from Judaea, founded communities outside it, first in Syria, Cilicia, and Cyprus, then in Asia Minor, Greece, and Rome, all in the space of about thirty years. From this Greek-speaking group came the Seven Hellenists in Acts 6, people like Joseph Barnabas, John Mark, Silas-Silvanus, and above all, Saulus-Paulus from Tarsus.

It was this 'Hellenistic-Jewish culture' of Jerusalem, and not that of Alexandria or Antioch, from which proceeded a Jewish movement that at last conquered the Roman empire. This special culture of the Holy City itself was ended suddenly by the catastrophe of 70 CE. But its fruit changed the world.

Conclusion

I come to the end: The Hellenization of Palestinian Judaism between the Persian period and the late Roman Empire—it does not end with the year 70—is an endless story taking place upon several quite different levels and with many even partially contrary perspectives. It always involved attraction and repulsion. It had quite another history and form than in Alexandria but it nevertheless created its own Jewish-Hellenistic culture in Jerusalem, which was violently destroyed by the catastrophe of 70 CE which gave world history another direction. Probably this Hellenistic culture in the Holy City was much richer than our very scanty and fragmentary sources let us know. The same could be probably said about Alexandria in an opposite way. Neither Philo of Alexandria, who was a unique personality, nor the later rabbis represent the whole truth. If the unabridged work of Jewish historians like Jason of Cyrene, Eupolemus, Justus of Tiberias and the Jewish parts of the great world history, and the autobiography of Nicholas of Damascus had been preserved we surely would know more about the spread of

Hellenistic civilization in the Jewish motherland. A strange thing is that we possess only very few official inscriptions from the time of Herod, his successors, and the Roman procurators. But Jerusalem was destroyed too thoroughly to make great epigraphical discoveries there. The numerous ossuary graffiti in Greek constitute an exception. The abundant wealth of the Qumran texts also gives too little information about the contemporary political, social, and cultural background or about the towns of the country, especially Jerusalem. The Essenes were not interested in worldly life; we can speak here of some sort of self-ghettoization. But in addition to the ossuaries, private documents of the Bar Kochba caves, and the later inscriptions from Beth Shearim in Galilee have brought a rich harvest. They confirm our picture from the social, legal, and linguistic side.

So as I said at the beginning, my thesis of *Judaism and Hellenism* can surely be supplemented, improved, and sometimes corrected. And I hope this will happen by new evidence again and again, but it must not be revised.

My conclusion is: The predominant Hellenistic civilization gave the Near East a new face up to the Arab conquest and renewed and continued its influence upon Jewish Palestine again after the miscarried "Hellenistic Reform" in 175 BCE, but could not further threaten the religious and ethnic identity of the Jews, but rather strengthened it and made it more creative and fruitful. It produced unique consequences for world history: it created Rabbinism and Christianity.

Notes

1. I have written a short autobiographical sketch on my way in scholarship with the title "A Gentile in the Wilderness. My encounter with Jews and Judaism," in *Overcoming Fear: Between Jews and Christians* (ed. J. H. Charlesworth; New York: Crossroad, 1993) 67–83.

2. M. Hengel, in collaboration with Christoph Markschies, *The 'Hellenization' of Judaea in the First Century after Christ* (trans. John Bowden; London and Philadelphia: SCM Press and Trinity Press International, 1989). The slightly enlarged German version is "Zum Problem der 'Hellenisierung' Judäas im 1. Jh. n.Chr.," in *Judaica et Hellenistica: Kleine Schriften I* (Tübingen: Mohr Siebeck, 1996) 1–90. Cf. "Die Begegnung von Judentum und Hellenismus

im Palästina der vorchristlichen Zeit" (1970), *Kleine Schriften I*, 151–69; "Die Hellenisierung des antiken Judentums" (with H. Lichtenberger, 1981), *Kleine Schriften I*, 295–314. Cf. also "Jerusalem als jüdische und hellenistische Stadt," in *Judaica, Hellenistica et Christiana: Kleine Schriften II* (Tübingen: Mohr Siebeck, 1999), 115–56 and (in collaboration with R. Deines) "Die Septuaginta als 'christliche Schriftensammlung', ihre Vorgeschichte und das Problem ihres Kanons," in M. Hengel and A. M. Schwemer, eds., *Die Septuaginta zwischen Judentum und Christentum* (WUNT 72; Tübingen: Mohr Siebeck, 1994) 182–284. About the problem of 'Hellenization' in Palestine see now the balanced judgment of N. Kokkinos, *The Herodian Dynasty* (JSPSup 30; Sheffield: Sheffield Academic Press, 1998) 79–84.

3. The English version is *Between Jesus and Paul: Studies in the Earliest History of Christianity* (London: SCM Press, 1983), esp. pp. 1–29, 129–56.

4. *Kerygma und historischer Jesus* (2d ed.; Zürich and Stuttgart: Zwingli Verlag, 1967) 9: " . . . dass die theologische Arbeit Bultmanns und die seiner Schüler unverändert im Mittelpunkt der Diskussion steht." This was related to the problem of the historical Jesus; it is also true for the discussion of the problems of history of religion, cf. p. 15: "Die deutsche Theologie ist heutzutage beinahe so von Bultmann her bestimmt wie vor einer Generation durch Karl Barth, wie durch Ritschl mehr als halbes Jahrhundert zuvor und wie noch früher durch Hegel. . . . Man hätte erwarten können, dass das Ergebnis dieser ersten Periode der deutschen Nachkriegstheologie eine Periode der Bultmann-Scholastik geworden wäre. . . . "

5. E. J. Bickerman, *The Jews in the Greek Age* (Cambridge, Mass., and London: Harvard University Press, 1988). About its genesis see A. I. Baumgarten in his 'biographical note' on p. 309-10. The initial version was completed in 1963 but E. Bickerman reworked it and "prepared the final revision during the last months before setting off for Israel in the summer of 1981, a trip from which he was not to return."

6. *Judaism and Hellenism* (London: SCM Press, 1974) 1:3.

7. See M. Hengel and A. M. Schwemer, *Paul between Damascus and Antioch* (London: SCM Press, 1997) 29–30.

8. Y. Shavit, *Athens in Jerusalem: Classical Antiquity and Hellenism in the Making of the Modern Secular Jew* (London: Vallentine, Mitchell, 1997). See the review of Mordecai Beck with the title "Hellenism Then and Now," *Jerusalem Post Magazine*, December 19, 1997.

9. (London: Thames and Hudson, 1990).

10. See A. Lemaire, "Der Beitrag idumäischer Ostraka zur Geschichte Palästinas im Übergang von der persischen zur hellistischen Zeit," *ZDPV* 115 (1999) 12–23: "Auf dieser Ebene [i.e., the local administration] verwandelt sich ein so berühmtes Ereignis wie die Eroberung durch Alexander d. Grossen in das Auswechseln des Namens einer Datumsformel" (21).

11. See M. Stern, *Greek and Latin Authors on Jews and Judaism* (Jerusalem: The Israel Academy of Sciences and Humanities, 1974) 1:47–52.; Josephus, *Ag. Ap.* 1.179–83. It must have happened in the forties of the fourth century BCE. Cf. now the deliberations of B. Bar-Kochba, "The Wisdom of the Jew and the Wisdom of Aristotle," in *Internationales Josephus-Kolloquium Münster 1997* (ed. J. U. Kalms and F. Siegert; Münsteraner Judäistische Studien 4; Münster: Lit, 1998) 241–50, which are perhaps a bit too skeptical. On the Diaspora in Asia Minor in Persian times see Hengel, *Kleine Schriften II*, 169.

12. *From Ezra to the Last of the Maccabees* (New York: Schocken Books, 1962) 20–31, esp. 21–24. About Greek money see Ezra 2:69 and Neh 7:69–71: *dark^emônîm* = drachmas.

13. *Kleine Schriften II*, 29. Possibly I dated the final redaction of the work a bit too late to the first half of the third century BCE. Bickerman fixes it about a hundred years earlier. But it is probably not the work of a single author but of a school.

14. From Ezra, 15.

15. *Die orientalisierende Epoche in der griechischen Religion und Literatur* (Heidelberg: Winter 1984).

16. (New York: Columbia University Press, 1971).

17. See L. Köhler and W. Baumgartner, *Lexicon in Veteris Testamenti libros* (Leiden: Brill, 1953) 192; *TWNT*, 6:727–45.

18. Eusebius, *P.E.* 13.12.8 (GCS 43.2, p. 195): ἡ καθ᾽ ἡμᾶς αἵρεσις.

19. *Mos.* 2.212, 215; *Spec.* 2.61ff.; *Legatio* 156, 245. Josephus also begins his *Antiquities* with the remarks that the Jewish creed is "highly philosophical" (1.25: λίαν φιλόσοφος).

20. M. Stern, *Greek and Latin Authors*, 1:248–50, number 96. Shortly before this he wrote that he taught Herod philosophy but the king soon abandoned his enthusiasm for (theoretical) philosophy "because of the abundance of goods that distracts (people in authority)."

21. M. Hengel, "The Qumran Essenes and Hellenism," in *Aspects of Religion in the Dead Sea Scrolls* (ed. J. J. Collins and R. Kugler; Grand Rapids: Eerdmans, 2000), 46–56.

22. M. J. Winn Leith, ed.; *Wadi Daliyeh I. The Wadi Daliyeh Seal Impressions* (DJD 24; Oxford: Claredon, 1997).

23. Y. Meshorer and S. Qedar, *The Coinage of Samaria in the Fourth Century BCE* (Jerusalem: Numismatics Fine Arts International, 1991) 16, 18, 51 (nr. 38).

24. Especially Hercules, the Phoenician Melkart (2 Macc 4:20) and Perseus, who was associated with Joppa and its Andromeda tradition. See *Judaism and Hellenism*, 1:72.

25. *Wadi Daliyeh I*, 21: "some thirty-nine different seal impressions can be labeled Greek . . . Some twenty-one are Near Eastern." Because the bullae are private and the coins official this may indicate that the personal taste was

more directed to the 'Greek fashion'. Because "of the Greek bullae, twenty-nine probable are ring impressions and then probably came from scaraboids or other types of stamps," while "among the Near Eastern bullae only three carry probable ring impressions" (23) we may suppose that the using of a Greek-styled ring seemed to be more 'progressive'. Cf. 26ff.

26. About the more conventional coins from Yehud see L. Mildenberg, "Yehud-Münzen" in H. Weippert, *Palästina in vorhellenistischer Zeit* (Handbuch der Archäologie II,1; München: C. H. Beck, 1988) 719–28; see also pls. 22–23. They are less elaborated and more dependent on the Attic coins with the owl. The only exception is the British Museum coin with the god upon the winged wheel. See H. Kienle, *Der Gott auf dem Flügelrad* (Göttinger Orientforschungen VI.7; Wiesbaden: Harrassowitz, 1975). The Yehud-coinage proceeds without interruption from the fifth century up to Ptolemy I.

27. *Ant.* 11.21, 325; see M. Hengel, *Juden, Griechen und Barbaren* (Stuttgart: KBW Verlag, 1976) 17ff.

28. Curtius Rufus 4.8.9–11; see *Juden, Griechen und Barbaren*, 19–21, and M. Mor, "The Samaritans and Bar-Kokhbah Revolt" in *The Samaritans* (ed. A.D. Crown; Tübingen: J. C. B. Mohr [Paul Siebeck] 1989) 19–31. There is a discrepancy about the names of the Macedonian governors between Arrian, *Anabasis* 2.13.7, who remains silent about the incident in Samaria, and Curtius Rufus 4.5.9 and 4.8.11.

29. *Wadi Daliyeh I,* 24.

30. F. Hüttenmeister and G. Reeg, *Die antiken Synagogen in Israel, Teil 2: Die samaritanischen Synagogen* (BTAVO Reihe B 12, 2; Wiesbaden: Reichert, 1977) 559, 565, 585, 612, 641, 645, 671. Cf. G. Davies, "A Samaritan Inscription with an expanded text of the Shᵉmaᶜ," *PEQ* 131 (1999) 3–19, which has a list of all Samaritan texts with the Shᵉmaᶜ and related texts.

31. Cf. Gen 34:2, 18, 26 and Euseb., *P.E.* 9.22.1. Because Theodotus is a Samaritan, he calls Sikima a ἱερὸν ἄστυ, a holy town. On euhemerism see *Sib. Or.* 3:110–60.

32. See the Samaritan Anonymous, Eusebius *P.E.* 9.17.5: ξενισθῆναί τε αὐτὸν (Abraham) ὑπὸ πόλεως ἱερὸν Ἀργαριζιν cf. 2 Macc 6:2 and the letter of the "Sidonians in Sichem," Josephus, *Ant.* 12.257–64: There ἱερὸν Διὸς Ἑλληνίου means: the temple of the most great and 'anonymous God' identical with the Greek Zeus. The letter shows an anti-Samaritan Jewish polemical revision.

33. Josephus, *Ant.* 12.257.

34. Euseb., *P.E.* 9.17.5.

35. P. Bruneau, "Les Israélites de Délos et la juiverie délienne," *Bulletin du correspondance hellénique* 106 (1982) 467–79; cf. R. Pummer in *The Samaritans* (ed. A. D. Crown; Tübingen: Mohr Siebeck, 1989) 150–51. Cf also S. Talmon, "A Masada Fragment of Samaritan Origin," *IEJ* 47 (1997) 220–32. Possibly some

Samaritans became allies of the Sicarii in Masada and brought their scrolls with them.

36. Justin, *Apol.* 26.2.4, 56.1ff.

37. See, e.g., G. Lüdemann, *Untersuchungen zur simonianischen Gnosis* (GThA 1; Göttingen: Vandenhoeck und Ruprecht, 1975); for a critical position: K. Beyschlag, *Simon Magus und die christliche Gnosis* (WUNT 10; Tübingen: Mohr, 1974).

38. Cf. *Apol.* 26.3. Cf. S. J. Isser, *The Dositheans* (SJLA 17; Leiden: Brill, 1976).

39. Cf. M. Hengel, *The Zealots* (Edinburgh: Clark, 1989) 197.

40. 2 Macc 6:8 probably only related to the inhabitants of Ptolemais; see *Judaism and Hellenism*, 2:192 n. 200.

41. K. Bringmann, *Hellenistische Reform und Religionsverfolgung in Judäa. Eine Untersuchung zur jüdisch-hellenistischen Geschichte (175–163 v. Chr.)* (Göttingen: Vandenhoeck & Ruprecht, 1983).

42. *Hellenistische Reform*, 12: "Anders ausgedrückt: War das Motiv in der beschriebenen Weise politisch oder religiös reformatorisch?"; cf. the criticism in the review of Bringmann's book by T. Fischer, "Zu einer Untersuchung der jüdisch-hellenistischen Geschichte," *Klio* 67 (1985) 350–55 (esp. 352) and S. Applebaum's review in *Gnomon* 57/2 (1985) 191–93: "The separation of politics and religion is anachronistic."

43. See M. Hengel, *The Zealots*, xi–xii = *Kleine Schriften I*, 351–57; and also R. Deines, *Die Pharisäer: Ihr Verständnis im Spiegel der christlichen und jüdischen Forschung seit Wellhausen und Graetz* (WUNT 101; Tübingen: Mohr Siebeck, 1997) 11, about the new tendencies in research about Pharisaism: "In Wahrheit ist jedoch lediglich eine gesellschaftspolitische Ideologie an die Stelle der religiösen Konfession getreten." Cf. M. Hengel and A. M. Schwemer, *Paulus zwischen Damaskus und Antiochien* (WUNT 108; Tübingen: Mohr Siebeck, 1998) 102 n. 416.

44. *Weltgeschichtliche Betrachtungen* (Stuttgart: A. Kröner, 1935) 108.

45. *Ag. Ap.* 2.165. Josephus knows that this is an unusual word: "Our lawgiver . . . was attracted by none of these forms of policy (i.e., monarchy, oligarchy, ochlocracy), but gave to his constitution (πολίτευμα) the form of what—if a forced expression be permitted—may be termed a 'theocracy', placing all sovereignty and authority (κράτος) in the hand of God." See now Ch. Gerber, *Ein Bild des Judentums für Nichtjuden von Flavius Josephus* (AGJU 40; Leiden: Brill, 1997) 338–59. We should not forget that already the translators of the LXX formed a new epithet for God, translating *Shaddai* and *Sabaoth* with παντοκράτωρ. The few pagan testimonies are later and under Jewish and Christian influence: See Lidell and Scott (9th ed.), 790, and R. Feldmeier, "World Rulers, kosmokratores," in *Dictionary of Deities and Demons in the*

Bible (ed. K. van der Toorn, B. Becking, and P. W. van der Horst; Leiden: Brill, 1995) 1707–9.

46. See Dan 9:27: "And he shall make strong a covenant for the many for one week." Cf. 11:30b, 32a. See J. A. Montgomery, *Daniel* (ICC; Edinburgh: Clark, 1960) 385.

47. Cf. στυγούμενος ὡς τῶν νόμων ἀποστάτης. Cf. 1 Macc 11:21: τίνες μισοῦντες τὸ ἔθνος αὐτῶν ἄνδρες παρανόμοι.

48. 4:18–20. The delegates got a bad conscience and contributed the money for the fitting out of ships.

49. See Köhler-Baumgartner, *Lexicon,* 1444, nr. 12; מרא שמיא Dan 5:23; see also *Paulus zwischen Damaskus und Antiochien,* 196 n. 794. See pp. 194–205 about "monotheistic tendencies among the Western Semites in the Hellenistic age."

50. 12:11 cf. 11:31; see Köhler-Baumgartner, *Lexicon,* 1447, 1513ff.

51. See O. Eissfeldt, *Kleine Schriften II* (Tübingen: Mohr, 1963) 431ff., cf. 191–92, 195ff. (= *ZAW* 57 [1939], 23, 28ff.). Eissfeldt mentions a parallel from Ugarit where a *bʿl knp* appears. See O. Plöger, *Das Buch Daniel* (KAT 18; Gütersloh: Mohn, 1965) 135 and Köhler-Baumgartner, *Lexicon,* 1447.

52. *The God of the Maccabees* (trans. H. R. Moehring; SJLA 32; Leiden: Brill, 1979) xii.

53. Tacitus, *Hist.* 5.8.2: "rex Antiochus demere superstitionem et mores Graecorum dare adnisus quominus taeterrimam gentem in melius mutaret. . . ." Stern has translated this as "King Antiochus endeavoured to abolish Jewish superstition and to introduce Greek civilization . . . " (*Greek and Latin Authors,* 2:28; cf. 2:47ff.). In reality, Antiochus IV was not the true 'enlightener' but the high priest Jason and later Menelaus and their aristocratic supporters.

54. Dan 11:21 "whom he deceives": a hint of the replacement of Jason through Menelaus, whose group of adherents is smaller but through the help of the king becomes strong. Cf. 9:27 and 11:30–32, the escalation of the conflict and the king's collaboration with those "who abandon the holy covenant" and "act wickedly against the covenant."

55. *Ant.* 12.237–41: Here Onias III gave the high priesthood to his brother Jesus/Jason, who was deprived of his post by the king, who gave it to a third younger brother, Onias, who accepted the name Menelaus. This confused account was possibly invented by an anti-Jewish Greek source, by analogy with the power struggle of relatives and brothers in the Hasmonaean high priestly family, down to Hyrcanus II and Aristobulus II.

56. *Ant.* 12.240.

57. Cf. 2 Macc 3:4, 11; 4:1, 23ff. Simon from the priestly order Bilga (according to the Old Latin [Balgeas] and Armenian text) was a brother of Menelaus and Lysimachus (4:39ff.) and they all together were partisans of the Tobiads in

Jerusalem. These were for their part enemies of their youngest brother, Hyrcanus, in Transjordan, who became an ally of Jason. Cf. *Ant.* 12.229–36; 2 Macc 4:26; 5:5–8. It is astonishing that 2 Maccabees and the totally independent Greek source of Josephus agree in details. See *Judaism and Hellenism* 1:279, 283; 2:185 n. 140; 187 n. 160.

58. About the replacement of guilty men by women see M. Hengel, *Rabbinische Legende und frühpharisäische Geschichte: Schimeon b. Schetach und die achtzig Hexen von Askalon* (Heidelberg: Winter 1984) 48–52.

59. See the introduction to *The God of the Maccabees*, xiii.

60. Cf. *Judaism and Hellenism*, 1:115–30.

61. Cf. the fragments in Clement of Alexandria, *Strom.* 5.99.3 and Euseb., *P.E.* 13.12.4; see C. R. Holladay, *Fragments from Hellenistic Jewish Authors* (Atlanta: Scholars Press, 1983) 3:162ff. Cf. *Strom.* 1.150 = *P.E.* 13.12.1ff.; *Fragments*, 152ff.

62. Cf. E. Bickerman, *The God of the Maccabees*, 113ff.

63. Euseb., *P.E.* 13.12.6–8; *Fragments*, 170–75; this translation is according to Holladay.

64. *Ep. Arist.* 16, 139. See R. Feldmeier, "Weise hinter 'eisernen Mauern': Tora und jüdisches Selbstverständnis zwischen Akkulturation und Abgrenzung im Aristeasbrief," in M. Hengel and A. M. Schwemer, ed., *Die Septuaginta*, 20–37.

65. *The God of the Maccabees*, 114.

66. 1 Macc 8:17; 2 Macc 4:13; cf. 11:24 : ἡ ἐπὶ τὰ ἑλληνικὰ μετάθεσις.

67. For further references see the index of *Judaism and Hellenism*, 2:306; see also B. Z. Wacholder, *Eupolemus: A Study of Judaeo-Greek Literature* (Cincinnati: Hebrew Union College-Jewish Institute of Religion, 1974) and *Fragments*, 1:93–156.

68. Josephus, *Ant.* 13.249; cf. *J.W.* 1.61; I. Shatzman, *The Armies of the Hasmonaeans and Herod* (TSAJ 25; Tübingen: Mohr, 1991) 31ff.; M. Hengel, "Jerusalem als jüdische *und* hellenistische Stadt," in *Kleine Schriften II*, 115–56 (esp. 137ff.). This happened probably after the siege of Jerusalem by Antiochus VII Sidetes ca. 134–132 BCE.

69. Josephus, *Ant.* 13.374, 378; *J.W.* 1.88. Cf. also *Ant.* 13.383, his nickname is Thrakidas.

70. *J.W.* 1.88.

71. *J.W.* 1.88; cf. *Ant.* 13.374. For John Hyrcanus, see *Ant.* 13.249, 296, 299 and *J.W.* 1.67.

72. *Ant.* 13.378: ὡς ὄντας ἕλληνας cf. *J.W.* 1.94.

73. *J.W.* 1.93.

74. *Ant.* 13.377.

75. Philo, *Quod Omn. Prob.* 75; *Ant.* 18.21. The population of Jewish Palestine was about 600,000–1,000,000.

76. *J.W.* 1.75, 77 = *Ant.* 13.307, 309.

77. *J.W.* 1.70; *Ant.* 13.301, see E. Schürer, *The History of the Jewish People in the Age of Jesus Christ* (3 vols.; rev. and ed. G. Vermes et al.; Edinburgh: Clark, 1979–86) 1:216ff. Priests who are also called kings (or princes) were found in Phoenicia and Syria. See *The History of the Jewish People*, 2:227 n. 2.

78. *J.W.* 1.123; *Ant.* 14.8–10. Antipater received the grant of Roman citizenship from Caesar; see the inscription from Kos, *Supplementum epigraphicum graecum XLV 1995* (Amsterdam: Gieben, 1923–) no. 1131. It was inherited by his son Herod: King Gaius Julius Herodes.

79. *J.W.* 1.113; cf. *Ant.* 13.411.

80. Cf. only *CIJ*, nos. 787 and 795, which are two relatively late inscriptions from Cilicia. Of the approximately 110 Greek names upon ossuaries in and around Jerusalem only two are theophoric. See L. Y. Rahmani, *A Catalogue of Jewish Ossuaries* (Jerusalem: Israel Academy of Sciences and Humanities, 1994) nos. 84 and 282: *Diodotos.*

81. M. Hengel and A. M. Schwemer, *Paulus*, 251–60 (esp. 258).

82. *Natural History* 5.70; see M. Stern, *Greek and Latin Authors*, 1:469, nr. 204. See also *Kleine Schriften II*, 123ff., 140ff., and *Kleine Schriften I*, 57–67.

83. *Greek and Latin Authors*, 1:477; Polybius in Josephus, *Ant.* 12.136; Philo, *Leg. ad Gaium* 281.

84. In Neh 10:33ff. we find only the obligation to pay one-third of a shekel by the people in Judaea for the temple and its offerings. In Ex 30:11–14 it is only a nonrecurring single payment for each Israelite over twenty; so it is understood in 4Q159. See *Qumrân Cave 4, I* (4Q158–4Q186) (ed. John Allegro; DJD V; Oxford: Clarendon Press, 1968) 6–9; Schuerer, *The History of the Jewish People*, 2:271; cf. Philo, *Legatio ad Gaium* 156, 216, 312; *Legatio ad Gaium* (ed. A. Pelletier; Les Oeuvres de Philon d'Alexandrie 32; Paris: Editions du Cerf, 1972) 364–66.

85. Suetonius, *Augustus* 98.2.

86. The famous Pilate inscription in Caesarea marked a second lighthouse at the eastern entrance of the harbor and was called Tiberieion; the other higher lighthouse at the other, western end of the mole was the 'Drusion', Josephus, *War* 1.412; *Ant.* 15.336. See the ingenious reconstruction of the inscription by G. Alföldy, "Pontius Pilatus und das Tiberieum von Caesarea Maritima," *Scripta Classica Israelica* 18 (1999) 85–108.

87. See now N. Kokkinos, *The Herodian Dynasty* (above n. 2).

88. See Martin Hengel, *Kleine Schriften I*, 171–95, 428–38, in his argument with E. Sanders. It is extremely improbable that the introduction of the prayer-house in Judaea goes back to a priestly initiative. The priests would then have created a rival institution to the temple.

89. *The Greek Minor Prophets Scroll from Nahal Ḥever (8HevXIIgr)* (ed. E. Tov; DJD 8; Oxford: Clarendon, 1990).

90. L. Y. Rahmani, *A Catalogue of Jewish Ossuaries* in the Collections of the State of Israel (Jerusalem: Israel Antiquities Authority, 1994).

91. See ibid, 53ff.: It became a widespread custom in the time before 70 CE and was later not restricted to Pharisees.

92. Ibid., 12.

93. Ibid., 13.

94. G. Avni and Z. Greenhut, ed., *The Akeldama Tombs: Three Burial caves in the Kidron Valley, Jerusalem* (IAA Report I; Jerusalem: Israel Antiquities Authority, 1996). About the inscriptions see pp. 57–72. (p. 66 no. 19).

95. About the Hellenists, see the references in the index of M. Hengel and A. M. Schwemer, *Paulus,* 533; Hengel, *Paul between Damascus and Antioch;* idem, *Between Jesus and Paul* (Philadelphia: Fortress, 1985) 1–29; idem, *The Pre-Christian Paul* (London: SCM, 1991).

Cult and Culture
The Limits of Hellenization in Judea

JOHN J. COLLINS

Sometime in the early second century BCE, the Jewish sage Jeshua ben Sira made the observation that all the works of the Most High come in pairs, one the opposite of the other (Sir 33:15; cf. 42:24). Or at least, that is how we tend to perceive things. In the study of ancient Judaism and early Christianity, two of the more durable binary oppositions have been Hellenism and Judaism, on the one hand, and Hellenistic (meaning Diaspora) and Palestinian Judaism on the other.[1] Both of these oppositions have been criticized repeatedly in recent years. Erich Gruen has argued eloquently that "'Judaism' and 'Hellenism' were neither competing systems nor incompatible concepts. It would be erroneous to assume that Hellenization entailed encroachment upon Jewish traditions and erosion of Jewish beliefs. Jews did not face a choice of either assimilation or resistance to Greek culture." Gruen's book deals primarily with the literature of the Diaspora, but he also points to the extensive Hellenization of Judea under the Hasmoneans, and questions whether Hellenism was ever an issue for the Maccabees.[2] In his classic study of thirty years ago, Martin Hengel argued that Palestinian Judaism, too, was Hellenistic Judaism.[3] In this regard, Hengel stood in the tradition of J. G. Droysen, who understood Hellenism as a syncretistic blending of Greek and oriental cultures.[4] But Hengel went on to discuss the "conflict between Palestinian Judaism and the spirit of the Hellenistic Age." He argued that the crisis of the Maccabean era led to a reaction in Judea, that put a brake on syncretism, fixed intellectual development on the Torah and precluded any fundamental criticism of the cult and the law.[5] The manifold evidence of Hellenistic influence in Judea notwithstanding, the corpus of literature that has come down to us from Judea in the Hellenistic era is very different from its counterpart from the Diaspora. Hellenistic culture was a manifold entity, and it was neither absorbed nor rejected whole. Consequently the question of Hellenism in the land of Israel calls for some differentiation between different aspects of Hellenistic culture.[6]

The Concept of Judaism

At the outset, however, it may be well to reflect for a moment on the other term of the pair, Judaism or Ἰουδαϊσμός, a term which, like Hellenism (in the cultural sense), first appears in the second book of Maccabees. Just as Ἑλληνισμός refers to a culture and way of life, so also did Ἰουδαϊσμός. In the words of Josephus, it is constituted οὐ τῷ γένει μόνον ἀλλὰ καὶ τῇ προαιρέσει τοῦ βίου, not by race alone but also by the choice of way of life.[7] Shaye Cohen has argued that this understanding of Judaism as a πολιτεία, or public way of life, dates from the Hasmonean period. Prior to that time, the term Ἰουδαῖος was an ethnic designation and meant "Judean" rather than "Jew in the religio-cultural sense. Ἰουδαῖοι in the Diaspora were similar to other ethnic groups such as the Idumeans who associated together and maintained their traditional customs. While our evidence supports a shift in linguistic usage and a corresponding shift in attitudes in the Hasmonean period, the idea of a distinctive Jewish way of life was established long before this. At the beginning of the Hellenistic period, Hecataeus of Abdera wrote his famous account of the inhabitants of Judea, in which he noted that their way of life (τὰς κατὰ τὸν βίον ἀγωγάς) differed from that of other peoples and was somewhat anti-social and hostile to foreigners.[8] The rights of Jews, or Judeans, to live according to their ancestral laws had been confirmed by Hellenistic rulers, most famously by Antiochus III when he took control of Jerusalem at the beginning of the second century BCE.[9] This way of life was, to be sure, that of an ἔθνος and the ethnic dimension of Judaism has always remained important. The ethnic dimension became less decisive in the Hasmonean period, but the way of life that became known as Judaism was well established long before the term Ἰουδαϊσμός was coined.

Like Hellenism, Judaism was a manifold entity and not all aspects of it were equally important. The way of life survived quite well in the Greek-speaking Diaspora and was not seriously threatened by the spread of the Greek language in Palestine. Neither was it imperiled by the adoption of Hellenistic style in literature or architecture, for example. In such matters, Erich Gruen is clearly right that "Jews were not obliged to choose between succumbing or resisting. Nor should one imagine a conscious dilemma whereby they had to decide how far to lean in one direction or other, how much 'Hellenism' was acceptable before they compromised the faith, at what point on the spectrum between apostasy and piety they could comfortably locate themselves."[10]

Conceptions of God

The conception and worship of God, what we would call religion, was a more sensitive area, but here again considerable rapprochement was possible. Philo's explanation of the first chapter of Genesis is representative of the theology of Alexandrian Judaism: "It consists of an account of the creation of the world, implying that the world is in harmony with the Law, and the Law with the world, and that the man who observes the law is constituted thereby a loyal citizen of the world, regulating his doings by the purpose and will of Nature, in accordance with which the entire world itself also is administered."[11] There were certainly precedents in the biblical tradition, especially in the wisdom literature, for "creation theology" that held that the will of God is reflected in nature. Hellenistic philosophy, however, especially Stoicism, permitted a much more systematic "natural theology," which was embraced by Jews like Philo and the author of the Wisdom of Solomon, even if it was not fully compatible with biblical ideas of revelation and election.[12] Fundamental to this theology was a belief in the unity of humankind and of the truth, and an acknowledgment that the truth disclosed in biblical revelation could also be approached, even if imperfectly, in other ways by poets and philosophers. A relatively early (second century BCE) formulation of this belief is found in the Letter of Aristeas. Aristeas explains to King Ptolemy: "These people worship God the overseer and creator of all, whom all men worship, but we, O King, address differently as Zeus and Dis" (*Ep. Arist.* 16). Aristeas is supposedly a Greek. Some scholars have argued that the identification was acceptable on the lips of a Greek but would not have been endorsed by Jews.[13] But we find an almost identical formulation in the roughly contemporary Jewish author Aristobulus, who emended the divine names Dis and Zeus in the passages he cited from Greek poets, "for their inherent meaning refers to God," and "the Zeus celebrated in poems and prose compositions leads the mind up to God."[14] From an early point, Greeks had sought correspondences between their deities and those of eastern peoples. The god of the Jews was sometimes identified with Dionysus, because the use of branches at the feast of Sukkoth was associated with the thyrsus in Bacchic festivals.[15] That identification was generally rejected by Jews, except perhaps for some apostates in the Maccabean era. But the high god Zeus, at least in his more philosophical formulations, was deemed a satisfactory counterpart to God Most High, even though Homeric mythology would undoubtedly have been problematic for most Jews.

Cultic Separatism

Jewish willingness to accept Zeus as an alternative name for God did not entail a willingness to participate in pagan cult. One of the most persistent charges against Jews by their gentile opponents was that of atheism, the refusal to worship the gods of the *polis* or state. This refusal, coupled with distinctive observances required by Jewish law, led to the view of Judaism as "somewhat anti-social and hostile to strangers," in the famous phrase of Hecataeus of Abdera. In the Hellenistic world, religion was deeply imbedded in culture and politics. The refusal of Jews to participate in pagan cults, and the frequent denunciations of idolatry in Jewish literature, has sometimes led to the impression that Jews were antagonistic to Hellenistic culture.[16] The impression is mistaken, however. Both Philo and the Wisdom of Solomon are vehement in their denunciations of idolatry,[17] but they nonetheless embrace Greek philosophy and the concept of a universal wisdom with enthusiasm. Philo famously declared that the Jews, though strangers, differed little from the citizens.[18] Synagogues were dedicated to Ptolemaic kings, and prayers were offered for Roman emperors. The project of Hellenistic Judaism in the Diaspora required that a distinction be made between cult and culture, however difficult it might be for some gentiles to accept it. Hellenistic culture was not an undifferentiated whole. Political allegiance only became problematic for Diaspora Jews in the Roman era, when relations with the rulers deteriorated. The use of the Greek language, or of Greek literary forms was never a problem. The author of 4 Maccabees, who preached strict adherence to the Jewish

Law at a time when relations between Jews and gentiles were at a low ebb, nonetheless wrote good Greek with a sophisticated rhetorical style. The language was simply a given, for Jews of the Diaspora, and many Greek ideas and modes of expression were part of the air they breathed. Cultic conformity, however, was a different matter. The Jews of the Diaspora might be said to have pioneered the distinction between cult and culture, which would play an important role in Western society in much later times.[19]

Despite the general compatibility of Judaism and Hellenistic culture, then, there were occasions on which Jews were confronted with a decision as to how much 'Hellenism' was acceptable, or how far traditional practices could be abandoned. Various Jews might draw the line at different points and customs, and institutions that were innocuous in some situations might take on symbolic significance at other times. For those who maintained a commitment to "the Jewish way of life," however, as distinct from apostates like Philo's nephew Tiberius Julius Alexander, a line was inevitably drawn at some point.

The Hellenistic Reform in Judea

The paradigmatic instance of a conflict between 'Hellenism' and 'Judaism' is the sequence of events that took place in Jerusalem in the reign of Antiochus IV Epiphanes, in the years 175–164 BCE.[20] These events entailed cultural changes, but also eventually cultic changes imposed by the Syrian king, and finally open warfare. This was clearly a case where a line was drawn and some practices were deemed unacceptable. It is important for our discussion to consider the point at which that line was drawn and the causes of the conflict.

The beginning of this sequence of events is described as follows in 1 Maccabees:

> In those days certain renegades came out from Israel and misled many, saying, "Let us go and make a covenant with the Gentiles around us, for since we separated from them many disasters have come upon us." This proposal pleased them, and some of the people eagerly went to the king, who authorized them to observe the ordinances of the Gentiles. So they built a gymnasium in Jerusalem, according to Gentile custom, and removed the marks of circumcision,

and abandoned the holy covenant. They joined with the Gentiles and sold themselves to do evil. (1 Macc 1:11–15)

A more detailed account is provided by 2 Maccabees. Here we find that the instigator was Jason, brother of the high priest Onias III, and that he obtained the high priesthood by promising to pay large sums of money to the king. He also paid for the privilege of building the gymnasium and registering "the Antiochenes in Jerusalem." The precise implications of this registration are not clarified. It is widely thought to entail the constitution of a Greek polis in Jerusalem, with a new list of citizens.[21] His innovations were initially greeted with enthusiasm, resulting in an extreme of Hellenization (ἀκμή τις ἑλληνισμοῦ) so that priests lost interest in the temple in preference for the gymnasium. Nonetheless, no conflict arose until Jason was usurped by Menelaus, whom he had entrusted with the tribute for the king. Menelaus then drove Jason into exile and had the legitimate high priest, Onias III, murdered.[22] When Antiochus Epiphanes was rumored to have died in Egypt, Jason attempted to regain control of Jerusalem. It was at this point, according to 2 Maccabees, that Antiochus thought that Judea was in revolt and sent in the troops.[23]

It is clear that Jason and Menelaus were attracted to some things Hellenistic, and that the gymnasium, the great symbol of Hellenistic culture and forum of Greek education, was welcomed by many people in Jerusalem.[24] We may agree then with Hengel that Hellenistic culture must have made considerable inroads in Judea already before the reform. Whether Jason's innovations reflected a new, hellenized, understanding of religion, however, is a controversial question. Elias Bickerman, in his classic book *The God of the Maccabees*, argued that it did.[25] Greeks were aware that other lawgivers besides Moses had claimed divine authority, and concluded that all such laws were of human origin. Jews had not always been separate from gentiles. There was a primeval age when separation did not exist. Hecataeus of Abdera explained the separation as an unfortunate but understandable reaction by Moses to his expulsion from Egypt. Other Greek writers held that separatist laws had been introduced later, by Moses' inferior successors. "A Hellenized Jew," wrote Bickerman, "could no more ignore these results of Greek scholarship than can an enlightened Jew of today ignore the results of scholarly criticism of the Bible."[26] Even observant Jews like

Philo maintained their allegiance to the Mosaic law by understanding it allegorically. Some of Philo's contemporaries no longer felt the obligation to observe the letter of the law at all. Bickerman argued that "we have only to retrace the line of thought of these Jewish Hellenists in order fully to understand the similar ideology of Jason and Menelaus in Palestine. They wanted to reform Judaism by eliminating the barbaric separatism, which had been introduced only late, and returning to the original form of worship, free of any distortion."[27] Writing in Germany in 1937, Bickerman drew an ominous analogy with modern Judaism: "The reformers under Epiphanes remind us of the Jewish reform movement during the forties of the nineteenth century, when men like G. Riesser, A. Geiger and I. Einhorn proposed the abolition of the dietary laws and declared circumcision not to be binding. They, too, were fascinated by the non-Jewish world around them and were impressed by the hypotheses of (Protestant) scholarship concerning the origin of the Pentateuch."[28] Bickerman ascribed this ideology not only to the original reform of Jason but also to Menelaus and the cultic innovations that followed. In his view "Menelaus and his partisans thus worshipped the heavenly god of their ancestors without temple and images, under the open sky upon the altar which stood on Mt. Zion. They were free from the yoke of the law, and in mutual tolerance they were united with the Gentiles. What could be more human, what could be more natural, than their desire to force this tolerance also upon those of their coreligionists who were still unenlightened?"[29]

Bickerman's view of the motives of the reformers has not won general acceptance. Isaak Heinemann argued that the Hellenism of the reformers, like that of other "Graeculi des Orients" was superficial and without intellectual foundations.[30] Victor Tcherikover stated bluntly: "The changes in the sphere of religion and culture were not the reason for the reform, but its consequences, and they involved no principles. . . ."[31] For him, the reform consisted of converting Jerusalem into a *polis*, primarily with an eye to economic advantage. Martin Hengel, however, rallied to Bickerman's defense on this point.[32] He points to "a whole series of significant philosophers and learned men in the second and first centuries in the Phoenician coastal cities," and notes that even an inland city like Gadara in Trans-Jordan had a significant tradition of Greek education. But there was no such tradition in Jerusalem prior to Jason's reform. There were, of course, traditions of learning, but they were either concerned with the transmission of sacred literature, or with traditional Near Eastern wisdom. Ben Sira has smatterings of Greek philosophy, but scarcely more. There is no Judean counterpart to the philosophical hermeneutic of Aristobulus or even to the sporadic allegorizing of Pseudo-Aristeas. No Judean author says that Zeus is another name for the true God.

Hengel's survey of Jewish literature written in Greek in the land of Israel in the Maccabean era yields only three authors, Jason of Cyrene, Eupolemus, and an anonymous Samaritan whose work is attributed to Eupolemus by Eusebius.[33] If we may judge by the abbreviation of his work in 2 Maccabees, Jason of Cyrene must have had a good Greek education, but it is unlikely that he received it in Jerusalem. As Hengel readily admits, "the very name of Jason of Cyrene . . . indicates that he was not a real Palestinian but either came from the Jewish Diaspora in Cyrenaica or at least spent a good part of his life there."[34] The attribution of the Samaritan work is disputed.[35] One of the surviving fragments is ascribed to Eupolemus by Eusebius, while the other is said to be from an anonymous work although it appears to be a briefer summary of the same source. In any case, Eupolemus is our only example of a Judean author who wrote in Greek in this period. He is plausibly identified with the figure mentioned in 1 Macc 8:17 as a Jewish delegate to Rome whose father had negotiated the charter of rights for Jerusalem with Antiochus III. His work "On the kings in Judea" is written in Greek and uses the LXX. On Hengel's own admission, it has "serious linguistic and stylistic deficiencies,"[36] but it shares an interest common in Hellenistic historiography in the origins of culture. Moses is portrayed as the first wise man, and is credited with the invention of the alphabet. He also says that Solomon gave a golden pillar to the king of Troy, who set it up in the temple of Zeus. This latter episode recalls an incident mentioned in 2 Macc 4:18–20, when Jason sent 300 drachmas for a sacrifice to Hercules at the quadrennial games at Tyre, but the envoys requested that the money be used for triremes instead. Hengel comments: "Perhaps in the background here is the conception of pre-Maccabean hellenists that the 'greatest God' (*theos megistos*) to whom Solomon owed his status as king, the God who gave him the commission to build the temple and whom Suron defined in his answer as 'creator of heaven and earth,' was in the last resort, as the one god, also identical with the Zeus of the Phoenicians and the Greeks."[37]

Eupolemus then provides some evidence that the kind of ideas postulated by Bickerman were current in Jerusalem in the early second century BCE. To say that Jason or Menelaus can be credited with such ideas remains a gratuitous inference. But the most interesting thing about Eupolemus, in any case, is that such a hellenized figure was chosen by Judas Maccabee for the mission to Rome. And that should hardly surprise us. A major qualification for such a mission was the ability to speak Greek. The quarrel of the Maccabees was not with the Hellenistic understanding of history, nor even with the correlation of Zeus Olympios and the God of Israel.[38]

While it is true that we only see the reformers through the eyes of their detractors, we must still make do with the evidence at our disposal. That evidence shows that both Jason and Menelaus, in turn, were ready to pay large sums of money for the control of Jerusalem. Presumably they hoped to gain enough financially to make the investment worthwhile. The background stories of the Tobiad family in Josephus also show far more interest in unscrupulous profiteering than in any kind of religious reform.[39] Menelaus' betrayal of Jason's trust in outbidding him for the priesthood and Jason's willingness to plunge Jerusalem into civil war further erode confidence in their intellectual idealism. Moreover, it is not clear that much education went on in Jason's gymnasium.[40] There was considerable curricular variety in the gymnasia of the Near East. Second Maccabees does not complain that people were reading Homer instead of the Torah, only that they were obsessed with the novelty of Greek athletics. While the account in 2 Maccabees may be distorted, it remains the only account we have. No doubt, the reformers were genuinely attracted to the trappings of Hellenism, but there is little evidence that their deeper motives were cultural or religious. I am inclined, then, with Tcherikover, to doubt that there were any principles involved other than power and profit.[41] Of course the pursuit of power and profit was typical of the Hellenistic world, but it was not in any way peculiar to Hellenistic culture.

Both the books of Maccabees imply that the reforms of Jason were significant violations of the Jewish way of life. First Maccabees claims that they "removed the marks of circumcision and abandoned the holy covenant" (1 Macc 1:15). Second Maccabees says that Jason set aside the constitution based on the ancestral laws which had been authorized by Antiochus III and "broke down the lawful manners of life, and introduced new customs forbidden by the law" (2 Macc 4:11). Even the Book of Daniel, which pays minimal attention to the cultural reforms and does not mention the gymnasium, refers to the Jewish leaders in this period as "violators of the covenant" (Dan 11:30: מרשיעי ברית). In the judgment of these authors, a line had been crossed and the new customs were incompatible with the Jewish way of life. It is not apparent, however, that this judgment was widely shared. The introduction of the gymnasium provoked no revolt. (Curiously, we are never told that it was torn down later, although neither are we ever told that it remained in existence. Herod held athletic contests, apparently in Jerusalem, and also had a hippodrome).[42] There is good reason to believe that Jews of Diaspora in the Ptolemaic era frequented the gymnasium.[43] Philo shows considerable familiarity with the institution,[44] and the education that he and other Diaspora writers had evidently received is most easily explained by their attendance at the gymnasium.[45] Whether the Hellenizers of the Maccabean era removed the marks of their circumcision has been disputed.[46] Such a procedure was certainly not required for participation in a gymnasium and even the putative reason for it, nudity, may not have been *de rigueur*. Such a practice, however, would go some way to explaining Daniel's designation of the reformers as "violators of the covenant" and the polemic against nudity in the Book of Jubilees.[47] But even epispasm, or abandonment of circumcision, was not necessarily tantamount to apostasy. These were instances where Jews may have differed as to what was an acceptable place to draw the line. In any case, the introduction of the gymnasium, while it may have been offensive to many Jews, was not the cause of the Maccabean revolt.

The Ideology of the Persecution

This brings us to the second major issue in the Hellenization of Jerusalem under Antiochus Epiphanes. Was the desecration of the temple by Antiochus Epiphanes integrally related to the program of the Hellenizers? Was the new worship on Mt. Zion a reflection of their theology? Bickerman held that it was: "The form of worship introduced by Epiphanes on Mt. Zion corresponded to the Greek conception of a reasonable religion of nature."[48] The persecution of traditional Jews arose from the desire of Menelaus and his cohorts "to force this tolerance also upon those of their coreligionists who were still unenlightened."[49] Hengel argued that

> The cult in the temple was also "reformed" in syncretistic fashion, presumably following the example of the more strongly Hellenized

Phoenicians. . . . Honour was given above all to the "supreme God of heaven," interpreted in a syncretistic and universalistic way. He was identified with Ba'al Shamem of the Phoenicians and Zeus Olympius of the Greeks. Presumably the radical reformers were influenced by the ideas of the Greek enlightenment, and perhaps they sought to restore the original "reasonable" form of worship of the deity without "superstitious" falsification. At the same time they sought the complete dissolution of the characteristics of Judaism and its consistent assimilation to its Hellenistic oriental environment.[50]

There were indeed Jews in the second century BCE who argued that the God of Israel was the same deity who was called Zeus by the Greeks. We have already considered the cases of pseudo-Aristeas and Aristobulus. These instances are somewhat later and in a different cultural context, in the Diaspora. Bickerman argued that "we have only to retrace the line of thought of these Jewish Hellenists in order fully to understand the similar ideology of Jason and Menelaus in Palestine."[51] It must be emphasized, however, that this identification did not entail "the complete dissolution of the characteristics of Judaism and its consistent assimilation to its Hellenistic oriental environment." On the contrary, Aristeas proceeds to denounce polytheism and idolatry and even to defend the rationality of the Jewish food laws. A willingness to entertain the legitimacy of some Greek conceptions of God was by no means tantamount to consistent assimilation.

Another relevant instance of *theocrasia,* or the identification of the God of Israel with a Greek deity, is provided by the action of the Samaritans. According to 2 Maccabees, when Antiochus Epiphanes renamed the Jerusalem temple in honor of Olympian Zeus, he also renamed the temple on Mt. Garizim in honor of Zeus Xenios, or "Zeus the god of strangers," "just as those who inhabited the place had requested" (2 Macc 6:2). Josephus, who does not appear to use 2 Maccabees in his account of this period, preserves a copy of the Samaritans' request, in which they are at pains to distinguish themselves from the Jews, and profess to be Sidonians by origin.[52] (It is possible that the request came from a group of Hellenized citizens rather than from the Samaritan people as a whole. The wealthy citizens of the Idumean town of Maresha also identified themselves as Sidonians).[53] Bickerman has defended the authenticity of the request, and the king's response, at length, although some doubts about the reliability of Josephus persist.[54] But here again, the identification of the God by a Greek name entailed no other changes in the religion, as far as we know.[55] Moreover, other Near Eastern cults, in Phoenicia and elsewhere, were given a veneer of Hellenistic names "without losing their identity or continuity."[56] The "Hellenistic enlightenment," then, which led to the identification of Greek and Semitic deities, does not in itself explain the disruptive events in Jerusalem.

Between the reorganization of Jerusalem by Jason and the reorganization of the cult by royal command some seven years later, several important events intervened. First was the usurpation of the high priesthood by Menelaus, who was not of the Zadokite line. Menelaus had evidently been an associate of Jason, but his agenda may have been quite different. In any case, he was hard pressed to pay the tribute that he had promised to the king, and resorted to the theft and sale of temple vessels. The first outbreak of fighting was occasioned by a popular demonstration against this plunder (2 Macc 4:39–42). A more serious outbreak followed, when a rumor spread that Antiochus had died in Egypt during his second invasion of that country. Jason, with a force of a thousand men attacked Jerusalem, and wrested control of it from Menelaus, who took refuge in the citadel. Then, "when news of these events reached the king, he thought that Judaea was in revolt" (2 Macc 5:11) and he sent in troops to take the city by storm.[57] The walls of the city were torn down, and a military garrison, the Akra, was established in the City of David. According to 1 Macc 1:34, "they stationed there a sinful people, men who were renegades." This garrison "collected all the spoils of Jerusalem." From this point on, there were open hostilities between Epiphanes and his Jewish subjects.[58]

Up to this point, the actions of the king are quite intelligible. The sacking of Jerusalem and establishment of the Akra were punitive measures, intended to punish Jerusalem for its putative revolt. The severity of the punishment was undoubtedly influenced by the fact that the king had been humiliated in Egypt by the Roman legate, Popilius Laenas.[59] This humiliation is clearly linked to the fury of the king in Dan 11:30: "Ships of the Kittim will come against him and he will be intimidated. He will return and rage against the holy covenant."[60] The difficulty arises with what happens next.

According to 1 Macc 1:41, "the king wrote to his whole kingdom that all should be one people and that all should give up their particular customs." Taken at face value, this statement is quite incredible.[61] As late as 166, Antiochus was still celebrating the multiplicity of gods worshipped in his dominion, at the great festival at Daphne.[62] He may have written to urge his subjects to "be one people," but no people other than the Jews were required to abandon their particular customs, and Jews in the Diaspora were not subjected to this requirement.[63] The alleged universality of the royal edict, then, must be rejected as an exaggeration. First Maccabees, however, goes on to describe how "the king sent letters by messengers to Jerusalem and the towns of Judah; he directed them to follow customs strange to the land" (1:44) and forbade the observance of the traditional cult. This statement is paralleled in 2 Maccabees 6, where an Athenian senator is sent to enforce the edict. This attempt to change the religion of a people is extraordinary in antiquity, and lends itself to no ready explanation. Some scholars have supposed that the edict was a punitive response to an escalating Jewish revolt, but the evidence of the books of Maccabees lends little support to this view.[64]

In view of the anomalous character of Epiphanes' edict in the context of Hellenistic policies, Bickerman argued that the initiative for the persecution came not from the king but from the hellenizing Jewish High Priest Menelaus.[65] He found some hints of this solution in the sources. In 2 Macc 13:4, Menelaus is put to death by Antiochus V Eupator, because he is identified by Lysias, a Seleucid general, as "the cause of all the trouble." According to Josephus (*Ant.* 12.384–85) Lysias made a more specific accusation: it was Menelaus who persuaded the king's father to compel the Jews to abandon their fathers' religion. Josephus wrote some two and a half centuries after the events, but he does not seem to have used 2 Maccabees as a source. Even if Lysias made the accusation, however, he was not an impartial witness. He wanted to relieve the Seleucid monarchy of responsibility for a disastrous sequence of events, and Menelaus was no longer a useful ally.

Bickerman accepted the view of Lysias, and found another, much less explicit, hint in Dan 11:30, which says that the king would pay heed to those who forsook the holy covenant. This position was endorsed by Hengel: "Neither the king nor his 'friends', who were certainly very little interested in the Jews, will have conceived such unusual ideas, which presuppose a knowledge of conditions within Judaism. This gives greatest probability to Bickerman's view that the impulse to the most extreme escalation of events in Judea came from the extreme Hellenists in

Jerusalem itself. . . . Thus Menelaus and the Tobiads who supported him appear as the authors of the edict of persecution."[66] One might add that some analogies for violent religious reform could be found in Jewish history, both in the earlier reform of King Josiah (2 Kings 22–23) and in the subsequent policies of the Hasmoneans.

Nonetheless, the fact remains that all our primary sources (Daniel, 1 and 2 Maccabees) ascribe primary responsibility to Antiochus Epiphanes. This is also true of the pagan sources. A letter of Antiochus V Eupator to Lysias, preserved in 2 Maccabees 11, acknowledges that "the Jews do not agree with my father's plan of converting them to Hellenic customs, but prefer their own way of life."[67] According to Diodorus, the king was offended by Jewish separatism and hostility toward gentiles, and "shocked by such hatred directed against all mankind, he had set himself to break down their traditional practices."[68] Tacitus says that "King Antiochus endeavored to abolish Jewish superstition and to introduce Greek civilization" but was prevented by war with the Parthians.[69] There are some parallels for the prohibition of customs that were perceived as barbaric, such as the Punic custom of human sacrifice.[70] Some centuries later, Hadrian would prohibit circumcision. The actions of Hadrian provide the closest analogy to those of Antiochus,[71] but it is possible that he had the Seleucid precedent in mind. Epiphanes had no such precedent, but he was known to be an impulsive character; hence the jibe that he was not *epiphanes,* a god made manifest, but *epimanes,* mad.[72] Jerusalem had incurred his wrath by seeming to rebel at the moment of his humiliation, and the Jews were widely perceived in the Hellenistic world as misoxenic and anti-social. It is not impossible that in his anger and wounded pride he took unprecedented measures against what he perceived as strange and alien people. Whether, or to what degree, he was encouraged in this by Menelaus is a question that we may never be able to answer.[73]

What appears to be relatively clear, however, is that the measures taken by Antiochus amounted to an attempt to suppress traditional Jewish observance, not to reform it: "It was impossible either to keep the Sabbath, to observe the ancestral festivals, or openly confess oneself to be a Jew" (2 Macc 6:6). Cultic practices introduced included not only the worship of Zeus Olympius but also of Dionysus, and we are told that many Jews sacrificed to idols. Both Zeus Olympios/Baʿal Shamem, as the god of heaven, and Dionysus were often taken as the pagan counterparts of the God of Israel, but if either of these cults was understood to continue the worship of the traditional God of Israel, then that worship was completely reconceived, to a degree that is without parallel elsewhere in Hellenistic Judaism. Some practices, such as eating pork, were apparently demanded precisely because they violated the Jewish law.[74] Tcherikover argued plausibly that the new cult in the temple was simply the cult practiced by the Syrian garrison, and Bickerman himself argued that the new order of worship was entirely un-Greek.[75] But then it can hardly have resulted from an enlightened, hellenized view of the history of religion,[76] and indeed it can only be taken as a very atypical instance of "Hellenism" at all.

I am inclined then to agree with Heinemann and Fergus Millar that a sharp distinction must be drawn between the Hellenistic reform of Jason, on the one hand, and the religious persecution of Antiochus Epiphanes on the other.[77] It was only the persecution, not the reform as such, that provoked the armed rebellion of the Maccabees. It was quite possible to have a gymnasium in Jerusalem without posing a threat to monotheism. If the survival of Judaism was imperiled in this period, it was not because of athletics or the Greek hat, or even nudity in the gymnasium. Still less was it threatened by enlightened Hellenistic views of history and religion. It was only when the traditional Jewish cult was proscribed and some Jews were compelled to participate in pagan worship that "Hellenism" (if the policies of Antiochus Epiphanes can be so described) became unacceptable to the majority of the Jewish people.

The Distinctiveness of Palestinian Judaism

Nonetheless, the fact remains that the corpus of literature that has come down to us from Palestinian Judaism is very different from its counterpart from the Diaspora. Jerusalem produced no philosopher of the stature of Philo. The Diaspora shows no evidence of the kind of preoccupation with minutiae of the law that we find in some of the scrolls from Qumran. In his *magnum opus* thirty years ago, Hengel suggested that the development of Judaism in the land of Israel could be explained to some degree as a reaction against Jason's reform and the subsequent persecution. "The failure of the attempt of the Hellenistic reformers to abolish the Torah by force in effect *fixed* intellectual development *on the Torah*," and "this fixation meant that any fundamental theological criticism of the cult and the law could no longer develop freely within Judaism."[78] Repudiation of Hellenism could take other forms besides armed rebellion against the Seleucids. At the same time, Hengel recognizes that in other respects the process of Hellenization continued, and indeed he insists that Palestinian Judaism can also be described as Hellenistic Judaism through the first century CE and later.[79]

It is clear that cultural Hellenization continued apace in Judea under the "phil-hellene" Hasmoneans and even more so under Herod.[80] The late Arnaldo Momigliano wrote: "The penetration of Greek words, customs, and intellectual modes in Judaea during the rule of the Hasmoneans and the following Kingdom of Herod has no limits."[81] And yet there were some limits. Josephus tells us of Herod that "because of his ambition . . . and the flattering attention which he gave to Caesar and the most influential Romans, he was forced to depart from the customs (of the Jews) and to alter many of their regulations, for in his ambitious spending he founded cities and erected temples—*not in Jewish territory, for the Jews would not have put up with this, since we are forbidden such things, including the honouring of statues and sculptured forms in the manner of the Greeks*—but these he built in foreign and surrounding territory."[82] Moreover, "he established athletic contests every fifth year in honour of Caesar, and built a theatre in Jerusalem, and after that a very large amphitheatre in the plain, both being spectacularly lavish but foreign to Jewish custom."[83] He even introduced Roman-style gladiatorial contests. These innovations drew criticism from "the natives" (ἐπιχώριοι). According to Josephus: "More than all else it was the trophies that irked them, for in the belief that these were images surrounded by weapons, which it was against their national custom to worship, they were exceedingly angry."[84] Herod eventually yielded by removing the ornaments. The pattern that we find here is rather similar to what we found in the Maccabean period. Athletic contests and theatrical performances might offend some people, but they could be tolerated. Idolatry, or the worship of pagan gods in Judean territory was intolerable to many. Again, the line would seem to be drawn between culture and cult. Josephus reports several similar incidents in the Roman era, such as the attempt to pull down the golden eagle from the temple shortly before Herod's death,[85] and Jewish resistance to the introduction of Roman standards into Jerusalem by Pontius Pilate[86] and to the installation of a statue of Caligula in the temple.[87]

The case of Herod shows the duality of Jewish reactions to Hellenism. On the one hand, the upper classes in Jerusalem, including many priests, embraced Hellenistic culture as enthusiastically as their counterparts in Alexandria, even if they left no comparable intellectual achievements (with the arguable exception of Josephus).[88] On the other hand, the people that Josephus calls "the natives," who presumably constituted the larger part of the population, looked on cultural innovations with suspicion, and sometimes with revulsion. Only idolatry or pagan worship would provoke a militant reaction, but there is also evidence for broader cultural aversion in Judea, in a way that is not attested in the Diaspora.[89] It is significant that Herod is not said to have built a gymnasium in Jerusalem. Presumably this institution had acquired negative associations for the "natives" after the debacle of the Maccabean era.

The negative reaction of some Jews against Hellenistic mores cannot be ascribed entirely to the experiences of the Maccabean era. Consider, for example, a passage in the *Book of the Watchers*, which is one of the oldest sections of the *Book of Enoch* and was almost certainly written before the Maccabean revolt.[90] There we are told that the fallen angels taught many things to human beings, including the making of weaponry and "the things after these, and the art of making them: bracelets, and ornaments, and the art of making up the eyes and of beautifying the eyelids, and the most precious and choice stones, and all kinds of coloured dyes. And the world was changed. And there was great impiety and much fornication and they went astray, and all their ways became corrupt" (*1 Enoch* 8:1–2). It is tempting to see in this passage an allegory of the cultural innovations of the Hellenistic age. The reaction of apocalyptic literature, such as we find in the *Book of Enoch,* is first to hope for a great judgment to cleanse the earth, and second to accompany Enoch in imagination in his ascent to heaven and his journey to the ends of the earth; in short to look for salvation in some other realm that has not been polluted.[91] Similarly, the Dead Sea sect withdrew to the wilderness to prepare the way of the Lord, since the temple was judged to be defiled, not only by Jason and Menelaus, but more immediately by the Hasmonean priests.[92] Whether the reaction of such people can reasonably be described as a "fixation on the Law" is debatable. The concerns of the Dead Sea sect certainly included halachic observance in great detail, and this was also true of their sectarian rivals, the Pharisees.[93] But they had other concerns, too, and their religion cannot be reduced to an obsession with the Law.

Perhaps the most penetrating insight in Hengel's great book, however, is that even those forms of Judaism that seem most resolutely anti-Hellenistic are nonetheless often influenced by Hellenistic culture in profound ways.[94] Both the Dead Sea sect and the Pharisees can be seen as variants of the voluntary associations that proliferated throughout the Hellenistic world.[95] The apocalyptic literature, while by no means typical of Hellenistic thought, has some significant analogues in the Hellenistic world.[96] Most important, it introduced into Jewish tradition the hope for individual salvation after death, which was typically Hellenistic, even if it was conceived here in new ways.[97] The world was indeed changed, and neither Judaism nor any other way of life in the ancient Near East could avoid the changes entirely.

Nonetheless, I submit that the most striking thing about the Jewish encounter with Hellenism, both in the Diaspora and in the land of Israel, was the persistence of Jewish separatism in matters of worship and cult. There was a limit to Hellenization, which is best expressed in the distinction between cult and culture. That distinction was extraordinary in the ancient world, but it would be paradigmatic for both Judaism and Christianity in later phases of Western history.

Notes

1. On the various roles of these distinctions in shaping the identity of modern Judaism see Yaacov Shavit, *Athens in Jerusalem: Classical Antiquity and Hellenism in the Making of the Modern Secular Jew* (The Littman Library of Jewish Civilization; London: Vallentine Mitchell, 1997).

2. Erich Gruen, *Heritage and Hellenism: The Reinvention of Jewish Tradition* (Berkeley: University of California Press, 1998) xiv, 1–40. Cf. Tessa Rajak, "The Hasmoneans and the Uses of Hellenism," in P. R. Davies and R. T. White, ed., *A Tribute to Geza Vermes: Essays on Jewish and Christian Literature and History* (JSOTSup 100; Sheffield: Sheffield Academic Press, 1990) 261–80; Lee I. Levine, *Judaism and Hellenism in Antiquity: Conflict or Confluence?* (Seattle: University of Washington Press, 1998) 33–95.

3. Martin Hengel, *Judaism and Hellenism: Studies in Their Encounter in Palestine in the Early Hellenistic Period* (Philadelphia: Fortress, 1974) 1.103–6.

4. J. G. Droysen, *Geschichte des Hellenismus* (2 vols.; Hamburg, 1836–43). Note the essay of Arnaldo Momigliano, "J. G. Droysen between Greeks and Jews," in idem, *Essays in Ancient and Modern Historiography* (Oxford: Oxford University Press, 1977) 307–23.

5. Hengel, *Judaism and Hellenism* 1. 306–9.

6. John M. G. Barclay, *Jews in the Mediterranean Diaspora* (Edinburgh: Clark, 1996) 82–102, distinguishes seven different aspects of Hellenism: political, social, linguistic, educational, ideological, religious, and material. Cf. Martin Hengel, *Jews, Greeks and Barbarians* (London: SCM, 1980) 60, who has a similar list.

7. *Ag. Ap.* 2.210. See Shaye J. D. Cohen, *The Beginnings of Jewishness* (Berkeley: University of California Press, 1999), 132–35.

8. Hecataeus, in Diodorus Siculus 40.3.4. M. Stern, *Greek and Latin Authors on Jews and Judaism* (Jerusalem: Israel Academy of Sciences, 1976) 1.26.

9. Elias Bickerman, "Le charte séleucide de Jerusalem," in idem, *Studies in Jewish and Christian History* (Leiden: Brill, 1980) 2.44–85; Victor Tcherikover, *Hellenistic Civilization and the Jews* (New York: Atheneum, 1970) 82–89.

10. Gruen, *Heritage and Hellenism,* xv. Martin Goodman, "Jewish Attitudes to Greek Culture in the Period of the Second Temple," in G. Abramson and T. Parfitt, ed., *Jewish Education and Learning* (Chur, Switzerland: Harwood Academic Publishers, 1994) 169 comments on the "lack of concern about encroaching Hellenism" and suggests that Jews in the Hasmonean period felt that Greek culture was "not really wholly alien."

11. *De Opificio Mundi* 3.

12. J. J. Collins, "Natural Theology and Biblical Tradition: The Case of Hellenistic Judaism," *CBQ* 60 (1998) 1–15.

13. Barclay, *Jews in the Mediterranean Diaspora,* 143; Gruen, *Heritage and Hellenism,* 216.

14. Eusebius, *P.E.* 13.13.3–8. Carl R. Holladay, *Fragments from Hellenistic Jewish Authors. III. Aristobulus* (Atlanta: Scholars Press, 1995) 173.

15. Plutarch, *Quaestiones Conviviales* 4.6; cf. Tacitus, *Hist.* 5.5.5.

16. See especially Barclay, *Jews in the Mediterranean Diaspora,* 181–228.

17. Philo, *De Decalogo,* 52–81; *De Vita Contemplativa* 3–9; *De Spec. Leg.* 1.13–29; 2.255; Wis 13–15. See J. J. Collins, *Jewish Wisdom in the Hellenistic Age* (Louisville, Ky.: Westminster, 1997) 209–13.

18. *De Vita Mosis* 1.34–36.

19. See further J. J. Collins, *Between Athens and Jerusalem* (revised edition; Grand Rapids, Mich.: Eerdmans, 2000).

20. For the following discussion of the events in the Maccabean era see my essay "The Hellenization of Jerusalem in the pre-Maccabean Era" (Publications of the Rennert Center; Ramat Gan: Bar Ilan University, 1999).

21. Tcherikover, *Hellenistic Civilization*, 161; Hengel, *Judaism and Hellenism* 1.277–8.

22. Dov Gera, *Judaea and Mediterranean Politics, 219–161 BCE* (Leiden: Brill, 1998) 49, 129–30, regards the murder of Onias III as fictional, but this position is surely hypercritical.

23. 2 Macc 5:11.

24. On the importance of the gymnasium in Hellenistic culture see Strabo 5.4.7; Pausanias 10.4; Jean Delorme, *Gymnasion* (Paris: Boccard, 1960).

25. Elias Bickerman, *The God of the Maccabees: Studies in the Origin and Meaning of the Maccabean Revolt* (Leiden: Brill, 1979) 85–88.

26. Bickerman, *The God of the Maccabees*, 86.

27. Ibid., 87.

28. Ibid. Bickerman was neither the first nor the last to make such analogies. See Shavit, *Athens in Jerusalem*, 306–14.

29. Bickerman, ibid., 88.

30. Isaak Heinemann, "Wer veranlasste den Glaubenszwang der Makkabäerzeit," *Monatsschrift für Geschichte und Wissenschaft des Judentums* 82 (1938) 145–72.

31. Tcherikover, *Hellenistic Civilization*, 169. Economic motives are also emphasized by Klaus Bringmann, *Hellenistische Reform und Religionsverfolgung in Judäa. Eine Untersuchung zur jüdisch-hellenistischen Geschichte (175–163 v. Chr.)* (Göttingen: Vandenhoeck & Ruprecht, 1983).

32. Hengel, *Judaism and Hellenism*, 1.299.

33. Hengel, *Judaism and Hellenism*, 1.88–99. Elsewhere he accepts a Palestinian origin as probable in the case of the epic poets, Philo and Theodotus. (*The Hellenization of Judaea in the First Century after Christ* [Philadelphia: Trinity Press International, 1989] 26–27), but regardless of their provenance there is no reason to date either of these works to the Maccabean era or earlier.

34. Hengel, *Judaism and Hellenism*, 1.95.

35. By Robert Doran, "Pseudo-Eupolemus," *OTP* 2.873–82, who ascribes the fragments in question to the Judean Eupolemus.

36. Hengel, *Judaism and Hellenism*, 1.92.

37. Ibid., 1.94.

38. Cf. Levine, *Judaism and Hellenism*, 39: "It has been contended that this revolt came in protest to the process of Hellenization in Judaea, but this was patently not the case."

39. *Ant.* 12.175–85; Hengel, *Judaism and Hellenism* 1.269–72. Gera, *Judaea and Mediterranean Politics*, 36–58, regards this story as a fiction, composed by a Jew in Ptolemaic Egypt, primarily because of biblical parallels with the story of Joseph. But while the story is stylized in light of biblical parallels, it is difficult to believe that it had no factual basis.

40. Robert Doran, "Jason's Gymnasium," in H. W. Attridge, J. J. Collins and T. II. Tobin, eds., *Of Scribes and Scrolls: Studies on the Hebrew Bible, Intertestamental Judaism and Christian Origins* (Lanham, Md.: University Press of America, 1990) 99–109.

41. *Pace*, Hengel, who insists that the Jerusalem aristocracy must have had some "politisch-religiöser Theorie." See the foreword to the third German edition of *Judentum und Hellenismus* (Tübingen: Mohr, 1988) xii.

42. *Ant.* 15. 268–76. Gruen, *Heritage and Hellenism*, 31, finds a very dubious reference to it in the *xystos* or covered collonade mentioned in Josephus, *J.W.* 2.344, which was connected to the temple by a bridge.

43. Louis H. Feldman, *Jew and Gentile in the Ancient World* (Princeton: Princeton University Press, 1993) 57–61.

44. Feldman, ibid., 60. See *De Agricultura* 111–21, among many other passages.

45. Alan P. Mendelson, *Secular Education in Philo of Alexandria* (Cincinnati: Hebrew Union College Press, 1982) 25–26. Cf. Philo's description of his education in *De Congressu* 74–76.

46. Doran, "Jason's Gymnasium," 106; Gruen, *Heritage and Hellenism*, 30.

47. Jub. 3:31.

48. Bickerman, *The God of the Maccabees*, 87.

49. Ibid., 88

50. Hengel, *Judaism and Hellenism*, 1.305. On the Hellenization of the Phoenicians see Fergus Millar, "The Phoenician Cities: A Case-Study of Hellenization," *Proceedings of the Cambridge Philological Society* 209 (1983) 55–71; idem, *The Roman Near East: 31 BC to AD 337* (Cambridge, Mass.: Harvard University Press, 1993) 264–95.

51. Bickerman, *The God of the Maccabees*, 87.

52. *Ant.* 12.5.5 §258–64. In Josephus, the new name of the temple is given as Zeus Hellenios.

53. I owe this suggestion to Hanan Eshel.

54. Bickerman, "Un Document Relatif a la Persécution d'Antiochos IV Épiphane," in *Studies in Jewish and Christian History*, 1.105–35. For the doubts, see Fergus Millar, "The Background of the Maccabean Revolution," *JJS* 29 (1978) 6. Josephus wrote some two and a half centuries after the events.

55. Seth Schwartz, "The Hellenization of Jerusalem and Shechem," in Martin Goodman, ed., *Jews in a Greco-Roman World* (Oxford: Clarendon, 1998) 40.

56. Millar, "The Background of the Maccabean Revolution," 6; Bickerman, "Un Document Relatif," 127–28. Bickerman comments: "En faisant appeler 'Zeus' leur dieu, les Samaritains n'introduisirent donc pas un culte grec dans le temple du Garizim ni changèrent leur religion traditionnelle."

57. This incident is probably identical with the attack led by Apollonius the Mysarch in 1 Macc 1:29, although 1 Maccabees does not mention Jason's coup. On the chronology of events, see still Bickerman, *The God of the Maccabees,* 104–11; also Bringmann, *Hellenistische Reform,* 39. A different sequence is accepted in Emil Schuerer, *A History of the Jewish People in the Time of Jesus Christ* (*175 BC to AD 135*) (rev. and ed. Geza Vermes and Fergus Millar; Edinburgh: Clark, 1973) 1.151; Jonathan A. Goldstein, *II Maccabees* (AB 41A: New York: Doubleday, 1983) 115. Gera, *Judaea and Mediterranean Politics,* 153–57, implausibly dates Jason's revolt to the time of Antiochus' first invasion of Egypt.

58. According to 2 Maccabees 5:27, Judas Maccabee and his followers withdrew to the wilderness before the outbreak of religious persecution, although 1 Maccabees relates their resistance specifically to the requirement of pagan sacrifice.

59. Polybius 29.27; Diodorus Siculus 31.2; Livy 45.12.3–6. See Otto Mørkholm, *Antiochus IV of Syria* (Copenhagen: Gyldendal, 1966) 94; Erich Gruen, *The Hellenistic World and the Coming of Rome* (Berkeley: University of California Press, 1984) 2.658–60; Gera, *Judaea and Mediterranean Politics,* 171–74.

60. J. J. Collins, *Daniel* (Hermeneia; Minneapolis: Fortress, 1993) 384.

61. Bickerman, *The God of the Maccabees,* 84; Tcherikover, *Hellenistic Civilization,* 181–84; Hengel, *Hellenism and Judaism,* 1.286–87.

62. Mørkholm, *Antiochus IV,* 99, 131–2; Gruen, *The Hellenistic World,* 660.

63. Second Macc 6:8–9 claims that a decree was issued at the suggestion of the citizens of Ptolemais, ordering the neighboring Greek cities to require their Jewish residents to adopt "Greek manners," but there is no record of such an initiative in the Diaspora.

64. Second Macc 5:27 says that Judas Maccabee and his followers escaped to the wilderness before the edict of persecution, whereas 1 Maccabees has his father Mattathias initiate the revolt by refusing to offer pagan sacrifice. Even 2 Maccabees, however, does not attribute militant action to Judas until after the edict was promulgated. Nonetheless, Tcherikover argued that "it was not the revolt which came as a response to the persecution, but the persecution which came as a response to the revolt" (Tcherikover, *Hellenistic Civilization,* 191). Similarly, Gera, *Judaea and Mediterranean Politics,* 227–28, argues that the proscription of Jewish religion was the king's "response to an ever deteriorating relationship between the Seleucid authorities and the Jews."

65. Bickerman, *The God of the Maccabees,* 83.

66. Hengel, *Judaism and Hellenism,* 1. 287, 289.

67. 2 Macc 11:22–26. See C. Habicht, "The Royal Letters in Maccabees II," *Harvard Studies in Classical Philology* 80 (1976) 1–18.

68. Diodorus 34–35.1.3.

69. Tacitus 5.8.2.

70. Bickerman, *The God of the Maccabees*, 77. The suppression of foreign rites, such as the Bacchanalia, in Rome, which Goldstein, *1 Maccabees* (AB 41; New York: Doubleday, 1976) 125–60, invokes as a paradigm, is not a particularly close parallel. Antiochus attempted to suppress a cult in its homeland.

71. Peter Schäfer argues that the comparison between Antiochus Epiphanes and Hadrian is "not a misguided one" in Schäfer, "Hadrian's Policy in Judaea and the Bar Kochba Revolt: A Reassessment," in Davies and White, *A Tribute to Geza Vermes*, 296. See also Schäfer, *Der Bar Kokhba-Aufstand* (Tübingen: Mohr-Siebeck, 1981) 48–49, and Martin Hengel, "Hadrians Politik gegenüber Juden und Christen," in *Ancient Studies in Memory of Elias Bickerman = JANES* 16–17(1984–85) 153–82.

72. Polybius 26.1.1. See Mørkholm, *Antiochus IV*, 181–82.

73. Bickerman's theory about the role of Menelaus is rejected by Tcherikover, *Hellenistic Civilization*, 184; Goldstein, *1 Maccabees*, 159; Millar, "The Background to the Maccabean Revolution," 17–21.

74. Goldstein, *1 Maccabees*, 158, suggests that the enforced eating of pork was due to the fact that the pig was a favored sacrificial animal of Dionysus.

75. Tcherikover, *Hellenistic Civilization*, 194–95; Bickerman, *The God of the Maccabees*, 75.

76. Cf. Tcherikover, *Hellenistic Civilization*, 195: "The Jewish Hellenists, if they had sought, as Bickermann believed, to convert the Jews to another faith, would have imposed on them not a Syrian but a Greek form of worship, in accordance with the education which they are alleged to have received."

77. Goodman, "Jewish Attitudes," 171, goes further, suggesting that "there was no connection," and that the authors of the books of Maccabees vilified the Hellenizing high priests for their own political reasons.

78. Hengel, *Judaism and Hellenism*, 1.308–9.

79. See especially his book, *The Hellenization of Judea*.

80. See especially Levine, *Judaism and Hellenism in Antiquity*, 33–95.

81. Arnaldo Momigliano, "Jews and Greeks," in idem, *Essays on Ancient and Modern Judaism* (Chicago: University of Chicago Press, 1994) 22

82. *Ant.* 15. 328–29, trans. Ralph Marcus, in the Loeb edition, emphasis added. See the comments of Arych Kasher, *Jews and Hellenistic Cities in Eretz Israel* (Tübingen: Mohr, 1990) 204–5. On Herod's building program see Duane Roller, *The Building Program of Herod the Great* (Berkeley: University of California Press, 1998).

83. *Ant.* 15.268–69.

84. *Ant.* 15. 276.

85. *J.W.* 1.648–50.

86. *J.W.* 2.169–74.

87. *J.W.* 2.184–203.

88. The Hellenization of the upper classes in Herodian Jerusalem is vividly shown by the archeological remains in the Jewish quarter. See N. Avigad, *Discovering Jerusalem* (Jerusalem: Shikmona, 1980) 81–202; Levine, *Judaism and Hellenism,* 48–51.

89. See Albert Baumgarten, *The Flourishing of Jewish Sects in the Maccabean Era: An Interpretation* (Leiden: Brill, 1997) 81–113 ("The Encounter with Hellenism and Its Effects").

90. See James C. VanderKam, *Enoch and the Growth of an Apocalyptic Tradition* (CBQMS 16; Washington, D.C.: Catholic Biblical Association, 1984) 111–14.

91. See John J. Collins, *The Apocalyptic Imagination* (revised edition; Grand Rapids, Mich.: Eerdmans, 1998) 47–59.

92. See John J. Collins, *Apocalypticism in the Dead Sea Scrolls* (London: Routledge, 1997).

93. Momigliano, "Jews and Greeks," 22–23, regarded "apocalyptic" and Pharisaism as the "two forces that combined, or in contrast with each other, draw a line between Judaism and Hellenism."

94. See especially Hengel, *Judaism and Hellenism,* 1.175–254.

95. For a perceptive discussion of both the similarities and the differences between Jewish sects and Greco-Roman voluntary associations see Albert Baumgarten, "Greco-Roman Voluntary Associations and Jewish Sects," in Goodman, ed., *Jews in a Graeco-Roman World,* 93–111.

96. See Hubert Cancik, "The End of the World, of History and of the Individual in Greek and Roman Antiquity," in J. J. Collins, ed., *The Encyclopedia of Apocalypticism. Volume 1. The Origins of Apocalypticism in Judaism and Christianity* (New York: Continuum, 1998) 84–125.

97. John J. Collins, "Apocalyptic Eschatology as the Transcendence of Death," in idem, *Seers, Sibyls and Sages* (Leiden: Brill, 1997) 75–97.

THREE

Jewish Perspectives on Greek Culture and Ethnicity

ERICH S. GRUEN

The encounter of Jew and Greek in antiquity continues to exercise a hold on scholarly attention and public imagination. The conquests of Alexander the Great spread Greek language and institutions all over the lands of the Near East, from Asia Minor to Iran where Jews were settled—including Palestine itself. The convergence of cultures was inescapable. Not only does it represent a historical confrontation of high significance, but the very terms "Hellenism" and "Judaism" have served as metaphors for a tension between reason and religion, between rationality and spirituality, through the ages.

The subject has, of course, attracted extensive scholarly treatment, with increased interest in recent years. But inquiry has proceeded largely on three fronts: (1) the influence of Hellenic language, literature, philosophy, historiography, and even religion upon the Jewish experience,[1] (2) the attitude of Greeks (or pagans more generally) toward Jews,[2] (3) the changing self-image of the Jews in the circumstances of a Hellenic world.[3] By contrast, little scrutiny has been applied to a related but quite distinct issue: the Jewish perception of Greeks.[4] Did the Jews have a clear and consistent sense of Greeks as an ethnic entity?

The very notion of "the Jews" carries its own perils. It would be illusory to imagine a monolithic group with a unitary viewpoint. The analysis here centers upon that segment of the Jews (no small one) for whom coming to grips with Hellenism was a matter of critical importance. As is well known, many Jews were thoroughly familiar with the Greek language, with Hellenic myths, traditions, religion, and institutions. They engaged in a protracted effort to redefine themselves within the terms of an ascendant Mediterranean culture that was largely Greek. How did they conceive of Greeks as a people, nation, or society and what relation did their concept or concepts have on the shaping of the Jews' own self-perception? Daunting questions. Relevant texts do not exist in abundance. A substantial number of Greek authors concerned themselves with Jewish customs, traits, and practices, their works cited by later authors or occasionally extant in fragments. But nothing comparable issued from the pens of Jewish authors about Greeks. Perspectives need to be pieced together from stray remarks, inferences, and implications. And they add up to no neat and tidy picture. The results, however, offer some intriguing insights into the mentality of Hellenistic Jews and their sense of interconnectedness with the dominant *ethnos* of the Mediterranean cultural world.

The Jews, on the face of it, might provide a useful "external" view of *Hellenismos*. In fact, however, they are, in an important sense, both "external" and "internal" witnesses. They represent a different culture, background, tradition, and history. Yet in the Hellenistic era, and indeed in the Greek East of the Roman period, the Jews were part and parcel of a Greek cultural community. That very fact, of course, was central to their grappling with a new sense of identity which they sought to articulate through the genres and the media familiar to Greeks while expressing the distinctiveness of their own character and achievement. Hence, Jews needed both to establish their own secure place within a Hellenistic framework and also to make it clear that they were not swallowed up by that prevailing cultural environment. The construct of Jewish identity in the Hellenistic world, therefore, an ongoing, complex, and shifting process, was tightly bound up with the construct of Greek ethnicity, i.e., the character, values, and beliefs of the Greek *ethnos* in Jewish eyes.

That these were constructs is inescapable. Although Jewish intellectuals could draw distinctions among Greek peoples, communities, and conventions, they frequently lapsed into broad characterizations and stereotypes. For obvious reasons. They had a definite agenda. In some form or other, Jews had to confront—or to formulate—those Hellenic traits from which they wished to disassociate themselves and, at the same time, to account for those characteristics which they had themselves embraced.

The texts discussed here, for the most part, were directed inward. Jews spoke largely to their own compatriots, striving to fashion a self-consciousness that could negotiate a cultural realm of alien origin. If Greeks read these works, so much the better. But few were likely to. The texts contributed to the articulation of Jewish identity by and for Jews.

Greeks regularly reckoned other *ethnē* as *barbaroi*, a familiar cliché of this subject. Jews suffered that disability, in Hellenic eyes, like everyone else. But they could also turn the tables. A striking text serves as suitable entrance into the inquiry. The author of the Second Book of Maccabees was a Hellenized Jew of the late second century BCE who composed his work in Greek, a writer thoroughly steeped in the traditions of Greek historiography.[5] His topic, however, was the background, circumstances, and consequences of the brutal persecution of Jews by the Hellenistic monarch Antiochus IV Epiphanes. The Jews resisted and retaliated under Judas Maccabeus. According to 2 Maccabees, they fought nobly on behalf of Judaism and, though few in number, ravaged the entire land and drove out the "barbarian hordes."[6] So the composer of this work, well-versed in the conventions of the genre, employed the standard Hellenic designation for the alien—but applied it to the Hellenes themselves. And it was not the only such occasion.[7] The pejorative contexts in which the term appears in 2 Maccabees make it clear that it signifies a good deal more than mere "speakers of a foreign tongue."

Biblical precedents, to be sure, could be drawn upon. The Canaanites carried a comparable stigma of barbaric backwardness, a necessary construct in order to justify their dispossession by the Hebrews. And the Philistines, fiercest of the Israelite foes, received a similar portrayal as savage idolators, thus to legitimize the triumph of Yahweh.[8] But the dire circumstances of the Maccabean era brought the Greeks sharply into focus. The cultivated author of 2 Maccabees expropriated the Hellenic characterization of "the Other" to his own purposes. The Greek *ethnos* itself could now be cast in that role.

A range of texts underscores the drive of Hellenistic Jews to brand the Greeks as villainous or ignorant aliens—or both. This would, of course, distinguish all the more conspicuously the advantages of being a Jew.

Apocalyptic literature served this purpose. The visions of Daniel received their current shape in the very era of the persecutions. And they speak in cryptic but unmistakable tones of the catastrophic evils brought by the rule of the Hellenic kingdom. The terrifying dream that paraded four huge beasts in succession represented the sequence of empires, the fourth most fearsome of all, a dreadful monster with iron teeth and bronze claws that devoured and trampled all in its path. That portent signified the coming of the Greeks, to culminate in the tenth and most horrific prince, plainly the figure of Antiochus Epiphanes, responsible for the abomination of desolation. The forecasts vouchsafed for Daniel, however, would end in triumph over the wicked, a divine intervention to sweep aside the brutal Hellenic Empire and bring about an eternal kingdom under the sovereignty of the Most High.[9] The Greeks here emblematize the mightiest of empires—and the one targeted for the mightiest fall.

That theme is picked up in the prophecies of the *Third Sibylline Oracle*. The Sibyl had venerable roots in pagan antiquity, but the surviving collection of pronouncements stems from Jewish and Christian compilers who recast them for their own ends. The contents of the *Third Sibyl* represent the earliest portion, almost entirely the product of Jewish invention, and some parts at least dating to the era of the Maccabees.[10] One group of verses echoes Daniel directly, employing some of the same imagery, with reference to the Macedonian kingdoms which impose an evil yoke and deliver much affliction upon Asia but whose race (*genos*) will be destroyed by the very race it seeks to destroy.[11] The text also repeats in different form the sequence of empires, including the Greeks as arrogant and impious and the Macedonians as bearing a fearful cloud of war upon mortals. Internal rot will follow, extending from impiety to homosexuality and afflicting many lands—but none so much as Macedon.[12] Elsewhere the Sibyl condemns Greeks for overbearing behavior, the fostering of tyrannies, and moral failings. She predicts that their cities in Asia Minor and the Near East will be crushed by a terrible divine wrath; Greece itself will be ravaged and its inhabitants dissolved in strife for gain.[13] In this bitter and wrathful composition, the Jewish author brands the people of Hellas as insolent, sacrilegious, and brutal, doomed to suffer the vengeance of the Lord.

The portrait is hardly less severe in the First Book of Maccabees. That work appeared first in Hebrew, the product of a strong supporter of the Hasmonean dynasty, composed probably late in the second century BCE.[14] The book opens with a harsh assessment of Alexander the Great, an arrogant conqueror whose campaigns brought slaughter and devastation in their wake. And his successors over the years delivered multiple miseries upon the earth.[15] The wickedness reached its peak, of course, with the arrival of Antiochus IV, symbol not only of evil but of the alien. The author of 1 Maccabees stigmatizes his measures as introducing the practices of the foreigner to the land of Judea.[16]

The stark contrast between Jew and Greek receives dramatic elaboration in the martyrologies recorded in 2 Maccabees. The elderly sage Eleazer resisted to the death any compromise of Jewish practice by spurning the cruel edicts of Antiochus Epiphanes, calmly accepting his agonizing torture. The same courage was exhibited by the devout mother who witnessed proudly the savage slaying of her seven steadfast sons and joined them herself in death, memorable testimony to Jewish faith and Hellenic barbarity.[17] The stories were retold many generations later, at a time when the fierce emotions of the Maccabean era were a distant memory. The torments inflicted upon Eleazer and the mother with her seven sons were elaborated in exquisite detail in a text preserved in some manuscripts of the Septuagint under the title of 4 Maccabees. The work was composed in Greek, probably in the first century CE by a Jew trained not in history but in Greek philosophy. He employed the martyrologies to illustrate Stoic doctrines of the command of reason over the passions. The author, therefore, ironically appropriated the Hellenic medium to convey Jewish commitment to the Torah by contrast with the irrationality and atrocities of the Greeks themselves.[18]

The abhorrence of philosophically minded Jews for the excesses of the Greeks surfaces almost inadvertently in another treatise roughly contemporary with 4 Maccabees. The so-called Wisdom of Solomon falls within the tradition of Jewish wisdom literature but comes from the hand of a Hellenized Jew thoroughly familiar with Greek philosophy.[19] Although the setting itself is strictly biblical, an interesting remark of the author bears notice for our purposes. He ascribes to the unspeakable Canaanites every form of loathsome practice, including orgiastic mystery rites, human sacrifice, and cannibalism. And he describes them in terms characteristic of participants in a Dionysiac *thiasos*.[20] The notorious Hellenic ritual thereby serves to epitomize barbaric behavior.

Jewish imagination went further still on this score. A full-scale story, almost entirely fictitious, depicted the lunatic crusade of a Hellenistic king against the nation of the Jews. And this time the villain was not Antiochus Epiphanes. The text appears in some of the manuscripts of the Septuagint, misleadingly entitled 3 Maccabees for it has nothing whatever to do with the history or legend of the Maccabees.[21] It depicts the mad monarch, Ptolemy IV, determined to eradicate the Jews of Egypt because their compatriots had denied him access to the Holy of Holies in the temple at Jerusalem. A frenzy of hatred drove Ptolemy to his scheme of genocide. He ordered subordinates to round up all the Jews in the land, confine them in the hippodrome outside Alexandria, and have them trampled en masse by a herd of crazed elephants drugged with huge quantities of frankincense and unmixed wine. But a happy ending concluded the tale. Ptolemy's dastardly plot was thrice thwarted, the final time when God's messengers turned around the great beasts to crush the minions of the king. The Jews ended in honor and triumph. But they had suffered a fearsome travail. The narrow escape only highlighted the hostility of those committed to the elimination of the Jews. Ptolemy's enmity did not stand alone. A group of friends, advisers, and soldiers urged the destruction of that *genos* which refused to conform to the ways of other nations.[22] And a far wider populace rejoiced at the prospect of Jewish demise, their festering hatred now given free rein in open exultation.[23] More significant, the Hellenized Jewish author of this work designates the Greeks themselves as "the aliens": ἀλλόφυλοι. And the exaltation of the Jews in the end elevates them to a position of authority, esteem, and respect among their "enemies."[24]

An incidental notice regarding one of the Jews' most notorious fictional antagonists warrants mention here. Haman, the grand vizier of the Persian king in the Book of Esther, endeavored to institute a policy of genocide against the Jewish nation. In the Greek additions to the Hebrew original, composed in the Hellenistic era, the wicked Haman, notably and significantly, is transformed into a Macedonian![25] The schema that pits Jews against Greeks, their opponents who stand outside the bounds of morality and humane behavior, persists in all these texts.

A comparable contrast appears in a far more unexpected place. The *Letter of Aristeas* narrates the celebrated legend of the translation of the Pentateuch into Greek. The job was done, so the story has it, at the directive of the cultivated King Ptolemy II, in collaboration with the Jewish high priest, and through the efforts of Jewish sages, experts in both languages—and in Greek philosophy besides—who were warmly welcomed and lavishly hosted by the Hellenistic monarch. No text seems better calculated to convey harmony and common objectives between the *ethnē*.[26] Yet all is not sweetness and light even here. In the warm glow of cultural cooperation that bathes most of the text, it is easy to forget the pointed words of Eleazer, the high priest, when he responded to queries by Greeks about the peculiar habits of the Jews. He affirmed in no uncertain terms that Jews alone held to monotheistic beliefs and that those who worship many gods engage in foolishness and self-deception. Idolators who revere images of wood and stone, he observed, are more powerful than the very gods to whom they pay homage, since they were themselves responsible for their creation. And he became quite explicit about those who manufactured myths and concocted stories: they were adjudged the wisest of the Greeks![27] It is hard to miss the irony there. Eleazer proceeded to declare that Moses, in his wisdom, fenced the Jews off with unbreakable barriers and iron walls to prevent any mingling with other *ethnē,* to keep them pure in body and soul, and to rid them of empty beliefs.[28] So, even the veritable document of intercultural concord, the *Letter of Aristeas,* contains a pivotal pronouncement by the chief spokesman for Judaism, who sets his creed decisively apart from the ignorant and misguided beliefs of the Greek *ethnos.*[29]

The contrast is elaborated at some length by Josephus. The historian distinguishes unequivocally between the virtues of the Jews and the deficiencies of the Greeks, a harsh critique of Hellenic behavior and institutions. The fact merits special notice. For Josephus notes at one juncture in the *Antiquities* that he addresses his work to Greeks, in the hope of persuading them that Jewish customs had been held in high esteem, protected by a series of Roman decrees.[30] But he records repeated interference by Greeks with the ancestral practices of the Jews and outright atrocities in Cyrenaica, Asia Minor, Alexandria, Damascus, Caesarea, and other cities of Palestine.[31] Josephus pulls no punches: the disposition of the Greeks is labeled as "inhumanity."[32]

In the *Contra Apionem* he developed the contrast at greater extent and on a different level. Josephus took aim even at Greek achievements in philosophy and law. He singles out Moses as most venerable of lawgivers, and speaks with scorn of Greeks who take pride in such figures as Lycurgus, Solon, and Zaleucus. They were Moses' juniors by several centuries. Indeed, Homer himself had no concept of law, an idea incomprehensible to the Greeks of his day.[33] Josephus proceeds later in the treatise to disparage Hellenic philosophy and education. The philosophers, he maintains, directed their precepts only to the elite, withholding them from the masses, whereby Moses' teaching encompassed all. Moses did not list piety as simply one among several virtues but subsumed all the virtues under piety, thus rendering them accessible to everyone. Whereas some Greek educational systems rest on verbal articulation of principles and others on practical training in morals, the Hebrew lawgiver alone blended both. Jews therefore escaped the imperfections and one-sidedness of both the Spartan and Athenian systems.[34] Josephus subsequently provides an extended excursus that brings the superiority of Jewish character, morality, and national qualities over the Greek into sharper focus. He places particular weight upon the Jews' faithful and consistent adherence to their own laws. To the Greeks such unswerving fidelity can hardly be imagined. Their history is riddled with inversions and deviations. Plato might have constructed a Utopian scheme to which readers could aspire, but those engaged in Greek public affairs themselves found his model laughably unrealistic. And it was not nearly as demanding as that which the Jews actually abide by![35]

For most Greeks, in fact, the semilegendary Spartan lawgiver Lycurgus and the sociopolitical structure that he installed in Sparta represented the exemplar to be imitated. The longevity of its system drew high praise throughout the Hellenic world. That record, however, prompted only scorn from Josephus. The endurance of the Lacedaemonian system was a mere trifle, not comparable to the two thousand years that had elapsed since the time of Moses—whose laws were still in operation. The Spartans themselves only held to their constitution while fortune smiled upon them, abandoning it when matters turned for the worse, whereas Jews remained steadfast throughout their vicissitudes and calamities.[36] The historian adverts to the record of martyrdom for the faith and the heroic resistance of the Jews to any effort to force them into betraying their traditions, even in the face of torture and execution. His rhetoric here spins out of control, denying that a single Jew had ever turned his back on the laws.[37] The subject evidently encouraged hyperbole.

Josephus exploited Hellenic writings themselves to drive home his point. Plato and other authors who censured their own poets and statesmen served his purposes nicely. They had already castigated the makers of public opinion for spreading preposterous conceptions of the gods. The myths multiplied deities without number, portrayed them in a variety of human forms, and had them engage in every type of licentiousness, misdemeanor, folly, and internecine warfare with one another. And, as if that were not enough, the Greeks grew weary of their traditional divinities and imported foreign gods by the score, stimulating poets and painters to invent new and even more bizarre images of worship.[38] No wonder Plato declared the precincts of his ideal state as off limits to all poets![39] Josephus reiterates once again the core of his thesis: Jews hold tenaciously to their laws and traditions, allowing neither fear of the powerful nor envy of the practices honored by others to shake their constancy.[40] There could be no stronger contrast with the inconstancy of the Greek character.

The celebrated lines of the apostle Paul allude directly to the antithesis between the *ethnē:* "There is neither Jew nor Greek, slave nor free, male nor female, for you are all one in Jesus Christ."[41] The string of contraries makes it clear that the two *ethnē* represented conventionally opposite poles. The same phraseology appears in another Pauline text: "We have all been baptized into one body and in one spirit, whether Jews or Greeks, slaves or free."[42] The distinctions held firm in Jewish circles. Paul had an uphill battle to surmount them.

So far the evidence seems clear and consistent. Jewish compositions constructed the Hellenes as foils, as aliens, as the "Other," thereby the better to set off the virtues and qualities of their own *ethnos*. One may note that this characterization crosses genre boundaries, appearing in apocalyptic texts, histories, apologetic treatises, and imaginative fiction. The diverse formulations range from the relatively mild strictures in the *Letter of Aristeas,* castigating Greeks for foolish and delusive idolatry, and Josephus' derisive blast at their irresolution, instability, and ludicrous concoctions of the divine, to the fierce portrayals of Hellenic character in texts like 1 Maccabees, in the apocalypic visions of Daniel and the *Third Sibyl*, in the martyrologies contained in 2 and 4 Maccabees, and in the fictive tale of 3 Maccabees, branding Greeks as barbaric, irrational, and murderous. All seems relatively straightforward and aggressively hostile.

But those constructs do not tell the whole story. Jewish perceptions (or at least expressed perceptions) of the Greeks were more complex, varied, and subtle. One might note, for instance, that Jewish writers did not frequently resort to the term *barbaroi* in referring to gentiles. The most commonly used phrase is a less offensive one: *ta ethnē*—"the nations." This occurs with regularity in 1 and 2 Maccabees, a phrase that can encompass Greeks but is by no means confined to them.[43] It can, of course, be employed pejoratively depending on context, as it frequently is in the Books of the Maccabees. But even there the term carries no inherently negative connotation. Indeed 1 Maccabees employs *to ethnos* repeatedly to refer to the Jewish nation itself, usually in circumstances of diplomatic correspondence between Jews and Hellenistic dynasts or Romans.[44] And, as is well known, Paul uses the phrase *ta ethnē* again and again, sometimes synonymously with "Greeks," usually with a broader denotation. But the term signifies no more than "those who are not Jews."[45] The construct is plainly malleable, not necessarily a vehicle of opprobrium.

Furthermore, in various Jewish authors and texts, Greek character and culture acquire a notably more positive aspect. But they do so because they are conceived as owing those qualities to the Jews themselves.

The approach can be illustrated through diverse examples. A fragment of the Hellenistic–Jewish historian Eupolemus has relevance here. His date and provenance are not quite secure—unless he is identical, as most assume, with the Eupolemus who was a member of Judas Maccabeus' entourage. That would place him in Palestine in the mid-second century BCE.[46] Whether the identification be accepted or not, Eupolemus' work certainly belongs in the circles of cultivated Jews writing in Greek in the Hellenistic period. Ancients accorded it the title of *On the Kings in Judaea*. But the coverage was wider. The pertinent fragment, in any case, concerns Moses. Eupolemus has him hand down the knowledge of the alphabet first to the Jews, from whom the Phoenicians acquired it, and they, in turn, passed it on to the Greeks.[47] The brevity of that passage does not justify lengthy exegesis. For our purposes, suffice it to say that it makes the Greeks indirect beneficiaries of the Hebrews rather than their antagonists. And this theme has resonance elsewhere.

The imaginative writer Artapanus, a Hellenized Jew from Egypt in the second or first century BCE, offers an interesting parallel.[48] His inventive re-creation of biblical stories includes an elaborate account of Moses' exploits that goes well beyond any scriptural basis. Apart from ascribing to Moses the inception of a host of Egyptian institutions and technologies, he also adds a Greek connection. The name Moses, Artapanus claims, induced Greeks to identify him with Musaeus, the legendary poet and prophet from Attica, son or pupil of Orpheus who stands at the dawn of Hellenic song and wisdom. Artapanus, however, gave a slight but significant twist to the legend. He has Musaeus as mentor of Orpheus, rather than the other way round.[49] Moses therefore becomes the father of Greek poetic and prophetic traditions. In striking contrast to the message delivered in Josephus' *Contra Apionem*, Artapanus does not disparage or reject those traditions but counts them as part of a Hebrew heritage.

A more obscure allusion in Artapanus has Moses receive the designation of Hermes by the Egyptian priests who honored him as interpreter of hieroglyphics.[50] The Hellenic aspect is not here in the forefront. Artapanus makes reference to the Egyptian version of Hermes, an equivalent to Thot, the mythical progenitor of much of Egyptian culture.[51] But his creative reconstruction clearly amalgamates the cultural strands. Artapanus writes ostensibly about Pharaonic Egypt but looks, in fact, to contemporary Ptolemaic Egypt. His Moses absorbs both Musaeus and Hermes and becomes the fount of Greek culture in the Hellenistic era.

Further fragments from another Jewish intellectual expand the perspective. Aristobulus, a man of wide philosophical and literary interests (though the depth of his mastery might be questioned), wrote an extensive work, evidently a form of commentary on the Torah, at an uncertain date in the Hellenistic period.[52] Only a meager portion of that work now survives, but enough to indicate a direction and objective: Aristobulus, among other things, sought to establish the Bible as foundation for much of the Greek intellectual and artistic achievement. Moses, for Aristobulus as for Eupolemus and Artapanus, emerges as a culture hero, precursor and inspiration for Hellenic philosophical and poetic traditions. But Aristobulus' Moses, unlike the figure concocted by Eupolemus and Artapanus, does not transmit the alphabet, interpret hieroglyphics, or invent technology. His accomplishment is the Torah, the Israelite law code. And from that creation, so Aristobulus imagines, a host of Hellenic attainments drew their impetus. Foremost among Greek philosophers, Plato was a devoted reader of the Scriptures, poring over every detail, and faithfully followed its precepts.[53] And not only he. A century and a half earlier, Pythagoras borrowed much from the books of Moses and inserted it into his own teachings.[54] Never mind that the Torah had not yet been translated into Greek by the time of Plato—let alone that of Pythagoras. Aristobulus had a way around that problem. He simply proposed that prior translations of the Bible circulated long before the commissioned enterprise of Ptolemy II, before the coming of Alexander, even before Persian rule in Palestine.[55] That, of course, is transparent fiction, compounding his concoction in order to save the thesis. But it was all in a good cause. It made Moses responsible for the best in Greek philosophy.

Other philosophers, too, came under the sway of the Torah. So at least Aristobulus surmised. The "divine voice" to which Socrates paid homage owed its origin to the words of Moses.[56] And Aristobulus made a still broader generalization. He found concurrence among all philosophers in the need to maintain reverent attitudes toward God, a doctrine best expressed, of course, in the Hebrew Scriptures which preceded (and presumably determined) the Greek precepts. Indeed, all of Jewish law was constructed so as to underscore piety, justice, self-control and the other qualities that represent true virtues—i.e., the very qualities subsequently embraced and propagated by the Greeks.[57] Aristobulus thereby brought the whole tradition of Greek philosophizing under the Jewish umbrella.

That was just a part of the project. Aristobulus not only traced philosophic precepts to the Torah. He found its echoes in Greek poetry from earliest times to his own day. The Sabbath, for instance, a vital part of Jewish tradition stemming from Genesis, was reckoned by Aristobulus as a preeminent principle widely adopted and signaled by the mystical quality ascribed to the number seven.[58] And he discovered proof in the verses of Homer and Hesiod. This required some fancy footwork. Aristobulus cavalierly interpreted a Hesiodic reference to the seventh day of the month as the seventh day of the week. And he (or his source) emended a line of Homer from the "fourth day" to the "seventh day." He quoted other lines of those poets to similar effect—lines that do not correspond to anything in our extant texts of Homer and Hesiod. It would not be too bold to suspect manipulation or fabrication.[59]

The creative Aristobulus also enlisted in his cause poets who worked in the distant mists of antiquity, namely the mythical singers Linus and Orpheus. Linus, an elusive figure variously identified as the son of Apollo or the music master of Heracles, conveniently left verses

that celebrated the number seven as representing perfection itself, asso-
ciating it with the heavenly bodies, with an auspicious day of birth, and
as the day when all is made complete.[60] The connection with the biblical
origin of the Sabbath is strikingly close—and too good to be true. Aristobulus summoned up still greater inventiveness in adapting or impro-
vising a wholesale monotheistic poem assigned to Orpheus himself.
The composition delivers sage advice from the mythical singer to his
son or pupil Musaeus (here in proper sequence of generations), coun-
seling him to adhere to the divine word and describing God as complete
in himself while completing all things, the sole divinity with no rivals,
hidden to the human eye but accessible to the mind, a source of good
and not evil, seated on a golden throne in heaven, commanding the
earth, its oceans and mountains, and in control of all.[61] The poem,
whether or not it derives from Aristobulus' pen, belongs to the realm of
Hellenistic Judaism. It represents a Jewish commandeering of Orpheus,
emblematic of Greek poetic art, into the ranks of those proclaiming the
message of biblical monotheism.

Aristobulus did not confine himself to legendary or distant poets.
He made bold to interpret contemporary verses in ways suitable to his
ends. One sample survives. Aristobulus quoted from the astronomical
poem, the *Phaenomena*, of the Hellenistic writer Aratus of Soli. Its
opening lines proved serviceable. By substituting "God" for "Zeus,"
Aristobulus turned Aratus' invocation into a hymn for the Jewish
deity.[62] Brazenness and ingenuity mark the enterprise of Aristobulus.
One can only imagine what inventive creations existed in those por-
tions of his work that no longer survive. The campaign to convert Hellenic writings into footnotes on the Torah was in full swing.

In that endeavor Aristobulus had much company. Resourceful
Jewish writers searched through the scripts of Attic dramatists, both
tragic and comic, for passages whose content suggested acquaintance
with Hebrew texts or ideas. And where they did not exist, alterations or
fabrications could readily be inserted. Verses with a strikingly Jewish
flavor were ascribed to Aeschylus, Sophocles, and Euripides, and others
to the comic playwrights Menander, Diphilus, and Philemon, again a
combination of classical and Hellenistic authors. The fragments are preserved only in Church Fathers and the names of transmitters are lost to
us. But the milieu of Jewish-Hellenistic intellectuals is unmistakable.[63]
Verses from Aeschylus emphasized the majesty of God, his omnipo-

tence and omnipresence, the terror he can wreak, and his resistance to representation or understanding in human terms.[64] Sophocles insisted upon the oneness of the Lord who fashioned heaven and earth, the waters and the winds; he railed against idolatry; he supplied an eschatological vision to encourage the just and frighten the wicked; and he spoke of Zeus' disguises and philandering—doubtless to contrast delusive myths with authentic divinity.[65] Euripides, too, could serve the purpose. Researchers found lines affirming that God's presence cannot be contained within structures created by mortals and that he sees all, but is himself invisible.[66] Attribution of comparable verses to comic poets is more confused in the tradition, as Christian sources provide conflicting notices on which dramatist said what. But the recorded writers, Menander, Philemon, and Diphilus, supplied usefully manipulable material. One or another spoke of an all-seeing divinity who will deliver vengeance upon the unjust and wicked, who lives forever as Lord of all, who apportions justice according to deserts, who scorns offerings and votives but exalts the righteous at heart.[67]

All of this attests to feverish activity on the part of Hellenistic Jews. Which of these texts are authentic but taken out of context and which were manufactured for the occasion can no longer be determined with confidence. No matter. The energy directed itself to discernible goals. Jewish writers appropriated, manipulated, reinterpreted, and fabricated the words of classical and contemporary Greek authors to demonstrate dependency on the doctrines of the Torah. These comforting fancies, of course, promoted the priority and superiority of the Jewish tradition. But, more interesting, they imply that the Hellenic achievement, far from alien to the Hebraic, simply restated its principles. The finest of Greek philosophers from Pythagoras to Plato, poets from Homer to Aratus, and even the legendary singers Orpheus and Linus were swept into the wake of the Jews.

A familiar story, but not one usually cited in this connection, underscores the point. Paul's celebrated visit to Athens can exemplify this genre of appropriation. The tale is told in the Acts of the Apostles.[68] Paul proselytized among the Jews and "God-fearers" in the synagogue— and with any person who happened to pass by in the *agora*. This upset certain Stoics and Epicureans who hauled him before the high tribunal of the Areopagus and questioned him about the new doctrine he was peddling.[69] Paul was quick to turn the situation to his own advantage—

and in a most interesting way. He remarked to the Athenians that they were an uncommonly religious people. He had wandered through many of their shrines and had found one altar inscribed to an "unknown god."[70] Of course, he was there to tell them precisely who that "unknown god" happened to be. Paul proceeded to speak of the sole divinity, creator of the world and all that is in it, a god who dwells in no temples and can be captured in no images.[71] The description plainly applies to the god of the Hebrew Bible, with no Christian admixture. Paul, like other inventive Jews, quoted Greek poetry to underpin his claims. So, he remarked to the Athenians, "as some of your own poets have said, 'We too are his [God's] children.'"[72] The poet in question happened to be Aratus of Soli, no Athenian. But that detail can be comfortably ignored. The parallels with other texts cited above are unmistakable. Paul deployed Greek poetic utterances as certification for Jewish precepts. And he cited a Greek dedicatory inscription as evidence for Hellenic worship of the right deity—even if the Athenians themselves did not know who he was.

This heartening construct of Hellenic dependence on Jewish precedents took hold over the generations. It did not await the Church Fathers for resurrection. Notably, and perhaps surprisingly, it appears in the work of Josephus. The Jewish historian, as we have seen, took pains to underscore differences between Jews and Greeks, to stress the stability of Jewish institutions and the durability of faith as against the multiple inadequacies of Hellenic practices. Yet Josephus also follows the line that many Greeks have embraced Jewish laws—though some have been more consistent in maintaining them than others. Indeed, he acknowledges, Jews are more divided from Greeks by geography than by institutions.[73] Like Aristobulus and others, he finds Greek philosophers hewing closely to the concept of God which they obtained from acquaintance with the Books of Moses—noting in particular Pythagoras, Anaxagoras, Plato, and the Stoics.[74] The prescriptions in Plato's *Republic* obliging citizens to study closely all the laws of their state and prohibiting social intercourse with foreigners in order to keep the polity pure for those who abide by its regulations came, according to Josephus, in direct imitation of Moses.[75] Toward the end of his treatise, *Contra Apionem,* Josephus makes even larger claims. Greek philosophers were only the first of those drawn to the laws of the Torah, adopting similar views about God, teaching abstinence from extravagance and harmony with one another. The masses followed suit. Their zeal for Jewish religious piety has now spread around the world so that there is hardly a single *polis* or *ethnos*, whether Greek or barbarian, unaffected by observance of the Sabbath, various Jewish practices, and even dietary restrictions. Indeed, they labor to emulate the concord, philanthropy, industry, and undeviating steadfastness characteristic of the Jews.[76] One may set aside the hyperbole. But Josephus' insistence on the Greek quest to duplicate Jewish ethics, religion, institutions, and customs is quite notable. And it seems poles apart from his drive elsewhere to underscore the distinctions between the *ethnē*.

At the very least, a tension, if not an inner contradiction, exists in Jewish perspectives on the people of Hellas. A strong strain emphasized the differences in culture and behavior between the peoples, categorized the Greeks as aliens, inferiors, barbarians, even savage antagonists. Other voices, however, embraced and absorbed Hellenic teachings, reinterpreting them as shaped by acquaintance with the Hebraic tradition and as offshoots of the Torah. From that vantage point, the Hellenic character becomes, through emulation and imitation, molded to the model.

For some Jewish intellectuals that was not enough. They postulated a still closer attachment, one that would give a common basis to the *ethnē*—a kinship connection. The postulate was imaginary but imaginative. Among Greeks, such a construct was standard fare. Hellenic cities and nations frequently cemented relations by tracing origins to a legendary ancestor from whom each derived.[77] A nice idea—and one the Jews were happy to pick up. Here, as elsewhere, they took a leaf from the Greek book.

This extraordinary link crops up more than once in the testimony. The most striking instance involves some unlikely partners: Spartans and Jews. Both peoples claimed Abraham as their forefather—so, at least, one tradition affirms. The claim appears in 1 Maccabees, asserted by King Areus of Sparta, evidently in the early third century BCE. He corresponded with the Jewish high priest and announced the happy discovery of a document that showed their people's common descent from the Hebrew patriarch. Areus conveyed his warmest wishes and employed language with biblical resonance: "Your cattle and possessions are ours, and ours are yours."[78] A century later, we are told, the

Hasmonean Jonathan, who succeeded his brother Judas Maccabeus as leader of the Jews, renewed contact with the Spartans, sending them a copy of Areus' letter. Jonathan called attention to the long-standing alliance between the two peoples, an alliance unneeded from a military point of view (for the Jews rely on the support of heaven to help them humble their foes) but emblematic of the kinship bonds between them. The message simply reasserted those bonds and noted that Jews never fail to remember the Spartans in their sacrifices and prayers. Jonathan asked nothing in return except resumption of contact and renewal of their brotherhood.[79] The Spartans graciously obliged with a missive that reached Jerusalem after Jonathan had been succeeded by his brother Simon c. 142 BCE. The letter hailed the Jews as brothers, sent warm greetings, expressed great pleasure at the revival of relations, and announced that the alliance and even the speeches by Jewish envoys had been inscribed on bronze tablets and deposited in the Lacedaemonian archives.[80]

What does it all mean? The subject has been treated at some length elsewhere and requires only a summary of the main issues.[81] Debate continues on the authenticity of Jonathan's correspondence. That matter can be set aside. Few will now deny the invention of Areus' letter—let alone the kinship ties between Jews and Spartans. The invention is plainly a Jewish one. The postulate of Abraham as ultimate forebear of both nations makes that clear enough. A Spartan might have opted for Heracles. Nor is Areus likely to have adopted biblical language in expressing the reciprocity of the relationship. And Jonathan, in transmitting a copy of Areus' letter, reestablishes contact by patronizing the Spartans: he assures them that the Jews have consistently sacrificed and prayed on their behalf—as is appropriate for brothers.[82] The Jews have the upper hand in this association, the benefactors rather than the beneficiaries.

An undeniable fact emerges. Jewish intellectuals conceived a kinship bond with Sparta. Ethnic differentiation evaporated. Abraham had sired both peoples. The traditions of Sparta—or, more properly, the image of Sparta—had obvious appeal in Judaea. The Lacedaemonians stood for martial virtue, voluntary sacrifice, order, stability, and the rule of law.[83] A Greek historian, Hecataeus of Abdera, had already described the measures of Moses in terms that his readers would recognize as resembling the acts of Lycurgus and the statutes of Sparta.[84] Josephus, in turn, acknowledges that Lycurgus as lawgiver and Lacedaemon as a model polity draw universal praise—although he is at pains to show, as we have seen, that Jewish stability and endurance have outstripped that model.[85] Those who invented the purported kinship affiliation plainly had the Spartan mystique in mind. Jews could now partake of it. Indeed, better than partake of it, they could take credit for it. Abraham was ultimately responsible.

Such a construct, of course, elided ethnic distinctions and denied discord between Hellenic and Hebrew cultures. The virtues ascribed to Spartan society reflected principles enshrined in the Bible. And the Hebrew patriarch symbolized the blending of the peoples from their origins.

Another tradition utilizes the figure of Abraham as progenitor to fuse the *ethnē* and the cultures on a still broader level. A Greek legend furnished the basis for it. Among the adventures of Heracles was one in which he grappled with the Libyan giant Antaeus and overcame him, a victory that emblematized the bringing of Hellenic civilization to barbarous Africa. An elaboration of the tale has Heracles wed the wife of Antaeus, a union from which descended a lineage through Sophax and Diodorus to the rulers of North Africa.[86] Jewish writers later fiddled with the story and transformed it—in an intriguing and illuminating way. The book of Genesis supplies a brief genealogy stemming from Abraham's marriage to Keturah. In the Hellenistic period that record was exploited and amalgamated with the legend of Heracles and Antaeus. In the new version, two of Abraham's sons by Keturah, Apher and Aphran, fought side by side with Heracles in subduing Antaeus. Heracles then married Aphran's daughter, producing a son, Diodorus, who later provided a grandson, Sophon, whence derived the name of a barbarian people, the Sophanes. The exploits of Apher and Aphran had still greater ramifications. The city of Aphra was named after the one, the whole continent of Africa after the other. And a third brother, Assouri, became the namesake of Assyria. This wonderfully imaginative construct is ascribed to an otherwise unknown writer Cleodemus Malchus.[87]

The identity of Cleodemus has generated substantial discussion which can be happily passed by here.[88] Only the text matters. Here again the tale has received an *interpretatio Judaica*, not an *interpretatio Graeca*. The line begins with Abraham, his son has the honor of a continent named after him, and Heracles' victory over the giant was made possible by the collaboration of Hebrew figures. The invention in this case is especially notable. Not only does the Greek legend of Heracles bringing civilization to a barbarous land metamorphose into one in which Abraham's progeny took part in the endeavor and bestowed their names upon national entities, but also the manipulated narrative now implies a kinship affiliation between Hebrews and Hellenes at the dawn of history. The greatest of Greek heroes marries into the patriarch's family. And together they are responsible for the ruling dynasty of North Africa—*barbaroi* though they be. Here is ethnic mixture indeed. The Jewish version absorbs the Heracles legend, links the nations, and even encompasses the *barbaroi*. This seems at the farthest remove from those texts in which the distinctions are vital and the Hellene as alien serves to highlight the superior values of the Jew.

A quite different variety of tale but one with comparable import warrants notice here: speculation on Jewish origins. Two versions supply a direct connection with the Greek world, one with the island of Crete, the other with a people of Asia Minor. Both survive amidst a list of hypotheses recorded by Tacitus—who, however, supplies neither sources nor significance.

In the view of some, says the Roman historian, the Jews were refugees from Crete who settled in distant parts of Libya at the time when Saturn had been driven from his realm by Jupiter. Tacitus notes the grounds for this conjecture, essentially etymological. Mt. Ida in Crete gave the name "Idaei" to its inhabitants, a name later barbarized into "Iudaei."[89] Whence derived this notion and how widespread it was we cannot know. It may well have stemmed from speculation by Greeks, a typical tendency to associate foreign peoples with Hellenic origins.[90] Jewish researchers may not have embraced the identification but would welcome the inferences that their people date to the earliest era of Greek mythology, that they share a heritage with the Hellenes, and even that they had an ancient foothold in Africa.[91]

The other tale was still more agreeable. It ascribed especially illustrious beginnings to the Jews: they were identified with the Solymoi, a Lycian people celebrated in the epics of Homer, whose name is reflected in the city they founded, Hierosolyma (Jerusalem).[92] The etymological assumption again accounts for the conclusion. A pagan source here, too, probably conceived the coincidence, standard fare for finding links between contemporary folk and Greek legend. It is unlikely that a Jew invented the idea that his ancestors' roots were in Asia Minor. But association with a Homeric people, particularly one described in the *Iliad* as "glorious" and as having given the Greek hero Bellerophon his toughest fight, would be congenial to the Jews—at least to those who regarded an ethnic amalgamation with nations honored in classical myths as an enhancement of their own cultural identity.[93]

Do we here reach an impasse? The texts seem to suggest inconsistency and ambivalence, if not outright self-contradiction, in Jewish perspectives on the people of Hellas. A strong strain in Jewish literature emphasized the differences in culture and behavior between the two peoples, categorizing the Greeks as aliens, inferiors, even savage antagonists and barbarians. Other voices, however, embraced and absorbed Hellenic institutions, finding them entirely compatible with Hebraic teachings. And still other traditions, invented or propagated by Jewish writers, far from stressing the contrast, brought the nations together with a blending of the races and the fiction of a common ancestor.

Is there an explanation for these discordant voices? Should one postulate a change over time in Jewish attitudes toward the Hellenes and Hellenic culture? Or was there perhaps a division within Jewish communities between those committed to the purity of the tradition, thus drawing a firm distinction between the cultures, and those inclined toward assimilation and accommodation? Neither explanation will do. In fact, supposedly different voices coexist in the same texts. So, the *Letter of Aristeas* proclaims a harmonious relationship between cultivated Greeks and learned Jews, a fruitful collaboration in the translation of the Pentateuch into *koine* Greek, but also presents a forceful reminder that idolatry still grips the Hellenes and that their childish beliefs distance them immeasurably from the genuine piety of the Jews.[94] Similarly, the dire forecasts of the Third Sibylline Oracle predict vengeance to be wreaked upon the aggressive and brutal Hellenic conquerors, repayment for their inner malevolence as well as their external aggrandizement. But the same work contains lines that indicate a reaching out by Jews to those Greeks who will repent and reform, a promise of divine favor in return for righteousness and piety, the expectation that Greeks will share with Jews in the glories of the eschaton.[95] And Josephus himself, as we have seen, not only draws the sharpest contrast between Hellenic deficiencies and Jewish virtues but also embraces the view that the noblest expressions of Greek philosophy cohere with the teachings of Moses.[96]

The matter is plainly more complex and more involved. The discrepancies and inconsistencies that we discern (or construct) may not have been so perceived by the ancients who viewed them with multiple visions. Could they both associate and contrast Jews and Greeks? Why not? The texts that betoken cultural conjunction in no way negate or compromise Jewish distinctiveness. On the contrary. They serve to underscore, rather than to undermine, Jewish superiority. In various formulations, the Greek alphabet arrived through a Jewish intermediary; poetic inspiration came from a Hebrew bard; the most sublime Greek thought derived from the teachings of the Pentateuch; Hellenic philosophers, dramatists, and poets who recognized the sole divinity, expressed lofty ethical precepts, and honored the Sabbath took their cue from the Torah; and even the Athenians unwittingly paid homage to the god of the Scriptures. These fictive inventions hardly dissolved the distinctions between Hebrews and Hellenes. Instead, they elevated the best in Hellenism by providing it with Hebrew precedents. The rest, by definition, fell short. All of this, and more, reflects energetic and often ingenious efforts to commandeer Hellenic achievements for Jewish purposes.

Nor is there any dilution of ethnic singularity in the tales that made kinsmen of Jews and Spartans or linked Heracles with biblical figures. Inventive Jewish writers exploited the Hellenic practice of signaling consanguinity among the nations by positing a common ancestor. But the Jews did it their own way: the mythical forefather was to be the Hebrew patriarch. That established the proper priority. The admirable qualities and the storied exploits of the Hellenes were enlisted to demonstrate the special eminence that attached to the *ethnos* of the Jews. This was no blend of the cultures. It was Jewish appropriation.

The strategy is neatly exemplified by an anecdote derived from the Mishnah. As the tale has it, Rabbi Gamaliel went to Acco, a largely gentile city on the coast of Palestine. There he took a bath in the bathhouse dedicated to Aphrodite and adorned by a statue of the goddess—no doubt in her most provocative pose. The rabbi was then asked by an astonished witness whether he was violating Jewish law by entering the sacred space of a pagan shrine and one marked by a statue of Aphrodite. Gamaliel had an answer: "The bathhouse was not built as an ornament for the statue, but the statue for the bathhouse; hence I did not come into Aphrodite's domain, she came into mine!"[97] The rabbi's reasoning may be a bit sophistical, but it was quite characteristic. Jews engaged in clever cultural aggrandizement.

The process, however, was not all one-sided. Greek writers did some appropriating of their own. As is well known, Greeks frequently traced the origins of some of their institutions and practices to peoples of the Near East, most particularly the Egyptians. Herodotus, of course, spoke with great respect of Egypt's ancient traditions and institutions to which Hellas owes a large debt.[98] Tales circulated later of Homer's birth in Egypt, of visits to Egyptian priests by Orpheus and Musaeus, by Lycurgus and Solon, by Pythagoras and Plato, all to take intellectual nourishment from that ancient land.[99]

Would the Greeks be willing to articulate a comparable debt to the Jews? A harder proposition. Few Greeks had any familiarity with Jewish history, literature, and traditions. Yet stereotypes and impressions existed. And, in fact, there are traces of a reciprocal recognition and of Hellenic concession to Jewish characteristics that could resonate with their own. Hecataeus of Abdera, writing in the late fourth century BCE, has an excursus on the Jews. Among other things, he makes some admiring remarks about Moses as law-giver, agricultural reformer, and initiator of a military system.[100] Hecataeus, to be sure, makes no claim that the Greeks learned anything from him. Nevertheless, the description of Moses as a proto-Lycurgus is striking. Of course, the version is an *interpretatio Graeca*, but it suggests at least a willingness to express an indirect affiliation.

In the perspective of several early Hellenistic authors, the Jews were a nation of philosophers.[101] That perception emerges most memorably in a story told of Aristotle by one of his pupils, Clearchus of Soli. According to the anecdote, Aristotle, while in Asia Minor, ran into a Jew from Coele-Syria whom he much admired for his learning and his impeccable character. Jews in general are known as philosophers, he said. And this particular one was especially notable. For he was *Hellenikos* not only in his speech, but in his very soul.[102] So the Jewish concept that the best in Greek philosophy derives from biblical roots is here mirrored by a Greek tale that has the Jew as quintessential philosopher. But the anecdote is given a Hellenic spin: the Jew has the soul of a Greek.

A two-way process existed, a mutual manipulation of crosscultural interchange, a double mirror. Hence it comes as no surprise to find in other Greek writers reverberations of, or parallels to, the thesis expressed by Aristobulus and Josephus. The late third century BCE historian and biographer of philosophers Hermippus of Smyrna remarked that Pythagoras imitated and made use of Jewish and Thracian doctrines and that he introduced many principles from the Jews into his philosophy.[103]

By the second century CE, Numenius of Apamea, a Neo-Pythagorean philosopher, could declare quite baldly: "What is Plato but Moses speaking in Attic Greek?"[104]

While Greeks acknowledged Moses' influence on Hellenic philosophy, however, the Jewish philosopher Philo turned that idea on its head. He has Moses himself not only learn arithmetic, geometry, music, and hieroglyphics from erudite Egyptians, but progress through the rest of his curriculum, presumably rhetoric, literature, and philosophy, with Greek teachers.[105] What itinerant Greek schoolmasters there might have been in Egypt in the late Bronze Age can be left to the imagination. In any event, there was a lively traffic in stories, whether filtered through *interpretationes Graecae* or *interpretationes Judaicae,* whereby the two *ethnē* reflected themselves in one another's culture.

Comparable inversions occur with respect to the slippery term *barbaros.* The Jewish author of 2 Maccabees, as we have seen, writing in Greek and in the genre of Hellenistic historiography, turned the tables on conventional practice and labeled the Greeks themselves as *barbaroi.*[106] That was ironic and pointed—but it did not become a dominant mode. Other Jewish writers embraced the long-established Hellenic antithesis that divided the world into Greeks and barbarians. It can be found, for instance, in Philo of Alexandria, who boasts of the widespread attraction of Jewish customs, applied in various parts of the world by both Greeks and barbarians—who reject the institutions of others within their own category.[107] Josephus employs the contrast regularly as a means of categorizing the non-Jewish world.[108] It appears also in Paul, who proclaims his message to "Greeks and Barbarians, the wise and the ignorant"—no pagan could have said it better.[109] Philo, in fact, can even adopt the Hellenic perspective wholesale and count the Jews among the *barbaroi!*[110] And while the Jewish philosopher in Egypt brackets Jews with barbarians, the Greek tax collector in Ptolemaic Egypt places Jews in the category of *Hellenes.*[111] Here is inversion upon inversion. And we have noticed already the unusual variant in Cleodemus Malchus' story about intermarriage between the houses of Abraham and Heracles: one of the descendants of that union gave his name to the "barbarian" Sophanes of Africa.[112] That is ethnic mixture indeed: not only linkage of Greek and Jew, but even a joint embrace of *barbaroi*. The counterpoint and transposition complicate matters considerably. But they also show with accuracy just how entangled was the reciprocity of the cultures. Jewish intellectuals, it appears, negotiated an intricate balance in their depiction of Greek ethnicity and culture. They simultaneously differentiated their nation from that of the Greeks and justified their own immersion in a world of Hellenic civilization. The differentiation, sharp though it might be, did not preclude imaginary kinship associations. And, on the other side of the coin, the thorough engagement with Greek culture did not mean compromise with the principles and practices of Judaism.

Jewish perspectives predominate in the texts here examined. But their discourse was not altogether lost on the Greeks themselves. The latter, who sought to enhance their stature by proclaiming a link with the venerable teachings of Egypt, also gave a nod in the direction of the Jews. It added yet another dimension to Hellenic self-perception to have Pythagoras and Plato acquainted with the Pentateuch, as they were with Egyptian learning. And even Aristotle could comfortably benefit from the erudition of a cultivated Jew—so long as he possessed the soul of a Greek. The double mirror captured the *ethnē*.

Notes

1. The most detailed and comprehensive study is still that of M. Hengel, *Judaism and Hellenism* (2 vols.; Philadelphia: Fortress, 1974). His conclusions on the extensive and early spread of Hellenism among the Jews, however, are challenged by L. Feldman, *Jew and Gentile in the Ancient World* (Princeton: Princeton University Press, 1993), especially 42–44, 416–22, and bibliographical references.

2. Enormous literature exists on this subject. The relevant texts are conveniently collected by M. Stern, *Greek and Latin Authors on Jews and Judaism* (2 vols.; Jerusalem: Israel Academy of Sciences, 1976). Among recent works, with references to earlier scholarship, see especially J. G. Gager, *The Origins of Anti-Semitism* (Oxford: Oxford University Press, 1985); Z. Yavetz, "Judeophobia in Classical Antiquity," *JJS* 44 (1993) 1–22; P. Schäfer, *Judeophobia: Attitudes*

toward *the Jews in the Ancient World* (Cambridge, Mass.: Harvard University Press, 1997).

3. The classic study is that of Y. Gutman, *The Beginnings of Jewish-Hellenistic Literature* (2 vols.; Jerusalem: Bialik, 1958, 1963 [Hebrew]). Cf. also J. J. Collins, *Between Athens and Jerusalem: Jewish Identity in the Hellenistic Diaspora* (New York: Crossroad, 1983; revised ed. Grand Rapids, Mich.: Eerdmans, 2000). A good general discussion may be found in D. Mendels, *The Rise and Fall of Jewish Nationalism* (New York: Doubleday, 1992). And see now E. Gruen, *Heritage and Hellenism* (Berkeley: University of California Press, 1998), with further bibliography.

4. The treatment by C. Sirat, "The Jews," in K. Dover, ed., *Perceptions of the Ancient Greeks* (Oxford: Blackwell, 1992) 54–78, is too broad and selective.

5. The work is itself an epitome of the now lost five-volume history of the Maccabees by Jason of Cyrene, plainly also a Hellenized Jew; 2 Macc 2:19–31. For a recent register of scholarship on 2 Maccabees, see E. Schürer, *The History of the Jewish People in the Age of Jesus Christ* 3.1 (rev. and ed. G. Vermes, F. Millar and M. Goodman; Edinburgh: Clark, 1986) 536–37.

6. 2 Macc 2:21: τοῖς ὑπὲρ τοῦ Ἰουδαϊσμοῦ φιλοτίμως ἀνδραγαθήσασιν, ὥστε τὴν ὅλην χώραν ὀλίγους ὄντας λεηλατεῖν καὶ τὰ βάρβαρα πλήθη διώκειν.

7. Cf. 2 Macc 4:25; 5:22; 10:4.

8. See the discussions of T. Dothan and R. Cohn, "The Philistine as Other: Biblical Rhetoric and Archaeological Reality," in *The Other in Jewish Thought and History* (ed. L. Silberstein and R. Cohn; New York: New York University Press, 1994) 61–73; and Cohn, "Before Israel: The Canaanites as Other in Biblical Tradition," in ibid., 74–90.

9. Daniel 2:31–45; 7:1–27; 8.1–26; 11:21–45; 12:1–3. This, of course, is not the place to explore these visions and their interpretations in detail. Among recent commentaries, see L. Hartman and A. Di Lella, *The Book of Daniel* (Garden City, N.Y.: Doubleday, 1978); J. J. Collins, *Daniel* (Hermeneia; Minneapolis: Fortress, 1993).

10. The chronology is complex and contested. A valuable recent treatment may be found in J. Barclay, *The Jews in the Mediterranean Diaspora* (Edinburgh: Clark, 1996) 216–25. The matter is taken up afresh in Gruen, *Heritage and Hellenism*, 271–83.

11. *Sib. Or.* 3: 381–400.

12. *Sib. Or.* 3: 166–90.

13. *Sib. Or.* 3: 202–04, 341–49, 545–55, 638–45.

14. On the date, see F.-M. Abel, *Les livres des Maccabées* (Paris: Lecoffre, 1949) xxviii–xxix; J. Goldstein, *1 Maccabees* (Garden City, N.Y.: Doubleday, 1976) 62–63; Schürer, *The History*, 3.1:181; J. Sievers, *The Hasmoneans and their Supporters* (Atlanta: Scholars Press, 1990) 3.

15. 1 Macc 1:9: ἔτη πολλὰ καὶ ἐπλήθυναν κακὰ τῇ γῇ.

16. 1 Macc 1:43–44: πορευθῆναι ὀπίσω νομίμων ἀλλοτρίων τῆς γῆς.

17. 2 Macc 6:18–7:41.

18. 4 Macc 4–18. For recent discussions of the text, with bibliography, see H. Anderson, "4 Maccabees," in *The Old Testament Pseudepigrapha* (ed. J. H. Charlesworth; Garden City, N.Y.: Doubleday, 1985) 2.531–43; Schürer, *The History*, 3.1: 588–93; J. W. van Henten, *The Maccabean Martyrs as Saviours of the Jewish People: A Study of 2 and 4 Maccabees* (Leiden: Brill, 1997) 58–82; D. deSilva, *4 Maccabees* (Sheffield: Sheffield Academic Press, 1998) 11–142.

19. See the excellent treatment by D. Winston, *The Wisdom of Solomon* (Garden City, N.Y.: Doubleday, 1979).

20. Wisdom of Solomon 12:3-5: καὶ σπλαγχνοφάγον ἀνθρωπίνων σαρκῶν θοῖναν καὶ αἵματος ἐκ μέσου μύστας θιάσου. Cf. Winston, *The Wisdom of Solomon*, 238–40, with references.

21. A valuable summary of scholarship on this text may be found in F. Parente, "The Third Book of Maccabees as Ideological Document and Historical Source," *Henoch* 10 (1988) 150–68. See, more recently, J. Mélèze-Modrzejewski, *The Jews of Egypt* (Philadelphia: The Jewish Publication Society, 1995) 141–53; Barclay, *The Jews in the Mediterranean Diaspora*, 192–203; and the excellent dissertation of S. Johnson "Mirror-Mirror: Third Maccabees, Historical Fictions and Jewish Self-Fashioning in the Hellenistic Period," Ph.D. diss., University of California, Berkeley, 1996.

22. 3 Macc 3:2; 3:6–7; 5:3; 6:23–24; 7:3.

23. 3 Macc 4:1: δημοτελὴς συνίστατο τοῖς ἔθνεσιν εὐωχία μετὰ ἀλαλαγμῶν καὶ χαρᾶς ὡς ἂν τῆς προκατεσκιρωμένης αὐτοῖς πάλαι κατὰ διάνοιαν μετὰ παρρησίας νῦν ἐκφαινομένης ἀπεχθείας. This attitude did not prevail, however, among all the Greeks in Alexandria itself; 3 Macc 3:8–10.

24. 3 Macc 3:6–7; 3:21.

25. Esther, Addition E, 10–14.

26. This work, of course, has generated a lengthening stream of publications. Among the servicable commentaries, see R. Tramontano, *La lettera di Aristea a Filocrate* (Naples: Ufficio succursale della civiltà cattolica, 1931); M. Hadas, *Aristeas to Philocrates* (New York: Harper, 1951); A. Pelletier, *Lettre d'Aristée à Philocrate* (Paris: Cerf, 1962); N. Meisner, "Aristeasbrief," *JSHRZ* 2.1 (1973) 35–87. Additional works cited in Schürer, *The History*, 3.1: 685–87.

27. *Ep. Arist.* 137: καὶ νομίζουσιν οἱ ταῦτα διαπλάσαντες καὶ μυθοποιήσαντες τῶν Ἑλλήνων οἱ σοφώτατοι καθεστάναι.

28. *Ep. Arist.* 139: ὁ νομοθέτης, ὑπὸ θεοῦ κατεσκευασμένος εἰς ἐπίγνωσιν τῶν ἁπάντων, περιέφραξεν ἡμᾶς ἀδιασκόποις χάραξι καὶ σιδηροῖς τείχεσιν, ὅπως μηθενὶ τῶν ἄλλων ἐθνῶν ἐπιμισγώμεθα κατὰ μηδέν, ἁγνοὶ καθεστῶτες κατὰ σῶμα καὶ κατὰ ψυχήν ἀπολελυμένοι ματαίων δοξῶν.

29. The same point about the folly of those whose objects of worship were fashioned by their own hands is made by Wisdom of Solomon 14–17, and Philo, *De Decalogo* 69.

30. Josephus, *Ant.* 16.174–75. Cf. C. Stanley, "'Neither Jew nor Greek': Ethnic Conflict in Graeco-Roman Society," *JSOT* 64(1996) 106-108.

31. See, e.g., Josephus, *Ant.* 16.160–61, 18.257–60, 19.300–12, 20.173–84. For additional references and discussion, especially on the outbursts against Jews by Greeks during the Great Revolt, see A. Kasher, *Jews and Hellenistic Cities in Eretz-Israel* (Tübingen: Mohr Siebeck, 1990) 245–87; Feldman, *Jew and Gentile*, 113–22.

32. Josephus, *Ant.* 16.161: τῆς τῶν Ἑλλήνων ἀπανθρωπίας.

33. Josephus, *Ag. Ap.* 2.154–56.

34. Josephus, *Ag. Ap.* 2.168–74.

35. Josephus, *Ag. Ap.* 2.220–24.

36. Josephus, *Ag. Ap.* 2.225–31, 2.279.

37. Josephus, *Ag. Ap.* 2.232–35, ἆρ᾽ οὖν καὶ παρ᾽ ἡμῖν, οὐ λέγω τοσούτους, ἀλλὰ δύο ἢ τρεῖς ἔγνω τις προδότας γενομένους τῶν νόμων ἢ θάνατον φοβηθέντας.

38. Josephus, *Ag. Ap.* 2.239–54.

39. Josephus, *Ag. Ap.* 2.256.

40. Josephus *Ag. Ap.* 2.271: καὶ τούτων ἡμᾶς τῶν νόμων ἀπαγαγεῖν οὔτεφόβος ἴσχυσε τῶν κρατησάντων οὔτε ζῆλος τῶν παρὰ τοῖς ἄλλοις τετιμημένων.

41. Gal 3:28: οὐκ ἔνι Ἰουδαῖος οὐδὲ Ἕλλην, οὐκ ἔνι δοῦλος οὐδὲ ἐλεύθερος, οὐκ ἔνι ἄρσεν καὶ θῆλυ· πάντες γὰρ ὑμεῖς εἷς ἐστε ἐν Χριστῷ Ἰησοῦ. See the expanded and more complex version in Col 3:11.

42. 1 Cor 12:13: καὶ γὰρ ἐν ἑνὶ πνεύματι ἡμεῖς πάντες εἰς ἓν σῶμα ἐβαπτίσθημεν, εἴτε Ἰουδαῖοι εἴτε Ἕλληνες εἴτε δοῦλοι εἴτε ἐλεύθεροι. Cf. also 1 Cor 10:32; Rom 1:16; 2:9–10; 3:9; 10:12; Acts 19:10; 19:17; 20:21; Stanley, "'Neither Jew nor Greek,'" 123. The Greeks are themselves made equivalent to τὰ ἔθνη; 1 Cor 1:22–24.

43. See, e.g., 1 Macc 1:11; 1:13; 1:14; 2:68; 3:10; 3:45; 3:48; 2 Macc 8:5; 12:13; 14:14–15.

44. See, e.g., 1 Macc 8:23; 10:25; 11:30; 12:3; 13:36; 14:28; 15:1–2; also 2 Macc 11:27. Note further the letter of Antiochus III, recorded or recast by Josephus, in which Judaea is an *ethnos* among other *ethnē; Ant.* 12.141–42: τῆς Ἰουδαίας και ἐκ τῶν ἀλλῶν ἐθνῶν.

45. So, e.g., Rom 3:29: ἢ Ἰουδαίων ὁ θεὸς μόνον οὐχὶ καὶ ἐθνῶν; similarly, Rom 9:24; 11:11–12; 11:25; 2 Cor 11:26; Gal 2:14–15. Cf. also Acts 4:27; 13:45–46; 14:5; 21:21. For the identification of Greeks with *ta ethnē*, see 1 Cor 1:22–24; Acts 14:1–2.

46. The fragments may be conveniently consulted in C. Holladay, *Fragments from Hellenistic Jewish Authors*. Volume 1: *The Historians* (Chico, Calif.: Scholars Press, 1983) 93–156, with notes and commentary. Among the important treatments of Eupolemus, see especially J. Freudenthal, *Alexander Polyhistor* (Breslau: Skutsch, 1875) 105–30; Gutman, *The Beginnings*, 73–94 (Hebrew); B. Z. Wacholder, *Eupolemus, A Study of Judaeo-Greek Literature* (Cincinnati: Hebrew Union College, 1974); D. Mendels, *The Land of Israel as a Political Concept in Hasmonean Literature* (Tübingen: Mohr, 1987) 29–46; G. Sterling, *Historiography and Self-Definition: Josephos, Luke-Acts and Apologetic Historiography* (Leiden: Brill, 1992) 207–22, with valuable bibliography. Some doubts on Eupolemus' origins and date are expressed by Gruen, *Heritage and Hellenism*, 139–41.

47. Eupolemus *apud* Eusebius, *Praeparatio Evangelica* 26.1: γράμματα παραδοῦναι τοῖς Ἰουδαίοις πρῶτον, παρὰ δὲ Ἰουδαίων Φοινίκας παραλαβεῖν, Ἕλληνας δὲ παρὰ Φοινίκων.

48. Fragments collected and commented upon by Holladay, *Fragments*, 1. 189–243. See the discussions of Freudenthal, *Alexander Polyhistor*, 143–74; Gutman, *The Beginnings*, 109–35 (Hebrew); C. Holladay, *Theios Aner in Hellenistic Judaism* (Missoula: Scholars Press, 1977) 199–232; Sterling, *Historiography and Self-Definition*, 167–86; Barclay, *Jews in the Mediterranean Diaspora*, 127–32.

49. Artapanus *apud* Eusebius, *Praeparatio Evangelica* 9.27.3–4: ὑπὸ δὲ τῶν Ἑλλήνων αὐτὸν ἀνδρωθέντα Μουσαῖον προσαγορευθῆναι. γενέσθαι δὲ τὸν Μώυσον τοῦτον Ὀρφέως διδάσκαλον. Cf. Holladay, *Theios Aner*, 224.

50. Artapanus *apud* Eusebius, *Praeparatio Evangelica* 9.27.6: ὑπὸ τῶν ἱερέων . . . προσαγορευθῆναι Ἑρμῆν, διὰ τὴν τῶν ἱερῶν γραμμάτων ἑρμενείαν.

51. On Artapanus' manipulation of the Hermes/Thot characteristics, see Gutman, *The Beginnings*, 120–22 (Hebrew); G. Mussies, "The Interpretatio Judaica of Thoth-Hermes," in *Studies in Egyptian Religion* (ed. M. Voss; Leiden: Brill, 1982) 97–108.

52. The fullest treatment of Aristobulus may be found in N. Walter, *Der Thoraausleger Aristobulus* (Berlin: Akademie, 1964). Among other worthy contributions, see Gutman, *The Beginnings*, 186–220 (Hebrew); Hengel, *Judaism and Hellenism*, 1.163–69; 2.105–10; N. Walter, "Aristobulos," *JSHRZ* 3.2: 261–79; Barclay, *Jews in the Mediterranean Diaspora*, 150–58. The whole subject has now been placed on a firmer footing by the excellent new edition of the fragments, with translation, notes, and bibliography by C. Holladay, *Fragments from Hellenistic Jewish Authors*. Volume 3: *Aristobulus* (Atlanta: Scholars Press, 1995).

53. Aristobulus *apud* Eusebius, *Praeparatio Evangelica* 13.12.1: φανερὸν ὅτι κατηκολούθησεν ὁ Πλάτωνν τῇ καθ' ἡμᾶς νομοθεσίᾳ καὶ φανερός ἐστι περιειργασμένος ἕκαστα τῶν ἐν αὐτῇ.

54. Aristobulus *apud* Eusebius, *Praeparatio Evangelica* 13.12.1: καθὼς καὶ Πυθαγόρας πολλὰ τῶν παρ' ἡμῖν μετενέγκας εἰς τὴν ἑαυτοῦ δογματοποιίαν κατεχώρισεν.

55. Aristobulus *apud* Eusebius, *Praeparatio Evangelica* 13.12.1.

56. Aristobulus *apud* Eusebius, *Praeparatio Evangelica* 13.12.3–4.

57. Aristobulus *apud* Eusebius, *Praeparatio Evangelica* 13.12.8. See Gutman, *The Beginnings*, 192–99 (Hebrew).

58. Aristobulus *apud* Eusebius, *Praeparatio Evangelica* 13.12.12. See, on this, Gutman, *The Beginnings*, 203–10 (Hebrew); Walter, *Der Thoraausleger*, 68–81; Holladay, *Fragments*, Volume 3, 230–32.

59. Aristobulus *apud* Eusebius, *Praeparatio Evangelica* 13.12.13–15; Clement, *Stromateis* 5.14.107.1–3. See the careful discussion of Walter, *Der Thoraausleger*, 1964: 150–58, with reference to the relevant Homeric and Hesiodic lines; cf. Gutman, *The Beginnings*, 210–12 (Hebrew); Holladay, *Fragments*, Volume 3, 234–37.

60. Aristobulus *apud* Eusebius, *Praeparatio Evangelica* 13.12.16: ἑβδομάτῃ δ' ἠοῖ τετελεσμένα πάντα τέτυκται. See Walter, *Der Thoraausleger*, 158–66; Hengel, *Judaism and Hellenism*, 1.166–67; Holladay, *Fragments*, Volume 3, 237–240.

61. Aristobulus *apud* Eusebius, *Praeparatio Evangelica* 13.12.4–5. Various versions of the poem are preserved by Christian authors in addition to Eusebius, and scholarly disputes over its transmission and over what counts as authentic Aristobulus remain unsettled. The subject now claims a whole new volume to itself: C. Holladay, *Fragments from Hellenistic Jewish Authors*. Volume 4: *Orphica* (Atlanta: Scholars Press, 1996).

62. Aristobulus *apud* Eusebius, *Praeparatio Evangelica* 13.6–7; cf. Clement, *Stromateis* 5.14.101.4b.

63. The fragments are collected by A.-M. Denis, *Fragmenta pseudepigraphorum graeca* (Leiden: Brill, 1970) 161–74. See the valuable discussion by Goodman in Schürer, *The History*, 3.1: 667–71, with bibliographies.

64. Pseudo Justin, *De Monarchia* 2; Clement, *Stromateis* 5.14.131.2–3; Eusebius, *Praeparatio Evangelica* 13.13.60.

65. Pseudo Justin, *De Monarchia* 2–3; Clement, *Stromateis* 5.14.111.4–6, 5.14.113.2, 5.14.121.4–122.1; Eusebius, *Praeparatio Evangelica* 13.13.38, 13.13.40, 13.13.48.

66. Clement, *Stromateis* 5.11.75.1; *Protrepticus* 6.68.3. The second passage is attributed by Pseudo Justin, *De Monarchia* 2, to the comic poet Philemon.

67. Clement, *Stromateis* 5.14.119.2, 5.14.121.1–3, 5.14.133.3; Eusebius, *Praeparatio Evangelica* 13.13.45–47, 13.13.62; Pseudo Justin, *De Monarchia* 2–5

68. Acts 17:16–33.

69. The author of Acts adds the snide remark that Athenians have nothing better to do with their time than to talk or hear about the latest fad; Acts 17:21.

70. Acts 17:23: Ἀγνώστῳ θεῷ.

71. Acts 17:24–26.

72. Acts 17:28: ὡς καί τινες τῶν καθ᾽ ὑμας ποιητῶν εἰρηκασιν: τοῦ γὰρ καὶ γένος ἐσμεν.

73. Josephus, *Ag. Ap.* 2.123: τῶν Ἑλλήνων δὲ πλέον τοῖς τόποις ἢ τοῖς ἐπιτηδεύμασιν ἀφεστήκαμεν.

74. Josephus, *Ag. Ap.* 2.168; cf. 1.162.

75. Josephus, *Ag. Ap.* 2.257: μάλιστα δὲ Πλάτων μεμίμηται τὸν ἡμέτερον νομοθέτην.

76. Josephus, *Ag. Ap.* 2.280–84.

77. An extensive collection of the epigraphic evidence on fictitious kinship connections between Greek states is now available in O. Curty, *Les parentés legéndaires entre cités grecques* (Geneva: Droz, 1995).

78. 1 Macc 12:23: τὰ κτήνη ὑμῶν καὶ ἡ ὕπαρξις ὑμῶν ἡμῖν ἐστιν καὶ τὰ ἡμῶν ὑμῖν ἐστιν.

79. 1 Macc 12:6–18.

80. 1 Macc 14:16–23. One other reference to the kinship exists, an allusion to the former high priest Jason, later an exile, who sought refuge in Sparta in reliance on the *suggeneia* between the nations; 2 Macc 5:9. Areus' letter and the exchange with Jonathan is given also by Josephus, following 1 Maccabees, with some additions and changes of wording; *Ant.* 12.225–27, 13.164–70.

81. See Gruen, "The Purported Jewish-Spartan Affiliation," in *Transitions to Empire: Essays in Greco-Roman History, 300–146 BC in Honor of E. Badian* (Norman: University of Oklahoma Press, 1996) 254–69, with references to earlier literature. Previous bibliographical summaries may be found in B. Cardauns, "Juden und Spartaner," *Hermes* 95 (1967) 317–18, n. 1; R. Katzoff, "Jonathan and Late Sparta," *American Journal of Philology* 106 (1985) 485, n. 1; C. Orrieux, "la 'parenté' entre Juifs et Spartiates," in *L'étranger dans le monde grec* (ed. R. Lonis; Nancy: Presses Universitaires de Nancy, 1987) 187, n. 7.

82. 1 Macc 12:11: ἡμεῖς οὖν ἐν παντὶ καίρῳ ἀδιαλείπτως ἔν τε ταῖς ἑορταῖς καὶ ταῖς λοιπαῖς καθηκούσαις ἡμέραις μιμνησκόμεθα ὑμῶν ἐφ᾽ ὧν προσφέρομεν θυσιῶν καὶ ἐν ταῖς προσευχαῖς ὡς δέον ἐστὶν καὶ πρέπον μνημονεύειν ἀδέλφων.

83. On the Spartan image, see F. Ollier, *La mirage spartiate* (2 vols.; Paris: de Boccard, 1933–1943); E. Tigerstedt, *The Legend of Sparta in Classical Antiquity*

(3 vols.; Stockholm: Almqvist & Wiksell, 1965, 1974, 1978); E. Rawson, *The Spartan Tradition in European Thought* (Oxford: Oxford University Press, 1969); N. Kennell, *The Gymnasium of Virtue* (Chapel Hill: University of North Carolina Press, 1995).

84. Hecataeus in Diodorus Siculus 40.3.6–7. Cf. Gruen, "The Purported Jewish-Spartan Affiliation," 260.

85. Josephus, *Ag. Ap.* 2.225–35.

86. On the various versions of the Greek tale, see Diodorus Siculus 1.17.21, 1.17.24, 4.17.4; Plutarch, *Sertorius* 9. Cf. N. Walter, "Kleodemos Malchas," *JSHRZ* 1.2 (1976) 116; R. Doran, "Cleodemus Malchus," in *OTP* 2. 884–85. The best analysis, exploring both classical and Jewish texts on North Africa, is that of Gutman, *The Beginnings* 2 (1963) 137–43 (Hebrew).

87. The text is preserved in Josephus, *Ant.* 1.239–41 and Eusebius, *Praeparatio Evangelica* 9.20.2–4, with some variations in the names. The biblical genealogy occurs in Gen 25.1–6.

88. Among the more important treatments, see Freudenthal, *Alexander Polyhistor,* 1875: 130–36; Gutman, *The Beginnings,* 2.136–37 (Hebrew); Walter, "Kleodemos Malchas," 115–18; Holladay, *Fragments,* 1.245–59; Doran, "Cleodemus Malchus," 883–87; Goodman, in Schürer, *The History,* 3.1: 526–29.

89. Tacitus, *Histories* 5.2.1: *Iudaeos Creta insula profugos novissima Libyae insedisse memorant, qua tempestate Saturnus vi Iovis pulsus cesserit regnis. Argumentum e nomine petitur: inclutum in Creta Idam montem, accolas Idaeos aucto in barbarum cognomento Iudaeos vocitari.*

90. Cf. E. Bickerman, "Origenes Gentium," *Classical Philology* 47 (1952) 65–81.

91. The learned might also recall that tradition had Zeus himself born in Crete; Hesiod, *Theogony* 470–80. And the age of Saturn would have the resonance of a golden era of stability. Cf. L. Feldman, "Pro-Jewish Intimations in Tacitus' Account of Jewish Origins," *Revue des Études Juives* 159 (1991) 339–46.

92. Tacitus, *Histories* 5.2.3: *Clara alii Iudaeorum initia: Solymos, carminibus Homeri celebratam gentem, conditae urbi Hierosolyma nomen e suo fecisse.*

93. The relevant Homeric passage is *Iliad* 6.184–85. In *Odyssey* 5.283, the bard mentions the "Solymian hills." The reference is picked up by the fifth century BCE poet Choerilus, who includes those dwelling in the Solymian hills among the Asian nations who marched with Xerxes against Greece. That passage is preserved by Josephus, a noteworthy point, for he interprets it (whatever Choerilus may have intended) as an allusion to the Jews and employs it as evidence for early Hellenic acquaintance with his people; Josephus, *Ag. Ap.* 1.172–75. The process neatly illustrates the adaptation of a Greek text for Jewish purposes. And it suggests that the tale of Jews as Solymoi could well have found its way into Jewish texts. The claim that a Jewish exegete made the initial identification is improbable; so I. Lévy, "Tacite et l'origine du peuple juif," *Latomus*

5 (1946) 334–39; M. Stern, *Greek and Latin Authors on Jews and Judaism* (2 vols.; Jerusalem: Israel Academy of Sciences, 1974) 2. 5–6. See Feldman, "Pro-Jewish Intimations," 351–54; 1993: 192, 520–22, who, however, goes too far in implying that Jews would have found the story unacceptable.

94. See above pp. 67–68.

95. *Sib. Or.* 3:545–72, 625–56, 732–61.

96. See above pp. 76–77.

97. M. Avodah Zarah, 3.4. A recent discussion by S. Schwartz, in P. Schäfer, *The Talmud Yerushalmi and Graeco-Roman Culture*, 1 (Tübingen: Mohr Siebeck, 1998), 203–17.

98. Cf. Herodotus 2.4, 2.43, 2.49–58, 2.82, 2.123, 2.167.

99. See, e.g., Isocrates, *Busiris* 28–29; Diodorus Siculus 1.68.2–4, 1.76.5–6, 96.1–3, 98.1–4; Plutarch, *Solon* 26.1.

100. Hecataeus, apud Diodorus Siculus 40.3.3–8.

101. Cf. Theophrastus, apud Porphyry, De Abstinentia 2.26; Megasthenes, apud Clement, Stromateis 1.15.72.5; Clearchus, apud Josephus, Ag. Ap. 1.176–83. The texts may be readily consulted in Stern, Greek and Latin Authors, vol. 1, numbers 4, 14, 15.

102. Clearchus, *apud* Josephus, *Ag. Ap.* 1.176–83: Ἑλληνικὸς ἦν οὐ τῇ διαλέκτῳ μόνον, ἀλλὰ καὶ τῇ ψυχῇ.

103. Hermippus, *apud* Josephus, *Ag. Ap.* 1.165: λέγεται γὰρ ὡς ἀληθῶς ὁ ἀνὴρ ἐκεῖνος πολλὰ τῶν παρὰ Ἰουδαίοις νομίμων εἰς τὴν αὐτου μετενεγκεῖν φιλοσοφίαν. Cf. Origen, *Contra Celsum,* 1.15.334. See H. Jacobson, "Hermippus, Pythagoras, and the Jews," *Revue des Études Juives* 135 (1976) 145–49, who suggests, somewhat speculatively, that Hermippus or his source got the information from a Jewish text in Greek that cited biblical passages. Cf. also Feldman, *Jew and Gentile,* 201–2.

104. Numenius, *apud* Clement, *Stromateis* 1.22.150.4: τί γὰρ ἐστι Πλάτων ἢ Μωυσῆς ἀττικίζων. The line is quoted in several other texts; see Stern, *Greek and Latin Authors* 2, no. 363a–e.

105. Philo, *De Vita Mosis,* 1.23.

106. See above p. 64.

107. Philo, *De Vita Mosis* 2.18–20: τῶν κατὰ τὴν Ἑλλάδα καὶ βάρβαρον.

108. See, e.g., Josephus, *J.W.* 5.17:"Ἑλλησι πᾶσι καὶ βαρβάροις; *Ant.* 4.12: οὔτε παρ᾽ "Ελλησιν οὔτε παρὰ βαρβάροις; *Ag. Ap.* 2.282: οὐ πόλις Ἑλλήνων ... οὐδὲ βάρβαρος.

109. Romans 1:14: "Ἑλλησίν τε καὶ βαρβάροις σοφοῖς τε καὶ ἀνοήτοις ὀφειλέτης εἰμί.

110. Philo, *De Vita Mosis* 2.27; *Quod Omnis Probus* 73–75.

111. *Corpus Papyrorum Raineri,* XIII, 4.109–201.

112. Cleodemus Malchus *apud* Eusebius, *Praeparatio Evangelica* 9.20.4.

The High Cost of a Good Education

ROBERT DORAN

Setting Up a Good Physical Plant

After Jason had agreed to pay the 150 talents to establish a gymnasium in Jerusalem, he must soon have realized that this was just the beginning of what he would have to pay out. Next he would have to locate an area for the gymnasium, and then build it. According to 2 Macc 4:12 he decided on an area "under the acropolis." B. Bar-Kochva has argued that the Akra, including the Ptolemaic Akra mentioned in the letter of Antiochus III (*Ant.* 12.138), was located on the southeastern hill of Jerusalem,[1] and that the gymnasium should probably be situated on the western hill which was unpopulated at this time.[2] Jason would thus have had the space on which to level out facilities for field events such as running and throwing the javelin and discus—the covered running-track (*xystos*) and the open-air tracks (*paradromis*). Jason would also have had to build the *palaestra,* an open space either square or rectangular framed by a colonnade behind which were rooms and spaces partially covered—the *apodyterion* where one put one's clothes, the *korykeion* or boxing-hall, the *konisterion* for periods of bad weather, the *loutron* for cleansing oneself after working out.[3] No doubt Jason would have wanted to do his community proud and would have ensured that the buildings looked sparkling. Even with this the cost did not stop. Who was to provide the oil? Who the fine sand? The oil supply would presumably not have been a problem in Judea, but where would one get an adequate supply of sand? Where would one find appropriate instructors and trainers? Who would pay them?

94

Finding the Right Curriculum

Once all these details had been ironed out and excellent, first-rate facilities with fine instructors had been equipped, the question of what would be done in them still arises. What Chrysis Pélékidis said apropos the ephebate is also appropriate for the gymnasium: It was multi-faceted, a military school, a school of civic preparation, a philosophical and literary school, a school for physical culture, a school in piety toward the gods.[4] To take these in order.

A) Military School

Marcel Launey made a thorough collection of the evidence which connected the gymnasium with the army and argued that even in the Hellenistic period the gymnasium prepared the citizen for war.[5] It is fascinating, for example, that an inscription from Babylonia from 109–108 BCE lists the ephebic and young men winners of contests with the bow, the javelin, the curved and the oblong shield.[6] Launey was roundly condemned by Jean Delorme,[7] whose most effective argument, and one echoed by Bezalel Bar-Kochva,[8] was that in the Hellenistic period one is dealing with a mercenary army, not a citizen army,[9] where the phalanx had displaced single, hand-to-hand combat. It is also interesting how the Theban generals Epaminondas and Philopoemen are said to have discouraged soldiers from taking part in gymnastic exercises.[10] However, they seem to have spoken not against exercises geared to military training but those which were moving toward the professionalization of athletics. Their concern echoed that earlier expressed by Euripides:

> Of the thousands of evils which exist in Greece there is no greater evil than the race of athletes. In the first place, they are incapable of living, or of learning to live, properly. How can a man who is a slave to his jaws and a servant to his belly acquire more wealth than his father? . . . What man has ever defended the city of his fathers by winning a crown for wrestling well or running fast or throwing a diskos far or planting an uppercut on the jaw of an opponent? Do men drive the enemy out of their fatherland by waging war with *diskoi* in their hands or by throwing punches through the line of shields? No one is

so silly as to do this when he is standing before the steel of the enemy. (Euripides, *Autolykos* frag. 282)[11]

Yet Plutarch will argue that "all these sports seemed to me to mimic warfare and to train for battle" (*Moralia* 639d), and that "military fitness is the aim of athletics and competition" (*Moralia* 639e). While one can agree with Delorme and Bar-Kochva that the gymnasium did not prepare one for the close maneuvers of the phalanx, the quick reflexes, agility, and ability to wrestle and feint would have been invaluable in hand-to-hand infighting. Thus I would maintain that, when we consider the gymnasium at Jerusalem, we have to take into account its character as military training.

While military training is an important and often neglected factor in the role of the gymnasium in Jerusalem, the main thrust of my paper will consider Pélékidis' other facets of the gymnasium.

B) School of Civic Preparation and Piety toward the Gods

Jean Delorme has clearly shown how the gymnasium was intimately connected to the religious and political life of the city.[12] As a reviewer of Delorme's book noted, "Each gymnasium had its own peculiar structure and layout, determined by natural features, immemorial religious associations, and the needs and ideas of the local community it served."[13] This sense of local pride in the culture and history of its city is what we need to keep in mind when looking at the gymnasium in Jerusalem. Unfortunately we do not have the curriculum followed at different cities. Clearly Homer was taught in many.[14] But what of a city which already had a long and unique literary and legal history? What would happen there when an educational institution like the gymnasium was introduced? Would it abandon its ancestral heritage? One small piece of evidence to suggest otherwise is the number of local histories written for specific cities. E. Bickerman showed how Sidon maintained its own local institutions when hellenized.[15] In the gymnasium library at Halicarnassus, copies were kept of the works of its two famous authors, Herodotus and the obscure C. Julius Longianus.[16] At Lamia the poetess Aristodama was given citizenship in gratitude for the epic poem she had composed and performed on the history of Lamia (*IG* 9.2.62). Beyond that, Stanley Bonner has shown how, at Rome, young Romans were taught their own language, laws, and literature alongside being given an entrée to Greek literature and rhetoric.[17] What would one expect to happen in Jerusalem under Jason? The author of the epitome may have the priests running helter-skelter to the gymnasium at the sound of the gong and abandoning their liturgical duties, but, as I have suggested elsewhere, this resembles other put-downs of physical exercises.[18] As Catullus says in Cicero's *De oratore:* "Although philosophers occupy all the gymnasia, yet their auditors are more eager to hear the gong (*discum audire*) than the philosopher. As soon as the gong sounds, even though the philosopher is in the middle of speaking about grave and important matters, they all abandon him to take an oil-rub" (2.5.21).

Given the role the ephebate played in the celebration of the civic religion of each city, is it not likely that Jason would have had the ephebes participate as far as possible in the festivals and processions that made up the cultic calendar of Jerusalem? It is, after all, a temple city whose income depended on an influx of visitors to the festivals. Would Jason have deliberately tried to turn off that cash flow by flouting the ancient festivals rather than making them more spectacular by ephebic participation? He is not accused of such an affront except in the most general polemic of the epitomist (2 Macc 4:10–17).[19]

C) Sketches for a Curriculum

It is well recognized that there is very little evidence for Judean schools in the pre-Christian period. James Crenshaw found little evidence for schools in early Israel; Shaye Cohen was equally skeptical from the evidence in rabbinic sources.[20] John Collins noted how literacy was required to be an authoritative teacher in the Dead Sea Scrolls (1QS 5:2; CD 14:6b–8; 13:2–4; 1QSb 3:22–27), and yet how a "school" in the context of the books of Proverbs, Job, and Qohelet would have the character of a group tutorial.[21] Can one glean anything about education in Second Temple times?

We do find instructions regarding education in 1QSa 1:6–9:

And this is the rule for all the armies of the congregation, for all native Israelites. From his youth they shall educate him in the book of HAGY, and according to his age, instruct him in the precepts of the covenant, and he will receive his instruction in their regulations; during ten years he will be counted among the 'boys.' At the age of twenty years, he will transfer to those enrolled to enter the lot amongst his family and join the holy community.[22]

Here membership in the community begins at age twenty, the age to pay the temple tax (Ex 30:14) and to be able to go to war (Num 1:3). It corresponds to the enrollment of the graduated ephebe into the ranks of a citizen. Prior to that the "boy" would have studied the traditional writings of his community, i.e., the Scriptures, and the statutes of the community. This presupposes that the boy would have begun to learn to read by about age seven, and the writing exercises uncovered by Naveh at Qumran testify to the learning of writing there.[23] 1QSa belongs to the first century BCE with its heightened sense of us vs. them, insiders vs. outsiders, and the strong need of indoctrination, but one suspects that these rules for education are not new but codify earlier practice.

Such a codification is not present, nor should it be sought, in the one teacher from Second Temple Judaism whose writing we have—Sirach. After listing various types of wise men—the instructor of many who is useless for himself, the skillful speaker who is hated, a man wise only for himself—Sirach sketches the compleat wise man: "A wise person instructs his own people, and the fruits of his good sense will be praiseworthy" (37:23).

This is how Sirach saw himself, as a teacher.[24] While he insists on the prerogatives of Aaron and his posterity ("In his commandments he gave [Aaron] authority and statutes and judgments, to teach Jacob the testimonies, and to enlighten Israel with his law"), Sirach spends only a small percentage of his work on priestly concerns. The end of the great hymn in Sirach 24 emphasizes that the wise man labors for all who seek out Wisdom (24:34; cf. Hebrew 30:26; Greek 33:17) Wisdom has been poured out on all God's creation, "upon all the living according to his gift; [God] lavished [Wisdom] upon those who love him" (1:10).

What educational process does Sirach recommend? First, that one lead a godly life; "To fear the Lord is the root of wisdom, and her branches are long life. . . . If you desire wisdom, keep the commandments, and the Lord will lavish her upon you" (1:20, 26). Here one might recall the strong links noted above between the gymnasion education and civic religion. Yet, while Sirach identifies Wisdom and the

Torah, there is little direct commentary on Torah, although there is some as in Sirach 17 with its retelling of Genesis 1–3. What we do find in Sirach is a different process at work.

> If you are willing, my child, you can be educated (παιδευθήσῃ) and if you apply yourself you can become clever. If you love to listen you will gain knowledge, and if you pay attention you will become wise. Stand in the company of elders. Who is wise? Attach yourself to such a one. Be ready to listen to every godly discourse, and let no wise proverbs escape you. If you see an intelligent person, rise early to visit him; let your foot wear out his doorstep. Reflect on the statutes of the Lord, and meditate at all times on his commandments. It is he who will give insight to your mind, and your desire for wisdom will be granted. (Sirach 6:32–37)

Here we find the emphasis on godly behavior, but it is linked with attaching oneself to someone known to be wise and with a keenness to study how others speak, presumably so one can imitate them. One has to remember proverbs. The same advice is given at 8:8–9: busy oneself with the proverbs of wise men; learn the tradition of the elders, and so learn how "to give answer when the need arises." The fullest statement comes at 38:34–39:10 when Sirach contrasts the activity of the scribe who needs leisure with that of those engaged in trades and crafts:

> How different the one who devotes himself to the study of the law of the Most High! He seeks out the wisdom of all the ancients, and is concerned with prophecies; he preserves the sayings of the famous and penetrates the subtleties of parables; he seeks out the hidden meanings of proverbs and is at home with the obscurities of parables. He serves among the great and appears before rulers; he travels in foreign lands and learns what is good and evil in the human lot. He sets his heart to rise early to seek the Lord who made him, and to petition the Most High; he opens his mouth in prayer and asks pardon for his sins. . . . Many will praise his understanding; it will never be blotted out. . . . Nations will speak of his wisdom, and the congregation will proclaim his praise.

Here three facets of the educational process are described: prayer and worship of God; experience of court life in foreign lands (cf. 34:9–11);

but what is also required is an acquaintance with traditional knowledge. To be wise, one must be versed in the writings of the people—the wisdom of the ancients and prophecies. The emphasis on discourse continues in the recommendation to focus on proverbs, riddles, and figures. This emphasis on listening to one's elders and garnering and examining proverbs is not peculiar to Sirach. Timothy Polk has shown how Ezekiel uses proverbs in his speeches: the prophet bases his arguments on them in speeches, but also rejects "accepted wisdom" in his vision of a new world.[25] No longer will the proverb apply: "The fathers have eaten sour grapes, and the children's teeth are set on edge."

What I want to stress here is that this use of proverbs and sayings of the wise in the educational process is not limited to Israelite culture. First of all, one must study with a teacher and frequent his house. Theognis, a Greek writer of the sixth century BCE, whose work was well known and with some of whose maxims Sirach may have been acquainted, begins his work to his friend Cyrnos:

> It is for your well-being, Cyrnos, that I am formulating these precepts which I, as a youth, received from good people. Be wise, and do not seek honor, fame and fortune by shameful and unjust acts. Know this. Then do not converse with base men, but always with good—eat and drink with them, sit with them and please those whose power is great. You will learn virtue from the virtuous. But if you mingle with base men, you will destroy your very spirit. So taught, frequent good people and you will some day say that I advised my friends well. (1.27–38)

In Plato's *Protagoras*, Hippocrates and Socrates go to the house where Protagoras the well-known teacher is staying. There the students of Protagoras follow him around hanging on every word. The students must be prepared to give up everything to follow their teacher and learn from him. Plato himself rejects simple book learning: "For this knowledge (philosophy) is not something that can be put into words like other sciences; but after long-continued intercourse between teacher and pupil, in joint pursuit of the subject, suddenly, like light flashing forth when a fire is kindled, it is born in the soul and straightway nourishes itself" (*Letter 7*. 341c).[26]

Secondly, the study of proverbs and figures is part of the training in argumentation among the Greeks. Aristotle places παραβολαί among the examples used by an orator as either inductive or indirect proof of his argument (Aristotle *Rhet.* 2.20, 1393a23–1394a18). In the *Topics,* one of his earliest works, Aristotle speaks of how one can be well equipped with reasonings:

> The means whereby we are to become well supplied with reasonings are four: (1) the securing of propositions; (2) the power to distinguish in how many senses a particular expression is used; (3) the discovery of the differences of things; (4) the investigation of likeness. . . . Propositions should be selected in a number of ways corresponding to the number of distinctions drawn in regard to the proposition: thus one may take in hand the opinions held by all or by most men or by the philosophers, i.e., by all, or most, or the most notable of them; or opinions contrary to those that seem to be generally held; and again, all opinions that are in accordance with the arts. We must make propositions also of the contradictories of opinions contrary to those that seem to be generally held, as was laid down before. (1.13–14, 105a23–105b18)[27]

Aristotle is here codifying and classifying common rules for argumentation, and one of his sources is "commonly held opinions," i.e., proverbs. Later, Aristotle was blamed by Isocrates' pupil Cephisodorus for not collecting proverbs (Athenaeus, *Deipnosophistae* 2.60d–e), whereas Diogenes Laertius (5.26) states that Aristotle authored works entitled *Parabolai* and *Paroimiai.* As Rudolf Pfeiffer noted:

> In his first anti-Platonic dialogue, *Peri Philosophias,* he regarded proverbs as 'survivals of a pre-literate philosophy' and treated them in a survey of early wisdom, together with the 'Orphics', the Delphic maxims and the precepts of the Seven Wise Men. He liked to embellish his later writings on rhetoric and politics with proverbial quotations. One of his pupils, Clearchus of Soli, enlarged his master's collection by writing two books of *Paroimiai* which for the amusement of his readers he cast in a literary narrative form; many others followed, who were content to arrange dry lists.[28]

Aristotle's emphasis on collecting commonly held opinions and investigating the limits of their applicability, i.e., the meaning of the terms of the propositions, resonates with Sirach's recommendation not to let a wise proverb slip by and to check out hidden meanings and obscurities in comparisons. Sirach's recommendation to seek out the sayings of notable men also resonates with what would later give rise to the manuals of *Progymnasmata*.[29] Such a comparison between Sirach's description of the educational process and that found in Athens is not meant to suggest any kind of derivation. The educational breakthrough of the Sophists and the cultural position of Athens led to more technical developments in science, historiography, geography, and rhetoric than took place in Jerusalem. The process recommended by Sirach and found in classical Greek writings reflects education in a traditional society. The emphasis on moral maxims continues at the basic level of the Greek educational process, however, as can be seen in the education manual from the third century BCE published by O. Guerard and P. Jouguet.[30] Within a traditional society, proverbs could be effectively used in courts to sway the verdict, as J. Messenger showed for Nigerian indigenous courts in the 1950s.[31] Sirach, too, is describing the traditional educational process in Judea. He writes in the traditional tongue to inculcate traditional values. But he is also doing more than that. He does not simply collect proverbs, but also groups them thematically, at times to form an argument. More important for our purposes, he evidences knowledge of Greek and Egyptian writings.[32] Scholars such as Alexander di Lella have argued that Sirach makes such sources authentically Jewish,[33] but one should reflect that Sirach is writing in the 180s BCE, about ten years before Jason builds his gymnasium. He is teaching the upper classes in Jerusalem and, as part of his syllabus, includes references to Greek and Egyptian literature. Possibly this means that he knows Greek and Demotic. Thomas Robert Lee, followed by Burton Mack, argued strongly that Sirach was aware of Greek rhetorical style.[34] Therefore, the one teacher of whom we have evidence of what he was teaching around the time of Jason's gymnasium in Jerusalem maintains a strong interest in Jewish traditional literature, using methods comparable to what we find in Greek education, and he is not averse to including in his course of instruction literature from other traditions (Sirach 39:4), nor does he discourage the study of foreign languages. In this, Sirach is not that different from what is going on in Rome at precisely the same time.[35]

I mentioned above that Sirach does not directly interpret the Torah. Later, in the Qumran scrolls, we will find evidence of Torah-exegesis.

But is there something before that might be relevant to what might have been appropriate in a Jewish gymnasium? Here I am being quite speculative, so bear with me. I wish to point to the retellings of the Bible as found in some works whose fragments are preserved in Greek.

a) Demetrius

Demetrius engages directly in questions about the Bible. Demetrius is frequently dated to the late third century BCE in Alexandria, but the basis for this dating and location have been soundly questioned by Erich Gruen.[36] Demetrius tried to establish chronological and genealogical order among the biblical events and the patriarchs and also answer difficulties which arise in reading the biblical text. How could Moses have married Zipporah, an Egyptian? Well, Zipporah really was a descendant of Abraham through Keturah's son Jokshan, and so Moses did not actually marry a foreigner. As Gruen notes, "Demetrius took up the tangles, reduced narrative to bare bones, assembled chronological data, straightened out genealogies, and supplied explanations for peculiar deeds and events. His work, or works, therefore, offered reassurance on the reliability of the Scriptures."[37] Further, Carl Holladay comments: "Perhaps the most notable characteristic of Demetrius' work is his biblicism. The LXX serves as his only source, and his knowledge of its contents is detailed and exact."[38] Gruen rightly questions that Demetrius required "Alexandrian techniques to engage in exegetical enterprise,"[39] yet the very questions Demetrius raises would have been at home in the world of Zenodotus, Callimachus, Eratosthenes, and Aristophanes of Byzantium, who had such a strong influence on the study of texts.[40] There is also reference to another writer, Philo, who disagreed with Demetrius.[41] Thus the tradition of close reading of the biblical text and investigation into the characters and chronology of events, part of the basic educational curriculum in the study of the Greek classics, was also being practiced on the Greek Bible by observant Jews. But for whom? Certainly for Jews, as Gruen emphasizes.[42] But was it part of an educational curriculum, as the master in Homeric philology, Dionysos son of Philotus, an Athenian, did in the gymnasium at Eretria?[43]

b) Aristobulus

A different set of questions concerning the Greek Bible is provided by Aristobulus. He interprets seeming anthropomorphisms in the Bible, explaining what it means for the Bible to say that God has hands and feet, that he stands and speaks.

> Therefore the lawgiver has employed a metaphor well for the purpose of saying something elevated, when he says that the accomplishments of God are his hands. And the establishment of the cosmos might well be called divine 'standing' in accordance with the elevated (level of meaning).

> For it is necessary to take the divine 'voice' not as a spoken word, but as the establishment of things.... And it seems to me that Pythagoras, Socrates, and Plato with great care follow him in all respects. They copy him when they say that they hear the voice of God, when they contemplate the arrangement of the universe, so carefully made and so unceasingly held together by God.[44]

Greek thinkers depend on Moses, they say the same things as Jewish writers but the Jewish sages say it more clearly and better (*PE* 13.12.10). Jews are a philosophical school "and the whole constitution of our Law is arranged with reference to piety and justice and temperance and the rest of the things that are truly good" (*PE* 13.13.8). The universal significance of Judaism is shown in that both Passover and Sabbath have cosmic significance—at Passover the sun and moon stand diametrically opposed to one another (*HE* 7.32.17–18), and the Sabbath observance agrees with the sevenfold structure inherent in the cosmos (*PE* 13. 12. 9–16). Aristobulus' work therefore arises out of a grammatical reading of the text which prompts philosophical questions, much as the Greeks tried to find deep meanings in Homer.[45] Again, to what audience is this directed? Does it correspond to a more advanced reading of the text than that of Demetrius, much as the curriculum in Greek studies moved on to a deeper level of reading after basic grammatical and rhetorical studies?

c) Ezekiel the Tragedian

Ezekiel the Tragedian poses a different problem. He worked "within the tradition of classical tragedy, influenced particularly by the plays of Aeschylus and Euripides."[46] R.G. Robertson arranged the fragments that remain into a pattern of five acts:[47]

Act I
> Scene 1 Moses' Monologue
> Scene 2 Moses' Dialogue with Zipporah

Act II
> Scene 1 Zipporah's Dialogue with ?
> Scene 2 Moses' Dream, and Jethro's Interpretation

Act III
> Scene 1 Moses' Dialogue with God
> Scene 2 Moses' Instruction to the People

Act IV
> Report of the Egyptian Messenger

Act V
> Elim, and the Report of the Messengers to Moses.

Ezekiel introduces characters unknown in the Bible—Chus and the Egyptian messenger—but follows the biblical narrative closely. "Ezekiel therefore has combined familiar conventions with striking novelty to create a complex picture. He nowhere disputes or denies the biblical account. But the admixture of the dream episode both magnifies the Moses figure and renders it more accessible to the dramatist's contemporary society. . . . The scene [wherein the Israelites encounter at Elim the legendary Phoenix] plainly involved the merging of a Jewish tale with Hellenic myth in creative fashion."[48] Like Robertson, I see no reason why it would not have been staged. But for whom? With Gruen,[49] I believe a Jewish audience, but I also suspect that the best location would be an educational center.

I have adduced these three examples, not to claim that they had anything to do with the gymnasium in Jerusalem but simply to suggest that they would fit easily into an educational system based on the Greek Bible. I do not think that either Jason of Cyrene or the epitomist would have been appalled by what they were doing, as they might have been by the work of Artapanus. Could they serve as analogues for the study of the Bible using techniques similar to those in fashion in Greek educational circles and yet maintaining Jewish pride in their own tradition? Are they not more likely analogues than Jewish ephebes running around spouting Homer and rejecting their tradition?

Getting a New Image

The image of the Judean as given by Hecataeus of Abdera was part flattering, part not so good. "Moses established sacrifices different from those of other nations, and different ways of living (τὰς κατὰ τὸν βίον ἀγωγάς), for because of his own expulsion he introduced a nonsocial way of life, hostile to foreigners (ἀπάνθρωπόν τινα καὶ μισόξενον βίον)" (as in Diodorus Siculus, *Bibliotheca Historica* 40.3.4). The Judeans needed to change their image.

Since I am primarily concerned here with 2 Maccabees and education, I don't have to discuss the highly poetical image at 1 Macc 1:15 (καὶ ἐποίησαν ἑαυτοῖς ἀκροβυστίας) of decircumcision. If some went through such an operation, it would certainly present a new image. I would like to raise just one question concerning decircumcision, however. Nissan Rubin has drawn attention to the decision in the Mishnah (Aboth 3.12) by Eleazar of Modin that someone who makes void the covenant of Abraham has no share in the world to come, and also that, after the Bar Kochva revolt, scholars decided that one who had undergone epispasm had to be recircumcised (although Rabbi Yehuda disagreed for those for whom it would have been life-threatening; Tosefta Shabbat 16.9). The Amoraim continued to discuss the issue as to whether the requirement to recircumcize was from the Torah or from the Sages (BT Yebamoth 72a).

R. Huna said: A mashuk is Pentateuchally permitted to eat terumah (אוכל בתרומה דבר תורה משוך) but has been forbidden to do so by Rabbinical ordinance because he appears to be like one uncircumcised. An objection was raised: The mashuk requires to be [re-]circumcized! Only by Rabbinical ordinance.

In Mekilta de-Rabbi Ishmael, one opinion was that

one who had been circumcised even one hour, even though the flesh turned and covered the crown, is not excluded from eating of the paschal lamb or of terumah.[50]

להביא את שנתקיימה בו מצות מילה אפילו שעה אחת על פי שחזר הבשר
וחפה את העטרה אינו מעבבו לא לאכול בפסח ולא לאכול בתרומה

Rubin argues that the procedure would have been relatively easy given the different method of circumcision at that time.[51] But the discussion among the Rabbis raises the question of whether those who had this procedure done at the time of Jason would have been within their rights. They had been circumcised as required by Genesis 17. Would undergoing this procedure void the covenant? It was a new question. The author of 1 Maccabees thought they did void the covenant, but was it a disputed question?

Back to 2 Maccabees. Changing names can also be a way of changing image—Joshua to Jason, Onias to Menelaus (*Ant.* 12.239). A scholarly consensus also has the name of Jerusalem being changed to Antiocheia at Jerusalem, a change about which I am unsure.[52] The main argument comes from 2 Macc 4:19: θεωροὺς ὡς ἀπὸ Ἱεροσολύμων Ἀντιοχεῖς ὄντας. There is inscriptional evidence, e.g., for Antiochenes from Pyramus, Ἀντιοχείοι ἀπο Πυραμου (*SIG* 585.286) as well as the list in *OGIS* 2.588.[53] Such a name change would not necessarily involve constitutional change. R. J. van der Spek has shown how πόλις could be used otherwise than for an independent city-state with a Greek type of government and institutions.[54] However, the meaning at 2 Macc 4:19 is linked to the meaning of 2 Macc 4:9: ἐὰν ἐπιχωρηθῇ διὰ τῆς ἐξουσίας αὐτοῦ γυμνάσιον καὶ ἐφηβεῖον αὐτῷ συστήσασθαι καὶ τοὺς ἐν Ἱεροσύλομοις Ἀντιοχεῖς ἀναγράψαι. I find that I prefer to translate this conditional clause: "if he were furnished by (the king's) authority to constitute a gymnasium and an ephebate for (the king) and to enroll the Antiochenes in Jerusalem." Here I take the pronoun αὐτοῦ, αὐτῷ to refer to the king, and the second to be a dative of interest. Usually the second is not translated, but, if one does translate it, then the meaning would be either that in general having a gymnasion in Jerusalem would be in the king's best interests, or, my favorite, that it refers to the dedication of the gymnasion to Antiochus IV, as in Halikarnassos there was the Philippeion, in Iasos the Ptolemaieion and the Antiocheion, in Miletus to Kapitonov. Of particular interest is the formula Βασιλεῖ Πτολεμαίῳ Ἀπολλοδώρῳ τὸ γυμνάσιον. Here, in Jerusalem, the Antiochenes would refer to the members of the gymnasion. Whatever the case, a clear sense of an openness to others and respect for the king is shown by this usage of Antiochenes in Jerusalem.

Second Maccabees 4:19 is of further interest. A θεωρός was an official representative of the city. Again, the epitomist provides only sparse information, and this is the only mention of these games at Tyre in this period, so one has to speculate as to what is going on. Into what context should we put this mission? Did Jason know that the games at Tyre were being held and that Antiochus IV was going to be there, and so he sent the embassy on his own initiative? If Jason did so on his own initiative, this evidences a clear decision to make connections with neighboring cities, perhaps imitating the alliance of Solomon with the king of Tyre, his covenant brother (1 Kgs 9:13). Even the envoys who disagreed with Jason vis-à-vis giving money for sacrifices to Heracles did agree to supply a ship to the Tyrian navy.[55] I myself am inclined to think that the sending of envoys to Tyre should be put in a different context, one known from inscriptions wherein the host city sends out invitations to those connected to the city by *suggeneia*. The Megarians sent envoys to Corcyra(?); the Akraiphians invited envoys to be sent from Thisbis, Orchomenes, and elsewhere to take part in the celebration of the Ptoia, in honor of the asylum granted to the sanctuary of Apollo Ptoios, and to offer sacrifice; the people of Cos sent to the cities of Camarina, Gelea, Messene, and elsewhere for the purpose of celebrating the Asclepieia in honor of the asylum granted to the sanctuary of Asclepios; and the de-crees from Magnesia at Meander were to celebrate games in honor of Artemis Leucophryen and the asylum of the city, and to offer sacrifice.[56] The combination of several factors—the presence of a king who sup-ported local traditions like the games at Tyre in honor of Heracles and who had recently permitted Jason to build a gymnasium, the later non-chalant assertion that Jason claimed *suggeneia* with the Spartans and that envoys are sent to the games and to offer sacrifice to the patron god of Tyre, Heracles— suggests to me that Jason's city—Jerusalem or An-tiocheia?—has been included on the invitation list, with the implication being that some kind of *suggeneia* was recognized, a relationship that seems to run through Heracles as Jason claims *suggeneia* with the Spar-tans (2 Macc 5:9).[57] A connection between the Judeans and Heracles is found in the work of Kleodemus Malchos (*Ant* 1.239–41; *PE* 9.20.2–4) where the sons of Abraham joined Herakles in his war against the Libyan giant Antaios, and Herakles ends up marrying the daughter of one of these sons. Erich Gruen[58] has stressed the Jewish quality of this fic-tive relationship, and argued that this tale "circulated among Jewish intel-lectuals around the turn of the second century" and disparages attempts, like those of Orrieux,[59] who propose earlier datings. I would argue, rather, that the fictive relationship, like the name change, is a convenient way to stress that Jews are not hostile to foreigners. While the tale as told by Kleodemus Malchos and the fictive correspondence with the Spartans found in 1 Maccabees stresses the superiority of the Jewish side of the relationship, one can well imagine tellings wherein the role of Heracles, who after all is the male member of the marriage relationship, would be stressed to advantage and so be acceptable to a Greek hearer.

The Cost

But this openness has its costs and risks. Once invited to the games, does it allow Judeans to participate in sacrifices to Herakles? According to the epitomist, a biased source, Jason thought so. Was there a debate present in Judaism about this issue? It seems so. The Jewish historian Eupolemus, whether he be identified with Judas Maccabeus' ambassador or not, wrote at the end of his retelling of the building of the Temple in Jerusalem by Solomon that "[Solomon] sent to Souran at Tyre the golden pillar, the one set up in the temple of Zeus at Tyre" (Eusebius, *PE* 9.34.18). Immediately after this statement, however, another Jewish historian, Theophilus, is quoted who claims, "Solomon sent to the king of the Tyrians the left-over gold. [The king] made a lifelike, full-length likeness of his daughter, and put the golden pillar as a covering to the statue" (Eusebius, *PE* 9.34.19). Whatever the exact meaning of what Theophilus has the Tyrian king do, he clearly wants to say that Solomon did not send a golden pillar, well-known in antiquity,[60] to him. Here one overhears echoes of a debate, similar to what the epitomist reports concerning Jason's intentions and the envoys' decision, as to what is appropriate behavior for Judeans.

That such a debate may have been taking place within Judaism may also be suggested by the LXX version of Ex 22:27a, to which Pieter W. van der Horst has drawn our attention.[61] Here the MT אלהים לא תקלל is translated by θεοὺς οὐ κακολογήσεις ("You shall not revile the gods"). Van der Horst points to passages in Philo (*De specialibus legibus* 1.53; *De vita Mosis* 2.203–4; *Quaestiones in Exodum* 2.5) that interpret this text in an apologetic mode so that the pagans may not speak disparagingly of Yahweh.[62] However, it is also interesting that other passages in Philo could allow a different, more positive, reading. Commenting on Gen 1:1, he writes:

> For it is indeed reasonable that [the heaven] should come into existence first, being both best of created things and made from the purest of all that is, seeing that it was destined to be the most holy dwelling-place of manifest and visible gods (θεῶν ἐμφανῶν τε καὶ αἰσθητῶν ἔμελλεν οἶκος ἔσεσθαι). (*De Opif.* 27–28)

Here Philo is no doubt referring to the sun and moon, but does it also allow for an understanding of θεός that is not limited to the one supreme God? When discussing Gen 1:26 ("Let us make man") Philo argues that this refers to God using others as fellow-workers who can be held responsible for the blameworthy deeds of humans (*Opif.* 72–76). Thomas Tobin has brilliantly untangled the various interpretations Philo gives of the creation of man,[63] and shown how the above reading, although found also in other Philonic works (*Conf.* 168–82; *Mut.* 29–32; *Fug.* 68–72), is anomalous.[64] It draws deeply from Plato's *Timaeus* 41a-44d. As Tobin comments:

> The identification of the figures to whom God speaks as God's powers (δυνάμεις) is not found in the *Timaeus,* but again it was a natural enough identification for a Jewish writer since the Septuagint often renders the Hebrew יהוה צבאות as κύριος τῶν δυνάμεων. It is to these heavenly powers then that God speaks (*Conf.* 171–73; *Mut.* 28–29; *Fug.* 69). It was also made easier by an identification, common during that period, of the traditional Greek gods with the various powers that either controlled the universe or served as the means by which the Supreme God exercised control. Such an identification is found in such diverse sources as Diogenes Laertius' description of Stoicism and the pseudo-Aristotelian treatise *De Mundo.* The interpretation of the phrase "Let us make man" of Gen 1:26 then clearly draws on the Timaeus and reflects a renewed interest in the interpretation of Plato.[65]

Does this anti-anthropomorphic interpretation, with which Philo is not satisfied, reflect the efforts of earlier interpreters? Is there therefore a strain in Judaism which would allow for some recognition of other deities, while certainly recognizing the supremacy of Yahweh?

The actions of Jason raise these questions of self-definition. Or perhaps I should say, the epitomist draws out these questions of self-identity when writing about Jason. As I have argued elsewhere,[66] the language at 2 Macc 4:10–17 resonates with other debates about changes in educational, not constitutional, systems. The emphasis of the epitomist on this issue makes sense, it seems to me, if we see him as fighting against such changes in his own community, i.e., against the participation of young Judeans in the gymnasia of Hellenistic cities. Inscriptional evidence for such a participation only surfaces at the beginning of the first century CE in Cyrene where a catalogue of ephebes contains a few clearly Jewish names.[67] Later, Jewish names are found in lists of ephebes in Iasos in Caria, and Korone in Messenia.[68] I would suggest that this practice may have been going on before the inscriptional evidence, and that the epitomist (Jason of Cyrene?) is warning against the practice.

What I have been trying to suggest in this paper is that perhaps Jason's 'reform' was not so radical as has been painted. Hellenization is at once too convenient and too amorphous a term to describe what was happening in pre-Maccabean Jerusalem. What I have been attempting to shape in this very speculative paper is a different framework into which to place those events. Rather than use the framework of the sources—Jason is a nasty Hellenizer, Judas Maccabeus a pious Torah observer—I want to allow Jason and Judas to co-exist in Jerusalem as Judeans. What one sees happening in our sources is a reaction to what transpired. Actions that Judeans used to do, e.g., Nicetas son of Jason, a Jerusalemite, donated 100 drachmas to the festival of the Dionysia in Iasos (*CIJ* II, no. 749), were being seen and condemned by others as not allowable. What was not condemned in the Torah, epispasm, was now being condemned. As Shaye Cohen urged in a festschrift for Professor Hengel, the Maccabean revolt spurred a process of reflection into what it meant to be a Judean.[69] It is to this process of self-identification that our sources introduce us, and enable us to see what was won, and what was lost.

Notes

1. Bezalel Bar-Kochva, *Judas Maccabeus: The Jewish Struggle against the Seleucids,* (Cambridge: Cambridge University Press, 1989) 445–65. See also the

discussion in Benjamin Mazar and Hanan Eshel, "Who Built the First Wall of Jerusalem?" *IEJ* 48 (1998) 268.

2. Bar-Kochva, *Judas Maccabaeus,* 447 n. 7.

3. For a full description see Jean Delorme, *Gymnasion. Étude sur les Monuments consacrés à l'Éducation en Grèce (dès origines à l'Empire romain)* (Paris: Boccard, 1960) 253–315. See also Doris Vanhove, "Le Gymnase" in Doris Vanhove, ed., *Le Sport dans la Grèce Antique: Du Jeu à la Compétition* (Bruxelles: Palais des Beaux-Arts, 1992) 57–77.

4. Chrysis Pélékidis, *Histoire de l'Éphébie Attique dès Origines à 31 avant Jésus Christ* (Paris: Boccard, 1962) 197.

5. Marcel Launey, *Recherches sur les Armées hellénistiques* (Paris: Boccard, 1950) 2.813–74.

6. Bernard Haussoulier, "Inscriptions grecques de Babylone" *Klio* 9 (1909) 353.

7. Jean Delorme, *Gymnasion,* 471–74.

8. Bezalel Bar-Kochva, *The Seleucid Army* (Cambridge: Cambridge University Press, 1976) 94.

9. When weighing Delorme's argument, one should take into account the inscription discussed by Paul Roesch, "Une loi fédérale béotienne sur la préparation militaire," *Acta of the Fifth International Congress of Greek and Latin Epigraphy. Cambridge, 1967* (Oxford: Blackwell, 1971) 81–88, wherein the ephebate in Boetia in the third century BCE meant obligatory military service as training for action in the phalanx.

10. Nepos, *Epaminondas* 2.4; 5.4 Plutarch, *Philopoemen* 3.2.

11. As translated in Stephen G. Miller, *Arete: Ancient Writers, Papyri, and Inscriptions on the History and Ideals of Greek Athletics and Games* (Chicago: Ares, 1970) 95–96.

12. Delorme, *Gymnasion,* 337–61.

13. R. E. Wycherley, review of *Gymnasion* by Jean Delorme, *JHS* 82 (1962) 201.

14. H. I. Marrou, *A History of Education in Antiquity* (New York: Sheed & Ward, 1956) 164–65, 187.

15. E. Bickerman, "Sur une inscription grecque de Sidon," *Mélanges syriens offerts à M.R. Dussaud* (Bibliothèque Archéologique et Historique 30; Paris: Guethner, 1939) 91–99. See also the comments of Luigi Moretti, *Iscrizioni Agonistiche Greche* (Rome: Signorelli, 1953) 108–11.

16. See Clarence A. Forbes, "Expanded Uses of the Greek Gymnasium," *Classical Philology* 40 (1945) 37.

17. Stanley F. Bonner, *Education in Ancient Rome* (London: Methuen, 1977) 1–37. See also the interesting comparisons Jonathan Goldstein drew between the Roman and Jewish position: "Jewish Acceptance and Rejection of Hellenism," *Jewish and Christian Self-Definition. Volume 2: Aspects of Judaism in the Graeco-Roman Period* (ed. E. P. Sanders et al.; Philadelphia: Fortress, 1981) 64–87.

18. Robert Doran, "Jason's Gymnasium" in *Of Scribes and Scrolls* (ed. Harold W. Attridge et al.: Lanham, Md.: University Press of America, 1990) 105–6.

19. On these verses, see Doran, "Jason's Gymnasium," 104–5.

20. James Crenshaw, "Education in Ancient Israel," *JBL* 104 (1985) 601–15. See now Crenshaw, *Education in Ancient Israel: Across the Deadening Silence* (Anchor Bible Reference Library; New York: Doubleday, 1998). Shaye Cohen, *From the Maccabees to the Mishnah* (Philadelphia: Westminster, 1987) 120–23.

21. J. J. Collins, *Jewish Wisdom in the Hellenistic Age* (OTL; Louisville: Westminster John Knox, 1997) 38.

22. Translation as in Florentino García Martínez & Eibert J. C. Tigchelaar, *The Dead Sea Scrolls Study Edition* (Leiden: Brill, 1997) 1.101.

23. J. Naveh, "A Medical Document or a Writing Exercise? The So-called 4Q Therapeia," *IEJ* 36 (1986) 52–55.

24. One has to agree with Benjamin Wright that Sirach is an elitist who sees himself as teaching future sages, i.e., those who have the time and leisure to pursue such studies. While he speaks of everyone seeking wisdom, he knows that few are able to do so. See Benjamin Wright, "The Discourse of Riches and Poverty in the Book of Ben Sira," *SBL Seminar Papers* (Atlanta: Scholars, 1998) 559–78.

25. Timothy Polk, "Paradigms, Parables and $M^e\check{s}al\hat{\imath}m$: On Reading the $M\bar{a}\check{s}\bar{a}l$ in Scripture," *CBQ* 45 (1983) 564–83.

26. For a discussion of later interactions between teachers and their students, see Richard Valantasis, *Spiritual Guides to the Third Century: A Semiotic Study of the Guide-disciple Relationship in Christianity, Neoplatonism, Hermetism and Gnosticism* (Minneapolis: Fortress, 1991).

27. Trans. W. A. Pickard-Cambridge in *The Works of Aristotle Translated into English* (ed. W. D. Ross; Oxford: Clarendon, 1928) vol. 1.

28. Rudolf Pfeiffer, *History of Classical Scholarship* (Oxford: Clarendon, 1968) 83–84.

29. See the collection by Ronald F. Hock and Edward N. O'Neil, *The Chreia in Ancient Rhetoric.* Vol. 1: *The Progymnasmata* (Atlanta: Scholars, 1986).

30. O. Guerard and P. Jouguet, *Un Livre d'Écolier du IIIe siècle avant J.-C.* (Cairo: Institut français d'Archéologie orientale, 1938).

31. John Messenger, "The Role of Proverbs in a Nigerian Judicial System," *The Study of Folklore* (ed. Alan Dundes; Englewood Cliffs, N.J.: Prentice-Hall, 1965) 299–307.

32. Jack T. Sanders, *Ben Sira and Demotic Wisdom* (Chico, Calif.: Scholars, 1983).

33. Patrick W. Skehan and Alexander di Lella, *The Wisdom of Ben Sira* (AB 39; New York: Doubleday, 1987) 50.

34. Thomas Robert Lee, *Studies in the Form of Sirach 44–50* (SBLDS 75; Atlanta: Scholars, 1986). Burton L. Mack, *Wisdom and the Hebrew Epic: Ben Sira's Praise of the Fathers* (Chicago: University of Chicago Press, 1985).

35. See the whole discussion in Stanley F. Bonner, *Education in Ancient Rome* (London: Methuen, 1977).

36. Erich S. Gruen, *Heritage and Hellenism* (Berkeley: University of California Press, 1998) 114–15.

37. Gruen, *Heritage*, 117.

38. Carl R. Holladay, *Fragments from Hellenistic Jewish Authors*. Vol. 1: *Historians* (Chico: Scholars, 1983) 52.

39. Gruen, *Heritage*, 117.

40. On these scholars, see Pfeiffer, *History*, 105–209. Both Holladay (*Fragments* 1.52) and John Collins [*Between Athens and Jerusalem: Jewish Identity in the Hellenistic Diaspora* (New York: Crossroad, 1983) 28] draw attention to the Greek influences on Demetrius.

41. See Clement of Alexandria, *Stromateis* 1.141.

42. Gruen, *Heritage*, 117–18.

43. IG XII, 9, 235, l.10–12.

44. Fragment 2 *PE* 8.10.9–10; fragment 4 *PE* 13.13.3–4. Translation by Adela Yarbro Collins, "Aristobulus" *OTP* 2.838, 840.

45. Félix Buffiere, *Les mythes d' Homère et la pensée grecque* (Paris: Les Belles Lettres, 1956).

46. Gruen, *Heritage*, 128.

47. R. G. Robertson, "Ezekiel the Tragedian," *OTP* 2.805.

48. Gruen, *Heritage*, 134–35.

49. Gruen, *Heritage*, 135.

50. Nissan Rubin, "Foreskin Pulling and the Rule of Folding," *Zion* 54 (1989) 106–8 (in Hebrew). The quotation is from Tractate Pisha, in the edition by Jacob Z. Lauterbach (Philadelphia: JPS, 1976) 1.120.

51. Rubin, "Foreskin," 110–12.

52. See Fausto Parente, "ΤΟΥΣ ΕΝ ΙΕΡΟΣΟΛΥΜΟΙΣ ΑΝΤΙΟΧΕΙΣ ΑΝΑΓΡΑΥΑΙ (II Macc. IV, 9) Gerusalemme è mai stata una POLIS?" *Rivista di storia e letteratura religiosa* 30 (1994) 3–38, who argues from a different tack than I do here.

53. G. Le Rider, *Suse sous les Seleucides et les Parthes* (Paris: P. Guenther, 1965) 410.

54. R. J. van der Spek, "The Babylonian City," in Amelie Kuhrt and Susan Sherwin-White, *Hellenism in the East* (Berkeley: University of California Press, 1987) 58.

55. One might note how the fleet of Rhodes was composed of vessels from its tributary islands. IG XI 4, 751 and 752–53. R. Etienne, "Les Étrangers et la politique: le rôle de Rhodes dans les Cyclades dans le premier tiers du IIe siècle av. J. C." in *L'Étranger dans le Monde Grec: Actes du colloque organisé par l'Institut d'Études Anciennes* (ed. Raoul Lonis; Nancy: Presses Universitaires de Nancy, 1988) 159–68.

56. All these have been conveniently found in Olivier Curty, *Les parentés legéndaires entre cités grecques* (Geneva: Libr. Droz, 1995) nos. 8, 10, 24, 25, 35, 46, 48, 55, 71, 80.

57. Curty notes how "le plus souvent, que les fondateurs de chaque cité soient parents." (*Les parentés legéndaires*, 216; see the whole discussion, 216–41).

58. Erich Gruen, "The Purported Jewish-Spartan Affiliation," in *Transitions to Empire: Essays in Greco-Roman History, 360–146 B.C.*, in honor of *E. Badian* (Robert W. Wallace and Edward M. Harris, eds.; Norman, Okla.: University of Oklahoma Press,) 254– 69.

59. Claude Orrieux, "La 'parenté' entre Juifs et Spartiates," in Raoul Lonis, *L'Etranger dans le monde grec*, 176–86.

60. Josephus cites Menander of Ephesus (*Ag. Ap.* 1.118; *Ant.* 8.145) for the golden pillar, while his citation of Dio (*Ag. Ap.* 1.113; *Ant.* 8.147) says only that the Tyrian king adorned the temple of Zeus with golden gifts. Herodotus 2.44 mentions a golden pillar which stood in the temple of Heracles.

61. Pieter W. van der Horst, "'Thou shalt not revile the gods.'" The LXX-translation of Ex 22: 28 (27), its background and influence" in idem, *Hellenism—Judaism—Christianity* (Kampen: Kok Pharos, 1994) 112–21. It originally appeared in the *Studia Philonica Annual* 5 (1993) 1–8.

62. Van der Horst, "'Thou shalt not revile . . .'" 115.

63. Thomas H. Tobin, S.J., *The Creation of Man: Philo and the History of Interpretation* (CBQ Monograph 14; Washington, D.C.: CBA, 1983).

64. Tobin, *Creation*, 30.

65. Tobin, *Creation*, 47–48.

66. Doran, "Jason's Gymnasium," 104–6.

67. Gert Luderitz, *Corpus jüdischer Zeugnisse aus der Cyrenaika* (Wiesbaden: Reichert, 1983) nos. 6, 7.

68. L. Robert, *REJ* 101 (1937) 85; IG V.1.1398: See L. Robert, *Hellenica* III 100f. V. Tcherikover also points to an inscription in Hypaipa near Sardis where a group of young men called themselves Ἰουδαῖοι νεωτεροι according to the usual division of Greek ephebes. *CPJ* 1.30, n.99.

69. Shaye J. D. Cohen, "Ioudaios: 'Judean' and 'Jew' in Susanna, First Maccabees, and Second Maccabees," in *Geschichte—Tradition—Reflexion. Festschrift für Martin Hengel zum 70. Geburtstag. Band 1. Judentum* (ed. Peter Schäfer; Tübingen: Mohr, 1996) 211–20. See also his "Religion, Ethnicity, and 'Hellenism' in the Emergence of Jewish Identity in Maccabean Palestine," *Religion and Religious Practice in the Seleucid Kingdom* (ed. Per Bilde et al.; Aarhus University Press, 1990) 204–23; "*Ioudaios to genos* and Related Expressions in Josephus," *Josephus and the History of the Greco-Roman Period: Essays in Memory of Morton Smith* (ed. Fausto Parente and Joseph Sievers; Leiden: Brill, 1995) 23–38.

The Honorary Decree for Simon the Maccabee (1 Macc 14:25–49) in Its Hellenistic Context

JAN WILLEM VAN HENTEN

In his epoch-making study *Judentum und Hellenismus,* Martin Hengel argues that there has been an intensive as well as diverse interaction between Jewish and Hellenistic cultures in the land of Israel in the Second Temple period. His thesis seems to be more plausible to me than the view of Louis Feldman and most of his other critics.[1] I agree with Hengel that in the Hellenistic period something principally new originated with respect to Judaism,[2] and that we can rightly speak of Hellenistic Judaism no matter whether we deal with Jewish sources from the diaspora or from the land of Israel. At the same time, it seems important to be aware of the pluriformity of Hellenistic Judaism in this connection and to nuance the kinds and intensity of the interactions between Hellenistic and Jewish cultures, on the one hand, and the contemporary processes of Jewish identity formations, on the other. In this contribution I would like to argue that we should build upon Hengel's study and strengthen the argument that Judaism was strongly influenced by the culture of the Greeks and the peoples surrounding the Jews in 'Israel' on the basis of two kinds of comparative analysis: (1) a diachronic comparison of related Israelite and Jewish sources; (2) a synchronic comparison of Jewish sources with related contemporary non-Jewish sources. The main part of the paper offers a case study of the second type of comparative reading and focuses upon a document in an important Jewish writing from Jerusalem, probably composed around 125 BCE. The honorary decree for Simon and his sons transmitted in 1 Macc 14:25–49 will be read in the light of four honorary decrees for

Ptolemaic kings composed by Egyptian priests and some other officials, following a suggestion of H. Bévenot and F.-M. Abel. The structure of 1 Macc 14:25–49 and these four Egyptian documents, as well as aspects of their content and function, will be discussed in detail. Correspondences and differences will be listed and evaluated. Finally, the ways of legitimization of the ruler's power in all five documents will be discussed, which allows us to compare a Jewish presentation of rulership with ideas about rulership in the contemporaneous culture of the Greco-Egyptian world.

At the beginning of his book, Hengel briefly discusses the concept of Hellenism. Following on the view of Johann Gustav Droysen, he characterizes Hellenism as a melting process of Greek and Oriental cultures and practices.[3] Afterwards, he sketches the political and economic interaction of "Palestinian Judaism" with the civilization of early Hellenism as well as the influence of Greek language and education on "Palestinian Judaism." These introductory chapters function as the framework for his extensive description and interpretation of the relevant Jewish sources. In the *pièce de résistance* of the book, chapter 3, he describes in painstaking detail how, in his opinion, Jewish thought has developed in interaction with Hellenistic culture. This discussion of many Jewish sources leads to an indication of a number of general characteristics of Hellenistic-Jewish culture, such as a trend toward rational thought, an interest in the patterns of history, nature, and human existence, individualization of religion, and anthropological conceptions focused on salvation.[4] Since the main focus here is on Hellenistic-Jewish sources, there is a danger of a circular argument. In order to avoid this danger I call for more comparative research in this connection. The thesis of an intensive and pluriform interaction between Jewish and non-Jewish cultures in the Hellenistic period can be strengthened by taking external points of reference into account. The changes of Jewish culture in the Hellenistic period as well as the correspondences and differences with non-Jewish cultures can be described with the help of two kinds of comparative research: (1) a thorough diachronic comparison of Jewish sources from the Hellenistic period and related earlier sources that belong to the Jewish cultural heritage, including, of course, the Hebrew Bible; and (2) a careful comparison of Hellenistic Jewish sources with contemporary non-Jewish sources originating in a related context.[5] On the basis of the first kind of comparison one can conclude to what extent Jewish ideas and practices changed and where continuities and discontinuities can be observed. Afterward one can start building a hypothesis about the causes of the changes observed. This analysis can be supplemented by synchronic comparative research, which would allow for conclusions about the extent of correspondences between the cultures of Jews and surrounding non-Jews as well as about unique features of Jewish culture. In the remaining part of this paper I will offer a case study of the second type of comparative research: a comparison of 1 Macc 14:25–49 and four Hellenistic Egyptian decrees in honor of Ptolemaic kings.

Structure and Content of 1 Macc 14:25–49

The decree for Simon and his sons seems to be an innovation in the Israelite and Jewish contexts. Jonathan Goldstein raises the issue of correspondences between 1 Macc 14:25–49 and Hebrew and Aramaic texts belonging to the traditions of Israel, and mentions only Neh 9–10 in this connection.[6] In my opinion, the people's confession of guilt and the covenant renewal described in Neh 9–10 differ greatly from the content and function of the decree in 1 Macc 14. As far as I can see, the content and function of all official documents in the Hebrew Bible seem to be rather different from those of the decree in 1 Macc 14. The differences make a diachronic comparative analysis superfluous. However, in order to avoid too hasty a conclusion, it may be wise to check whether significant vocabulary parallels used in connection with the decree do exist in older Israelite or Jewish texts.

The decree is framed by verses indicating that it was engraved on bronze tablets and stones (possibly pillars) on Mount Zion (14:27), in a conspicuous place within the precincts of the sanctuary (14:48) as well as in the treasury itself (14:49). The vocabulary connected with the decree and its motivation as given in 1 Macc 14:25, thanking Simon and his sons, seems to be unique in the Septuagint. Vocabulary that is similar to the procedure indicated in 1 Macc 14, though, can be found in Jewish writings from the second century BCE. Some of the closest parallels stem from other passages in 1 Maccabees. Χάρις occurs frequently in the Septuagint, for example in the phrase εὑρίσκω χάριν ἐναντίου + personal pronoun "find favor with person X" (1 Macc 10:60; 11:24), but there is just one other passage with the combination χάριν ἀποδίδωμι as found in 1 Macc 14:25. 3 Macc 1:9 refers to thank offerings (καὶ χάριτας ἀποδούς) for the Jerusalem temple by Ptolemy IV after a brief report of the Battle of Rapphia (217 BCE, see below). The Greek text of Ben Sira contains three references of ἀνταποδίδωμι and χάρις (3:31; 30:6 and 32[35]:2), and there are several passages with χάρις and δίδωμι (e.g., Prov 4:9; 13:15; Bar 2:14; Dan 1:9 LXX), but the content of none of these passages is close to the decision of the Jewish people to thank Simon and his sons, as mentioned in 1 Macc 14:25. Likewise, the verb καταγράφω "write down, write against, engrave" is used elsewhere in the Septuagint,[7] but only once with the meaning "engrave" as in 1 Macc 14:27, and in a different context (Exod 32:15). The word δέλτος "writing-tablet" occurs elsewhere within the Septuagint only in 1 Maccabees (8:22; 14:18, 27, 48).[8] Στήλη is sometimes the translation of מצבה in the Septuagint (e.g., Exod 23:24). The phrase occurs once in the context of an engraved decree. Third Macc 2:27 refers to a decree by King Ptolemy, which affected the Jews greatly, inscribed on a stone (στήλη, not necessarily a pillar, see for example the Rosetta stone): ". . . he (Ptolemy) set up a stone on the tower in the courtyard with this inscription: 'None of those who do not sacrifice shall enter their sanctuaries, and all Jews shall be subjected to a registration involving poll tax and to the status of slaves . . .'" (3 Macc 2:27–28; cf. 7:20).[9] Γραφή (1 Macc 14:27, 48) refers to an engraved text in Sir 45:11 (εἰς μνημόσυνον ἐν γραφῇ κεκολαμμένῃ) as well as in 1 Macc 8:22; 12:21, and 3 Macc 2:27. Finally, the word ἀντίγραφον "copy" (1 Macc 14:27, 49) often refers to a copy of an official letter, which is sometimes made public at a conspicuous place. The references to such copies are roughly contemporaneous with the decree of 1 Macc 14 (Est 8:13; 1 Macc 11:37).[10] Thus, my conclusion that the decree in 1 Macc 14 is an innovation in the Jewish context is confirmed by the analysis of the earlier usage of a sample of the relevant vocabulary.

The decree for Simon is embedded in the narrative of 1 Maccabees by an introduction which contains notices about the location of the decree and its copies, corresponding to the last verses of the decree (14:25–27, 48–49).[11] Several scholars have expressed doubts about the decree's authenticity. The most probable view seems to be that 1 Macc 14:27–49 goes back to an actual decree that has been adapted and embedded in 1 Maccabees.[12] The immediate cause for the decree is given in 14:25 by the phrase "these words," which refer to the documents of the Romans and the Spartans given or indicated in 14:16–23. The people (δῆμος) take the initiative to thank "Simon and his sons."[13] That not only Simon but also his sons are being honored is repeated in 14:49. These extended honors may be an adaptation by the 1 Maccabees' redactor in order to legitimize the position of Simon's successor, John Hyrcanus. First Maccabees presents a coherent and extensive picture of the Maccabean dynasty which is rounded off with John Hyrcanus.[14]

The first element of the decree itself is the date: "On the eighteenth day of Elul, in the one hundred seventy-second year, which is the third year of the great high priest Simon (140 BCE)" (14:27).[15] The second element is the reference to a great assembly of the priests, the people, the leaders of the people and the elders of the country.[16] The location of the assembly is given in the last two words of verse 27: ἐν ασαραμελ.[17] It probably concerns a transcription of the Hebrew אל עם חצר, referring to the temple court surrounding the priestly court.[18] This matches the references to Mount Zion and the temple surrounding in 14:26, 48. It is difficult to establish who exactly is responsible for the decree. Some of the categories of the Jewish representatives present during the assembly are mentioned again in the text, like the people (ὁ λαός, 14:35, 44, 46)[19] and the priests (14:41, 44), but other names are mentioned as well.[20] Simon's partner in the decree, however, seems to be quite clear: the people or the Jews and the priests are mentioned together three times (14:41, 44, 47). On the other hand, another entity seems to be responsible for the decree, since 14:28 uses—after the reference to the assembly—an enigmatic brief phrase: ἐγνώρισεν ἡμῖν. The problem is: who has made known to whom? If we anticipate for a moment the discussion of the Egyptian decrees, which clearly point to the priests being present during the assembly, an analogous procedure in Jerusalem would make the priests logical candidates, but that neither fits the singular ἐγνώρισεν nor other data in the decree.[21] The "us" in 14:28 may refer, therefore, to the δῆμος that planned to thank Simon and his sons (cf. the first person plural form ἀποδώσομεν in 14:25). The singular may be explained, though, by assuming that the convention here used is that the official(s) who make(s) known is/are indicated only vaguely (i.e., ὁ γνωριστής).[22]

The body of the decree starts with the preamble (*considerans*) introduced by ἐπεί "since" (14:29). This section offers the grounds for the decision formulated later: a survey of Simon and his brothers' deeds, including warfare against the Jewish people's enemies (14:29, 31–33, 36), the protection of the temple (14:29; cf. 14:31, 42) and the law (14:29), as well as the great honor brought to the Jewish people (14:29). Simon's glorious deeds are listed in detail (14:32–40) with a focus upon his military actions, but the decree does not tell anything about his sons. The list is interrupted by the reference to the people's (ὁ λαός) decision to make him its leader and high priest in 14:35, which may be linked to the decision of the δῆμος in 14:25.

The second part of the body (14:41ff.) offers the decision of the decree. The transition of the preamble to the decision has been discussed by several scholars.[23] A *terminus technicus* which would indicate the beginning of the decision (see below) is missing. Sometimes the ὅτι of 14:41 has been deleted in order to solve this problem.[24] In that case, the decision is clearly given from 14:41 onwards: "The Jews and the priests have resolved that Simon should be their leader and high priest forever. . . ."[25] It is quite clear that the content of the decision seems to be described from 14:41 onward.[26] An earlier version of the decree may not have had the ὅτι of 14:41, but the textual evidence does not justify a deletion of the ὅτι in 14:41.[27] I would like to propose another interpretation in order to solve this problem. Verse 41 is the continuation of verse 40, which starts with "For he/it had heard that. . . ."[28] The subject of ἤκουσεν is usually taken to be the Seleucid king Demetrius,[29] who confirmed Simon's high priesthood and made him one of his Friends according to 14:38–39. 14:40 is subsequently interpreted as the motivation for Demetrius' decisions. This interpretation is improbable for several reasons: (1) Demetrius' motivation is already indicated in 14:38 by κατὰ ταῦτα, "in view of these things," referring to the data mentioned in 14:35–7;[30] (2) it is improbable that hearing of the alliance between the Jews and the Romans would form Demetrius' major motive for his policy toward Simon and the Jews;[31] (3) taking Demetrius as subject of ἤκουσεν would lead to a contradiction between this section of the decree and its context in chapter 14, since Demetrius was put into custody by the Parthian king Arsaces according to 14:3, while the person(s) who heard about the Romans later on in the chapter were the Jewish δῆμος (14:25, see above); (4) it seems highly improbable that the continuation of 14:40, 14:41–49, should be read as Demetrius' motivation, which would be the implication of Demetrius as subject of ἤκουσεν in verse 40. My alternative interpretation takes as point of departure that the reference to the alliance of Romans and Jews in 1 Macc 14:40 should be linked to the decree's introduction in 14:25. This intro seems to present the recent

Spartan and Roman documents as the immediate cause for the decree.[32] Therefore, in the version of the decree transmitted to us, the decision seems to be introduced by a reference to the Roman alliance as indicated in 14:16–24. The decision itself is probably given in an indirect way in 14:40–49, and ends with the indication of the place where the decree and its copies would be put (14:49).[33] Thus, in the present context the δῆμος of the Jews seems to have confirmed, by the reference to its hearing (14:40), the decision by the Jews and the priests indicated in 14:41–49. The essentials of the decision concern the Jews and the priests' acceptance of Simon's leadership, power, and *insignia*, the confirmation by the entire people and Simon's acceptance (14:46–47).[34] The indication of the way of publication as the decision's final element acknowledges the homage mentioned in the decree's introduction (14:25).

Structure and Content of the Egyptian Priestly Decrees

Several scholars have referred to non-Jewish documents as parallel material of 1 Macc 14:25–49. Grimm mentions Greco-Egyptian and Roman monuments with reports about the glorious deeds of rulers such as Ptolemy Euergetes I and Augustus.[35] Bévenot suggests that 1 Macc 14:25–49 corresponds to the Greco-Egyptian inscriptions of Canopus and Rosetta.[36] Abel also mentions these inscriptions side by side with a reference to many honorary inscriptions issued by councils and cities from the mainland and islands of Greece.[37] Bartlett notes without offering references: "Memorial inscriptions describing votes of thanks to public servants were common in the hellenistic world, and we see again how far Maccabean Judaea had accepted hellenistic practices."[38] Goldstein presupposes that the decree was originally composed in Hebrew, but notes at the same time that there are hardly any documents from Semitic peoples that correspond to 1 Macc 14. He mentions only Neh 9–10 in this respect: "Our document has many parallels in Greek honorific inscriptions and surely imitates them in many respects. Nevertheless, the original was written in Hebrew and drew very much on Hebrew and Aramaic patterns. We have very few examples to tell us how the Semitic peoples drew up communal resolutions. Of the parallels, only Nehemiah 9–10 is probably free from Greek influence."[39] Abel is the only scholar, as far as I can see, who offers references to parallel vocabulary in inscriptions in his commentary on 1 Macc 14:25–49. He notes, for example, that the phrase χάριν ἀποδιδόναι is common in inscriptions and that inscriptions were sometimes engraved on bronze plaquettes.[40] Unfortunately, he does not elaborate the correspondences between the decree for Simon and his sons and the Egyptian priestly decrees. Of course, it is useful to compare 1 Macc 14:27–49 with various kinds of honorary decrees from the Greco-Roman period.[41] However, the decree in 1 Macc 14 and the four priestly decrees have a few very specific elements in common, which calls for a discussion on its own: (1) the benefactions of the ruler are not listed in a document issued by the ruler himself, but by an assembly of representatives of the people; (2) these assemblies have taken place in a temple compound, and (3) all documents probably have been bi- or trilinguals.

The four priestly decrees from Egypt discussed below deserve detailed attention, since their structure is much closer to the structure of 1 Macc 14:27–49 than is the case with the other parallel documents referred to. The inscriptions concerned date from the second half of the third century or the beginning of the second century BCE. The relevant texts are four tri- or bilingual decrees, that is, documents issued in a hieroglyphic, Demotic, and in most cases also a Greek version. Some of them have survived in several copies.[42] They are priestly decrees intended for all important Egyptian temples. It concerns:

(1) the Canopus decree of 238 BCE in honor of Ptolemy III Euergetes, his wife Berenice II and their daughter Berenice, who died at nine years old;[43]

(2) the Memphis decree of 217 BCE, also called the Raphia decree because of the references to the Battle of Raphia in 217, commemorated in this honorary decree for Ptolemy IV Philopator;[44]

(3) the Memphis decree of 196 BCE in honor of Ptolemy V Epiphanes, commemorating his coronation, inscribed on the famous Stone of Rosetta;[45]

(4) the Alexandria decree of 186 BCE (also in honor of Ptolemy V), which is usually called the Second Philae decree. This decree was issued at Alexandria and found in the Isis sanctuary of the temple island of Philae in the far south of Egypt.[46]

I will concentrate on the Greek versions of these documents (for number 4 no Greek text is available).[47]

The structure of all four decrees consists of five sections, while sections three and four contain the body of the decree:

(1) date;
(2) reference to the assembly of those who issued the decree;
(3) motivation for the decision;
(4) the decision itself;
(5) provisions for the publication of the decree.

Ad 1. Date

The date is indicated by the year of the king, who is usually mentioned with a collection of traditional titles (e.g., Rosetta Greek ll. 1–4), as well as by references to eponymous priests and priestesses of the ruler cults (e.g., Rosetta Greek ll. 4–6). The month and the day on which the decree has been issued is given according to the Macedonian and Egyptian calendars.[48] The introduction of the oldest of the four decrees, the Canopus decree, reads as follows: "In the ninth year of the reign of Ptolemy, son of Ptolemy and Arsinoe the Brother-and-Sister Gods, the priest of Alexander and the Brother-and-Sister Gods and the Benefactor Gods being Apollonidas son of Moschion and the canephore of Arsinoe Phildadelphos being Menekrateia daughter of Philammon, on the seventh of the month Apellaios, the seventeenth of the Egyptians' month Tybi . . ." (trans. Bagnall and Derow).[49] This date refers to the ninth regnal year of Ptolemy III Euergetes as well as to months and days according to the Macedonian and Egyptian calendars and can be converted to March 7, 238 BCE. The date is complemented by the reference to the eponymous priest of Alexander and the Ptolemaic ruler Apollonidas, son of Moschion. The introduction of the Canopus decree confirms the extension of the ruler cult for Alexander to the second Ptolemaic couple (Ptolemy II Philadelphos and Arsinoe I) with *Theoi Adelphoi* as its cult name, as well as to the ruling couple Ptolemy III Euergetes and Berenice II (as the *Theoi Euergetai*).[50] Menekrateia, daughter of Philammon, is the second eponymous priestly figure. Her title *canephore* ("basket-bearer") indicates that she was the priestess of Arsinoe I, the deified wife of Ptolemy II Philadelphos. The Raphia and Rosetta decree add a collection of traditional Egyptian royal titles to the introduction, which are also given in the Greek versions.[51] The Rosetta decree, for example, reads: "the one who received the kingdom from his father, lord of the diadems, very glorious, the one who has established order for Egypt, the pious one to the gods, victorious over his antagonists, the one who has restored life for humankind, the lord of the festival of thirty years" (my trans.).[52] The significant change from the Canopus decree, which offers only Greek titles, to the Raphia and Rosetta decrees with collections of pharaonic titles has been interpreted by some scholars as evidence of an Egyptianization of the Ptolemaic view of kingship.[53]

Ad 2. Reference to the assembly in a temple

The second part of the introductory section starts with a reference to the decree itself, in the Greek versions indicated by ψήφισμα, "Decision."[54] Next a reference to the assembly is given. All decrees have been issued by an assembly of various categories of priests coming from, at least in principal, all Egyptian temples. The location of the assembly is a temple in one of Egypt's centers of administration, the old Memphis, or the new capital, Alexandria. A good example is offered by the Rosetta stone (Greek ll. 6–8):[55] "Decision. There being assembled the Chief Priests (ἀρχιερεῖς) and Prophets (προφῆται) and those who enter the inner shrine of the robing of the gods (οἱ εἰς τὸ ἄδυτον εἰ<σ>πορευόμενοι πρὸς τὸν στολισμὸν τῶν θεῶν), and the Fan-bearers (πτεροφόραι) and the Scribes of the House of Life (ἱερογραμματεῖς) and all other priests from the temples throughout the land who have come to meet the king at Memphis for the feast of the assumption by Ptolemy, the Ever-living, the Beloved of Ptah, the God Epiphanes Eucharistos, of the kingship in which he suceeded his father, they being assembled in the temple in Memphis on this day declared (συναχθέντες ἐν τῶι ἐν Μέμφε(ι) <ἱ>ερῶι τῆι ἡμέραι ταύτηι εἶπαν). . . ."[56] The hieroglyphic version of the Raphia decree specifies the Ptah temple as the priests' assembly's location (l. 5). Incidentally, a reference to other Egyptians implies that in fact all Egyptian subjects were at least invited to involve themselves. Rosetta stone Greek ll. 52–53 notes that non-priests could also participate in the honors for the king: "and private individuals shall also be allowed to keep the festival and set up the aforementioned shrine and have it in their homes, performing the aforementioned celebrations yearly, in order that it may be known to all that the men of Egypt magnify and honor the God Epiphanes Eucharistos the king,

according to this law" (see further below). The grounds for the honors
for the king referred to in the third section of the decrees mention benefactions for temples, priests as well as all other subjects of Egypt, which
may indicate that the priests act as representatives of the Egyptian
population.[57]

Ad 3. Motivation for the decision (Greek versions: Canopus ll.
7–20; Raphia ll. 7–30; Rosetta ll. 9–36)

As far as the extant Greek versions are concerned, the motivation
(*considerans*) of the decree starts like the document in 1 Macc 14 with
"since" (ἐπειδή, Canopus l. 7; Rosetta l. 9; cf. Raphia Demotic version
l. 7; Philae II Hier. l. 4; 1 Macc 14:29). The most important reason for
honoring the king is his benefactions toward the Egyptian temples, the
people who live in them and all his other subjects.[58] The Rosetta stone
reads for example: "Whereas . . . king Ptolemy has been a benefactor
both to the temples (κατὰ πολλὰ εὐεργέτηκεν τὰ θ' ἱερά)[59] and to
those who dwell in them, as well as all those who are his subjects" (ll.
9–10). The Raphia decree refers to the king's care for the temples damaged during Antiochus III's invasion and for the statues taken away by
the Medes.[60] The Philae decree mentions a gift of gold, silver, and precious stones for the decoration and restoration of damaged temples, as
well as benefits to Apis, Mnevis and other sacred animals.[61] The Raphia
decree refers to similar gifts in combination to a note that the king had
spent a huge amount of gold pieces (300,000) as crown money on his
army (Greek fragment A on the second stone, ll. 14–22).[62] In connection
with the military operation against the rebels in Lycopolis, the Rosetta
stone notes "financing these actions with a considerable amount of
money."[63] A second proof of what Pestman calls "decent administration"
are measures connected with taxes and privileges.[64] Taxes are being decreased or abolished, and privileges for the temples reconfirmed.[65]

A third cluster of benefactions concerns the supposedly successful
struggles against foreign or indigenous opponents. The Canopus decree
still refers to the king's fighting for Egypt and bringing peace in a brief
and general way (Canopus Greek l. 12), but later Ptolemies figuring in
the decrees were involved in heavy military conflicts. The Raphia decree
pays a lot of attention to Ptolemy IV's triumph over Antiochus III at
Raphia, a city southwest of Gaza (Raphia Demotic ll. 10–15; 20–21;
23–25). The Rosetta stone commemorates the successful recapture of

the city of Lycopolis (Rosetta Greek ll. 20–28), but shows at the same time that Ptolemy V's position was not very strong, since he agrees to grant privileges and other measures to reduce the burden on the subjects and even offers amnesty to former rebels (Greek ll. 19–20). Finally, the second Philae decree describes Ptolemy's long-awaited triumph over the rebels of the south, including the arrest of the indigenous rebel king Chaonnophris/Anchwennefer (Hier. ll. 4–5; 9–12; Demotic ll. 3–4; 7–9). In connection with 1 Macc 14, it is of interest that the decrees note several times that the king spent great amounts of his own money on temples as well as on military campaigns.[66] Apart from these three types of reasons, some of the decrees refer to specific other measures as well.[67] This section is rounded off with the thanks of the gods to the king.[68]

Ad 4. Decision[69]

The decision is introduced by formulae like "the priests of the country are pleased to increase the already existing honors paid in the sanctuaries to King Ptolemy and Queen Berenice . . ." (δεδόχθαι τοῖς . . . ἱερεῦσιν . . . τιμὰς . . . αὔξειν . . . , Canopus Greek ll. 20–22, cf. l. 54); "It is the pleasure of the priests of all the temples in the country to increase greatly the existing honors of the ever-living King Ptolemy . . ." (ἔδοξεν τοῖς ἱερεῦσι τῶν κατὰ τὴν χώραν ἱερῶν πάντων τὰ ὑπάρχοντα τ[ίμια πάντα] τῶι αἰωνοβίωι βασιλεῖ Πτολεμαίωι . . . ἐπαύξειν μεγάλως, Rosetta ll. 36–37). The decision clearly has a religious dimension and results in extensions of the ruler cult. The Rosetta stone refers to setting up images of the king in every temple, paying homage to him three times a day, setting up statues and golden shrines which were carried out with those of the other gods during processions, festal days in commemoration of the king's regnal day as well as his birthday, monthly as well as annually, and finally to an additional name for the eponymous priests ("priest of the god Epiphanes Eucharistos").[70]

Ad 5. Publication

The last part of the decision concerns the publication of the decree. Most of the decrees were published on stelae of hard stone (Rosetta Greek ll. 53–4: . . . εἰς στήλας σ]τερεοῦ λίθου). The famous Rosetta stone as well as several of the other stones discussed here show that such stones did not necessarily have the form of a pillar.[71] The formulation of the oldest decree is slightly different. Canopus ll. 73–75 refers to a stone or a bronze monument: "The person who has been appointed as the overseer of every sanctuary and chief priest as well as the scribes of the sanctuary must write down this decision on a monument of stone or bronze (εἰς στήλην λιθίνην ἢ χαλκήν) in holy Egyptian as well as Greek characters [that is hieroglyphic, Demotic, and Greek script] and set it up at the most conspicuous location of the temples of the first, second, and third category, in order that the functioning priests manifestly honor the gods Euergetai (King Ptolemy and Queen Berenice) and their children, as is right" (my trans.).[72]

Comparison

It is obvious that the contents of 1 Macc 14:27–49 and the four priestly decrees are quite different, since different kinds of rulership as well as religious views and practices are at stake. Nevertheless, the basic structures of all five documents seem to be rather similar. They contain four or five sections: a date according to the Greek and the indigenous calendars, a reference to an assembly of priests or priests as well as other representatives of the people, a motivation, a decision to honor the ruler and, finally, an indication of the decree's publication (see above). First Macc 14:27 refers to the Babylonian and Jewish month Elul, to the 170th year of the Seleucid era as well to the third year of Simon's high priesthood. The dates in the priestly decrees are double in a different way, referring to the year of the Ptolemaic king and to eponymous priests as well as to Greek and Egyptian months (see above). Besides, in all four Egyptian decrees the assembly of the priests, as well as the publication of the decree, takes place in a temple context. The priestly decrees may help us to understand the corresponding data in 1 Macc 14 better. The analogy would confirm the interpretation that the words ἐν ἀσαραμελ (1 Macc 14:27) should not be connected with the preceding reference to Simon's high priesthood,[73] but with the great assembly mentioned in 14:28. In that case, the words would form the beginning of the decree's second section, pointing to the location of the meeting: "In the court of the people during a great assembly of the priests . . . (a decree was issued)." The court of the people, within the temple area,[74] as the meeting's location and the decree's publication at a conspicuous place in the precincts of the temple are perfectly logical, since the decree involved all Jews and not only the priests. The Egyptian decrees mention, apart from the king, priests as the only participants in the assembly but, like 1 Macc 14, the decrees involve the entire Egyptian population. The priests act as representatives of the people (see §3).[75] This conclusion is supported by the place of publication of the second Philae decree. The decree itself refers to this place as follows: "setting it up in the court of the (common) people in the sanctuary . . ." Hier. ll. 17–18; "and it shall be set up in the place of the multitude of (the) temple . . . ," Demotic ll. 14–15; trans. Müller).[76] This information corresponds with the actual location of the Philae decree. With another bilingual decree, it was located on the wall of the so-called House of Birth standing in the large court of the Isis temple in Philae between the first and second pylons.[77] This location could still be observed at the beginning of the twentieth century, since the temple island of Philae remained more or less intact up to the construction of the Assuan reservoir.[78] The large court with the House of Birth functioned as the temple's front hall and must have been accessible to all believers. Thus, the reference to this court as the court of the common people matches its function.[79]

Like 1 Macc 14:27–49, the body of the priestly decrees consists of two main sections: motivation and decision. The Egyptian documents are quite clear in this respect and show corresponding terminology separating the various sections from each other. The structure of 1 Macc 14:27–49 is less clear. Part of the technical terminology of the priestly decrees can be found in 1 Macc 14, with the ἐπεί "since" as the introduction of the considerans as the most clear specimen (1 Macc 14:29; see also above).[80] The analogy with the priestly decrees implies that 1 Macc 14:27–49 may have a section with the decision, although the transition to this section is difficult to establish (see §2). The correspondences with the Egyptian decrees do, however, support the interpretation of 1 Macc 14:40/41–49 as the section containing the decision of the honorary decree. At the same time, it is clear that the contents of the decision sections differ greatly. The Egyptian texts focus upon the religious honors of the king and queen linked to the ruler cult,[81] whereas 1 Macc 14:27–49 confirms Simon's leadership, including the high priesthood. Finally, the rare publication of the decree in 1 Maccabees on bronze tablets seems to be an imitation of the Romans (1 Macc 8:22; 14:18). Only one of the Egyptian priestly decrees refers to a bronze monument as an alternative to a stone one (Canopus Greek ll. 73–75). On the other hand, the partial analogy between the priestly decrees and 1 Macc 14:27–49 may support the attractive assumption that the decree on which the document in 1 Maccabees was based has been a bilingual or trilingual one like the Egyptian decrees (i.e., a decree in Aramaic and Greek or Aramaic, Hebrew, and Greek characters), although solid evidence is missing for this assumption.[82]

I have suggested above that in the present context of 1 Maccabees the immediate reason for issuing the decree for Simon and his sons seems to be the tribute paid by the Romans after his enlightening career. Customary occasions for the priestly decrees are the celebration of the king's birthday and regnal day,[83] which differ from the situation in 1 Macc 14, but also the king's military victories, which match Simon's success. Moreover, the grounds for honoring the ruler in 1 Macc 14 and the priestly decrees correspond in several ways. The Ptolemies are being honored first and foremost for their restoration and improvement of temples, the reduction of taxes, confirmation of temple privileges and the restoration of peace and order (see above §3). Despite cultural and religious differences and apart from the taxes, we find a similar cluster of reasons in 1 Macc 14:27–49. Simon protected the Jerusalem temple (14:31–32, 36; cf. 14:29), triumphed over the people's enemies (14:31–32; cf. 14:29) and created a stable and peaceful situation (14:36). He fortified the towns of Judah, as well as Beth-Zur, Joppa and Gazara (14:33–34). He also removed the gentiles from the citadel in the city of David, settled Jews in it, and fortified it for the safety of the country and the city (14:36–37). The liberation festival in commemoration of this victory (1 Macc 13:52) is not mentioned in the decree of chapter 14, but corresponds to the festivals founded by Ptolemy IV Philopator and Ptolemy V Epiphanes in commemoration of their triumphs over Antiochus III and the rebels from the south, respectively.[84] The tenor of the brief characterization of Ptolemy IV Philopator in the Raphia decree Greek l. 2 ". . . very glorious, pious towards the gods, savior of humans, triumphant over his antagonists, who returned the order in Egypt, restored the sacred affairs and secured the laws established by the three times very great Hermes . . ." corresponds with the brief description in 1 Macc 14:29 of the role of Simon and his brothers, who "exposed themselves to danger and resisted the enemies of their nation, in order that their sanctuary and the law might be preserved; and they brought glory to their people."[85] Proper administration and taking care of subjects, priests and others, underlie the reasons for honoring the ruler. Thus, the ruler is honored because of his deeds. 1 Macc 14:35 states this explicitly by commemorating that the people made Simon its leader and high priest "because he had done all these things (διὰ τὸ αὐτὸν πεποιηκέναι πάντα ταῦτα)." Likewise, the Ptolemaic king was only assured of acceptance and honors from the non-Greek population because of his successful administration, indicated, among other things, by the cult names *Soter* and *Euergetes*.[86] The striking detail that Simon acts as financer of the state and pays the wages of his soldiers and the expenses of their arms (14:32) is paralleled by several Ptolemaic kings, according to the priestly decrees.[87] This presentation of rulership implies that the ruler personifies the state. Günther Hölbl suggests that this view is typical of the Hellenistic ideology of rulership: "Während dem ptolemäischen Pharao das Kollektiv der ägyptischen Priester als rechtlich selbständig handelnde Grösse gegenübertritt (. . .) , verkörpert der ptolemäische Basileus wie sein seleukidischer Kollege das Prinzip des Staates allein in seiner Person."[88]

Thus, an important aspect of the decree in 1 Macc 14, that the status of the ruler is dependent of his deeds, corresponds with a trend in the depiction of the Ptolemaic king in the Egyptian priestly decrees. Furthermore, this topic of 1 Macc 14:27–49 is shared with other passages in 1 Maccabees about the position of the Maccabees as leaders of the Jews. This is the point of Mattathias' last words to his sons in 2:49–69, a passage which is linked to the honorary decree in chapter 14 from a compositional viewpoint.[89] First Maccabees notes of Mattathias and his friends already in 2:47, "the work prospered in their hands" (cf. 14:36 about Simon). The hymn of praise for Judah in 3:3–9 points in the same direction, by highlighting that Judah "embittered many kings, but . . . made Jacob glad by his deeds (ἐν τοῖς ἔργοις αὐτοῦ, 3:7)."[90] On the basis of the comparison between 1 Macc 14:27–49 and the priestly decrees from Ptolemaic Egypt, I would like to argue that the legitimization of Simon's leadership is a new development in Hellenistic Judaism, corresponding to a trend in depicting the ruler's image in Ptolemaic Egypt as presented by the priestly decrees.[91] This view of Simon as ruler may have been articulated because of the interaction of Jewish and non-Jewish elites in Egypt and Judea.[92]

The decision, finally, brings honor to the ruler and affects his position by confirming or even enhancing his power and status. The priestly decrees and 1 Maccabees go their own ways here, which is understandable because of the different contexts. The Egyptian documents contain arrangements for the veneration of the ruler, and in the case of the Canopus and Philae II decrees also his wife, as the people's side of the mutual beneficiary relationship between ruler and subjects. The decree's decision section usually starts with a phrase indicating the confirmation or extension of honors already existing (see §3). Nevertheless, 1 Macc 14 seems to reconfirm Simon's position as political and military leader as well as high priest (14:35, 38, 41–42)[93] in an analogous way and offers him the power of an autocratic ruler. Simon's power implies a role as the people's father, who could treat the Jewish state as his family estate.[94] Again, this presentation of Simon's rulership seems to correspond to a trend in the Ptolemaic ideology of kingship, which, of course, went even one principle step further by the foundation and expansion of the ruler cult. Through the cult of the Ptolemaic dynasty the function of rulership was firmly linked to the Ptolemaic family, which personified in its turn the Egyptian state.[95]

First Macc 14:25–49 conveys the impression that the Jewish priests and people took the initiative to appoint Simon as high priest and leader and to honor him by giving him great power and magnificent *insignia*. When we read the Egyptian priestly decrees in their historical contexts, we become aware of two things: (1) the king probably orchestrated his own honors, and (2) his powers were limited despite the benefactions listed in the decrees. Three out of four decrees were issued during or just after serious crises. The battle at Raphia was hardly a victory for Ptolemy IV, as is apparent from Polybius 5.82–86 and even from the decree itself. Ptolemy had to make peace with Antiochus after a rebellion of his Egyptian military forces.[96] The Rosetta stone and the Philae II decree reflect events from a rebellious period of about twenty years, in which several indigenous leaders set themselves up as successors of the pharaohs.[97] The concessions made by Ptolemy V to priests and other subjects, including amnesty to former opponents (Rosetta Greek ll. 19–20) and to the rebel king Chaonnophris/Anchwenncfer, at the request of the priests,[98] show that there was a balance of power that the king had to accept. At the same time, the decrees present the king as the great benefactor of Egypt and make extensive use of the old royal mythology depicting him as the royal god Horus, who avenged the death of his father Osiris on the enemy god Seth-Typhon. Just one example out of several is the description of Ptolemy IV's battle against Antiochus III in terms of the traditional Egyptian royal mythology: "Es geschah im Jahre 5 am 1. Pachons, da zog er aus Pelusium und kämpfte mit König Antiochos in einer Stadt, die man Raphia nennt, nahe dem Grenzfelde Ägyptens, das im Osten von Bethelea und Pasanfr liegt. Am 10. des genannten Monats besiegte er ihn in ruhmvoller Weise. Die unter seinen Feinden, die in dieser Schlacht bis in seine Nähe vordrangen, die tötete er vor sich, wie Harsiesis vordem seine Feinde geschlachtet hat ..." (Raphia Demotic ll. 10–12, trans. Spiegelberg).[99] In short, the priestly decrees seem to have been intended, therefore, as a double legitimization of the Ptolemies as kings of Egypt: through the ruler's deeds and through the presentation of these deeds as being in line with the tradition of the old royal god Horus.[100]

In the light of the Egyptian priestly decrees, one wonders whether the honorary decree for Simon also has been issued at his own instigation, or that of his sons, in order to legitimize his or their position and power, which were still disputed by some of the Jews.[101] Notwithstanding the considerable differences, 1 Macc 14:27–49 and the four Egyptian priestly decrees seem to show not only formal correspondences but are similar also in presenting the ruler and legitimizing his position. I hope that my comparative synchronic analysis is a convincing illustration of the kind of research called for at the beginning of this paper. As I have indicated, the decree for Simon seems to be an innovation within Hellenistic-Jewish traditions of the Second Temple period. The comparison of 1 Macc 14:25–49 and the priestly decrees allows us to conclude, in my opinion, that notwithstanding the fact that Simon's leadership is presented as a counterforce to Greek (Seleucid) rulership, it can also be understood as the outcome of a lively interplay between Jewish and non-Jewish Hellenistic views and conventions about political power and rulership.

Appendix

Greek fragment A on the second Raphia stone, Greek text according to Bernand, *La prose*, no. 14 1.39, and my translation

καὶ τᾶλλα τὰ νομιζόμενα
πρὸς τὴν τοιαύτην ὑποδοχὴν
στεφανηφοροῦντες καὶ πανη-

γυρίζοντες μετὰ θυσιῶν καὶ
5 σπονδῶν καὶ προθεσέων· εἰσ-
ελθών τε ὁ βασιλεὺς εἰς τὰ ἱερὰ
καὶ θύσας ἀνέθηκεν προσόδους
αὐτοῖς χωρὶς τῶν προανακει-
μένων ὑπ' αὐτοῦ καὶ ἱεροῦ κόσμου
10 χρυσοῦ καὶ ἀργυροῦ πολὺ πλῆθος,
καὶ τῶν ἐν τοῖς ἀδύτοις ἱερῶν
ἀγαλμάτων τά τε λείποντα ἐξ ἀρ-
χαίων χρόνων καὶ τὰ προσδεόμενα
ἐπανορθώσεως ἀνενεώσατο, χορη-
15 γήσας εἰς ταῦτα πολὺ πλῆθος χρυσί-
ου καὶ ἀργυρίου καὶ λίθων πολυτε-
λῶν καὶ τῶν ἄλλων {πολυτελῶν
καὶ τῶν ἄλλων}, ὧν χρεία ἦν, καίπερ
πολλῆς αὐτῶι δαπάνης γεγενημέ-
20 νης ἐν τῆι στρατείαι καὶ ἐστεφανω-
κότος αὐτοῦ τὰς δυνάμεις χρυσῶν
μυριάδων τριάκοντα, τῶν τε ἱερῶν
καὶ τῶν περὶ τὰ ἱερὰ διατριβόντων
καὶ τῶν ἄλλων τῶν ἐν τῆι χώραι
25 τὴν πᾶσαν ἐπιμέλειαν ἐποιήσατο
εὐχαριστῶν τοῖς θεοῖς ἐπὶ τῶι συν-
[τελ]έσαι αὐτοὺς ἃ ἐπηγγείλαντο
[αὐτωι· Ἀ]γαθῆι Τύχηι δεδόχθαι
[τοῖς κα]τὰ τὴν χώραν ἱερεῦ-
30 [σιν τάς τε π]ροϋπαρχούσας τιμὰς
[ἐν τοῖς ἱεροῖς βα]σιλεῖ Πτολεμαίωι
[καὶ βασιλίσσηι Ἀρσινό]ηι θεοῖς Φιλο-
[πάτορσιν καὶ τοῖς γονεῦ]σιν αὐτῶν
[θεοῖς Εὐεργέταις καὶ τοῖς προ]γόνοις

[The Context: the Egyptians' reception of the victorious Ptolemy IV returning from the Battle of Raphia]

. . . and the other things that are usual for such a reception, wearing a
wreath and celebrating a festival with sacrifices and (5) drink-offerings
and (other) offerings. And the king entered the sanctuaries and sacrificed, and he dedicated income to them independent from what was

dedicated by him before, as well as a great multitude of sacred decorations of (10) gold and silver. And the sacred statues in the innermost sanctuaries that were missing from old times and those that needed restoration he set in order again, (15) supplying for them a great multitude of gold, silver, precious stones and the other necessary things, in spite of his great expenses made (20) during the expedition and the crown money of 300,000 gold pieces he had given his forces. (25) He paid full attention to the sanctuaries and to those who are busy in connection with the sanctuaries and the others in the country, thanking the gods for fulfilling what they had announced (to him. To Good) Fortune. (The) priests of the country are pleased (30) to (extend greatly) the honors (in the sanctuaries that) existed before for King Ptolemy (and Queen Arsinoe), the Gods Loving (their Father, their parents), (the Gods' Benefactors, their) ancestors, (34) (the Gods' Loving Brother and Sister, and the Gods' Saviors . . . [the Greek text breaks off at line 34, the words between brackets in the translation from line 28 onward have been added on the basis of the Demotic version].

Notes

Abbreviations

GELS=J. Lust, E. Eynikel, K. Hauspie, *A Greek-English Lexicon of the Septuagint* (2 vols.; Stuttgart: Deutsche Bibelgesellschaft, 1992–1996).

OGIS=W. Dittenberger, *Orientis graeci inscriptiones selectae* (2 vols; Leipzig: Hirzel, 1903–1905)

SB=*Sammelbuch griechischer Urkunden aus Ägypten* 1915-

SEG=*Supplementum epigraphicum graecum* 1923-

1. M. Hengel, *Judentum und Hellenismus: Studien zu ihrer Begegnung unter besonderer Berücksichtigung Palästinas bis zur Mitte des 2.Jh.s v.Chr.* (WUNT 10; Tübingen: J. C. B. Mohr, 1969; 2nd ed. 1973; 3rd ed. 1988). The second and third German editions from 1973 and 1988 offer more references and secondary literature, but the content remains close to that of the first edition. In the preface to the third edition, Hengel deals briefly with Louis Feldman and some of his other critics, see pp. xi–xiv. I warmly thank Prof. P. W. Pestman (Leiden) and Dr. K. A. Worp (Amsterdam) for their help and comments to the draft of this contribution.

2. *Judentum und Hellenismus*, 3: "Im 'Hellenismus' entstand—durch die Begegnung des Griechentums mit dem Orient—etwas grundsätzlich Neues, das sich von dem Zeitalter der griechischen Klassik unterschied; ähnlich wie das Judentum . . . in der hellenistischen Zeit durch die Begegnung und Auseinandersetzung mit den politisch-sozialen und geistigen Mächten dieser Epoche eine allmähliche, tiefgreifende Umwandlung erfuhr, auf Grund derer es sich in wesentlichen Punkten von seinen alttestamentlichen Vorformen unterscheidet." Cf. p. 193: "Das gesamte Judentum ab etwa der Mitte des 3. Jh.s v.Chr. müsste im strengen Sinne als "hellenistisches Judentum" bezeichnet werden. . . ."

3. *Judentum*, 2–5. Cf. J. G. Droysen, *Geschichte des Hellenismus* (3 vols; Gotha: Perthes, 1877–78; 2nd ed.). Droysen's view has been heavily criticized by scholars who consider "Hellenism" basically as a process of Grecization, see, e.g., C. Préaux, *Le monde hellénistique: La Grèce et l'Orient* (323–146 av. J. C.) (2 vols; Paris: Presses Universitaires de France, 1978); R. Bichler, *'Hellenismus': Geschichte und Problematik eines Epochenbegriffs* (Darmstadt: Wissenschaftliche Buchgesellschaft, 1983).

4. *Judentum*, 369; 454. Cf. p. 566: "Gemeinsam war der rationale, empirische Charakter, die universalistische Tendenz, das Interesse an der göttlichen Ordnung des Kosmos und die betont anthropologisch-ethische Blickrichtung."

5. Cf. F. Millar, "The Background to the Maccabean Revolution: Reflections on Martin Hengel's 'Judaism and Hellenism,'" *JJS* 29 (1978) 1–21, esp. pp. 2–6.

6. J. A. Goldstein, *I Maccabees: A New Translation with Introduction and Commentary* (AB 41; New York: Doubleday, 1976) 501; Cf. U. Rappoport, "על התייונותם של החשמונאים" ['The Hasmonean State and Hellenism'], *Tarbiz* 60 (1990–91) 477–503, esp. p. 494.

7. *GELS* 2.232 s.v. See Exod 17:14; 32:15; Num 11:26; 1 Chron 9:1; 2 Chron 20:34; 1 Esd 2:16; Job 13:26; Sir 48:10; Hos 8:12 and 1 Macc 9:22.

8. *GELS* 1.98.

9. Unless specified otherwise, the NRSV has been used for the Bible and for writings incorporated in the Septuagint. H. Anderson, "3 Maccabees (First Century B.C.): A New Translation and Introduction," *The Old Testament Pseudepigrapha* (2 vols; ed. J. H. Charlesworth; London: Darton, Longman & Todd, 1985) 2.519 and *GELS* 2.439 prefer to translate στήλη with "pillar".

10. See 1 Esd 6:7; 8:8; Est 3:13–14; 4:8; 8:12a, 12s, 13; Ep Jer. 1; 1 Macc 8:22; 11:31, 37; 12:5, 7, 19; 14:20, 23; 15:24.

11. N. Martola, *Capture and Liberation: A Study in the Composition of the First Book of Maccabees* (Acta Academiae Aboensis ser. A 63.1; Åbo: Åbo Akademi, 1984) offers an extensive analysis of the composition of 1 Maccabees.

12. One of the observations which support this view are the contradictions between the decree and its immediate context, which are noted, among

others, by C. L. W. Grimm, "Das erste Buch der Maccabäer," *Kurzgefasstes exegetisches Handbuch zu den Apokryphen des Alten Testaments* (6 vols; eds. O. F. Fritzsche and C. L. W. Grimm; Leipzig: S. Hirzel, 1851–1860) 3.219–20, and Goldstein, *I Maccabees*, 501 and 504. See further the discussion by J. Sievers, *The Hasmoneans and Their Supporters* (Atlanta: Scholars Press, 1990) 120–21.

13. Δῆμος seems to be a political designation of the Jewish people, as in 2 Macc 11:34, Van Henten, *The Maccabean Martyrs as Saviours of the Jewish People: A Study of 2 and 4 Maccabees* (JSJ Sup 57; Leiden: Brill, 1997) 193 n. 32.

14. S. Joubert and J. W. van Henten, "Two a-typical Jewish Families in the Greco-Roman Period," *Neotestamentica* 30 (1996) 121–40, esp. pp. 127–32.

15. About the dates referring to the first and third year of Simon in 1 Macc 13:42; 14:27, see Sievers, *Hasmoneans*, 110–12.

16. Ἐπὶ συναγωγῆς μεγάλης ἱερέων καὶ λαοῦ καὶ ἀρχόντων ἔθνους καὶ τῶν πρεσβυτέρων τῆς χώρας.

17. Ἐν indicates the location, as usual in honorary inscriptions in the opinion of F.-M. Abel, *Les livres des Maccabées* (Paris: J. Gabalda, 1949) 257.

18. So already H. Ewald, *Geschichte des Volkes Israel* (7 vols; Göttingen: 1864–1868) 3.524; C. F. Keil, *Commentar über die Bücher der Makkabäer* (Leipzig: Dörffling und Franke, 1875) 230. See also Abel, *Livres*, 257. K.-D. Schunck, "1. Makkabäerbuch," *JSHRZ* 1.4.287–373, esp. p. 358, is dissatisfied by all existing interpretations and assumes a textual corruption. He thinks that the original text had something like "the city of the people of God" or "Jerusalem."

19. J. T. Nelis, *I Makkabeeën uit de grondtekst vertaald en uitgelegd* (De Boeken van het Oude Testament 6; Bussum: J. J. Romen, 1972) 238, assumes that λαός and δῆμος are synonyms in 1 Macc 14:25–49. Cf. the beginning of 14:35 with 14:25.

20. 1 Macc 14:41: οἱ Ιουδαῖοι καὶ οἱ ἱερεῖς τὸ ἔθνος: 14:28, 29, 30, 32 (twice), 35 (twice).

21. Grimm, "Das erste Buch," 214, assumes a wrong translation of the Hebrew original here (a hophal form interpreted as a hiphil) and proposes to write ἐγνωρίσαμεν ὑμῖν with the Syriac version and mss 19, 64, 93. Keil, *Commentar*, 231, Schunck, "1. Makkabäerbuch," 358, and Goldstein, *I Maccabees*, 503, follow him.

22. Abel, *Livres*, 257. B. Risberg, "Textkritische und exegetische Anmerkungen zu den Makkabäerbüchern," *Beiträge zur Religionswissenschaft* 2 (1918) 6–31, esp. pp. 15–16, suggests the reading ἐγνωρίσθη, followed by Schunck, "1. Makkabäerbuch," 358; Goldstein, *I Maccabees*, 503; 509; Sievers, *Hasmoneans*, 121–22. The introduction of the decree offers us still another possibility, since ἐγνώρισεν might refer to the δῆμος in 14:25. In that case Simon and his sons may well be indicated by "us" in 14:28, since the δῆμος wished to thank Simon and his sons. This interpretation would solve another difficulty further on: the transition of the preamble to the decision (see below), but the first person

plural pronoun does not match the references to Simon in the third person in the decree.

23. Most scholars assume that there are two main sections, but there is some difference of opinion about the beginning of the second section, see H. Bévenot, *Die beiden Makkabäerbücher übersetzt und erklärt* (Die Heilige Schrift des Alten Testaments 4.4; Bonn: Peter Hanstein, 1931), 157–58; Abel, *Livres*, 254–55, 257, 260–62; J. C. Dancy, *A Commentary on I Maccabees* (Oxford: Blackwell, 1954) 183; Nelis, *I Makkabeeën*, 236–37 (who assumes that the second section starts with 14:46, but also would like to change the sequence of the verses including 14:41–45 in the decision of the decree); Goldstein, *I Maccabees*, 503.

24. Grimm, "Das erste Buch," 216; Keil, *Commentar*, 233; E. Kautzsch, "Das erste Buch der Makkabäer," *Die Apokryphen und Pseudepigraphen des Alten Testaments* (ed. E. Kautzsch; 2 vols; Tübingen: Mohr, 1900) 1.76; Abel, *Livres*, 260; Dancy, *Commentary*, 185; J. R. Bartlett, *The First and Second Books of the Maccabees* (The Cambridge Bible Commentary on the New English Bible; Cambridge: Cambridge University Press, 1973) 195, 197; Goldstein, *I Maccabees*, 507; Schunck, "1. Makkabäerbuch," 359; Martola, *Capture*, 231 n. 8; Sievers, *Hasmoneans*, 123 n. 79. B. Niese, "Kritik der beiden Makkabäerbücher nebst Beiträge zur Geschichte der makkabäischen Erhebung," *Hermes* 35 (1900) 268–307; 453–527, esp. p. 463, maintains the ὅτι and argues that the decree does not establish Simon's high priesthood, but presupposes it.

25. Sievers, *Hasmoneans*, 124–27, offers a detailed discussion of Simon's powers.

26. With Bévenot, *Makkabäerbücher*, 157; J. C. VanderKam, "People and High Priesthood in Early Maccabean Times," *The Hebrew Bible and Its Interpreters* (eds. W. H. Propp, B. Halpern, and D. N. Freedman; San Diego: Eisenbrauns, 1990) 205–25, esp. p. 213, with references. Cf. οἱ Ἰουδαῖοι καὶ οἱ ἱερεῖς εὐδόκησαν, 14:41; εὐδόκησεν πᾶς ὁ λαός, 14:46, and καὶ ἐπεδέξατο Σιμων καὶ εὐδόκησεν, 14:47. Nelis, *I Makkabeeën*, 237 argues that the decision starts with verse 46.

27. It is missing only in cod. 71.

28. Cod. A reads ἠκούσθη instead of ἤκουσεν.

29. See, e.g., NRSV l.c., Abel, *Livres*, 259; Dancy, *Commentary*, 185; Bartlett, *First and Second Books*, 195, 197; Nelis, *I Makkabeeën*, 240; Goldstein, *I Maccabees*, 487; Schunck, "1. Makkabäerbuch," 359.

30. Cf. Grimm, "Das erste Buch," 216.

31. With Dancy, *Commentary*, 185.

32. Cf. Bévenot, *Makkabäerbücher*, 158–59; Bartlett, *First and Second Books*, 197.

33. Abel, *Livres*, 254–55, 257, 260–61, also assumes that 14:49 forms the end of the decree. K.-D. Schunck, *Die Quellen des I. und II. Makkabäerbuches*

(Halle: VEB Max Niemeyer Verlag, 1954) 35, notes that the treasury also functioned as archive of the high priest.

34. Sievers, *Hasmoneans*, 105–6, rightly argues that the great assembly only confirmed Simon's high priesthood and did not appoint him as high priest.

VanderKam, "People," 211–19, links 1 Macc 14:27–49 to 1 Macc 13:1–9 and argues that Simon received the high priesthood during the meeting described in 13:1–9 from ὁ λαός, which he takes to be Simon's military companions. Objections to this ingenious view are that the redactor of 1 Maccabees remains silent about such a chain of events and that the λαός does not necessarily refer to soldiers in the decree. A more probable assumption is that Simon, like Jonathan (1 Macc 10:20) and several others of his predecessors, was appointed by the Seleucid ruler and that his high priesthood was afterwards confirmed by the Jews, as Eric Gruen pointed out to me in his oral response to this paper.

35. Without offering many details, he refers to the Monumentum Adulitanum (the Adoulis inscription, *OGIS* 54), the Tabulae Triumphales, the Monumentum Ancyranum and the Tabula Heracleensis, which reports the powers transferred to Vespasian by the Senate, Grimm, "Das erste Buch," 212.

36. Bévenot, *Makkabäerbücher*, 156: "ähnliche Ehrentafeln in den Kanopund Rosetta-Inschriften."

37. Abel, *Livres*, 254–55.

38. Bartlett, *First and Second Books*, 196.

39. Goldstein, *I Maccabees*, 501. He considers two inscriptions important parallel documents of 1 Macc 14:27–49: a Greek text of the politeuma of Idumean refugees living in Memphis honoring a certain Dorion (*OGIS* 737, 112 BCE) and a Phoenician document from the community of the Sidonians living in Piraeus (96 BCE). The first document has been discussed, among others, by U. Rappoport, "Les Iduméens en Égypte," *RPh* 3rd series 43 (1969) 73–82, and D. Thompson Crawford, "The Idumenans of Memphis and the Ptolemaic politeumata," *Atti del XVII congresso internazionale di papirologia* (3 vols; Naples: Centro Internazionale per lo Studio dei Papiri Ercolanesi) 1069–75. G. Lüderitz, "What is the Politeuma?" *Studies in Early Jewish Epigraphy* (AGJU 21; ed. J. W. van Henten and P. W. van der Horst; Leiden: Brill, 1994) 183–225, esp. p. 199, interprets the politeuma as "the decision taking body of the city," which implies that Dorion was honored by the city of Memphis as well as by the Idumeans from that city. See the criticism by J. Bingen, "Épigraphie grecque d'Égypte: La prose sur pierre," *Chronique d'Égypte* 69 (1994) 152–67, esp. pp. 157–58. The second text can be found in H. Donner and W. Röllig, *Kanaanäische und aramäische Inschriften* (Wiesbaden: Harrassowitz, 1966–1969, 2nd ed.) no. 60.

40. Abel, *Livres*, 255.

41. As Edgar Krentz points out in his response to this paper elsewhere in this book. Relevant texts would also be the Φιλάνθρωπα-decrees of the

Ptolemies with lists of the king's benefactions. See G. Hölbl, *Geschichte des Ptolemäerreiches: Politik, Ideologie und religiöse Kultur von Alexander dem Grossen bis zur römischen Eroberung* (Darmstadt: Wissenschaftliche Buchgesellschaft, 1994) 139. Sievers, *Hasmoneans*, 122, assumes an analogy with the senatus consultum of 69 CE, which confirmed Vespasian's powers and emperorship (H. Dessau, *Inscriptiones Latinae Selectae* no. 244). This document is, however, limited to a description of Vespasian's powers and not at all an honorary inscription.

42. W. Huss, "Die in ptolemäischer Zeit verfassten Synodal-Dekrete der ägyptischen Priester," *ZPE* 88 (1991) 189–208, offers a survey of the relevant documents, a brief description of their contents as well as full references to copies and editions. See also P. W. Pestman, "De 'Steen van Rosette': wat staat er eigenlijk op?" *Vreemdelingen in het land van farao* (ed. P. W. Pestman et al.; Zutphen: Terra, 1985) 43–54.

43. Six copies. Greek version in *OGIS* I no. 56; *SB* no. 8858; *SEG* 18 no. 634; recent reeditions of the Greek version are offered by E. Bernand, *Inscriptions grecques d'Égypte et de Nubie au Musée du Louvre* (Paris: Éditions du CNRS, 1992) no. 1, and A. Bernand, *La prose sur pierre dans l'Égypte hellénistique et romaine* (2 vols; Paris: Éditions du CNRS, 1992) nos. 8–10 (commentary and references: 2.30–36). The Demotic text has been edited by W. Spiegelberg, *Der demotische Text der Priesterdekrete von Kanopus und Memphis (Rosettana)* (Heidelberg: Winter, 1922) 3–37; the hieroglyphic version by K. Sethe, *Hieroglyphische Urkunden der griechisch-römischen Zeit* (3 vols; Urkunden des ägyptischen Altertums 2; Leipzig: Hinrichs, 1904) 125–54. Canopus was located at the coast near Alexandria. Further references: Huss, "Synodal-Dekrete," 192; 201.

44. Three copies. H. Gauthier and H. Sottas, *Un décret trilingue en l'honneur de Ptolémée IV* (Cairo: IFAO, 1925) 32–40 and 2–7 offer editions of the Demotic and hieroglyphic versions. A reedition of all extant Greek fragments, Spiegelberg's translation of the Demotic version and a commentary on the three versions of this decree is given by H.-J. Thissen, *Studien zum Raphiadekret* (Beiträge zur klassischen Philologie 23, Meisenheim am Glan: Anton Hain, 1966); a reedition of the Greek fragments, translations and a commentary by Bernand, *La Prose*, nos. 12–14, 1.36–42; 2.37–44. Further references: *SEG* 8 no. 504a; 18 nos. 632–33; Huss, "Synodal-Dekrete," 194; 202. The Greek version of the Raphia decree is transmitted in fragments on three stones and a papyrus (PMünchen 3.1 no. 45). The first and the third stone as well as the papyrus offer only the introduction of the decree with part of the date and the royal titles (stone 1: *SB* no. 4244; *SEG* 8 no. 504a; Bernand, *La Prose*, no. 13; stone 3: *SB* no. 10039; *SEG* 18 no. 633; PMünchen: J. C. Shelton, "45. Königstitulatur des Ptolemaios Philopator," *Griechische Urkundenpapyri der Bayerischen Staatsbibliothek München Teil I* (ed. U. Hagedorn, D. Hagedorn et al.; Stuttgart:

Teubner, 1986) 3–6 with references; these three fragments can also be found in Thissen, *Studien*, 10–11). The second stone offers two fragments of the decree itself, corresponding with Demotic version lines 27–33 and 39–40; *SB* no. 7172; *SEG* 8 no. 467; Thissen pp. 20 and 24; Bernand, *La Prose*, no. 14.

45. Three copies. Greek version: *OGIS* I 90; *SB* nos. 8232; 8299; *SEG* 8 nos. 463; 784; 16 no. 855; 33 no. 1357. A recent reedition of the Greek versions offers Bernand, *La Prose*, nos. 16–18 (commentary: 2.46–56). The Demotic version has been edited by Spiegelberg, *Priesterdekrete*, 38–65; the hieroglyphic one by Sethe, *Urkunden*, 3.169–98. Further references: Huss, "Synodal-Dekrete," 195; 202. Rosetta was located near the coast in the Nile delta, east of Canopus. Several English translations have been published, including in C. Andrews, *The Rosetta Stone* (London: British Museum Publications, 1981) 25–28.

46. Initially, the first Philae decree (dating from 185/4), which concerns the enthronement of the living Apis bull, was considered older than the second Philae decree, which may date from September 12, 186 BCE. Only one copy of the second Philae decree has been transmitted to us. It is inscribed on the wall of the House of Birth of the Isis temple on the island of Philae. There are, however, three fragments of the hieroglyphic version. The hieroglyphic version has been edited by Sethe, *Urkunden*, 3.214–30; both Demotic and hieroglyphic versions as well as their translations are in W. M. Müller, *The Bilingual Decrees of Philae* (Egyptological Researches 3; Washington: Carnegie Institution, 1920) 57–88. Further references: Huss, "Synodal-Dekrete," 196; 202.

47. Huss, "Synodal-Dekrete," discusses several other priestly decrees, of which often only small fragments have survived. In his opinion, the latest of these decrees may date from 112 BCE, see pp. 199–200.

48. Canopus Greek ll. 1–3: year indicated by year of the king and priests; Raphia Greek ll. 1–7 (Stone 1 and 3; PMünchen ll. 1–13); Demotic ll. 1–5; Rosetta Greek ll. 1–6; Philae II Hier. lacuna; Demotic ll. 1–3 (year 19 conjectured on the basis of Philae I).

49. Βασιλεύοντος Πτολεμαίου τοῦ Πτολεμαίου καὶ Ἀρσινόης, θεῶν Ἀδελφῶν, ἔτους ἐνάτου, ἐπὶ ἱερέως Ἀπολλωνίδου τοῦ | Μοσχίωνος Ἀλεξάνδρου, καὶ θεῶν Ἀδελφῶν καὶ θεῶν Εὐεργετῶν, κανηφόρου Ἀρσινόη[ς] Φιλαδέλφου Μενεκρατείας τῆς | Φιλάμμονος, μηνὸς Ἀπελλαίου ἑβδόμηι, Αἰγυπτίων δὲ Τῦβι ἑπτακαιδεκάτηι . . . (ll. 1–3). See R. Bagnall and P. Derow, *Greek Historical Documents: The Hellenistic Period* (Chico, Calif.: Scholars Press, 1981).

50. Ptolemy IV Philopator integrated the independent cult for the first couple (Ptolemy I Soter and Berenice I) with this ruler cult, which was afterwards extended to later couples up to the ruling one, Hölbl, *Geschichte*, 88.

51. Discussions of these titles found in Thissen, *Studien*, 27–46; C. Onasch, "Zur Königsideologie der Ptolemäer in den Dekreten von Kanopus

und Memphis (Rosettana)," *Archiv für Papyrusforschung* 24/25 (1976) 137–55; C. G. Johnson, "Ptolemy V and the Rosetta Decree: The Egyptianization of the Ptolemaic Kingship," *Ancient Society* 26 (1995) 145–55, and Shelton, "45. Königstitulatur."

52. Rosetta Greek ll. 1–2: καὶ παραλαβόντος τὴν βασιλείαν παρὰ τοῦ πατρός, κυρίου βασιλειῶν, μεγαλοδόξου, τοῦ τὴν Αἴγυπτον καταστησαμένου καὶ τὰ πρὸς τοὺς θεοὺς εὐσεβοῦς, ἀντιπάλων ὑπερτέρου, τοῦ τὸν βίον τῶν ἀνθρώπων ἐπανορθώσαντος, κυρίου τριακονταετηρίδων. Cf. the first lines of the various Greek versions of the Raphia decree.

53. Thissen, *Studien*, 80–81; Onasch, "Königsideologie." For a criticism of this view: Johnson, "Ptolemy V." The discussion depends partly on one's estimation of the intensity of the interaction between king and priests and the involvement of the king with his Egyptian subjects. The decrees may have been the result of a compromise between king and priests, which would make the interpretation of Thissen and Onasch more probable, but the evidence is too meager for a definite conclusion.

54. Canopus Greek l. 3; cf. l. 74; Rosetta Greek l. 7; cf. l. 53.

55. See also Canopus Greek ll. 3–7; Raphia Demotic ll. 5–7; Philae II Hier. l. 4; Demotic l. 3.

56. Trans. Andrews, slightly changed. Cf. the enumeration of the categories of priests in Canopus Greek ll. 3–4: οἱ ἀρχιερεῖς καὶ προφῆται καὶ οἱ εἰς τὸ ἄδυτον εἰσπορευόμενοι πρὸς τὸν στολισμὸν τῶν θεῶν καὶ πτεροφόραι καὶ ἱερογραμματεῖς καὶ οἱ ἄλλοι ἱερεῖς οἱ συναντήσαντες ἐκ τῶν κατὰ τὴν χώραν ἱερῶν....

57. Cf. Pestman, "Steen van Rosette," 46.

58. Canopus Greek ll. 7–19; Rosetta Greek ll. 9–12; Raphia Demotic ll. 17–20; 21–23; 26.

59. Cf. εὐεργετέω Canopus ll. 8–9; εὐεργεσία l. 18; Rosetta l. 9; cf. 11; 34. Also Raphia Demotic ll. 7, 26, 30; Philae II Hier. ll. 5–8; 10; Demotic ll. 4–7; 8. Thissen, *Studien*, 34; 51; 58–60.

60. Raphia Demotic ll. 28–29; Greek fragment A of the second stone, ll. 9–18.

61. Philae II Hier. ll. 7–8; Demotic ll. 5–7; also Raphia Demotic ll. 18; 28–29; Rosetta Greek ll. 33–35.

62. See for the Greek text of this fragment and a translation the appendix to this article.

63. Rosetta l. 25: χορηγήσας εἰς αὐτὰ χρημάτων πλῆθος οὐκ ὀλίγον. Cf. χορηγία Canopus l. 10, Thissen, *Studien*, 65.

64. Pestman, "Steen van Rosette," 47.

65. E.g., Rosetta Greek ll. 12–19; 28–31.

66. Raphia Demotic ll. 18; 28–30; Greek fragment A ll. 14–25; Rosetta ll. 11, 21, 25, 33–34; Philae II Hier. ll. 7–8; 11; Demotic ll. 5–7.

67. The Canopus-decree also praises the beneficial measures to counter the hunger because of the insufficient rising of the Nile, including the importation of grain from Syria, Phoenicia, Cyprus and other regions (Greek ll. 13-20).

68. Canopus Greek ll. 19-20; cf. Raphia Demotic l. 30; Greek fragment A ll. 26-28; Rosetta Greek ll. 35-36; Philae II Hier. ll. 8-9; Demotic l. 7.

69. Canopus ll. 20-73; Raphia Demotic ll. 30-42; Greek fragment A ll. 28-34; fragment B ll. 1-15; Rosetta Greek ll. 36-53. Cf. Philae II Hier. ll. 12e-17c; Demotic ll. 10a-14d (increasing of the honors of king and queen, including the setting up of statues of both of them in "the (twofold) holi[est!] place(s) of every adytum(!), on (i.e., bearing) his name, (in) the court of the multitude of the temple" (Hier. ll. 14b-c)/ "[. . . in] every temple, in the place which (is) (the most) prominent of the temple" Demotic l. 11e).

70. This title refers to the two cult names of Ptolemy V, who were both interpreted in line with the old Egyptian royal ideology, implying that the king was the appearance of the royal god Horus as well as the "perfect one," L. Koenen, "Die Adaptation ägyptischer Königsideologie am Ptolemäerhof," *Egypt and the Hellenistic World* (Proceedings of the International Colloquium Leuven—24-26 May 1982; Studia Hellenistica 27; ed. E. Van 't Dack, P. Van Dessel, and W. Van Gucht; Leuven: Katholieke Universiteit Leuven-Peeters, 1983) 143-90, esp. pp. 157, 168; Hölbl, *Geschichte,* 147. In the Raphia decree the fourth section also includes a festival to commemorate the victory at Raphia (Demotic ll. 36-38). Cf. Raphia Demotic l. 17: "Manche gaben ihm einen Goldkranz, indem sie verkündeten (versprachen), ihm eine Königsstatue aufzustellen und ihm einen Tempel zu bauen" (trans. Spiegelberg).

71. See for example the photographs of the second Raphia stone in Thissen, *Studien* Ill. 1, 3 and 4, and the descriptions of the stones in Bernand, *La Prose,* 2.30; 32; 37; 40-1; 46; 54-5.

72. Cf. Philiae II Hier. ll. 17-18; Demotic ll. 14-15.

73. As is still argued by Sievers, *Hasmoneans,* 120 n. 67.

74. About the most probable explanation of ασαραμελ see §2.

75. Bernand, *La Prose,* 2.48, notes in connection with the Memphis decree of 196 (Rosetta) that the reasons for honoring Ptolemy V Epiphanes concern all his subjects.

76. Cf. the Philae II decree about the location of the statue and image of king and queen: in "the (twofold) holi[est!] place(s) of every adytum(!), on (i.e., bearing) his name, (in) the court of the multitude of the temple" (Hier. ll. 14b-c).

77. A picture of the Isis temple with an indication of the decree's location is found in G. Haeny, "A Short Architectural History of Philae," *BIFAO* 85 (1985) 197-233, esp. p. 225 with fig. 4.

78. About the temple island of Philae, see E. Vassilika, *Ptolemaic Philae* (Orientalia Lovaniensia analecta 34; Leuven: Peeters, 1989); D. Arnold, *Die*

Tempel Ägyptens: Götterwohnungen, Kultstätten, Baudenkmäler (Zürich: Artemis & Winkler, 1992) 91–93 with references.

79. About the temple court for the laity, see Müller, *Bilingual Decrees*, 79 n. 3; H. Bonnet, *Reallexikon der ägyptischen Religionsgeschichte* (Berlin-New York: De Gruyter, 1971; 2nd ed.) 783; Thissen, *Studien*, 69.

80. Rosetta Greek ll. 6–8: οἱ ἀρχιερεῖς ... συναχθέντες; cf. 1 Macc 14:28 ἐπὶ συναγωγῆς μεγάλης ἱερέων....

81. Hölbl, *Geschichte*, 99–105.

82. Martin Goodman made this suggestion during the conference.

83. E.g., Canopus Greek ll. 5–6; 25: birthday on February 8 and regnal day on February 28; Rosetta Greek ll. 7, 44–48: commemoration of the king's (second) accession to the throne. See §3.

84. Raphia Demotic ll. 36–38; Philae II Hier. ll. 15b-16d; Demotic ll. 12e–13e.

85. NRSV: "... to their nation."

86. Hölbl, *Geschichte*, 84.

87. See §3 for references.

88. Hölbl, *Geschichte*, 83.

89. Joubert and Van Henten, "Jewish Families," 129–30.

90. Also 3:4. See J. C. H. Lebram, *Legitimiteit en charisma. Over de herleving van de contemporaine geschiedschrijving in het jodendom tijdens de 2e eeuw v. Chr.* (Leiden: Brill, 1980). Van Henten, "The Song of Praise for Judas Maccabaeus: Some Remarks on I Maccabees 3:3–9," *Give Ear to My Words: Psalms and other Poetry in and around the Hebrew Bible: Essays in Honour of Professor N. A. van Uchelen* (ed. J. Dyk; Amsterdam: Societas Hebraica Amstelodamensis, 1996) 199–206.

91. Of course, one cannot exclude the possibility that similar correspondences occur in related documents from other peoples surrounding the Jews.

92. The variant readings in 1 Macc 14:35, the verse which interrupts the list of Simon's benefactions by a reference to an earlier decision by the people to make Simon its leader, are of interest in this connection. NRSV translates: "The people saw Simon's faithfulness (τὴν πίστιν with ed. Rahlfs and ed. Kappler) and the glory that he had resolved to win for his people . . . (NRSV: "nation"). Some of the Greek manuscripts and the Vulgate read or presuppose τὴν πρᾶξιν referring to Simon's deeds and cod. V combines both readings. Grimm, "Erste Buch der Maccabäer," 215, proposes to read with these textual witnesses πρᾶξιν. His suggestion that πίστιν originates from a wrong interpretation of the abbreviation PN (such an abbreviation was not usual as far as I know) or under influence of the πίστιν later in the verse is followed by Keil, *Commentar*, 232, and Dancy, *Commentary*, 185. Bartlett, *First and Second Books*, 196, interprets *pistis* as patriotism; Abel, *Livres*, 259, considers the reading πίστιν certain,

but notes at the same time that πρᾶξιν would fit very well; Goldstein, *I Maccabees*, 504, reads τὴν πίστιν . . . καὶ πρᾶξιν with cod. V.

93. See §2 with the refererence to Sievers, *Hasmoneans*, in footnote 25.

94. Joubert and Van Henten, "Jewish Families," 131.

95. Hölbl, *Geschichte*, 88. For an interesting discussion of Jewish and non-Jewish elements in the presentation of Hasmonean rulership, see Rappoport, "Hasmonean State," 494–501.

96. Raphia Demotic l. 25, as interpreted by Thissen, *Studien*, 62.

97. C. Préaux, "Esquisse d'une histoire des révolutions égyptiennes sous les Lagides," *Chronique d'Égypte* 11 (1936) 522–52; F. Übel, "ΤΑΡΑΧΗ ΤΩΝ ΑΙΓΥΠΤΙΩΝ. Ein Jenaer Papyruszeugnis der nationalen Unruhen Oberägyptens in der ersten Hälfte des 2. vorchristlichen Jahrhunderts," *Archiv für Papyrusforschung* 17 (1962) 147–62; P. W. Pestman, "Harmachis et Anchmachis, deux Rois indigènes du temps des Ptolemées," *Chronique d'Égypte* 40 (1965) 157–70. W. Peremans, "Les révolutions égyptiennes sous les Lagides," *Das ptolemäische Ägypten* (ed. H. Maehler and V. M. Strocka; Mainz: von Zabern, 1978) 39–50; W. Clarysse, "Hurgonaphor et Chaonnophris, les derniers pharaons indigènes," *Chronique d'Égypte* 53 (1978) 243–53.

98. Hölbl, *Geschichte*, 139.

99. Other associations of the king and Horus can be found in the Raphia decree Demotic ll. 32; 35–36; 41; on the stele bearing the decree Ptolemy is portrayed on horseback, killing the captive enemy kneeling before him like Horus killing his opponent Seth-Typhon, Thissen, *Studien*, 53–56; 63; 67–73; 78 and illustrations 1 and 2. The picture shows at least some assimilation of Greek and Egyptian views, since the eye-catching horse is a Greek contribution to this old combat scene of Egyptian myth. Cf. the statues referred to in the Philae II decree Hier. ll. 13f–15b; Demotic ll. 11c–12e, and Rosetta Greek ll. 10; 26; 38–39.

100. Thissen, *Studien*, 29; 33; 37; Koenen, "Adaption"; Onasch, "Königsideologie."

101. Sievers, *Hasmoneans*, 124–25, argues that the decree in 1 Macc 14 was intended to counter opposition to Simon.

SIX

The Honorary
Decree for Simon
the Maccabee

EDGAR KRENTZ

First Macc 14:25–49 gives the text of a decree honoring Simon Mac*f*abeus (καὶ τοῦτο τὸ ἀντίγραφον τῆς γραφῆς, 14:27; cf. 14:49). It introduces the decree by saying that the people heard the accounts of Simon's and his family's accomplishments ('Ως δὲ ἤκουσεν ὁ δῆμος τῶν λόγων τούτων, 14:25). In thanks (τίνα χάριν ἀποδώσομεν) for the liberty he won in war (ἔστησαν αὐτῷ ἐλευθερίαν, 14:26) they engraved bronze tablets and placed them on stelai on Mt. Zion (κατέγραψαν ἐν δέλτοις χαλκαῖς καὶ ἔθεντο ἐν στήλαις ἐν ὄρει Σιων). The decree itself opens with the date ('Οκτωκαιδεκάτῃ Ελουλ ἔτους δευτέρου καὶ ἑβδομηκοστοῦ καὶ ἑκατοστοῦ—καὶ τοῦτο τρίτον ἔτος ἐπὶ Σιμωνος ἀρχιερέως μεγάλου ἐν ασαραμελ, 14:27) and the legal formula enacting it (ἐπὶ συναγωγῆς μεγάλης ἱερέων καὶ λαοῦ καὶ ἀρχόντων ἔθνους καὶ τῶν πρεσβυτέρων τῆς χώρας ἐγνώρισεν ἡμῖν, 14:27). There follows the reason for the decree (ἐπεί, 14:27): the people saw Simon's trustworthiness and public reputation (καὶ εἶδεν ὁ λαὸς τὴν πίστιν τοῦ Σιμωνος καὶ τὴν δόξαν, 14:35) and appointed him their leader and high priest (ἔθεντο αὐτὸν ἡγούμενον αὐτῶν καὶ ἀρχιερέα, 14:35). Finally, the decision is made by the Jews and the priests (οἱ Ιουδαῖοι καὶ οἱ ἱερεῖς εὐδόκησαν) to appoint Simon their lifelong leader, high priest (ἔθεντο αὐτὸν ἡγούμενον αὐτῶν [ethnarch? cf. 14:47] καὶ ἀρχιερέα)[1] and military commander (τοῦ εἶναι ἐπ' αὐτῶν στρατηγόν, 14:42), with supreme authority in religious (περὶ τῶν ἁγίων), political, and military affairs (ἐπὶ τῆς χώρας καὶ ἐπὶ τῶν ὅπλων καὶ ἐπὶ τῶν ὀχυρωμάτων, 14:42). All should obey him; in his name edicts were to go forth (v. 43). They granted him symbols of honor, purple and gold clothing (ὅπως περιβάλληται πορφύραν

146

καὶ χρυσοφορῇ, 14:43). Both people and priests were legally bound to obedience (14:44, 45). The decree ends with the decision of the people that Simon act in accordance with their decree (εὐδόκησεν πᾶς ὁ λαὸς θέσθαι Σιμωνι ποιῆσαι κατὰ τοὺς λόγους τούτους, 14:46). Simon agreed to be high priest, general, and ethnarch of the Jews and priests, in charge of everything (v. 47). They (people and priests?) engraved the decree on bronze tablets and placed it in a conspicuous place inside the temple precinct, with a copy in the treasury (14:48, 49). The decree is clearly honorific, ascribing a high position to Simon with congruent symbols.

Prof. J. Willen van Henten illuminated the decree in 1 Macc 14:25–49 (dated 140 BCE) by comparing it to four decrees honoring Ptolemaic rulers, (dating from 238, 217, 196, and 186 BCE) which antedate the decision in 1 Macc 14. Each owes its origin to priestly activity.[2] I will supplement his contribution by citing other texts from the same era, drawn from laws and decrees from Syria and Asia Minor in the collection edited by Charles Michel.[3] A number of inscriptions fall into this same period: (1) the Ionian Confederation honoring Antiochus I (ca 266 BCE);[4] (2) Elea honoring Attalos III (135 BCE);[5] (3) Ilion honoring Antiochus I (ca 277 BCE);[6] (4) Antioch on the Orontes honoring Eumenes II (175 BCE);[7] (5) Akragas honoring Demetrius of Syracuse (210 BCE);[8] (6) decree honoring Zeno, commander under Ptolemy Soter (290 BCE).[9] And one might add, though it is much later, the decree of the league of Asian cities honoring Caesar Augustus (9 BCE).[10]

Professor van Henten identifies five recurrent sections in these honorary decrees: (1) date; (2) reference to the assembly of those who issue the decree; (3) motivation for the decision.[11] I should prefer to name this the preamble, since it is really a part of the enactment. Decrees regularly put the term ψήφισμα before this statement;[12] (4) the decision itself; and (5) provisions about the publication of the decree. He also finds these five sections or features in the text of 1 Macc 14:25–49. Here there are some problematic areas.[13]

I appreciate the attention to form, since it is one method of categorizing a text's genre and function. These five recurrent components are the standard structure in Ptolemaic, Syrian, and Asian inscriptions. In short, this is the generic form for an honorary decree, shared also by the decree in 1 Maccabees.

But some questions arise. (1) The date is clearly present in the Simon decree (14:27). There is an enigmatic phrase in 1 Macc 14:27, ἐν ἀσαραμελ. Van Henten interprets the phrase as a transcription of the Hebrew הצר עם אל, meaning "in the temple court surrounding the court of priests."[14] This is a possible, but problematic interpretation, since it is not normal to name a location at this point in an honorific inscription.[15] But other interpretations are at least possible. The new edition of Schürer offers the following note:

The mysterious words ἐνσαραμελ or ἐνασαραμελ have been interpreted as part of the titulature; see Derenbourg, *op. cit.*, pp. 450–51. Σαραμελ, presumably הצר עם אל = ἐθνάρκης. But the ἐν preceding it remains a puzzle. Possibly σεγεν = סגן stood here originally, corresponding to the Greek στρατηγός (cf. vol. II, §24, 3). See R. H. Charles, *Apoc.* I, p. 119. Abel, *in loc.*, sees in the phrase a geographical expression עם אל חצר 'Courtyard of the People of God'. For a full discussion, see Schalit, *op. cit.*, Anhang XIV, although his own theory, ἐν ασαραμελ = ἐν ασαρᾷ (= עזרה) μεγάλη, 'in the great Temple courtyard', seems far-fetched.[16]

Jonathan Goldstein offers an interpretation based on Greek epigraphy. He argues that the EN is a corruption of KAI, since K was easily confused with E and AI read as N. He then interprets it to mean "Prince of God's people."[17] The enigmatic words remain enigmatic: temple court? ethnarch? prince? general or leader? This is quicksand on which it is difficult to erect an edifice.[18]

(2) The assembly members in 1 Maccabees are a problem. 1 Macc 14:28 speaks of a συναγωγὴ μεγαλή of priests, people, rulers of the ἔθνος, and elders. The Asian and Syrian inscriptions involve the people (the δῆμος) in the passing of the decree. The regular formula being ἀγαθῇ τυχῇ· ἔδοξεν τῇ βουλῇ καὶ τῷ δημῷ . . . or δέδοχθαι. The four decrees from Ptolemaic Egypt result from an assembly of priests and other religious functionaries. Do these priestly groups function as governmental bodies? That is, are they able to make decrees that also involve the citizen body (the δῆμος) in the process of enactment? Are these Egyptian decrees, which relate primarily to celebrations of the ruler within temple precincts, true parallels in terms of the legal bodies— assuming the great synagogue in 1 Maccabees was such a legal body.

First Macc 14:25 credits the people with the initiative in the enactment. Is it possible that the great synagogue meant the people and priests were the equivalent of the people and the archons of the people and the elders were the equivalent of the council? In short, the four names in 1 Macc 14:28 are puzzling. It is striking that later in the text of 1 Macc 14 the priests seem to disappear and the author speaks of the people, the δῆμος, taking the initiative about the decree.[19] The Asian and Syrian decrees are much closer to 1 Maccabees in this regard. The decree of Ilion honoring Antiochus I, for example, begins τύχηι τῆι ἀγαθῆι, δεδόχθαι τῆι βουλῆι καὶ τῶι δήμωι.[20]

(3) The preamble of the decree gives the motivation for the decision in typical fashion. Van Henten cites the use of ἐπεί, ἐπειδή in decrees honoring rulers to introduce the preamble, a usage which runs throughout the entire geographic region of these decrees, from Sicily to Egypt. Inscriptions often have the longer, more formal form ἐπειδή.[21]

The grounds for the decree list the benefactions performed by the honored ruler. Thus when Ilion honors Antiochus I, it is because of his zeal (σπουδή) and respect for his position (φιλοτιμία) that led him to inaugurate peace and set the affairs of the cities in order, that is his virtue (ἀρετή).[22] Antiochus honors Eumenes because he demonstrated virtue, a well-disposed mind, and the ideal of goodness (ἀρετῆς ἕνεκεν καὶ εὐνοίας καὶ καλοκἀγαθίας ἣν ἀπεδείξατο).[23] Eumenes was a model of benefaction, εὐεργεσία. 1 Maccabees follows the format in naming the benefactions of Simon.

(4) The decree proper (item 4) is introduced by some form of the verb δοκέω. The Rosetta inscription uses the phrase ἀγαθῆι τυχῆι, ἔδοξεν τοῖς ἱερεῦσι τῶν κατὰ τὴν χώραν ἱερῶν πάντων. ... In the Asiatic inscriptions the regular formula reads ἀγαθῆι τυχῆι, ἔδοξεν τῆ βούλη καὶ τῷ δημῷ. ... The Canopus inscription has a variation of the formula: ἀγαθῆι τυχῆι, δεδοχθαι τοῖς κατὰ τὴν χώραν ἱερεῦσι. The formula lists those who actually perform the legal procedure to enact a decree (a δόγμα). Recall the use of this formula in Acts 15: 22, 28: ἔδοξεν γὰρ τῷ πνεύματι τῷ ἁγίῳ καὶ ἡμῖν. ...

The Maccabees text is here problematic in several respects: it does not include the formula for legal enactment (a *terminus technicus*, as van Henten points out).[24] There may be the *bath qol* of that decision in 14:41 (οἱ Ἰουδαῖοι καὶ οἱ ἱερεῖς εὐδόκησαν), 46 (εὐδόκησεν πᾶς ὁ λαός), and 47 (καὶ ἐπεδέξατο Σιμων καὶ εὐδόκησεν) where the verb εὐδόκησεν is used, a variation on the verb δοκέω, as van Henten points out. In addition, there is nothing that corresponds to the ἀγαθῆι τυχῆι wish or the invocation of a god before the decision is reported. And one highly significant verbal complex is also completely absent, the use of the adjective εὐεργέτης and the noun εὐεργεσία. To be sure, *die Sache ist wohl da.* But the vocabulary that runs through the Canopus decree is not. The language of the decree is "mixed." There is clear evidence of formal legislative terminology—as the form is also there. But there is also—and I stress this—clear narrative style. The word ἐγνώρισεν in 14:28 is puzzling in context. The people "saw" (εἶδεν) his trustworthiness and appointed (ἔθεντο) him leader, high priest, etc. (14:35). "And they said (καὶ εἶπεν)" that the decree should be put on bronze tablets (14:48). These are all narrative statements, not legal enactments. The language is not carried through consistently.

(5) Provisions about the publication of the decree. The decision to set up a stele of stone or bronze is perfectly normal, both in Egypt and in Asia/Syria. The Ilion decree in honor of Antiochus I decrees that a gold equestrian statue of the ruler be set up ἐν τῷ ἐπιφανεστάτῳ τόπῳ ἐπὶ βήματι, with an inscription honoring him as benefactor and savior (εὐεργέτην καὶ σωτῆρα).[25] The inscription honoring Eumenes II from Antioch on the Orontes directs that "the decree be inscribed on stone stelai, set up in the agora by the statues of king Antiochus, in the temple of Athena Nikephoros, and in the temple of Apollo at Daphne."[26] The use of agora or temple as a prominent place to display a honorific decree is normal.

Some years ago Frederick Danker described the semantic field of honorific decrees:

> In brief, about eight centuries separate Homer and the flowering of Hellenistic Christian communities, yet the cultural phenomenon of interplay between people of excellence and those on whom they make their impact finds continuous celebration, with a fairly consistent pattern of themes and diction developing in the last five centuries preceding the reign of Caesar Augustus.[27]

There is no doubt that 1 Macc 14:25–49 uses this semantic field, the language of honorific inscriptions—whether one reads those from Egypt or elsewhere in the Greek-speaking Hellenistic world. But one cannot argue that Egypt is the primary source of this language. μία χέλιδων ἔαρ οὐ ποίει, "One swallow does not make a spring," as the old Greek proverb puts it. The legal formula for passing a decree is just too different. First Maccabees was originally written in Hebrew, according to Solomon Zeitlin and Goldstein.[28] That means that the language of the Greek text is shaped partly by the Semitic original and partly by the unnamed translator of our Greek text.[29] I agree with Prof. van Henten that the permanent appointment of Simon as high priest and ethnarch, functionally king, probably happened at Simon's "own instigation." And I would add that the translator, working at a later date, shaped the Greek text to support the heirs of Simon's claim to the hereditary kingship, signaled by permission to issue coinage (1 Macc 15:6).[30] By casting, somewhat incompletely, the elevation of Simon into the language of enkomiastic decrees honoring Hellenistic rulers, the author of 1 Maccabees positioned Simon's heirs well and thus served the Hasmonean dynasty's ongoing claim to regal status.[31]

Notes

1. Only until a trustworthy prophet arose (ἕως τοῦ ἀναστῆναι προφήτην πιστὸν).

2. See his paper in this volume for details.

3. Charles Michel, *Recueil d'inscriptions grecques* (Bruxelles: H. Lamertin, 1900); ibid., *Recueil d'inscriptions grecques, supplément* (Bruxelles: H. Lamertin, 1912–1927; reprint, Chicago: Ares, 1976). I will also give the number of the inscription from *OGIS* = Wilhelm Dittenberger, *Orientis Graeci Inscriptiones Selectae*. 2 vols. Hildesheim: Georg Olms Verlagsbuchhandlung, 1960 (= Leipzig, 1903).

4. Michel no. 486, *OGIS* no. 222.

5. Michel no. 515; *OGIS* no. 332.

6. Michel no. 525; *OGIS* no. 219.

7. Michel no. 550; *OGIS* no. 248.

8. Michel no. 553; this inscription from Sicily falls outside the immediate geographic area.

9. Michel, no. 1480.

10. *OGIS* no. 458.

11. Actually, this should be regarded as part of the decree itself.

12. See, for example, the Canopus decree (*OGIS* 56.3), Rosetta decree (*OGIS* 90.7), and, much later, the Priene inscription (*OGIS* 458.27).

13. On the form of decrees, see A. G. Woodhead, *The Study of Greek Inscriptions* (Cambridge: Cambridge University Press, 1967) 37–39; on 61 he notes the development of the preamble and the type of honors bestowed.

14. Van Henten refers to H. Ewald and F. M. Abel, *Livres,* 257.

15. So Jonathan A. Goldstein, *1 Maccabees.* AB 41 (Garden City, N.Y.: Doubleday, 1976) 501.

16. Emil Schürer, *The History of the Jewish People in the Age of Jesus Christ* (*175 B.C.–A.D. 135*). A New English Version revised and edited by Geza Vermes and Fergus Millar. Vol. I (Edinburgh: T. & T. Clark, 1973) 193–94, note 13.

17. Goldstein, 502–502. He cites the Syriac version in support.

18. J. C. Dancy, *A Commentary on I Maccabees* (Oxford: Basil Blackwell, 1954) 184 comments that Bevan follows Daremberg and translates the phrase "Prince of the People of God," the Hebrew equivalent of the Greek ethnarch. Dancy himself notes the ἐν before the term and inclines to "in the assembly of the people of God"—though Daremberg's interpretation fits the context better.

19. See 1 Macc 14:35, 46

20. Michel 525, line 14, 15 = *OGIS* 219.

21. Woodhead, 38–39, suggests that ἐπειδή is the usual term.

22. Michel 525, lines 9, 10 = *OGIS* 219.

23. Michel 550, lines 31, 32, p. 414 = *OGIS* 248, lines 33, 34.

24. Dancy, 183, comments that "it is not quite clear in this decree where the dividing line falls between the two [the benefactions of the honor and the decree itself] (see. 41 n.), but vv. 32–37 clearly belong to the former, vv. 41–45 to the latter." It is the absence of the technical terms that is responsible for the unclarity.

25. Michel 525, lines 36–38 + *OGIS* 219.

26. Michel 550, lines 52–56 + *OGIS* 248. See also the decree of Elea honoring Attalus III, which directs the placing of an inscribed marble stele in the precinct of Asklepius, in front of the temple (ναός), Michel 515, lines 59–62 + *OGIS* 332.

27. Frederick Danker, *Benefactor: Epigraphic Study of a Graeco-Roman and New Testament Semantic Field* (St. Louis: Clayton Publishing House, 1982) 20.

28. *The First Book of Maccabees,* English translation by Sidney Tedesche, introduction and commentary by Solomon Zeitlin (New York: Harper & Brothers for The Dropsie College, 1950) 33–34; Goldstein, 501.

29. I have not addressed all problems of interpretation in this brief paper, only those that bear on the formal analysis of it as an honorific decree.

30. Victor Tcherikover, *Hellenistic Civilization and the Jews* (Philadelphia: The Jewish Publication Society of America; Jerusalem: The Magnes Press, 1959) 250. There is no numismatic evidence that Simon ever acted on this permission. Hasmonean coinage begins with Aristobulus I.

31. Contrast the attitude expressed in Psalms of Solomon 17 which objects to a non-Davidic monarch.

SEVEN

Greek in Jewish Palestine in Light of Jewish Epigraphy

PIETER W. VAN DER HORST

I, Justus, the son of Leontius and of Sappho, lie [here] dead,
[I] who, after having plucked the fruit of all [kinds of] wisdom,
left the light, [and left also] my poor parents in endless mourning,
and my brothers too, alas, in my Beth She'arim.
And having gone to Hades, I, Justus, lie here now
with many of my own kindred, since mighty Fate so willed.
—Be of good courage, Justus, [for] no one is immortal.[1]

This epitaph of a boy with a Latin name, the son of a father with a Greek name and a mother with a Greek name (that of the best-known Greek poetess at that), is written in Homeric hexameters; it follows a number of well-known Greek conventions in the composition of epitaphs; it mentions Hades and Moira (the Greek goddess of Fate). Yet, it is Jewish! It was written by a Jew in the first half of the third century CE and it was found in the impressive catacombs of the rabbinic city of Beth She'arim, where famous rabbis were also buried since the beginning of the third century. And Justus—or at least his family— apparently felt at home there: the stone speaks, with "evident pleasure,"[2] of "*my* Beth She'arim" (line 4). Here we see our topic in a nutshell. But it is a topic that bristles with problems.

The study of the Hellenization of Palestine in the light of epigraphical sources is hampered right from the start by a very serious handicap. This handicap is that there is no comprehensive corpus of all the epigraphic material from the land of Israel covering the period between Alexander the Great and Muhammad. If we want to base our argument on a comprehensive survey of inscriptions for this near-millennium, we are completely at a loss, since one would have to consult many hundreds of books, periodicals, and museum catalogues in order to get an overview of the evidence. Collecting and publishing all this material would be a mammoth task far beyond the capabilities of one scholar; only a team would be able to do so. Most fortunately there is such a team now, but the project is still in its infancy (alas for me). The *Corpus Inscriptionum Iudaeae/Palestinae* (*CIIP*) will be a new corpus of all inscriptions, in all languages, arranged topographically, found in Israel (including the West Bank, Gaza, and the Golan Heights) and dating from the fourth century BCE to the seventh century CE. I owe this description to Professor Jonathan Price from Tel Aviv University, who initiated the whole enterprise. The corpus will include a full reediting of every text, a drawing or photograph, textual apparatus, English translation, and commentary. The estimate is that there will be between 6,000 and 7,000 texts in the corpus.[3] This is exactly the tool we need if we want to carry out the type of investigation that is the topic of this paper. But we simply do not have it now, so we will just have to make do. But what *do* we have?

As to the Jewish material, we have first of all the old Frey.[4] In the much maligned second volume of his *Corpus Inscriptionum Iudaicarum* (henceforth *CIJ*), he collected some 530 Jewish inscriptions from Palestine. This is still, in spite of all its shortcomings,[5] a very valuable collection, but when we compare the number of 530 texts to the estimated 1,800 texts in the provisional database of Jonathan Price (which admittedly is still incomplete), we can gauge how great the progress in this field has been in the past six decades or so. To mention only the most important partial collections that have appeared after 1952 and pertain to ancient Palestine, we have the group of epitaphs edited by B. Bagatti and J. T. Milik in their book *Gli scavi del Dominus Flevit* (*Monte Oliveto—Gerusalemme*). *Parte I: La necropoli del periodo romano* (Jerusalem: Franciscan Publishing House, 1958). We also have the fine volumes with the epitaphs from Beth She'arim by B. Mazar, *Beth She'arim I: Report on the Excavations 1936–1940* (Jerusalem: Massada, 1973), by M. Schwabe and B. Lifshitz, *Beth She'arim II: The Greek Inscriptions* (New Brunswick: Rutgers University Press, 1974), and by N. Avigad, *Beth She'arim III: Report on the Excavations during 1953–1958* (Jerusalem: Massada, 1976). There are two other important books in modern

Hebrew: J. Naveh, *On Stone and Mosaic. The Aramaic and Hebrew Inscriptions from Ancient Synagogues* (Jerusalem: Sifriyat Ma'ariv, 1978) and its Greek counterpart by L. Roth-Gerson, *The Greek Inscriptions from the Synagogues in Eretz-Israel* (Jerusalem: Yad Yitzhak ben Zvi, 1987). An important new collection can also be found in the publication by R. Hachlili of the epitaphs of the so-called Goliath family in Jericho ("The Goliath Family in Jericho: Funerary Inscriptions from a First-Century A.D. Jewish Monumental Tomb," *BASOR* 235 [1979] 31–65). And finally, there is the recent collection of ossuaries and their inscriptions by L. Y. Rahmani, *A Catalogue of Jewish Ossuaries in the Collections of the State of Israel* (Jerusalem: Israel Academy, 1994).[6] For the rest of the material one has to consult a very wide variety of scholarly journals over which most of the new finds are scattered (but especially the *Israel Exploration Journal* and the *Revue Biblique*), and the annual installments of the 'Bulletin Epigraphique' in the *Revue des études grecques* (since 1938) for the Greek material. The best way to keep track of new Jewish inscriptions in Greek, however, is to consult the section "Palaestina" in the annual *Supplementum Epigraphicum Graecum* (=*SEG*), even though, inevitably, it is always lagging years behind.[7] For tracing new inscriptions in Hebrew and Aramaic the *Bulletin d'épigraphie sémitique* (*BES*), published in the periodical *Syria* (since 1967) is the best tool.[8]

There is a considerable overlap between some of the above-mentioned collections that has to be taken into account. When we add up what we have in the volumes mentioned here and subtract the overlapping items, we arrive at a total of some 900 inscriptions, which is still a very far cry from the 1,800 in the *CIIP* database. The situation is still worse as far as Christian and Pagan material is concerned, and that is a good reason to limit ourselves here to the Jewish evidence in order not to complicate things further, although it is important to keep in mind that, if we leave the Jewish material aside, "from the third century BCE we find almost exclusively Greek inscriptions in Palestine."[9] And these run into the thousands (possibly some 6,000).

When we now try to establish the percentage of Greek inscriptions in the Jewish evidence, we find that of Frey's 530 inscriptions 315 (60 percent) are in Greek (several of them in fact being bilingual).[10] Of the 43 inscriptions from the cemetery of Dominus Flevit, 12 are in Greek (29 percent). In Beth She'arim, however, of the 246 epitaphs no less than 218 are in Greek (88 percent). Of the 32 tomb inscriptions of the Goliath

family, 17 are in Greek, which is 53 percent. And of Rahmani's 240 inscribed ossuaries, 87—16 of which are bilingual—are in Greek (37 percent).[11] These percentages vary widely, from 29 to 88 percent (and we
will have to come back to that), but anyway the overall average of Greek
inscriptions is slightly more than 53 percent.[12]

How does this compare to the average in the provisional database
of the *CIIP*? The percentage of Greek inscriptions in this comprehensive collection has not yet been established, but Professor Price was so
kind to let me know that his provisional estimate is that "of the Jewish
inscriptions well over half, I would say even 70 percent, have some Greek
writing on them."[13] He adds the important observation that this includes not only the inscriptions which are exclusively Greek but also the
considerable number which are bilingual, containing both Greek and
Hebrew or Aramaic. Interestingly enough, Latin makes no appearance
in the Jewish inscriptions from Palestine.[14] If for safety's sake we round
off Price's impression that the Greek material is well over half, maybe
even 70 percent to—say—60 percent, we see something very significant.
This is not only rather close to the average of 53 percent that we have
just arrived at, but it is also exactly the percentage of Greek inscriptions
in the old collection of Frey. So even though in the past 65 years[15] the
material has more than tripled, the numerical ratio of Greek and non-
Greek material has not changed at all![16] And that is a striking and very
important observation.

If more than half of the Jewish epigraphic material from the period
between Alexander and Muhammad is in Greek, what does that tell us?
Can we readily draw the conclusion that for more than half of the
Jewish people in their homeland their native language was Greek, not
Aramaic?[17] That would be overhasty, for we first have to address the
question of the representativeness of this material. Can we say, for instance, with Lee Levine, on the basis of the fact that some 37 percent of
the Jerusalem ossuaries are in Greek, that "we can *safely* [italics added]
set this number as the minimum percentage of those inhabitants in the
city who preferred Greek"?[18] Can we follow Martin Hengel who, on the
basis of some 40 percent Greek ossuary inscriptions in Jerusalem concludes as follows: "Auch wenn man davon ausgeht, daß Ossuarin-
schriften überwiegend von Gliedern der Mittel- und Oberschicht stam-
men, so darf man doch annehmen, daß ca. 10–15 percent der damaligen
Bewohner Jerusalems als Muttersprache Griechisch sprachen"?[19] Should

we agree with Baruch Lifshitz, who confidently states: "La proportion des textes épigraphiques grecs par rapport à la quantité des inscriptions découvertes à Jérusalem témoigne de l'emploi de la langue grecque par une partie assez considérable de la population de la ville"?[20] These are very difficult questions, the more so if we take seriously Josephus' somewhat enigmatic remark, "Our people do not favour those who have mastered the languages of many nations" (*Ant.* 20.264).[21]

Demographers of the ancient world constantly have to struggle with the problem of the scarcity and the questionable representativeness of the sources. To give an example: Of the various classes into which ancient Greek and Latin inscriptions fall, by far the largest numerically is that of epitaphs. In many tens of thousands of these inscriptions the age at death is mentioned. But, as a specialist in the epigraphy and demography of the Roman Empire has calculated,[22] even so we only know the age at death of about .015 percent of all people in the first five centuries of the Empire. (He made the calculation on the basis of the assumption that in 500 years there are approximately 16 generations, each of which on average counted some 20 million people; this total of some 320 million divided by the total number of inscriptions with age indication yields .015 percent). Even if these numbers needed to be substantially corrected, the overall picture would hardly change. We will always remain far below 1 percent of the total population. This fact raises the serious problem of how representative this less than 1 percent is for the population of the Empire as a whole.[23] As a matter of fact, that completely depends upon whether or not we can clearly get into the picture the possible distorting factors in the data at our disposal. There are distorting factors, although to what extent they really distort our picture is a matter of ongoing debate. Let us review here only the most important of them and try to find out how these factors may have influenced our Jewish material from Palestine.

Although it is certainly true that the only area in which the influence of Hellenistic culture upon the Jewish people can be more or less quantified is the realm of epigraphy,[24] we have to ask what is the statistical status of our data. To begin with the number of inscriptions as compared to the number of Jews in our period, we have to concede that it is indeed only an extremely tiny minority for whom we have their epitaphs or honorary inscriptions. If we take our period, spanning almost a thousand years, to have comprised about thirty-three generations (thirty years for one generation, for the sake of convenience), and if we take a generation as averaging one million Jews (in Palestine only, that is),[25] then we have 900 inscriptions for 33 million Jews: that is to say, one inscription for every 37,000 Jews. Even if the average number of Jews per generation would have to be further reduced or if we would take the ca. 1,800 inscriptions of the *CIIP* project as our basis, we would not even reach .025 percent. From a statistical point of view that is a hopeless situation, for what can we say about the 99.975 percent of other Jews whose tombstones or honorary inscriptions have not been preserved, if ever they had one? To put it another way: Is it possible that the Greek inscriptions belong only to a very tiny upper class of less than 1 percent of the Jews whereas the vast majority of the people would never phrase their inscriptions in Greek? This is an extremely improbable suggestion, it would seem to me, for the following reasons.

Many Jews were definitely too poor to erect tombstones inscribed with epitaphs, but that does not necessarily imply that the inscribed stones we do have all derive from the upper classes. There is ample evidence that the epitaphs in Greek represent a wide stratum of the population.[26] There is a great difference between a metrical epitaph in Homeric hexameters engraved upon luxurious and expensive sarcophagi with elaborate decorations on the one hand and poorly scratched names on potsherds or wall-plaster that marked the graves of deceased on the other (and we have many of the latter sort). The former is a manifestation of wealth and status; the latter is usually the contrary (though not necessarily so). To be sure, "the desire to emulate Graeco-Roman mores (and the means to do so) was far more pronounced among the upper than the lower social strata,"[27] but there are numerous very simple and poorly executed tombstones with inscriptions in poor Greek that undeniably stem from these lower strata of Jewish society. The persons who had their tombstones in Beth She'arim inscribed with Greek epitaphs include not only rabbis and public officers but also merchants and craftsmen.[28] Lieberman already wrote that "the very poverty and vulgarity of the language of these inscriptions shows that it was spoken by the people and not written by learned men only."[29] As to the many synagogue inscriptions in Greek collected by Lea Roth-Gerson,[30] there can be little doubt that most of them were meant to be read by the regular visitors of these buildings, that is, the common people who were members of the local community, who were supposed to be able to make sense of them. And no doubt they were. As Goodenough re-marked: "The Jews who went to the synagogues . . . admired the Aramaic or Hebrew but read the Greek."[31]

In this connection it is important to notice that it is not only in Jewish, but also in Samaritan synagogues that dedicatory or honorary inscriptions were in Greek. The seven inscriptions uncovered in the re-cently excavated Samaritan synagogue in El-Khirbe are all in Greek.[32] And that is not an isolated case. In Ramat Aviv, to the north of Tel Aviv, an excavation of an ancient Samaritan synagogue has yielded three in-scriptions: one in Samaritan Aramaic, two in Greek, the only complete one reading: "Blessing and peace be upon Israel and upon this place, Amen." And also in another Samaritan synagogue in ancient Palestine, in Beth Shean-Scythopolis, three of the four inscriptions found there are in Greek, only one in Samaritan Aramaic.[33] This evidence corrobo-rates the impression we get on the basis of the Jewish material.[34] It may be an exaggeration to say with A. W. Argyle, "To suggest that a Jewish boy growing up in Galilee would not know Greek would be rather like suggesting that a Welsh boy brought up in Cardiff would not know English,"[35] but it is certainly not as far from the truth as many of his critics would claim.[36]

Moreover, the epigraphic material itself should not be considered in isolation. Papyri,[37] the legends of coins,[38] and the literary sources[39] also suggest strongly that many Jews in Judaea and the Galilee were able to speak or understand Greek, even if they did not belong to the upper classes. There is, for instance, the much debated and very significant Greek papyrus letter by Soumaios from the Bar Kochba archive (one of the three that are in Greek, P. Yadin 52 = SB VIII 9843).[40] However great its problems of interpretation may be,[41] it almost certainly does imply that the author (perhaps Bar Kochba himself or at least one of his fellow soldiers) was not able to write Hebrew or Aramaic and for that reason wrote the letter in Greek (ἐγράφη δὲ Ἑληνιστὶ διὰ τ[ὸ ...]μαν μὴ εὑρηθῆναι Ἑβραεστὶ γράψασθαι). Even though of the some thirty docu-ments in this archive the vast majority (90 percent) are deliberately in Hebrew and Aramaic,[42] which is quite understandable in a religiously motivated and nationalist revolt, there are three documents in Greek. And there can be little doubt that this was due to the fact that for many (but how many?) Palestinian Jews, Greek, the *lingua franca* of the Near East in the Roman period, had become the language of their daily life, even for the followers of the Jewish leader of the second revolt against Rome who used the archaic Hebrew script on his coins.[43] This letter from the Bar Kochba archive demonstrates that this did not apply to the cultural elite only, for the letter was written in a sloppy hand and bristles with spelling errors. Moreover, Soumaios expected his Jewish addressees to be able to read the Greek letter, besides the other ones addressed to them in Hebrew and Aramaic.[44] Similar observations could be made, *mutatis mutandis*, on the Murabba'at papyri and the documents from the Babatha archive, the majority of which are in Greek.[45] In this connection it is telling that of the 609 papyri from the Roman Near East in general found outside Egypt—the *vast* majority of which are from Roman and Byzantine Palestine—some 325 are in Greek: that is almost 55 percent![46]

The important observation in rabbinic literature, to the effect that in Caesarea Maritima (and certainly also elsewhere) synagogue services were conducted in Greek, leads to the same conclusion,[47] which in its turn is confirmed by the famous Justinian *Novella* 146 (of the year 553 CE).[48] Also, the fact that so many inscriptions are bilingual, containing Hebrew or Aramaic with Greek translation, may be an indication that for many Greek was more readily understandable than the other two languages. Telling, too, are the finds of Greek documents in Qumran, Masada, and other sites of the Judaean desert, and the thousands of Greek loanwords in rabbinic literature (and several even in the Copper Scroll from Qumran).[49] But all this has already been so eloquently and elaborately argued by Martin Hengel that it is superfluous to go into the matter again.[50] It is not unimportant to observe that none of our sources ever mention the presence of interpreters in situations where Palestinian Jews had to talk with Greeks.[51] "There is no sign that the acquisition of Greek was felt as very difficult,"[52] though many may never have arrived at a level higher than what was necessary to keep up simple conversations with Greek fellow townsmen without being able to write Greek. Here the general question of literacy comes in, but in view of a lack of a comprehensive study of literacy in ancient Judaism—a real desideratum![53]—we have to leave that matter aside. Let me only remark that it was not only literate people with knowledge of Greek who erected inscribed tombstones. As a matter of fact anyone could do that, since the texts on the stones were generally incised by professional stonecutters who had a large number of stock phrases to provide their clients with examples. Here it is important to keep in mind the distinction between bilingual speakers and literate bilinguals: i.e., inability to write does not necessarily imply inability to speak a language.[54]

Another factor that may distort our picture is the fact that a majority of the inscriptions were found in urban centers, not in the countryside, so that the figures we have may yield averages that do not accurately reflect either cities or countryside, although they certainly do reflect cities more accurately than the countryside.[55] What was true for major cities, such as Jerusalem, Caesarea, Jaffa, Sepphoris, let alone Scythopolis (which belonged to the Decapolis)[56] and other Hellenistic cities,[57] need not necessarily apply to the many small towns and villages in Judea and the Galilee.[58] "It is quite possible to interpret the paucity of Greek inscriptional data in Upper Galilee as reflecting a genuine linguistic conservatism, if not a conscious attempt to preserve a dominant Semitic ambience."[59] Unfortunately, we have hardly any means to establish with any precision how great the differences in this respect between city and countryside were. We do know, however, that the Roman administration passed on imperial decrees in inscribed form to the local population, not in Latin but in Greek, assuming that these edicts could be read not only by inhabitants of the greater urban centers. The famous *Diatagma Kaisaros* from the village of Nazareth is a clear case in point.[60] Here at least a good many of the local Galileans were expected to be able to read it.[61]

A further distinction that has to be made is of a chronological nature. There can be little doubt that the process of Hellenization was, in general, a progressive one. To quote Lee Levine, "The degree of Hellenization was clearly of a different order in the first to fourth centuries CE than in the third to first centuries BCE."[62] Even though the production of Jewish literature in Greek seems to have decreased after 70, the proportion of Greek inscriptions as compared to Hebrew and Aramaic ones increases (except in Jerusalem, where there is a drop-off of epitaphs in general after 70). It would seem that what once was limited to certain circles or strata of society gradually permeated into other societal areas as well.

One could also wonder whether perhaps the preponderance of Greek in the epitaphs has to do with the genre. It is a well-known fact that the genre of *carmina sepulcralia* was a Greek creation, and Greek genres had fixed rules as to form, language, and style. Perhaps this fact also caused Greek to predominate as the language of tomb inscriptions. That is very implausible, however, for although it certainly applied to tomb inscriptions with metrical poetry—of which we have only two instances in Jewish Palestine[63]—it did not apply to the other forms, for example, the many instances of only the name of the deceased, whether or not followed by the age at death, a form that, moreover, also had its predecessors in Hebrew and Aramaic as early as biblical times.[64] So the constraints of genre did not play a role as distorting factor as far as the knowledge and use of Greek in inscriptions by Jewish inhabitants of ancient Palestine is concerned. We can therefore assume that people recorded the names of their deceased in Greek because Greek was their first language (or at least because they were fully bilingual).[65]

A special case is the disproportionally great number of Greek epitaphs from the catacombs of Beth She'arim. A proportion of almost 90 percent is all the more striking since the city was a rabbinic center of great renown and several famous rabbis were buried there. It is tempting to see this high percentage in light of the fact that precisely on account of the fame of the city as a prestigious center of rabbinic learning, many Jews from the diaspora wanted to be buried there. And indeed, there are quite a number of Greek inscriptions from Beth She'arim that clearly indicate that the deceased did not originate in Palestine. We find ten epitaphs of men and women from Palmyra, Byblos, Tyre, Sidon, Beirut, and Antioch (BS 2 nos. 92, 100, 137, 141, 147, 148, 164, 172, 199, 221), all of them from Syria.[66] It is clear that we have to do here with immigrants from the neighboring country, although it must remain uncertain for what reason they left Syria and settled in Beth She'arim. Was it in order to be buried in the neighborhood of the great rabbis, or was it for a more down-to-earth reason such as trade interests, or for other reasons? Be that as it may, it is not a matter of surprise that these inscriptions from diaspora Jews are in Greek. But it should immediately be added that this accounts only for ten out of 218 inscriptions, that is, less than 5 percent. From a theoretical point of view it cannot be ruled out that many of the remaining 208 Greek epitaphs also derive from diaspora Jews who do not identify themselves as such, but that seems extremely unlikely. As a matter of fact many of the deceased are explicitly said to have originated from other places in Roman Palestine, and for the rest of the inscriptions the most natural assumption is that the deceased were locals.[67] And most of these also used Greek as the language of their inscriptions, which was very probably also their daily language. This seems to be corroborated by the metrical epitaph with which I started this paper (BS II 127). Let us now briefly have a closer look at it.

As I already indicated above, the most striking thing about this exceptional epitaph is that the deceased indicates that he is a native from Beth She'arim ('my Beth She'arim') and at the same time he presents us with the most thoroughly Greek epitaph in ancient Palestine one could imagine. To be sure, it is exceptional, but there it is. It is Greek not only in its Homeric language, but also in its form and contents, although it should be conceded that from a metrical point of view the poem is far from faultless. From a morphological point of view, however, the poem is remarkably free from errors, apart from one instance of iotacism (line 6). This poetic inscription is a clear demonstration that (at least some) Palestinian Jews were not only quite familiar with the Greek language but also with Greek literature, for the poem is full of Homeric phraseology and diction. This is one of the two poetic inscriptions from Beth She'arim (for the other one see BS 2.183).[68] It is written in alternating dactylic hexameters and pentameters (disticha), as is usual in epigrams. The deceased speaks in the first person, which occurs very often in pagan Greek funerary epigrams. In line 1 Λεοντείδης for 'son of Leontios' is already an imitation of Homeric patronymics (cf. Ἀτρείδης for 'son of Atreus'). In line 2 the intentionally emphatical πάσης σοφίης ('all wisdom' or 'every sort of wisdom' or 'all kinds of wisdom') is important, since it seems to indicate that it was not only Jewish wisdom (i.e., Torah study, which flourished at Beth She'arim) but also secular Greek learning in which Justus had been educated. In Greek epigrams *sophia* is often used for 'excellence in one of the arts or in learning'—it was used, for instance, of poets, orators, and jurists—whereas in Jewish tradition, wisdom (*hokhma*) had a wide range of religious overtones.[69] It is therefore not accidental that it is in the concept of *sophia* that we see the two worlds of Judaism and Hellenism reaching out to each other here. "The man described in this epigram was educated both in Greek and Jewish learning. . . . The Jew Justus, a citizen of that town which was for many decades a center of Jewish scholarship, and apparently also the author of the inscription, used this expression in the sense accepted in his Hellenized environment."[70] In line 3 λιπεῖν φάος ('leaving the light' for 'dying') is a Homeric expression (*Od.* 11.93), as is ἀκαχημένους, 'mourning' (*Od.* 9.62, 105, 565, etc.). Αὐτοκασίγνητος for 'brother' in line 4 is very common in Homer. Βέσαρα (line 4) for Beth She'arim occurs also in Josephus (in the form Βήσαρα, *Life* 118–19). With the expression 'in my Beth She'arim,' the author would seem to express the Jewish idea of being laid to rest among one's own people.[71] 'To go to Hades' in line 5 in the sense of 'to die' is common both in Homer and in Greek funerary epigraphy. In Jewish writings 'Hades' had lost its religious-mythological meaning (God of the underworld); hence the LXX translators used it to render *she'ol*, and it occurs ten times in the New Testament. Μοῖρα κραταίη in line 6 (a typically Homeric verse ending) would at first sight seem to be more difficult to reconcile with Jewish ideas. Moira was, since Homer, the Greek goddess of fate, but apparently Justus sees no problem in using the term, in the tradition of Greek epigrams, to say that it was his destiny to die young. The θάρσει formula in line 7—which is from a different speaker—is a too much debated and too extensive matter to deal with here in any detail.[72]

Now it should be noted that this is not the first time we come across Homeric poetry in the land of Israel. From several centuries earlier, probably from the second century BCE, we have the epic poems of Philo and Theodotus, both of them probably of Palestinian provenance.[73] The fact that we do not have any other traces of this kind of literary activity from the centuries between these two poets from the second century BCE and the third century CE in which the two metrical epitaphs in Beth She'arim were written may be striking to the uninitiated, but to anyone familiar with the vicissitudes of the tradition history of ancient literature and epigraphy in general and Jewish literature and epigraphy in Greek in particular this is not as telling as one might be inclined to think. There may, or may not, have been a much greater production of Homeric poetry (Sosates is a case in point: we know only his name, all his works are lost),[74] or of Greek literature in general, or of Greek epitaphs, or even of just Greek words on tombstones, in Hellenistic-Roman Palestine than we will ever be able to know, but these two key points—Greek Homeric poetry in both the second century BCE and the third century CE—should make us aware of the potential there was in principle.

How far have we come? Not much further than our predecessors, I am afraid. Can we still subscribe to the verdict of one of the greatest experts in the linguistic situation of Roman Palestine, Haiim Rosén, "daß die κοινή [Griechisch] in weitestem Ausmaß unter den Juden Palästinas verbreitet war" and that "bis in die einfachsten Volksschichten hinab der Gebrauch des Griechischen zu beobachten [ist]"?[75] It is hard to say yes or no, but our evidence does not fully warrant such far-reaching conclusions. Yet I am inclined to put it this way: The burden of proof is on the shoulders of those scholars who want to maintain that Greek was not the lingua franca of many Palestinian Jews in the Hellenistic-Roman-Byzantine period, in view of the fact that more than 50 percent, maybe even some 65 percent, of the public inscriptions is in 'the language of Japheth.' The minimalist interpretations that have been put forward by several scholars (Feldman, Rajak, Grabbe, the new Schürer) have turned out to be unconvincing. It is on the basis of the sketched evidence that as early as 1965 the great Jewish epigrapher Baruch Lifshitz was able to conclude: "The Greek language and Greek culture had penetrated all the Jewish communities of the Greek east."[76] Rosén and Lifshitz are probably by and large right, but their statements should be qualified by adding that this does not imply that a majority, or even a large minority, of Jews were monolingual Greek-speakers. For most, or at least many, of the Jews in Palestine, Greek most probably remained a second language, certainly outside the urban areas.[77] We may tentatively conclude that Roman Palestine was a largely bilingual, or even trilingual, society[78]—alongside the vernacular Aramaic (and, to a much lesser extent, Hebrew), Greek was widely used and understood—but we have to add that the degree of use and understanding of the Greek language probably varied strongly according to locality and period, social status, and educational background, occasion and mobility.[79] As far as we can see, however, opinions will remain divided over this issue.[80]

Notes

1. The Greek text is:
   Κεῖμαι Λεοντείδης νέκυς Σαφοῦς υἱὸς Ἰοῦστος
   ὃς πάσης σοφίης δρεψάμενος καρπὸν
   λεῖψα φάος, δειλοὺς γονέας ἀκαχημένους αἰεί,
   αὐτοκασιγνήτους τε, οἴμοι, ἐν οἷς Βεσάροις
   καί γ' ἐλθὼν εἰς Ἅδην Ἰοῦστος (. . .) αὐτόθι κεῖμαι,

σὺν πόλλοισιν ἑοῖς, ἐπὶ ἤθελε Μοῖρα κραταίη.
—Θάρσει, Ἰοῦστε, οὐδεὶς ἀθάνατος.
2. Thus the editors, M. Schwabe and B. Lifshitz, *Beth She'arim II: The Greek Inscriptions* (New Brunswick: Rutgers University Press, 1974) 107. The inscription is no. 127 in their collection.

3. Other scholars involved in the project include Benjamin Isaac, Hannah Cotton, Leah di Segni, Ada Yardeni, Werner Eck, Alla Stein, and Israel Roll.

4. J.-B. Frey, *Corpus Inscriptionum Judaicarum*, vol. 2 (Vatican City: Pontificio istituto di archelogia cristiana, 1952). Vol. 2 covers Asia and Africa. Vol. 1, which was published in 1936 but was reprinted with an extensive Prolegomenon by Baruch Lifshitz in 1975 (published by Ktav), covers Europe. I leave out of account here the still older and more outdated collections by J. Oehler, "Epigraphische Beiträge zur Geschichte des Judentums," *Monatsschrift für Geschichte und Wissenschaft des Judentums* 53 (1909) 292–302, 443–52, 525–38; S. Klein, *Jüdisch-Palästinisches Corpus Inscriptionum* (Vienna: Löwit, 1920); and P. Thomsen, *Die lateinischen und griechischen Inschriften der Stadt Jerusalem* (Leipzig: Hinrichs, 1922).

5. See L. Robert, *Bulletin Epigraphique III* (*1952–1958*) (Paris: Les Belles Lettres, 1974) no. 24 (pp. 101–4).

6. One might add recent publications such as the book by R. C. Gregg and D. Urman, *Jews, Pagans, and Christians in the Golan Heights: Greek and Other Inscriptions of the Roman and Byzantine Eras* (SFSHJ 140; Atlanta: Scholars Press, 1997), but that is a collection of not only Jewish, but also pagan and Christian epigraphical material; it will be left out of account here also because for too many of these 240 inscriptions the religious affiliation cannot be established at all.

7. Very useful also is F. Bérard et al., eds., *Guide de l'épigraphiste* (3rd ed.; Paris: Editions Rue d'Ulm, 2000).

8. It is also useful to check the Hebrew journal *Hadashot Arkheologiot*. See further my *Ancient Jewish Epitaphs* (Kampen: Kok Pharos, 1991) 13–15.

9. M. Hengel, *Judaism and Hellenism* (London: SCM Press, 1974) 1:58.

10. In 1974 Mussies counted 440 Jewish inscriptions in Greek in Palestine on the basis of *CIJ* and *SEG;* see G. Mussies, "Greek in Palestine and the Diaspora," in S. Safrai and M. Stern, eds., *The Jewish People in the First Century 2* (CRINT 1.2; Assen: Van Gorcum, 1976) 1042.

11. Roth-Gerson's book is left out of account here since it contains only Greek inscriptions.

12. I do not know the basis for Lee Levine's statement that "the overall percentage of Greek inscriptions in Roman-Byzantine Palestine jumps to over 55 percent" (L. I. Levine, *Judaism and Hellenism in Antiquity: Conflict or*

Confluence [Seattle/London: University of Washington Press, 1998] 180), but he is certainly very close to the truth. For if we would add to these statistics the fact that the still unpublished collection of 30 ossuaries from Scythopolis all contain only Greek inscriptions, the average percentage indeed "jumps to over 55 percent"!

13. E-mail communication of 18 Dec. 1998. Price cautiously adds, "but don't hold me to this!"

14. Cf. the remark by H. B. Rosén: "Das Lateinische konnte sich den palästinischen Sprachen nicht als Prestigesprache gegenüberstellen, nicht nur weil es in Palästina auf ein bereits fest verankertes und eingewurzeltes Griechisch gestoßen ist, sondern wohl eher deshalb, weil dieses Griechisch Träger einer spezifischen Landes- und Nationalkultur war, die man heute jüdischen Hellenismus nennt, und weil die Sprachen Palästinas Ausdrucksmittel einer mehr als tausendjährigen Literatur waren, welche der lateinischen weder an geistigem Prestige noch an Verwurzelung im Volke in irgendeiner Weise nachstand" ("Die Sprachsituation im römischen Palästina," in idem, *East and West: Selected Writings in Linguistics*, vol. 1 [München: Wilhelm Fink, 1982] 489; cf. ibid. 493–94).

15. Even though *CIJ* II was published only in 1952, Frey's volume reflects the "Stand der Forschung" of the early thirties of our century.

16. The percentage of Greek inscriptions in the Jewish Diaspora is about 85 percent. See my *Het Nieuwe Testament en de joodse grafinscripties uit de Hellenistisch-Romeinse tijd* (Utrecht: Faculteit der Godgeleerdheid, 1991).

17. On Aramaic as the principal spoken language of Palestine see E. Schürer, *The History of the Jewish People in the Age of Jesus Christ* (4 vols.; Edinburgh: Clark, 1979) 2:20–28 (with bibliography). For a similar discussion about the choice of language for Jewish epitaphs in Italy see D. Noy, "Writing in Tongues: The Use of Greek, Latin and Hebrew in Jewish Inscriptions from Roman Italy," *JJS* 48 (1997) 300–11; and L. V. Rutgers, *The Jews in Late Ancient Rome: Evidence of Cultural Interaction in the Roman Diaspora* (Religions in the Greco-Roman World 126; Leiden: Brill, 1995) 176–209.

18. Levine, *Judaism and Hellenism in Antiquity*, 76.

19. Hengel, "Der vorchristliche Paulus" in M. Hengel and U. Heckel, eds., *Paulus und das antike Judentum* (Tübingen: Mohr, 1991) 257–58. In his "Jerusalem als jüdische und hellenistische Stadt," in idem, *Judaica, hellenistica et christiana: Kleine Schriften II* (Tübingen: Mohr, 1999) 147, Hengel speaks of 10 to 20 percent.

20. Lifshitz in "Jérusalem sous la domination romaine," *ANRW* 2.8 (1977) 459. Cf. also M. Hadas, *Hellenistic Culture: Fusion and Diffusion* (New York / London: Columbia University Press, 1959) 36: "The most forceful evidence that Greek had become the vernacular comes from epigraphy."

21. See T. Rajak, *Josephus: The Historian and His Society* (London: Duckworth, 1983) 46–50.

22. M. Clauss, "Probleme der Lebensalterstatistiken aufgrund römischer Grabinschriften," *Chiron* 3 (1973) 395–417, here 411.

23. See, e.g., R. MacMullen, "The Epigraphic Habit in the Roman Empire," *American Journal of Philology* 103 (1982) 233–46.

24. Thus Levine, *Judaism and Hellenism*, 180.

25. To be sure, this number is an estimate and also two million or half a million could be a reasonable estimate, but for the present purposes that hardly makes a difference. In the scholarly literature on the subject the estimates vary from half a million to five million; see the surveys in A. Byatt, "Josephus and Population Numbers in First Century Palestine," *Palestine Exploration Quarterly* 105 (1973) 51–60; and G. Stemberger, "Juden," *Reallexikon für Antike und Christentum* 19 (Lieferung 147, 1998) 172. By assuming a Jewish population of one million we keep on the safe side; so does R. H. Pfeiffer, *History of New Testament Times* (New York: Harper, 1949) 189.

26. See J. Barr, "Hebrew, Aramaic and Greek," in W. D. Davies and L. Finkelstein, eds., *The Cambridge History of Judaism* (Cambridge: Cambridge University Press, 1989) 2:102 with n. 4. The same applies to the Jewish epitaphs of Rome; see H. J. Leon, *The Jews of Ancient Rome* (Peabody: Hendrickson, 1995; reprint of the 1960 ed.) 75–92, and Rutgers, *Jews of Late Ancient Rome*, passim. Feldman's theory that so many ossuaries have inscriptions in Greek only to prevent non-Jews from molesting the graves is not convincing. See L. H. Feldman, *Jew and Gentile in the Ancient World: Attitudes and Interaction from Alexander to Justinian* (Princeton: Princeton University Press, 1993) 14 and 22 (the whole first chapter of this book, pp. 3–44, is directed against Martin Hengel).

27. Levine, *Judaism and Hellenism in Antiquity*, 24.

28. See R. Hachlili, *Ancient Jewish Art and Archaeology in the Land of Israel* (Handbuch der Orientalistik. Erste Abteilung, Nahe und der Mittlere Osten 35; Leiden: Brill, 1988) 103.

29. S. Lieberman, *Greek in Jewish Palestine* (New York: Feldheim, 1965) 30. See also the conclusion of J. N. Sevenster, *Do You Know Greek? How Much Greek Could the First Jewish Christians Have Known?* (NovTSup 19; Leiden: Brill, 1968) 183. A comparable instance of that category is the motley mixture of graffiti in the necropolis of Maresha/Marissa, which were definitely scratched there by common people, for the Greek is vulgar and has many orthographic errors, but it is Greek these people (partly Idumaeans, partly Phoenicians) wrote. See *SEG* 8.247–61 and *SEG* 42.1439–54, with Rosén, "Sprachsituation," 504, and Sevenster, *Do You Know Greek?* 112–13.

30. See her book mentioned above in the text. More than one-third of the synagogue inscriptions from Israel are in Greek.

31. E. R. Goodenough, *Jewish Symbols in the Greco-Roman Period* (New York: Pantheon Books [Bollen Foundation], 1954) 2.123.

32. *SEG* 42.1423–29.

33. See G. Reeg, *Die antiken Synagogen in Israel, II: Die samaritanischen Synagogen* (Wiesbaden: Reichert, 1977) 572–73, 631. See now also *SEG* 42.1474 for another new Greek inscription from a Samaritan synagogue in Israel.

34. For a wider survey of Samaritan evidence for Hellenistic influence see my essay "Samaritans and Hellenism" in my *Hellenism—Judaism—Christianity: Essays on Their Interaction* (2nd ed.; Leuven: Peeters, 1998) 49–58.

35. A. W. Argyle, "Greek Among the Jews of Palestine in New Testament Times," *NTS* 20 (1973/74) 88.

36. The whole debate is summarized by G. H. R. Horsley, *New Documents Illustrating Early Christianity* (Macquarie University: The Ancient History Documentary Research Centre, 1989) 5:21.

37. See S. E. Porter, "The Greek Papyri of the Judaean Desert and the World of the Roman East," in S. E. Porter and C. E. Evans, eds., *The Scrolls and the Scriptures. Qumran Fifty Years After* (Sheffield: Sheffield Academic Press, 1997) 293–316; and H. M. Cotton, W. E. H. Cockle, and F. G. B. Millar, "The Papyrology of the Roman Near East: A Survey," *Journal of Roman Studies* 85 (1995) 214–35.

38. Though they are hard to use for the present purpose because coins were instruments of propaganda. See Y. Meshorer, *Jewish Coins of the Second Temple Period* (Tel Aviv: Am Hasefer, 1967); Y. Meshorer, *City Coins of Eretz Israel and the Decapolis* (Jerusalem: Israel Museum, 1985). Cf. the remarks by J. C. Greenfield, "The Languages of Palestine, 200 BCE–200 CE," in H. H. Paper, ed., *Jewish Languages: Theme and Variations* (Cambridge, Mass.: Association for Jewish Studies, 1978) 147 and by F. E. Peters in his response, ibid., 161.

39. For a short survey of Palestinian Jewish writings in Greek see S. E. Porter, "Jesus and the Use of Greek in Galilee," in B. Chilton and C. A. Evans, eds., *Studying the Historical Jesus* (NTTS 19; Leiden: Brill, 1994) 139–42. Also Hengel, *Judaism and Hellenism*, 88–102.

40. *Editio princeps* by B. Lifshitz, "Papyrus grecs du désert de Juda," *Aegyptus* 42 (1962) 240–56. Reeditions include J. A. Fitzmyer, "The Languages of Palestine in the First Century A.D." in idem, *A Wandering Aramean: Collected Aramaic Essays* (Missoula: Scholars Press, 1979) 29–56, here p. 36 (now conveniently reprinted in S. E. Porter, *The Language of the New Testament: Classic Essays* [Sheffield: Sheffield Academic Press, 1991] 126–62, here p. 142).

41. Good recent surveys of the debate and assessments of the problems are B. Rochette, "Le SB VIII 9843 et la position du grec en Palestine aux deux premiers siècles après J.-C.," *Archiv für Papyrusforschung* 44 (1998) 42–46; and L. Devillers, "Le lettre de Soumaïos et les Ioudaioi johanniques," *Revue Biblique* 105 (1998) 556–81.

42. See F. Millar, *The Roman Near East, 37 BC–AD 337* (Cambridge, Mass./ London: Harvard University Press, 1993) 545–52, for a useful survey of all the documents, with the update by Cotton, Cockle, and Millar, "The Papyrology of the Roman Near East," 229–31.

43. L. Mildenberg, "Der Bar-Kochba-Krieg im Lichte der Münzprägungen," in H. P. Kuhnen, ed., *Palästina in griechisch-römischer Zeit* (Handbuch der Archäologie II 2) (München: Beck, 1990) 357–66; idem, *The Coinage of the Bar Kochba War* (Aarau/Frankfurt: Verlag Sauerländer, 1984).

44. In view of this data it is hard to understand how the great papyrologist Herbert Youtie could state, "Greek never became a vital linguistic factor in Palestine comparable to Hebrew or Aramaic." See his response to Jonas Greenfield in Paper, ed., *Jewish Languages*, 157.

45. See P. Benoit, J. T. Milik, and R. de Vaux, eds., *Les grottes de Murabba'at* (2 vols.; Oxford: Oxford University Press, 1961) and N. Lewis, *The Documents from the Bar Kokhba Period in the Cave of Letters: Greek Papyri* (Jerusalem: Israel Exploration Society, 1989). Of the 36 documents in the Babatha archive, 26 are in Greek.

46. Based on Cotton, Cockle, and Millar, "The Papyrology of the Roman Near East."

47. *j. Sotah* 7.1.21b and other references in S. C. Reif, *Judaism and Hebrew Prayer* (Cambridge: Cambridge University Press, 1993) 350 n. 47; W. F. Smelik, *The Targum of Judges* (Oudtestamentische studiën 36; Leiden: Brill, 1995) 6–7; and Levine, *Judaism and Hellenism*, 160–61. On Caesarea and the dominant position of Greek there including among Jews, see B. Lifshitz, "Césarée de Palestine, son histoire et ses institutions," *ANRW* 2.8 (1977) 490–518. Cf. also K. G. Holum, *King Herod's Dream: Caesarea on the Sea* (New York and London: Norton, 1988). On "the Greek of the synagogue" see the chapter with this title in Lieberman's *Greek in Jewish Palestine*, 29–67.

48. On this *Novella* see A. Linder, *The Jews in Roman Imperial Legislation* (Detroit: Wayne State University Press, 1987) 402–11, who conveniently presents the text with translation and commentary.

49. For the Greek loanwords in the Copper Scroll see Schürer, *History*, 2:78. For the rabbinic traditions about the young men of the House of the Patriarch who studied the Greek language and Greek 'wisdom' see S. Lieberman, *Hellenism in Jewish Palestine* (New York: The Jewish Theological Seminary of America, 1962) 100–14. On the general issue of the Patriarchs' knowledge of the Greek language and Greek 'wisdom' see my essay "The Last Jewish Patriarch(s) and Graeco-Roman Medicine" (forthcoming).

50. See his *Judaism and Hellenism*; idem, *The 'Hellenization' of Judea in the First Century after Christ* (London: SCM Press, 1989) passim (now in expanded German version in his *Judaica et hellenistica: Kleine Schriften I* [Tübingen: Mohr, 1996] 1–90); idem, "Der vorchristliche Paulus," 177–294, esp. 256–65; and

finally his "Jerusalem als jüdische und hellenistische Stadt," 115–56. For a good summary of criticisms of Hengel's position (with bibliography) see L. L. Grabbe, *Judaism from Cyrus to Hadrian* (2 vols.; Minneapolis: Fortress, 1992) 1:150–53.

51. Thus, Mussies, "Greek," 1056.

52. Barr, "Hebrew," 103.

53. See, e.g., B. Spolsky, "Triglossia and Literacy in Jewish Palestine of the First Century," *International Journal of the Sociology of Language* 42 (1983) 95–109. Dr. Catherine Hezser from Berlin is preparing a full-scale study of the problem of literacy among Jews in the ancient world.

54. Cf. Horsley, *New Documents*, 5:24. Grabbe overlooks this when he concludes overhastily that the use of Greek was "confined to a particular segment of the population, namely, the educated upper class" (*Judaism*, 1: 158). Cf. also the same minimalist position in Schürer, *History*, 2:74.

55. On this also Rosén, "Sprachsituation," 490.

56. Thirty ossuaries of Jews found in Scythopolis have only inscriptions in Greek! See G. Fuks, "The Jews of Hellenistic and Roman Scythopolis," *JJS* 33 (1982) 409–10.

57. See the chapter on the Hellenistic cities in Schürer, *History*, 2:85–183.

58. It has to be added, however, that there do not seem to be significant regional variations in the sense that there is more Hebrew material in Jerusalem or more Greek in the coastal areas, as Prof. J. Price reminds me in a private communication. For a similar distinction between urban areas and countryside in neighboring Phoenicia, see J. D. Grainger, *Hellenistic Phoenicia* (Oxford: Clarendon Press, 1991) 77–83, 108–11 et aliter. Cf. also F. Millar, "The Problem of Hellenistic Syria," in A. Kuhrt and S. Sherwin-White, eds., *Hellenism in the East* (London: Duckworth, 1987) 110–33.

59. E. M. Meyers and J. F. Strange, *Archaeology, the Rabbis and Early Christianity* (London: SCM Press, 1981) 91.

60. See my *Ancient Jewish Epitaphs*, 159–61, and the detailed study by B. M. Metzger, "The Nazareth Inscription Once Again," in idem, *New Testament Studies: Philological, Versional, and Patristic* (NTTS 10; Leiden: Brill, 1980) 75–92. The recent study by E. Grzybek and M. Sordi, "L'Edit de Nazareth et la politique de Néron à l'égard des chrétiens," *Zeitschrift für Papyrologie und Epigraphik* 120 (1998) 279–91, is unconvincing.

61. See Meyers and Strange, *Archaeology*, 84; Sevenster, *Do You Know Greek?*, 117–21.

62. Levine, *Judaism and Hellenism in Antiquity*, 26.

63. I collected these and the other metrical inscriptions by Jews in "Jewish Tomb Inscriptions in Verse," in J. W. van Henten and P. W. van der Horst, eds., *Studies in Early Jewish Epigraphy* (AGJU 21; Leiden: Brill, 1994) 129–47; reprinted in van der Horst, *Hellenism—Judaism—Christianity*, 27–47. There is

one other metrical inscription from Palestine, in Marissa, but it is not Jewish (see *SEG* 8.244).

64. See, for instance, K. A. D. Smelik, *Writings from Ancient Israel: A Handbook of Historical and Religious Documents* (Edinburgh: T. & T. Clark, 1991) 152–55 and in G. I. Davies, *Ancient Hebrew Inscriptions* (Cambridge: Cambridge University Press, 1991).

65. See also the verdict by Joseph Fitzmyer in "The Languages of Palestine," 35: "It is unlikely that the language chosen for most of these crudely incised identifications was merely the *lingua franca* of the day. Rather, they bear witness to the widespread and living use of Greek among first-century Palestinian Jews." Cf., however, Rajak, *Josephus*, 57: "Now those who put Greek on their tomb need not be Greek speakers, just as Latin on English gravestones was not put there by Latin speakers, but adopted because it was associated with worship and study." Ibid.: "Greek was the language of some Jews in Jerusalem."

66. S. Safrai, "Relations between the Diaspora and the Land of Israel," in S. Safrai and M. Stern, eds., *The Jewish People in the First Century* (CRINT 1.1; Assen: Van Gorcum, 1974) 194 and J. J. Price, "The Jewish Diaspora of the Graeco-Roman Period," *Scripta Classica Israelica* 13 (1994) 173. In other Greek funerary inscriptions from Israel we also find Jews from abroad, especially from Alexandria (e.g., *CIJ* 918, 928, 934; but cf. also 882, 889, 910, 925, 931, 954 [?], 991; Dominus Flevit no. 9).

67. See Z. Weiss, "Social Aspects of Burial in Beth She'arim: Archeological Finds and Talmudic Sources," in L. I. Levine, ed., *The Galilee in Late Antiquity* (New York/Jerusalem: The Jewish Theological Seminary of America, 1992) 357–71.

68. Also, the other Homeric poem (BS 2.183) does not give any indication that the deceased or his family derived from elsewhere than Beth She'arim.

69. See, *inter multos alios*, R. E. Murphy, "Wisdom," *Anchor Bible Dictionary* 6 (1992) 920–31; and E. E. Urbach, *The Sages: Their Concepts and Beliefs* (Jerusalem: Magnes Press, 1975) Index *s.v.* 'wisdom.' Schwabe-Lifshitz, *Beth She'arim*, 2:100, mention several Jewish parallels to the expression *pasa sophia*.

70. Schwabe-Lifshitz, *Beth She'arim*, 2:99–100, esp. 101, where they rightly emphasize that "in this one hexameter [read: pentameter!] concepts from two different worlds meet and are combined."

71. Thus, Schwabe-Lifshitz, *Beth She'arim*, 2:107. The use of ὅς or ἑός as in line 6 for ἐμός is a late-epic feature.

72. See my *Ancient Jewish Epitaphs*, 121–22.

73. C. R. Holladay, *Fragments from Hellenistic Jewish Authors II: Poets* (Atlanta: Scholars Press, 1989) 70–72 and 208–10. Cf. now also E. R. Gruen, *Heritage and Hellenism: The Reinvention of Jewish Tradition* (Berkeley/Los Angeles: University of California Press, 1998) 120–27.

74. See S. J. D. Cohen, "Sosates, the Jewish Homer," *HTR* 74 (1981) 391–96.

75. Rosén, "Sprachsituation," 510.

76. "L'hellénisation des Juifs en Palestine," *RB* 72 (1965) 520–38, quote at 538. Cf. also his "Du nouveau sur l'hellénisation des Juifs de Palestine," *Euphrosyne* n.s. 3 (1970) 113–33 and Lieberman, *Greek in Jewish Palestine*, 39: "We have seen how deeply Greek penetrated into all the classes of Jewish society of Palestine."

77. Thus also Mussies, "Greek," 1058. Cf. Fitzmyer, "Languages of Palestine," 46.

78. See B. Spolsky, "Jewish Multilingualism in the First Century: An Essay in Historical Sociolinguistics," in J. A. Fishman, ed., *Readings in the Sociology of Jewish Languages* (Leiden: Brill, 1985) 35–51, esp. 40–41, where trilingualism ('triglossia') is stressed. See also Ch. Rabin, "Hebrew and Aramaic in the First Century," in S. Safrai and M. Stern, eds., *The Jewish People in the First Century* (CRINT 1.2; Assen: Van Gorcum, 1976) 1007–39. But cf. R. Schmitt, "Die Sprachverhältnisse in den östlichen Provinzen des Römischen Reiches," *Aufstieg und Niedergang der Römischen Welt* 2.29.2 (Berlin/New York: W. de Gruyter, 1983) 554–86, here 576: "Man wird die Sprachgemeinschaft dieses Landes mit gutem Recht als bilingual bezeichnen dürfen."

79. See G. H. R. Horsley, *New Documents*, 5:19, though he says that this consensus view is "an uneasy one."

80. I owe special thanks to Professor Jonathan Price of Tel Aviv University, who was so kind not only to send me information about the *CIIP* project but also to read the first draft of this paper and to send me his valuable critical remarks. Also my colleagues Dr. Gerard Mussies and Dr. Leonard V. Rutgers cheerfully volunteered to comment upon the first draft of this paper. Finally, I wish to express my gratitude to Dr. James N. Pankhurst, who kindly checked my English. It is self-evident that all remaining errors are mine.

Greek
at Qumran

JAMES C. VANDERKAM

Widespread use of Greek is exactly what we should expect and do, in fact, find in the land of Israel in the Hellenistic period. The value, negative or positive, that was attached by different groups to the Greek language during the time, say, of Antiochus IV need not have been shared in other periods. The combined literary, numismatic, and inscriptional evidence shows that Greek was widely used and does not indicate that this was considered objectionable. The case of Greek at Qumran is instructive in this regard.

The presence of Greek texts at Qumran—apparently ones that were carefully prepared and that were indeed used—is eloquent testimony about the strength of Greek influence on the Jewish population of Palestine. The Qumran community was atypical in that it probably had an unusually high percentage of literate members (perhaps all members were literate). Also, it was in some ways a very conservative group, one wedded to the ancient traditions of the Scriptures (as they understood them), and one that seems to have cherished a work like *Jubilees* which puts such a premium on Hebrew. *Jubilees* offers an important comment about the status of the Hebrew language in a passage in which the angel of the presence is receiving orders from the Lord concerning Abram:

> Then the Lord God said to me: "Open his mouth and his ears to hear and speak with his tongue in the revealed language." For from the day of the collapse it had disappeared from the mouth(s) of all mankind. I opened his mouth, ears, and lips and began to speak Hebrew with him—in the language of creation. He took his fathers' books (they were written in Hebrew) and copied them. From that time he began

to study them, while I was telling him everything that he was unable (to understand) (12:25–27a).[1]

4Q464 (4QExposition on the Patriarchs) contains a passage that seems to reflect the ideas expressed in *Jubilees* 12.[2] Frag. 3 i, as does frg. 1 (the same could be true for frg. 2), deals with Abra(ha)m. In line 5 there is possibly a reference to "confused" and line 7 preserves the word "forever", but the clearer evidence comes in lines 8–9 which the editors translate as:

> r]ead the holy tongue
> I will make] the peoples pure of speech

They note that the words of line 9 are from Zeph 3:9: "At that time I will change the speech of the peoples to a pure speech, that all of them may call on the name of the Lord and serve him with one accord" (cf. also Isa 19:18). The verse occurs in a condemnatory context in which Jerusalem is criticized for not having learned a lesson from the destruction of other nations. The preceding verse reads: "Therefore wait for me, says the Lord, for the day when I arise as a witness. For my decision is to gather nations, to assemble kingdoms, to pour out upon them my indignation, all the heat of my anger; for in the fire of my passion all the earth shall be consumed" (3:8). Thus the change to a single pure language for the nations will occur following the great judgment predicted by Zephaniah. The Qumran fragment does not name the one language as Hebrew, but that is the likely referent.[3] According to *Jubilees,* all spoke a single language at first (see 3:28) which, in light of 12:26, was certainly Hebrew; the confusion of tongues introduced at Babel changed the situation (10:24–25). The Qumran fragment suggests that in the future all will again speak the one pure language—Hebrew.

Yet, even at Qumran—despite the group's conservative nature, its several copies of *Jubilees* and one of 4Q464, and its widespread use of Hebrew—Greek texts are found. Perhaps it is worth recalling in this context the requirement for the Guardian of all the camps in the *Damascus Document:* He "shall be from thirty to fifty years old, one who has mastered all the secrets of men and the languages of all their clans" (*CD* 14:9–10; it is partially preserved in 4Q266 10 i 2–3; 267 9 v 13–14).[4] Not surprisingly, at Qumran more than 700 of the 850 or so manuscripts are written in Hebrew, the "revealed language", the "language of creation". But, according to Emanuel Tov's latest version of the inventory list of the Qumran texts, another 100 or so are copied in Aramaic, and 27 Greek texts have been identified.[5] That is, about 3 percent of the texts are in Greek. Eight of these come from cave 4; five of those eight have been identified as copies of Greek biblical texts and three are unidentified.

4Q119 4QLXXLeviticus[a] (probably first century BCE)

4Q120 pap4QLXXLeviticus[b] (probably first century BCE, though it could be later)

4Q121 4QLXXNumbers (late first century BCE, early first century CE)

4Q122 4QLXXDeuteronomy (second century BCE)

4Q126 4QUnidentified gr (first century BCE, possibly early first century CE)

4Q127 pap4QParaExodus gr (first century BCE or early first century CE, possibly earlier)[6]

4Q350 4QAccount gr (the text is copied on the back of frg. 9 of 4Q460 [4QNarrative Work and Prayer] written in Hebrew) is a ledger, with no complete words

4Q361 4QpapUnidentified Fragment gr.[7]

Ulrich notes that there are no clear errors in 4Q119, although the scribe did correct a small lapse at one point, and that the manuscript "penetrates further behind the other witnesses to provide a more authentic witness to the Old Greek translation."[8] 4Q120 contains few errors and at one place a later scribe corrected a letter.[9] 4Q121 has two possible scribal errors, and the scribe has made only two or three corrections.[10] That is, these are copies that were carefully inscribed, and efforts were made to fix what was faulty in them once they were made.

The remaining 19 Greek texts come from cave 7 where all the surviving texts are in Greek and all (apart from the last) are written on papyrus. When the cave 7 texts were published by M. Baillet in 1962, the first two were identified as Exode and Lettre de Jérémie; 7Q3–5 were called Textes bibliques (?); and 7Q6–18 were designated as Fragments divers. 7Q19 (Empreintes de papyrus) consists of imprints left by papyrus fragments on three lumps of clay.[11] Some of the Greek fragments from cave 7 have received an extraordinary amount of attention because J. O'Callaghan and others have claimed they were from copies of New Testament books, but that thesis seems not to be faring very well, and only 7Q5, identified by some as from Mark 6:52–53, remains as a possibility.[12] Several of the previously unidentified numbers have now been more securely explained as fragments of a Greek version of the *Epistle of Enoch*. It seems as if 7Q4 1, 7Q12, 7Q8, and 7Q13 are from the same manuscript of the Epistle, so that the overall number of manuscripts from cave 7 will have to be reduced, probably by three.[13] As a result, there are perhaps 24 or 25 Greek manuscripts at Qumran. Naturally, we do not know how they got there, but their dates (second–first century BCE and first century CE) raise the possibility that they were copied at the site.

Mention should also be made of a few other cases where Greek letters appear in texts found at Qumran. In the Copper Scroll (3Q15) Greek letters are present in the first four columns of the text; they are always at the ends of lines and always at the end of the description of a particular treasure: KEN in col. 1:4; CAG in 1:12; HN in 2:2; ΘE in 2:4; DI in 2:9; TP in 3:7; and one uncertain letter followed by K in 4:2.[14] The function of these letters remains unknown.[15] Some Greek letters are also found in the Cryptic A script in which several manuscripts were copied.[16] For example, 4Q186 (4QHoroscope) scatters some Greek letters into a text mostly written in other scripts;[17] cf. also 4QPs[b] frg. 5 (the letters in לאל "look like Greek and Latin letters in mirror writing with Hebrew values [α = א and L = ל]"[18]); and 4QCant[b] (where several scribal markings may be Greek letters).[19]

What are we to make of the Qumran situation? It shows that even in a community like this (if cave 7 was associated with Qumran and there is no reason to doubt this) there were some members who read the scriptures in Greek, although the relative numbers of manuscripts written in the three languages of Qumran indicate that Greek was hardly the dominant one. At the very least we have no reason for thinking it was condemned or banned. Some years ago, A. R. C. Leaney wrote an essay about "Greek Manuscripts from the Judaean Desert."[20] He said regarding the Greek texts in caves 4 and 7: "We can at least say that together these two caves suggest an interest in the Greek Pentateuch and in a wider range of scriptures in the Greek language. This care for the Greek Bible is confirmed when more detailed study reveals that the manuscripts are evidence for concern about the text of that Bible. . . ."[21] After surveying varieties of texts in Greek—written by or about Jews—

he noted that the writers "were related to 'Hellenism' in a great variety of ways. While some entertained a lively interest in Hellenistic ideas, to write in Greek was perfectly consistent with a desire to maintain or reassert the Jewish claim to be unique and inviolable people of God."[22] Indeed, some texts, such as the Greek Additions to Esther, show that more conservative views were expressed in the Greek passages than in the Hebrew text of the book. He went on to conclude that we should "rest content with the obvious fact that the evidence suggests that habitual readers of scriptures in Greek were among the members of the sect."[23]

In a more recent study, L. Greenspoon[24] has commented that "relatively little has been written on the implication of these Greek biblical texts for our understanding of the Qumran community and of the wider Palestinian context in which they were found and, presumably, used."[25] In a rather speculative way he adds to Leaney's conclusions that Greek readers and speakers were probably always a minority at Qumran. "... [A]nd it is probable that at least some at Qumran were not completely convinced of the validity of transmitting the divine word in a 'foreign' language. This raises the possibility that there never were large numbers of Greek biblical manuscripts at Qumran or that—with the exception of Pentateuchal texts—some felt free to dispose of 'the Septuagint' in ways that have left few, if any, traces."[26] Possibilities such as these should also be kept in mind when attempting to draw inferences from the information that has survived.

Regarding many questions raised by these Greek texts (and the Greek Minor Prophets Scroll from Naḥal Ḥever), one can do little more than speculate. The evidence indicates, however, that Greek was sufficiently widely used and accepted to make its presence felt among an unusual, traditional, and learned group like the one at Qumran.

Notes

1. The translation is from VanderKam, *The Book of Jubilees* (2 vols.; CSCO 510–11, Scriptores Aethiopici 87–88; Louvain: Peeters, 1989) vol. 2.

2. E. Eshel and M. Stone, "Exposition on the Patriarchs," in *Qumran Cave 4 XIV: Parabiblical Texts, Part 2* (consulting ed. J. VanderKam; DJD 19; Oxford: Clarendon, 1995) 215–30; see also their essay, "The Holy Language at the End of

Days in Light of a New Fragment Found at Qumran," *Tarbiz* 62 (1993) 169–77 (Hebrew).

3. See Eshel and Stone, "4QExposition on the Patriarchs," 219–21 for a discussion of the passage and for references to other texts that associate Hebrew with the words in Zephaniah.

4. The translation is from G. Vermes, *The Complete Dead Sea Scrolls in English* (New York/London: Allen Lane/The Penguin Press, 1997) 143.

5. See "Appendix III: A List of the Texts from the Judaean Desert" in *The Dead Sea Scrolls after Fifty Years: A Comprehensive Assessment* (ed. P. Flint and J. VanderKam; 2 vols.; Leiden/Boston/Köln: Brill, 1998, 1999) 2.669–717.

6. 4Q119–127 were published in P. W. Skehan, E. Ulrich, and J. E. Sanderson, *Qumran Cave 4 IV Palaeo-Hebrew and Greek Biblical Manuscripts* (DJD 9; Oxford: Clarendon, 1992) 161–242.

7. 4Q350 is published by H. Cotton in *Qumran Cave 4 XXVI Cryptic Texts and Miscellanea*, Part I (DJD 36; Oxford: Clarendon, 2000) 294–95; 4Q361 is included on pl. lxi of H. M. Cotton and A. Yardeni, *Aramaic, Hebrew and Greek Documentary Texts from Naḥal Ḥever and Other Sites with an Appendix Containing Alleged Qumran Texts* (DJD 27; Oxford: Clarendon, 1997). Yardeni considers the pieces of letters on the two lines of 4Q361 to be indecipherable (p. 284) and does not transcribe it. She maintains that 4Q342–46a, 348, 351–60a are not from Qumran cave 4, but her case is not equally convincing in each instance (see p. 283).

8. DJD 9.163.

9. DJD 9.168.

10. DJD 9.188.

11. M. Baillet, J. T. Milik, and R. de Vaux, *Les 'petites grottes' de Qumran* (DJD 3; Oxford: Clarendon, 1962) 142–46.

12. He first announced the identification in "Papiros neotestamentarios en la cueva 7 de Qumrân?" *Bib* 53 (1972) 91–100.

13. See E. Muro, "The Greek Fragments of Enoch from Qumran Cave 7 (7Q4, 7Q8, and 7Q12 = 7QEn gr = Enoch 103:3–4, 7–8)," *RevQ* 18 (1997) 307–12; E. Puech, "Sept fragments de la Lettre d'Hénoch (1 Hén 100, 103 et 105) dans la grotte 7 de Qumrân (= 7Hén gr)," *RevQ* 18 (1997) 313–23. For earlier attempts at identification, see G. W. Nebe, "7Q4:Möglichkeit und Grenze einer Identifikation," *RevQ* 13 (1988) 629–33; Puech, "Notes sur les fragments grecs du manuscrit 7Q4 = 1 Hénoch 103 et 105," *RB* 103 (1996) 592–600.

14. See J. T. Milik, "Le rouleau de cuivre provenant de la grotte 3Q (3Q15)," DJD 3.221.

15. See A. Wolters, "The Copper Scroll," in *The Dead Sea Scrolls after Fifty Years*, 1.305; he does suggest that each may be the beginning of a proper name.

16. For this script, see S. J. Pfann, "298. 4QcryptA Words of the Maskil to All Sons of Dawn" in *Qumran Cave 4 XV Sapiential Texts, Part 1* (consulting ed.

J. A. Fitzmyer; DJD 20; Oxford: Clarendon, 1997) 7 and 9–13. On p. 7 n. 19 he lists seven manuscripts in Cryptic A: 4Q186, 249, 250, 298, 313, 317, and 324c.

17. J. Allegro, *Qumrân Cave 4 I (4Q158–4Q186)* (DJD 5; Oxford: Clarendon, 1968) 88–91.

18. E. Tov, "Scribal Markings in the Texts from the Judean Desert" in *Current Research and Technological Developments on the Dead Sea Scrolls* (ed. D. W. Parry and S. D. Ricks; STDJ 20; Leiden/New York/Köln, 1996) 61.

19. Tov, "Scribal Markings," 67–68, 76.

20. In *Studies in New Testament Language and Text: Essays in Honour of George D. Kilpatrick on the Occasion of His Sixty-fifth Birthday* (ed. J. K. Elliott; Leiden: Brill, 1976) 283–300.

21. "Greek Manuscripts," 283.

22. "Greek Manuscripts," 289.

23. "Greek Manuscripts," 291.

24. "The Dead Sea Scrolls and the Greek Bible" in *The Dead Sea Scrolls after Fifty Years,* 1.101–27.

25. "The Dead Sea Scrolls and the Greek Bible," 111.

26. "The Dead Sea Scrolls and the Greek Bible," 113.

NINE

Galileans, Phoenicians, and Itureans

A Study of Regional Contrasts in the Hellenistic Age

SEAN FREYNE

Historians of the Greco-Roman period have become increasingly aware that terms such as Hellenization and Romanization need suitable qualification if their accounts are not to be distorted by unhelpful generalizations. Various distinctions have been proposed— conscious and unconscious, active and passive, imposed and freely assimilated forms of Hellenism.[1] In addition, Fergus Millar in particular has indicated a further aspect of the complex process of cultural interchange between East and West in the wake of Alexander's conquests, namely, the survival of the older, Semitic cultures, side by side with, or alternatively, cloaked in Greek dress.[2] Millar freely acknowledges that in order to gauge this aspect of the matter properly we need data on the pre-Greek cultures of the Near East, data which in many cases is singularly lacking. Despite this situation, Millar's own programmatic study of the Roman Near East, based on regional variations, is highly suggestive, covering a broad canvas and pointing out significant contrasts in the reception of Greece and Rome in the East, based on geographical, political, and cultural differences.[3]

It is this aspect of the issue of Hellenization that I would like to explore further here—on a much smaller canvas to be sure—attempting to identify ethnic contrasts on a regional basis when faced with the new situation. Galilee not only participated in Jewish culture, as we shall claim, within the limits of Eretz Israel, but on an East/West axis it also partook of a regionalism characterized by diverse ethnic populations with very different lifestyles within a territory that ranged from the Mediterranean to the Euphrates. Indeed, the emergence of the very name *galil haggoyim* (Isa 8:23) shows an early awareness of the tension that this twofold pull implied for the inhabitants of the northern region in the period of Assyrian political and cultural control in the eighth century BCE. It is surely no accident that the same tension comes to expression in the second century BCE at the height of the Greek cultural domination as described in the First Book of Maccabees (Γαλιλαία ἀλλοφύλων [1 Macc 5:15]). The Phoenicians to the west and the Itureans to the east were Galilee's nearest neighbors in this later period according to our literary sources, but whereas these are ethnic descriptions, Galilee is primarily a geographic one, thus giving rise over the last two centuries to a lively debate about the ethnic makeup of the population there.[4]

By discussing the special instance of Galilee in the Hellenistic period within a wider context it is hoped to clarify this question, as well as other issues regarding its social and cultural ethos which have surfaced in recent discussions. These are often prompted by extraneous considerations that have more to do with twentieth-century concerns than with accurate historical profiling. However, the introduction of regional variations into the discussion of Hellenization is intended not just for the sake of adding one more qualification to that overused term, but rather with a view to uncovering some of the real issues that were at stake within this particular instance of cultural interchange that fascinates and preoccupies us all. To what extent might it be the case that Galilee's cultural affiliations and ethnic allegiances were shaped by Phoenician encroachment or Iturean expansion on the region south of Hermon, as the Seleucid control began to loosen in the mid-second century BCE? And if either or both of these alternatives were the case, in what recognizable forms might they have expressed themselves—as vestiges of an older, Semitic lifestyle and its presuppositions, or as mediums of the Greek language and culture, as this had already been mediated by the Ptolemies throughout the previous century? How might the emerging Judean state and its ideology of territorial expansion have viewed such developments, and what were the chances that, as it sought to realize the Deuteronomic ideal of the land, it might encounter an older population sympathetic to its objectives? What, if any, contribution to the later cultural mix did the various dynastic changes from the Assyrian to the Persian period make, even prior to Alexander's conquests? These are some of the questions that a regional approach to our topic give rise to, questions that are far easier to pose than to answer in any definitive way.

The Phoenicians

Let us begin with the Phoenicians since, despite the absence of a national literature, we are relatively well informed about them, due to their maritime activity, the rise of a significant Diaspora within the Mediterranean world, and their frequent contacts with the Greeks long before Alexander's day. Indeed, it is to this familiarity with and respect for their cultural achievements among the Greeks that Millar attributes the fact that, unlike elsewhere, the signs of a "deliberate effort at Hellenization of Phoenicia are markedly slight."[5] By Hellenization here and elsewhere, Millar has in mind, not the natural fusion of material cultures through the adoption of architectural and other forms, such as pottery and the like, based on regional skills and local materials, but the conscious introduction of Greek constitutions to older cities as well as the establishment of new ones and the imposition of new forms of religious belief and practice as a replacement for the older Semitic ones. Such policies often went hand in hand with changes in the vernacular language of the region and the arrival of new settlers designed to control or "enlighten" the natives.

The accounts of the earlier relations between the Phoenicians and the Israelites suggest a situation of inequality, one in which separate Israelite ethnicity came under threat (Judges 1:31f.; 5:17), or where Solomon was dependent on the goodwill of Hiram, king of Tyre, in order to establish and maintain the Jerusalem temple (1 Kings 5:1–12; 9:10–13). In this latter instance, not merely was an annual tax paid in terms of wheat and oil, but Galilean territory "in the land of Cabul" was also ceded to the Tyrians. In the eighth century an even more serious problem emerged in that the Israelite cult came under threat from an aggressive policy of syncretization under Jezebel, giving rise to Elijah's famous contest with the priests of the Baal of Carmel (1 Kings 18). The identity of this deity has been widely discussed, but certain features of the narrative, particularly the taunts of the sleeping god, or the god absent on a journey, bear a striking resemblance to the profile that later emerges of Melqart, the god of Tyre, rather than to the more general Baal Shamem, who was featured at the head of the pantheon in the seventh-century treaty of Esharhaddon, king of Assyria with the king (*baal*) of Tyre.[6] The extent to which these patterns of aggressive colonization may have been further facilitated by the Hellenistic spirit is something that we shall return to in the final section of this paper.

In the light of Millar's statement previously cited, how are we to characterize the Phoenician encounter with Hellenism? It is noteworthy that with the exception of Akko, none of the Phoenician coastal cities changed its name. As Elias Bickerman had previously noted, it is not at all evident that the older Phoenician cities received Greek charters[7] and Josephus mentions the presence of records at Tyre, dating back to the reign of Hiram (*Ag. Ap.* 1.155–58). While this claim may simply be based on the demands of Greek historiography rather than actual fact, it nevertheless shows a consciousness of their own past and a desire to remember that past that was resistant to the ideology of the Greco-Macedonian empire. The fact that the Phoenician language continued to be used in inscriptions and on coin legends is a further indication of a certain cultural conservatism, even when Greek had increasingly become the language of administration and commerce in the region generally, already in the Persian period.[8] The claim of Philo of Byblos to have translated an earlier Phoenician history by one Sanchuniathon presents a similar problem to Josephus' Tyrian records. Recent opinion seems to be that the work is indeed to be dated to the Hellenistic era, but again it reflects a concern with its own past on the part of Hellenistic Phoenicia. The fact that some correspondence has been established between Philo's account of Phoenician religion and the Canaanite and Hittite mythology that has been discovered this century, suggests that he had access to ancient traditions.[9]

The idea of continuity in Phoenician religion from the pre-Hellenistic to the Hellenistic age would seem to be supported by a consideration of the *interpretatio Graeca* as this appears on inscriptions, especially bilingual ones, both in the homeland and in the Diaspora. Thus, one second-century BCE dedicatory inscription from Malta is addressed to Lord Melqart, Lord of Tyre, "because he listened to the call of the two brothers 'BD'SR and 'SRSMR". Both are theophoric names related to the Egyptian god Osiris, but in the Greek version of the inscription they are rendered by the names Dionysus and Serapis, the former being identified with Osiris according to Herodotus, and the latter being his Egypto-Greek name.[10] In the Greek rendering, the dedicants are described as Tyrians, and Lord Melqart is translated as *Herakles archegetes*. This same identification is also found in a first-century BCE bilingual inscription from the northern Phoenician town of Arados. In this instance the son of the religious affairs commissioner makes a dedication as gymnasiarch to Hermes and Herakles, according to the Greek text. In the Phoenician version, however, he is given his Semitic name, Astharthut, again a theophoric name related to the goddess Astarte, who is closely connected with Melqart within the Phoenician pantheon. Of considerable interest is that whereas the name Hermes is simply transliterated as L'RM, Herakles is rendered Melqart.[11]

Both inscriptions show how the two worlds of Greece and Phoenicia are intimately intertwined in religious matters, not merely in terms of personal theophoric names, but also by the fact that a person bearing a Semitic name could hold the office of gymnasiarch, with all the connotations of Hellenistic culture that the office implies, and yet wish to honor his native god by its Semitic name as well as by the Greek equivalent. Clearly, in these instances at least, the two worlds are not seen to be opposed to each other. The emergence of individual city gods such as Melqart at Tyre or Eshmun at Sidon might be compared to the notion of the patron god of the Greek city, the giver of its charter, and indeed the Phoenician cities maintained their independence from each other even prior to the Hellenistic age. Melqart had clearly emerged within the Tyrian pantheon before the Greek period, the circumstances of his supplanting the more universal and chthonic deity, Baal Shamem, being unclear.[12] Whereas in the Esharhaddon treaty Baal Shamem as well as Baal Malage and Baal Saphon are in the first rank of Phoenician deities, with Astarte, Eshmun, and Melqart belonging to the second grade, the Israelite prophet Ezechiel in the sixth century, if not already Elijah in the eighth, seems to regard Melqart as the god of Tyre (Ezek 28: 4–9).

Indeed, the identification of Melqart and Herakles must have taken place already by the Persian period. Herodotus describes how his search for Herakles took him to Tyre, knowing that there was a sacred sanctuary to the god there, which, the priests of the god informed him, had dated from the foundation of the city over 2000 years earlier. He also discovered at Tyre a second shrine to Herakles of Thasos, and on arriving at that island learned that this had been established by the Phoenicians on their search for Europa, the daughter of Agenor, the king of Tyre. Thus, the father of Greek history is aware that the Phoenician Herakles (i.e., Melqart) is older than the Greek Herakles, the son of Amphitruon, and acknowledges that there are two gods of the same name, the one Olympian and the other a hero (*History* 2.44). The information which Herodotus claims to have been given at Tyre and Thasos shows a desire to have the patron of the city associated with its very foundation in the remote past. In fact the name itself, Melqart, is derived from *melek/*king, and hence it is plausibly assumed that the god is none other than the figure of the founding king, in line with the west-Semitic cult of the divinized royal ancestors, thus supplanting the more impersonal Baal Shamem. Philo of Byblos indirectly supports this derivation in his allusion to a similar distinction to that of Herodotus, namely, that the Phoenicians worship both humans who have been their benefactors and the planets, "so that for them some gods were mortal and some immortal" (*PE* 1. 9.29).

This identification of Melqart with Herakles, as well as that of Eshmun with Asklepios at Sidon, was not a random decision, but rather relates to the specific traits of both the Phoenician gods and their Greek counterparts. Eshmun was a healing god, as is suggested by his name from the root *šemĕn* ("oil"), and his sanctuary at Sidon was located near a stream that was reputed to have healing properties. His identification with Asklepios, the Greek god of healing was, therefore, natural and obvious.[13] The Melqart/Herakles identification may be attributed to Phoenician colonists in the West, rather than to Greek traders, if the story of Herodotus regarding the sanctuary of the god at Thasos deserves any credence. Again, the linkage appears to be well thought through on the basis of the biography of both gods. Both are divinized heroes and their victory over death was cultically celebrated—by the spring rite of the *egersis* in the case of Melqart, which Josephus reports (*Ant.* 8.146), and by the offering of quails to Herakles, since according to the legend, after having been killed by the Tryphon, he was restored to life through being given a quail by Iolaus. Both engaged in travel, Herakles as the bringer of peace and order and Melqart as the founder of cities throughout the Mediterranean world.[14] Thus, the epithet ἀρχηγητής, normally reserved for Apollo, was an appropriate one, as in the Malta inscription already discussed, where it renders the Phoenician *baal ṣur* ("lord of Tyre"). The role of Melqart in founding Phoenician colonies in the Greek islands, North Africa, Italy, and Spain can be documented from literary and inscriptional evidence, most notably in the account by Diodorus of the Carthaginians bringing tithes annually to his shrine in the mother city, in order to appease his wrath (Diodorus Siculus 20.14. 2–20). Indeed, so important was this role for Herakles/Melqart that Diodorus can describe him as being *para tois apoikois* ("among the colonists").[15] We shall later see that this aspect of the Tyrian god's activities is quite significant in assessing the city's cultural influences on Galilee.

This brief discussion of the Phoenician encounter with Hellenistic culture shows that it was not by any means a hostile or invasive experience. Millar is certainly correct in stressing the importance of earlier contacts and the reputation that the Phoenicians had acquired in the Greek world, going back to Homer. This gave them an advantage when a new and, insofar as we can judge, more pervasive and invasive cultural shift occurred after Alexander. The fact that Tyre had resisted him for a considerable length of time did not result in any serious consequences for the city subsequently. The degree of independence associated with the minting of one's own city coins which both Tyre and Sidon enjoyed from the late second century BCE until the reign of Nero in the first century CE expressed itself in their ability to retain historical memories of their past and to express these in games, rituals, *some* sense of their independent ethnicity based on language, and possibly even in the retention of records. The fact that in all probability their chief god, Melqart, had received an *interpretatio graeca* from Phoenician colonists rather than having an alien understanding imposed by others proves to be an interesting contrast with the Jews that will be discussed further at a later stage.

The Itureans

If our information about the Phoenicians in the Hellenistic age is relatively secure though sketchy, the situation with regard to the Itureans is quite different. Nevertheless, it seems important to pursue them as far as our sources will allow, since Galilee is one of the places where they are to be found in the second century BCE. This piece of information is based on Strabo's report of Timagenes, preserved by Josephus, who reports that the Hasmonean, Aristobulus I, gave them the option of either undergoing circumcision or of leaving the region (*Ant.* 13.318–19). We shall examine this information more fully in the next section, but here it should be noted that it has been taken to support the conclusion that the Iturean territory in Palestine "must have included Galilee, or most of it."[16] Recently, Richard Horsley has provided a novel interpretation of Josephus' account by distinguishing between the Itureans who ruled the territory and were driven out by the Hasmoneans, and the native

Galileans who were of Israelite stock and whose forcible (re-)circumcision should be seen as part of their domination by the Jerusalem/Judean temple state.[17] Thus, the Itureans were either near neighbors of, or the actual inhabitants of, the Hasmonean state in the Hellenistic period, and any study of the effects of Hellenization in the region calls for an examination of their profile on a larger scale.

The difficulty in tracking down the Itureans is partly due to the sources, but also because of the seminomadic lifestyle of at least some of their members. Already in the early Persian period they are to be found in northern Transjordan, where the Israelite tribes of Reuben, Gad, and half Manasseh are reported to have encountered various Arab tribes, including Jetur, who elsewhere is numbered among the sons of Ishmael (1 Chron 5:18–22; Gen 25:13–15).[18] Our best source for the later period is Strabo, who locates the Itureans (and other Arabs) in the mountainous regions overlooking the plain of Marsyas, between the Lebanon and Anti-Lebanon ranges, and later he also locates them in the region of Damascus (Strabo, *Geog.* 16.755f.). In both instances it is their lawless lifestyle that he describes, often living in mountain caves and harassing the farmers of the plain, or robbing the merchants plying their trade between Arabia Felix and Damascus, a picture that is also corroborated by Josephus (*Ant.* 15.344–48). By Strabo's own day in the reign of Augustus this threat had been overcome, he claims, due to "good government established by the Romans, and through the Roman soldiers that are kept in Syria." This clearly refers to the establishment of Berytus as a Roman *colonia* by Augustus in 15 BCE and the stationing of Roman legionaries in its territory, including the Beqa' valley. As part of the same policy he had earlier, in 23 BCE he transferred the territory of Trachonitis, Batanea, and Auranitis to the control of Herod the Great, after the governor of Syria had routed the robbers from the region (Josephus, *Ant.* 15.343), much to the chagrin of Zenodorus, the Iturean chief who was then in charge of the region and who in addition had once again resorted to banditry to increase his income. On his death in 20 CE, the remaining territories which he controlled, namely, Banias and Ulatha (Huleh) and their territories were also assigned to Herod, thus effectively bringing to an end the Iturean political presence south of Hermon and Damascus, even though Herod had to deal with another outbreak of banditry in Trachonitis later by establishing a colony of Idumeans in the region (Josephus, *Ant.* 16.271–75; cf. *OGIS* 424).

It would, however, be inaccurate to see the Itureans merely as marauding nomads lacking in political and administrative skills. Admittedly, the material remains such as Khirbet Zemel do suggest more primitive forms of dwelling, dating from the late second century CE, and so-called Golan or Iturean ware is roughly produced and betrays less-developed ceramic techniques than other locally produced ware in the general region.[19] In all probability we should think of a dimorphic society on the basis of the archaeological evidence from the Hauran, that is, partly settled and partly nomadic or seminomadic, moving around in the Arabian steppe in the eastern Leja, but not necessarily at odds with each other.[20] It is in the territory north of Damascus that the Iturean kingdom of Chalcis is to be located, probably also including Baalbek/Heliopolis, even though the site of Chalcis itself has not been definitively established.[21] It is possible that the Itureans had been able to gain a permanent foothold in the Beqa' region as early as the Persian period, since we hear of Arabs in the region of the Anti-Lebanon harassing Alexander during his campaign against Tyre in 333 BCE. The fact that the name of the first Iturean ruler mentioned in the sources bears the dynastic name of Ptolemy, son of Mennaeus, might suggest that already in the third century BCE some Itureans had come into direct contact with Greek influences. Certainly, like the Hasmoneans in Judea, they were able to avail of the breakup of the Seleucid dynasty to gain a firmer foothold in the region during the second century BCE. It is during Pompey's incursion into Syria that Ptolemy, son of Mennaeus, comes into view, when on payment of 1,000 talents, he was restored to his kingdom of Chalcis (Josephus, *Ant.* 14.39, 128).

Ptolemy continued to rule until 40 BCE, clearly as a vassal of Rome, and using the titles *ethnarchos et archiereus* on his coins. This latter title has been taken to mean that he regarded himself as controlling the most important cultic site in the territory, namely Baalbek, thereby emulating the Hasmoneans in Judea.[22] Twice he attempted to take Damascus, but was repulsed, first by the Nabatean king Aretas III, and later with the aid of the Hasmonean, Aristobulus II (*Ant.* 13.392, 418). Despite these reverses, he continued to engage in regional politics, forging links with the Hasmoneans through marriage and supporting Aristobulus' son Antigonus and the Parthians in the civil war against Herod the Great. However, unlike Herod and the Nabateans to the south, he was not able to secure his dynasty as a client of Rome. As already mentioned, the southern part of Ptolemy's erstwhile territory fell to Herod the Great, passing through the hands of Cleopatra first and then Ptolemy's grandson, Zenodorus, whereas Chalcis itself was divided into the ethnarchies of Abilene and Iturea (cf. Luke 3:1), eventually being integrated into the Roman province of Syria in the second century. Rome's apparent lack of confidence in Ptolemy's successors controlling this troubled region, which was so important for east-west and north-south caravan routes through Damascus, might suggest that the Itureans were resistant to influences coming from the west and sought to maintain a cultural independence also. Throughout the first century it was thus left to Herodian princes (Philip, Agrippa I, his brother, Herod of Chalcis, and Agrippa II), all educated in Rome and having close ties there, to ensure the stability of the region.[23] Even then, the example of some Idumeans maintaining their allegiance to their native god Kos as a way of refusing full allegiance either to Judea or to Rome in the person of Herod (*Ant.* 15.253–58), shows the continued importance of traditional religion. In addition, the archaeological evidence from the Hauran in terms of inscriptions, architectural forms, and ceramic patterns shows that although the medium was Greek and the administration Roman, the village culture of southern Syria was able to combine some traditional values with the new reality of life.[24] Once again, Millar states the issue succinctly, if cautiously: "We may note that both Strabo and Dio Cassius describe some of the inhabitants as 'Arabs'; but what they mean by that remains obscure. Nor can we be certain whether rural temples built in classical forms, whose known worshippers used Greek when they put up inscriptions, did not embody older local traditions and forms of belief. It must nonetheless be significant that such hypothetical older traditions could now be expressed in Greek forms."[25]

One way to proceed is to examine the evidence emanating from various sites in the territories known to have been inhabited by Itureans. Even though Baalbek may have been under the control of Ptolemy, son of Mennaeus, this site has yielded little of its pre-Roman past and is, therefore, of no direct value for this enquiry. Other sites in the region are more promising, however, especially Niha (Aramaic Nihatha), where the remains of two temples have been discovered, one of them being among the oldest temples in Syria.[26] The later of the two, dating probably from the mid-second century CE, attests to the fusion of older traditions with Roman colonial presence since the foundation of the colony of Berytus under Augustus. Of particular interest is a relief of a priest, Narkisos, son of Casios, who is described as an honorary decurion (*bouleutikos*) of the colony of Heliopolis (*IGLS* VI 2935), yet his dress and pose are decidedly oriental: "la frontalité occidentale s'allie au hieratisme oriental," as J.-P. Rey-Coquais describes it.[27] Two Latin inscriptions are also significant. One is a votive dedication by the prophetess Hochma to the god Hadranus, "having fasted from bread for 20 years by order of the god" (*IGLS* VI.2928). Another is bilingual (Latin and Greek) from a funerary monument erected to the *Dea Syr(ia) Nihat(ena)* by a veteran with the name Sextus Allius Jullus, the goddess being given her old Syrian name *Atargatis* in the Greek rendering (*IGLS* VI.2929). Clearly, Hadranus is closely related to Atargatis and one is tempted to see here traces of the old Syrian weather gods, Hadad and Atargatis, who were honored in an early Hellenistic inscription in the region of Ptolemais/Akko also.[28] At nearby Hosn Niha we meet another local god, Mifsensus, in an inscription relating to the discharge of an offering to this god by nine members of the local council on behalf of the village and the worshipers (*IGLS* VI 6.2946). Significantly, five of the nine names are clearly Semitic, the other four being Roman. Like those at Niha itself, this inscription is in a temple that architecturally is similar to that of Jupiter Heliopolitanus at nearby Baalbek. Thus, at these rural sanctuaries of the Beqa', local conservatism in religious matters is still being maintained even by those who regard themselves as Roman colonists, at the very time in the second century CE that Heliopolitan Jupiter is supplanting local deities in the whole region.[29] Unfortunately, we have no information on the cult of the older sanctuary at Niha, nor can we speak of the native Semites as Iturean. Nevertheless, the pattern of local conservatism that these relatively late inscriptions betray at a shrine, which must have been within their erstwhile territory, suggests that it may still be possible to identify traces of their worship in other contexts.

Another location where local cult sites have been discovered is in the Hermon region, territory bordering on—if not actually belonging to—the Itureans' possessions in the Huleh and Banias regions. Shimon Dar, who has both surveyed sixty-four sites in the whole region and engaged in archaeological work at several of the more important locations, has confidently identified these sites as Iturean, a conclusion that has been challenged on the basis of the lack of clear ethnic identity markers for the inhabitants of the region by the archaeologist of Banias, Zvi Uri Ma'oz.[30] Har Senaim, only four kilometers from Banias, is particularly important, however, because irrespective of its dating, it represents a virtual high place of relatively primitive and humble dimensions when compared with other rural temple sites in Syria. Two cult complexes were discovered, the coin profile of the upper one suggesting a date from the Hellenistic/early Roman times, though in the absence of stratified digs, this, too, has been challenged by Ma'oz. The complex consists of an enclosure with a number of rooms and courtyards with cisterns, leading to an open space hewn out of a rock. From this point there is a magnificent view of the valley below, with two *stelai,* suggesting that this was the primary place of worship within the complex. More than a dozen *stelai* in all were found within the whole complex, some standing *in situ* in pairs and some lying on the ground. At the lower complex the outlines of two adjacent temples were found, one of them without a roof and embodying the rock as the possible cult object. Fragments of decorated columns, cornices, and architraves as well as a number of statues of eagles lay strewn around the complex, and also a small bronze incense burner and a basalt altar. A relief of Helios with seven rays emanating from his head was found on one of three altars located in a secluded spot. In addition several Greek inscriptions, dated to the second century CE, were also discovered, making it possible to suggest a larger social and cultural context for this complex.[31]

While the criticism of Dar's too easy identification of this site with the Itureans has some validity, Ma'oz does agree that Har Senaim represents a unique cult site with primitive features in terms of its worship and layout. The pairs of *stelai* of unequal height probably represent male and female deities, either of Arabian or Phoenician background. They also partake of the aniconic tradition of ANE worship which identifies the gods with rocks, stones, or other natural objects, especially associated with mountain tops and high places.[32] As late as Eusebius, Hermon was known as a place of pagan worship, and there is the inscription to the *theos megistos k(ai) hagios* found on the summit of the mountain top, discovered by Sir Charles Warren in 1870.[33] The fact that the Har Senaim cult sites should probably be dated later than Dar suggests only heightens their significance in terms of the larger religious situation of the region, including nearby Banias. In such a context, they almost seem out of place and time. Har Senaim is only one of several cultic sites identified by Dar within a small radius of each other, suggesting that the religious culture of Hermon had continued the older idea of local *baalim* being worshipped at separate sites, rather than the more generalized worship of a god such as Zeus/Baal Shamem or Helios/ Sol Invictus that began to assert itself in the Hellenistic and Roman periods. On that basis it might be possible to distinguish between the upper and lower complexes at Har Senaim, just as the two temples at Niha seem also to reflect such a development. While the *theos megistos* of the Warren inscription points in the direction of Baal Shamem, the Helios relief with the seven rays emanating from its head is similar to several medallions found in Baalbek and points to an Arabic background.[34] Thus the altar relief of Helios at Har Senaim might be an indicator of Iturean influence there after all.

Space does permit an examination of a third site with possible Iturean connections, namely Sia in the Hauran, where a temple of Baal Shamem retained its Semitic character despite its social role on behalf of the Roman presence in the east on the borders of desert, steppe, and settled land. Again, however, the only case that can be made for Iturean presence there is circumstantial, namely, the information that this whole region was once inhabited by brigands who can reasonably be identified with the Itureans and their lifestyle, as this is known to us from Strabo. Though our search for the Itureans as bearers of a pre-Hellenistic culture has proved inconclusive, it has not been futile in terms of the larger theme of this paper. The comparison with the Phoenicians is highly instructive. Whereas they were able to maintain clear traces of their pre-Greek past in cultural terms and a degree of independence politically under both the Hellenistic monarchs and Rome, a distinctive Iturean culture has virtually vanished under the weight of Greek and Roman presence in the East. There are obvious reasons for such contrasting fates of the two ethnic groups, based on their respective pasts and previous achievement of separate cultural identity. The seafaring activities of the Phoenicians are the envy of the Jews, as Josephus' thinly veiled comments in the *Contra Apionem* indicate (*Ag. Ap.* 1.60), but the Itureans surface from the anonymity of other Arab tribes mentioned in passing in our sources only because of their precarious lifestyle and the fact that they were a possible frustration to Rome's ambitions in the East. Even if we were to suppose that the kingdom of Chalcis and the other territories were populated solely by Itureans, a claim that Ma'oz contests, we should still have to acknowledge that they have left very few unambiguous traces of their pre-Greek past in terms of language, religion, or distinctive ethos, in striking contrast to their Nabatean "cousins" in the south. Politically, they were no more successful in making the transition that other neighboring peoples had made in accommodating themselves to Roman rule in the East. Perhaps we shall find the missing traces in Galilee! For what it is worth, one clue might be the fact that among the defenders of Jotapata in 66 CE is a certain Neteiras (*War* 3.233), a name also found on one of the inscriptions from Har Senaim.[35] What is in a name?

Galilee and Galileans

Earlier it was suggested that the name "Galilean" was not primarily an ethnic marker in a manner similar to "Phoenician" or "Iturean," despite Josephus' use of the phrase *ethnos ton Galilaion* on two occasions (*War* 2.510; 4.105), a usage which is important to Horsley in building his case for separate identities for Galileans and Judeans.[36] It is true that the name Galilee does have a certain *implied* ethnic connotation. The Hebrew *hag-galil*, the Greek translation of which is *Galilaia* in the LXX (and *Galila* in the Zenon papyri) originally means "the circle," and with the addition of *ethnon allophulon* (Isa 8:23 LXX; 1 Macc 5:15), the phrase is deemed to denote the early Israelite experience living in the hill country and surrounded by hostile Canaanite city states.[37] It was appropriate, therefore, for the nationalistic author of 1 Maccabees to recall the Isaian phrase (but translating *goyim* by *allophulon* rather than by *ethnon* as in the LXX) in his account of the hostility experienced by Jerusalem worshipers living in the northern region in the wake of Antiochus IV's decree in the mid-second century BCE. Indeed, this same experience recurred almost two hundred years later on the eve of the first revolt, and Josephus' list of cities where Jews suffered is mainly centered on Galilee: Scythopolis, Ptolemais, Tyre, Hippos, Gadara, and the territory of Agrippa II, i.e., Batanea, Hauran, and Trachonitis (*War* 2.477–83). It could be argued that these depictions of Galilee and its inhabitants emanate from a Jerusalem-based perspective and are highly apologetic in tone and that the situation was more complex. The real issue becomes one of describing more accurately the ethnographic mix in Galilee and the role which the phenomenon we call Hellenism played in shaping or reshaping religio-cultural affiliations of the population there.

This general question raises a number of other more specific ones, as already indicated. To begin with, it would be important to know the general situation in Galilee prior to Alexander in order to estimate properly the changes which occurred in his wake. Two contrasting answers have been given to this question in the scholarly debates about Galilee. On the one hand, it has been claimed that in the eighth-century BCE Assyrian conquest of the north, Galilee fared rather better under Tiglathpilesar III in 732 BCE than did Samaria and its immediate environs under Sargon II in 721, in that only a small section of the ruling elite in the north was deported, whereas Samaria itself was depopulated and replanted by foreigners. On the basis of this analysis of the literary record, Alt claimed that people of Israelite stock and allegiance continued to dwell in Galilee, and that these remained largely undisturbed throughout subsequent regimes. Thus, when the opportunity presented itself in the wake of the Maccabean wars of expansion, the Galileans entered the ἔθνος τῶν Ἰουδαίων, as it were, by right. More recently, Richard Horsley has also supported the Galilean Israelites remaining in place through the centuries, but unlike Alt, he sees the Hasmonean conquest as imposing the "laws of the Judeans" on an unwilling and unreceptive population in the north.[38]

While Alt and Horsley rely on the literary evidence, a very different picture emerges from recent reports of archaeology in Galilee. Thus, Zvi Gal's survey of lower Galilee finds a major break in the settlement of the region in the seventh/sixth centuries, that is, coinciding with the Assyrian conquest and its aftermath. It was only in the Persian period that the number of settlements in this region begins to increase again. This evidence seems to correlate well with the Assyrian annals and inscriptions, so that Horsley's summary dismissal of Gal's findings is unwarranted.[39] In addition to Gal's findings in lower Galilee, account should also be taken of the surveys of Upper Galilee conducted by M. Aviam and others on behalf of the Association for the Archaeological Survey of Israel.[40] From this it emerges that a village culture began to appear in Upper Galilee in the Persian and early Hellenistic periods (93 sites in all), with further increases in the Roman and Byzantine periods, not merely in Galilee, but in the Golan also.[41] This upward curve in the number of settlements should be attributed to internal Jewish migration, with the need for new settlements and military outposts, following on the Maccabean expansion, and the move to the north of many southern Jews as a consequence of the second revolt. Archaeology cannot always decide definitively on the Jewish ethnicity of individual settlements, since we do not know how widespread the use was in the early Hellenistic period of such later instrumentalities of Jewish faith as *miqwoth*, synagogues, and dietary regulations requiring certain kinds of kitchenware. Nevertheless, some assumptions can be made, as for example, that sites which can be clearly identified as Jewish for a later period (e.g., Meiron, Gush Halav, Khirbet Shema, and Nabratein), in all probability were Jewish earlier also, even when definitive artifactual evidence may be lacking.[42] Aviam has also noted that in several instances sites were abandoned in the early Hellenistic period, and at bedrock in others. Hasmonean coins predominate, thereby supporting the further assumption that non-Jewish sites such as Har Mizpeh Yamim had to be abandoned contemporaneously with new Hasmonean foundations taking root in the region.[43]

In the light of this new information it seems difficult to maintain the Alt/Horsley line of a continued Israelite presence in the north from the seventh to the second century BCE. Indeed, it is debatable if such a specific ethnic identity could have been maintained in the absence of a central place of Yahweh worship locally, other than Gerizim or Jerusalem. There is no indication that Galileans showed any interest in the former during the Persian period, and, at least in Horsley's view, they were supposed to be independent of the latter.[44] Once it is accepted that the region was relatively underinhabited at the beginning of the Hellenistic age, the issue of Hellenism in Galilee is very different from the situation which obtained in nearby Phoenicia. The Phoenician coastline was dotted with cities and lesser foundations that already in the Persian period had established free association through trade and commerce with the Greek world, and in the case of Tyre in particular had embarked on a program of setting up Phoenician colonies in the west under the patronage of their city god Melqart.[45] The arrival of Alexander must certainly have been seen as an interruption: he was strongly opposed at Tyre for seven months and at Gaza. Nonetheless, they and other cities were able to retain something of the status they had acquired previously under the Persians, and presumably they soon began to be organized along the lines of Greek cities—as the change of Akko's name to Ptolemais indicates—though the extent to which older institutions may have continued must remain an open question, as we have seen. Under the Ptolemies, Tyre and Ptolemais, as the two closest Phoenician cities to Galilee, functioned as important ports for produce from the interior for export to Egypt, as we learn from the Zenon papyri. Presumably also their territories were extended, but the number of fortresses between the territory of Ptolemais and Galilee such as Cabul and Tefen[46] suggests that the latter was separately administered as γῆ βασιλική even when some native landowners were still operating there, as Tcherikover rightly acknowledges.[47]

The Ptolemaic administration introduced many different forms of Greek officialdom into Galilee, as can also be discerned from the Zenon correspondence, and we would have to suppose that some of these were non-Semites, even though the case of Toubias in Perea should make one cautious of drawing hard lines between Greeks and non-Greeks in terms of cultural accommodation, at least among the upper echelons of the native population. We must also assume that throughout the third century BCE various cult centers such as Har Mispe Yamim also emerged.[48] This site, located on a spur of Mt. Meron, is in the center of Galilee, and as its name implies, overlooks both the Jordan valley and the Mediterranean coast. The site comprises a walled enclosure with two structures, which on the basis of pottery finds can be dated to the Persian period. One of the rooms is cultic in purpose, having a paved floor, stone benches for seating and a raised altar with steps leading up to it. In the Hellenistic period it underwent changes with the temple area, becoming an open courtyard but still continuing as a cultic site with a large quantity of animal bones being discovered.

Of special significance are a number of bronze artifacts discovered at the site: a decorated situla or bronze votive vessel, an apis bull, a recumbent ram, and a prancing lion cub. The decoration of the situla includes a representation of a male making an offering to a number of Egyptian gods who are identified by name in Egyptian. A Phoenician inscription has been added secondarily, which dedicates the object to Astarte "because she heard my voice" on behalf of one *bd 'smn*, a theophoric name meaning "in the hand of Eshmun," the Sidonian god. The excavators assign the finds to the Persian period, but suppose that they continued to be used in the Hellenistic period when the site was finally abandoned with signs of destruction of the apis bull and also a slate figurine of Osiris, Horus, and Isis. This one site clearly illustrates several stages of Galilean life in the Hellenistic period. Its foundation in the Persian period alerts us to the need for caution in drawing rigid lines between various periods and cultures in the world of the Ancient Near East, but the site's continued use and adaptation in the Hellenistic period associates it with the strong Ptolemaic presence in Galilee during the third century BCE. Since the Phoenician inscription is added secondarily to the situla, it is uncertain when precisely this reuse of the object occurred, but the Phoenician (Sidonian?) coloring is unmistakable, and illustrates how Galilee in the early Hellenistic age was open to religio-cultural influences from various outside locations. Finally, the destruction of the site and its non-use subsequently underlines the impact of the Hasmonean expansion on Galilean life and society.

The issue of Hellenism in Galilee then becomes a question of how the Hasmoneans dealt with the region from the mid-second century onward, rather than one of how an older established Semitic people coped with a new wave of culture coming from the Greek world for the first time. As Tessa Rajak has argued convincingly, the Hasmoneans combined an active acceptance of certain aspects of Hellenism in areas such as coinage, architecture, and military organization, together with a militantly nationalistic outlook that expressed itself in a war of conquest of what were perceived to be the national territories.[49] Thus Simon could be represented as articulating Hasmonean territorial policy as follows: "We have taken neither foreign land or seized foreign property, but only the inheritance of our fathers, which at one time had been unjustly taken by our enemies. Now that we have the opportunity we are firmly holding the inheritance of our fathers" (1 Macc 15:33). Likewise, the court historian Eupolemus also reflects this ideology of conquest, drawing not on the patriarchal narratives but on the biblical past of David and Solomon. Among the nations round about that David is said to have conquered are the Phoenicians and the Itureans. At a later point he has Solomon ordering various regions, including Galilee, to provision the builders of the temple (*PE* 9.30.3–4; 33).

By way of conclusion to this paper we must now briefly examine the impact of these policies on both the Phoenician and Iturean presence in Galilee in the light of the earlier discussion of their developments in the Hellenistic age.

A. The Phoenicians in Galilee

The dangers of assimilation, territorial encroachment, and religious competition were all aspects of previous history, on the basis of the biblical accounts (Judg 1:31f.; 5:17; 1 Kings 8 and 18). Indeed, the fact that some of the so-called Hellenizers had sought to emulate the days of Jezabel by joining in the celebration of Melqart was a clear indication of the attraction of Tyre in particular for certain elements of the Jerusalem aristocracy (2 Macc 4:18–20). But how far could the Hasmonean wars of conquest go? According to Ezekiel's description of the ideal land, the western boundary was the Great Sea, ignoring the Phoenician presence entirely. Visionary literature was one thing, the reality of politics another. Thus, while Simon rescued some Jews living in the region of Ptolemais and that city was subsequently attacked by Alexander Jannaeus, it was never captured (1 Macc 5:15, 21–23; *Ant.* 13.324–34); the later account of Jannaeus's attack on Tyre is probably not accurate. If military dominance was not an option, cultural exclusion was, and recent archaeological evidence from Galilee can help to fill out that picture in a highly informative way, through an analysis of coins and pottery.

(a) Coins: The preponderance of Tyrian coins at all the excavated sites of Galilee, upper and lower, has given rise to a lively debate. Initially, the Meiron team, working on upper Galilean synagogue sites (Meiron, Gush Halav, and Khirbet Shema') drew far-reaching conclusions about the trade patterns between this region and Tyre. In particular, Richard Hanson's discussion of the coin finds (adopted and supported by Eric Meyers) at the three sites concludes that: "Tyre was the centre of economic influence for a peripheral area that included Upper Galilee in its orbit. The villagers of Upper Galilee were marketing their oil and other products in the direction of Tyre, and receiving Tyrian money in return."[50] This picture, they believe, merely confirms that of Josephus, who describes John of Gischala's entrepreneurial skills as follows: "He then bought up that commodity (oil), paying Tyrian coin of the value of four Attic drachmas for four amphorae, and proceeded to sell half an amphora at the same price" (*War* 2.592; cf. *Life* 74f., where, however, there is no mention of Tyrian coins being used and only Jews in Caesarea Philippi, not Syria, are in question). A later study by Joyce Raynor and Yaakov Meshorer repeats Hanson's conclusions: "Of the Phoenician cities, Tyre continued to be the focus of economic activity and contact with the populace of Meiron. Almost one-quarter of all city coins found at Meiron are Tyrian, many more than from any of the other mints represented. Tyrian influence on the Upper Galilee was continuous and substantial."[51] Meyers was less certain of the dominance of Tyre in the region as a whole when the profile of Nabratein, another village site in the region, subsequently excavated, was brought into the picture. Here the orientation appeared to be more toward the east, rather than toward the Phoenician cities, especially Tyre.[52] Others, too, express caution. Thus, Dan Barag, while agreeing with the Tyrian influence in upper Galilee, feels that the picture could be inflated by the fact that of all the mints producing coins in the region, Tyre was by far the most prolific and operated under the least restrictions in the Roman period. Thus the number of coins emanating from Tyre at these and other sites might not necessarily be an accurate indication of the trading patterns of the city, since mints such as Ptolemais/ Acco, not to speak of Sepphoris or Tiberias, were never authorized to issue coins on the same scale.[53] The comments of Uriel Rappaport are along similar lines. He finds that the presence of Tyrian silver coins at Meiron does not support the views of Hanson and others of large-scale trade between the region and Tyre, but is merely a sign that "Galilee drew mainly on Tyre for its supply of small change."[54] Rappaport's comments seem to raise the question of the scale of trading with Tyre rather than the fact itself. However, Richard Horsley, in a sharply worded critique of the received position of Tyrian influences, argues that the very model which it presupposes, namely that of a free-market economy, is inappropriate and anachronistic. He points rather to the conflictual situation revealed in the hostility at the outbreak of the first revolt between Galilean Jews and Kedasa, "the strong inland village of the Tyrians, always at feud and strife with the Galileans" (*War* 4.105). He queries Josephus' indication that the dispute was partly ethnic-religious (*War* 2.459), and points to the fact that fugitives from the Tyrian region joined the Jewish rebels in 66 CE, reported elsewhere by Josephus as indicative of the ongoing politico-economic situation of conflict, based on Tyre's "dependence for food on villages of the interior, some of which it controlled and other of which it could pressure."[55] The situation at the outbreak of the first revolt may not be the best indicator of earlier relations, however. Undoubtedly, there was a pattern of encroachment by Tyre in particular on the interior at various junctures, but equally there is evidence of Israelites/Jews living in its territory. The situation varied considerably from one period to another, and the danger of using sociological models is that they lead to discarding of evidence that does not fit the particular mold being applied. It may be true that all ancient economies were politically controlled, but there is plenty of evidence even from Ptolemaic times, when state monopoly was the general policy, suggesting that some degree of free market trading also occurred, certainly on local and regional levels. I do not see any reason, therefore, to reject entirely the idea of Upper Galilean peasants trading with Tyre, possibly indeed by means of middlemen, such as John of Gischala, operating through the countryside and at local markets.

Moving from Upper to Lower Galilee opens up a further dimension to this discussion of coins and trading patterns, in view of the recent publication of findings from two important sites, Iotapata (Yodefat) and Gamala. A rather different profile emerges from these two locations, despite their similar strong nationalistic leanings during the first revolt and the fact that neither site was inhabited after 67 CE. At Gamala, a considerable amount of Tyrian coins have been found, covering the whole period from 126 BCE–66 CE, 721 in all, 36 of which are silver shekels and 7 half-shekels. In addition, 128 coins of Sidon have been discovered at the same site. However, this considerable number of Phoenician coins has to be set in the context of the large number of Hasmonean coins there (3,883, or 62.9 percent of the total).[56] The predominance of these coins is in itself not surprising, in that the presence of Hasmonean coins at bedrock is common at many sites in both Upper and Lower Galilee, as already noted, following Aviam. What is surprising is that the Hasmonean and Phoenician coins at Gamala cover the same period, even though the city's pro-revolt stance is expressed by striking its own coin of the revolt with the legend "For Redemption" and on the reverse "Jerusalem the H(oly)."

At Jotapata, David Adan Bayewitz and Mordachai Aviam have detected a definite change in the coin patterns, by contrast. Unlike the simultaneous usage of native Jewish and Phoenician coins at Gamala, there is an abrupt change from Seleucid and Phoenician autonomous coins (Tyre, Sidon, and Ptolemais) to Hasmonean coins only, toward the end of the second century BCE. This disappearance of Phoenician city coins from the last decade of the second century BCE (110 BCE), linked to the change to native Jewish coins, has been judged by the excavators as coinciding with a population shift which they base on other grounds, from "inhabitants tied to the Phoenician coastal cities in the 2nd century to those who avoided contact with those cities," namely, people who were closely aligned to the Hasmonean kingdom. This conclusion receives additional confirmation from the presence of stepped pools, similar to those found in Jerusalem, fragments of stone jars and the absence of any imported fine ware or figurative art, all indicators of a conservative, religiously observant ethos which is concerned about matters of ritual purity.[57]

The contrast between these two sites in terms of contacts with the Phoenician cities, despite the similar Jewish character of both, is certainly striking. It is possible to imagine Jotapata adopting an inward-looking stance in the early Hasmonean period, in view of the hostilities between them and Ptolemais in particular as described in 1 Maccabees. In this regard it is perhaps noteworthy that of the coins of this city prior to the Hasmonean takeover, those of various Seleucid kings and autonomous coins from Ptolemais-Akko (not Tyre) predominate, representing 41.2 percent of the total number of coins found in the whole excavation. One explanation for its subsequent conservatism might therefore be the location in contrast to that of Gamala: the one relatively vulnerable to Phoenician encroachment from the coastal plain; the other, though bordering on the Dekapolis, well-removed from any Phoenician threat. Nevertheless, one could have expected a greater range at Jotapata also in the first century CE, when the Jewish territory had been recognized by the new overlords, the Romans. In this regard, the comparisons with nearby Sepphoris will be of considerable significance when the coins from the various excavations at that center are published and can be studied comparatively.

(b) Ceramics: The recent analysis of Phoenician pottery by Andrea Berlin provides an alternative window on the situation we are exploring. Her highly significant study of the distribution of Phoenician semi-fine ware originated from an examination of the pottery of Tel Anafa.[58] This was a Hellenistic Phoenician outpost in the Huleh valley, where coins of Sidon and Tyre continue to predominate into the early Roman period (first century BCE), after which the settlement appears to have ceased. Only three Hasmonean coins were found in the total collection there so that it never came within the Jewish orbit, unlike Gamala. The ware in question is used for various types of vessels, chiefly for table use. Its Phoenician origins have been established through comparative analysis of similar ware from Um el-Amed and Tyre, with this latter site being the likely place of production. What makes the discovery and identification of this ware particularly valuable is the fact that it can be dated to a very specific period—from late second century BCE to mid-first century CE, but not continuing into the middle Roman period—on the basis of stratified discovery of shards of the ware at three different sites: Dor, Shiqmona, and Tel Anafa.

Berlin has traced the distribution patterns of this ware according to three different types which she believes may have been marketed separately: (i) baggy jars for carrying oil and wine; (ii) serving vessels such as jugs and table amphorae which would have been sold empty, and (iii) personal ware—ointment pots, juglets, unguentaria and small amphoriskoi. The first two types show a very similar distribution pattern—sites along the coast from Tyre to Ascalon and in the Akko plain along the Carmel ridge, together with a cluster of sites in the Huleh valley, including Tel Anafa, Dan, and Tel Wawiyat. The third type, which would have been filled and sold for their contents, have a somewhat wider range of distribution, because they were more easily portable in larger quantities. Thus, in addition to the sites where the first two types are found, this one is also to be had at three sites east of the Sea of Galilee, not far from Gamala–Ein Gev, Horvat Kanaf, and Tell es Shuna, as well as in the Greek islands. What is quite remarkable about this pattern, which Berlin emphasizes, is the absence of any of these types from sites in Galilee, even though its vendors clearly moved from Akko-Ptolemais to the Jezreel valley along the Carmel ridge, thus skirting the borders of Lower Galilee, and likewise in the north, they would have traveled inland to the Huleh, just north of the upper Galilean boundary of the first century. When one compares the distribution map of this ware with the political map of the region in the early Roman period, the convergence between the distribution sites and the territories assigned to the Phoenician cities is remarkably close indeed. Thus, the obvious conclusion is that the ware in question was used by Phoenicians, and particularly in the culturally mixed Huleh basin, where, Berlin suggests, it might be considered as an example of "identity-conscious social grouping" by people seeking to maintain a feeling of cultural identity and connectedness at some distance from their roots.

A comparison of the distribution patterns of the Phoenician fine ware as presented by Berlin with that of the Phoenician coins previously discussed presents some interesting convergences and differences. The resistance to the Phoenician fine ware in lower Galilee would seem to correspond to the disappearance of Phoenician coins at Jotapata in the same period. Galilee developed its own centers for production of household wares and storage jars at Shikhin and Kefr Hanania from the mid-first century BCE, so that the domestic needs of the region were fully taken care of from within Galilee itself and there was, therefore, no need for this type of imported ware, even from nearby Phoenicia. Yet, if the shift in population at Jotapata is to be seen as bringing with it definite changes in religio-cultural attitudes, as has been suggested, then it seems likely that these same factors were operative in the choice of household wares also, especially since the Kefr Hanania ware was commended because of its thermal resistance, thus making the observance of the purity of vessels more manageable (*b. Shabb* 120b). At the same time, the more open attitude to Phoenician trade as exemplified by the coin profile at Gamala is matched by the presence of some of the Phoenician ware in that region, if not in Gamala itself.

In Upper Galilee, however, matters appear to be quite different. The coin patterns and the semifine ware distribution do not converge, since as we have seen, no trace of the semifine ware was discovered at any Galilean site, and, in fact, the household needs as well as the larger storage jars of Meiron, Kh. Shema, Nabratein, and Sasa, all Upper Galilean Jewish sites, were serviced by Kefr Hanania. Such a discrepancy between the coin and pottery profiles of these centers might appear to call for a revision of the trading links which were projected on the basis of the coins alone. However, this need not necessarily be the case, since the Kefr Hanania ware was also found at such non-Jewish sites as Hippos-Susita and Tel Anafa, and so was capable of competing with wares produced elsewhere, even at non-Jewish sites.[59] It might also mean that selling to non-Jews was less of a problem than purchasing from them, especially if the exchange could take place at a local market, rather than in the pagan city itself.

B. Itureans and Galilee

The literary evidence for an Iturean presence in Galilee has already been alluded to. Even if Schürer's claim that most of Galilee was inhabited by them seems an overstatement, we might still have expected to find traces of their presence there subsequently. The Idumeans in the south, who also underwent enforced circumcision, appear to have maintained some forms of separate ethnic identity, either as zealous Jews during the first revolt or as continuing the worship of their native god Qos (*War* 4.345–53; 6.387; *Ant.* 15.253–58), but there is no similar profile for Itureans in later Jewish history. This may mean that, as Josephus' report intimates, they availed themselves of the option of leaving the territory, moving farther north and east. The nearest location to Galilee in which we find them is in Ulatha and Paneas, the territory that passed to Herod the Great on the death of Zenodorus in 20 BCE, and it is from there that continued Iturean influence on Galilee could be expected to emanate. Even there, however, it is difficult to be certain about the extent of and significance of their presence. The borders of political Galilee did not extend that far north, and on the basis of later Jewish settlement patterns, it is clear that boundaries between Jews and non-Jews in this region were rigidly observed. Thus, no remains of Jewish synagogues have been found north of the line running through Sasa, Baram, and Qazyon, a line that corresponds in the main to the political borders of Roman Galilee as described by Josephus (*War* 3. 35–40).[60] Immediately above that line is Kadesh, the border town, which, Josephus says, once belonged to Galilee, but which in his day was a strong inland fortress of Tyre, "always at war with the nation" (*War* 2.459; 4.105). It boasted a second-century CE temple decorated in typical Hellenistic style and dedicated to the "holy sky god," that is, in all probability, Baal Shamem.[61] It is surely significant that further expansion, in terms of distinctive Jewish settlements, took place, not in Upper Galilee but in the Golan, thus maintaining the separate cultural and cultic identities that had emerged in the area over the centuries.

A major difficulty in identifying the Itureans is the lack of unambiguous evidence from the material culture, as already discussed. Traces of the so-called "Iturean" or "Golan" ware have been found, mostly in Upper Galilee, but also at Jotapata, where a number of storage jars have been uncovered, one almost complete example of which stands one meter high.[62] These *pithoi* date from the Hellenistic period, but even if, as seems likely, they are to be identified as Iturean ware, they do not necessarily mean an Iturean occupation of the site, since such jars were part of the ceramic koine of the region, prior to the emergence of Shikhin and Kefr Hanania as local production centers, and the masonry at Jotapata is Phoenician rather than Iturean, as these have been identified from Dor and Kh. Zemel, respectively. Remains of similar pottery were found at Tel Dan also in the Hellenistic levels, and it would be highly significant if the famous bilingual inscription, "to the God who is in Dan," could be attributed to Iturean use of the sanctuary, although any such identification would be purely conjectural. The Hermon sanctuaries are, we claimed, the best evidence for Iturean cult sites in our present state of knowledge. Their remoteness and archaic features are striking, especially when compared with nearby Banias, where the cult of Pan at the grotto dates from 200 BCE. Herod the Great had a temple built there dedicated to Augustus, immediately after being put in charge of the territory of Zenodorus. Josephus' description of this temple is in sharp contrast to the still primitive cult complexes of the Hermon villages.

One aspect of the Iturean lifestyle which was their hallmark elsewhere, namely brigandage, is perhaps the closest that they came to leaving a direct trace of their ongoing presence in Galilee and its environs. As governor of Galilee, the youthful Herod the Great earned his spurs with the Romans by routing a band of brigands and killing their leader, the ἀρχιληστής Hezechias, who was operating on the borders of Syria (War 1.204–6; Ant. 14.158–60). According to Josephus, the praises of Herod were sung throughout the villages and cities of Syria, since they had long wanted to be rid of this threat to their possessions. The episode raised the ire of certain anti-Herodian factions in Jerusalem, however, and Herod was accused of violating Jewish law by his unauthorized action in putting people to death. Hezechias is, of course, a Jewish name; years later, his son Judas led a revolt on Sepphoris after the death of Herod in 4 BCE. The character of this revolt has been variously understood as one of popular kingship, or the remnants of Hasmonean resistance to Herodian rule.[63] At any event it is the nature and theater of Hezechias' action that prompts the suggestion of a possible Iturean connection, for that earlier episode (47 BCE), since the event has the hallmarks of their activity in the Beqa valley as described by Strabo, giving rise to the establishment of Berytus as a Roman colonia (Geog. 16.755). Were such a supposition to be upheld, it would open up an interesting, but not altogether unlikely vista of alliances between Hasmoneans and Itureans. Less than ten years later, Ptolemy, son of Mennaeus, the Iturean prince of Chalcis, joined forces, as we have seen, with the last of the Hasmoneans, Antigonus, in attempting to oust the newly appointed king of the Jews, Herod. Hezechias, either experiencing directly Herod's exaction of extra taxes in Galilee for Rome's war effort against the Parthians, or anticipating the worst for his own ilk as a Hasmonean landowner in Galilee, with the rise of Antipater and his family, may indeed have engaged in brigandage on "the borders of Syria," but his underlying motives were political—the maintenance of Hasmonean control. In this objective he could rely on the Itureans support. Drawing once again on the Idumean parallel, Herod was opposed there also, and the Idumeans proved to be staunch Jewish nationalists in the struggle against Rome a century later. Such a supposition of Galilean-Hasmonean and Iturean alliance against the Herodians is, therefore, quite plausible within the power politics of the time, but clearly only conjectural. Perhaps it is worth noting that Josephus emphasizes the fact that Herod came to the attention of the Romans because of his conduct of this affair, particularly in view of the fact that over twenty years later Augustus was to turn to him again in ridding the region of the destabilizing Iturean menace, not just in Transjordan but in Upper Galilee itself.

Conclusion

This attempt at a regional study of Hellenism and its impact on indigenous peoples of the ANE with differing histories has yielded some interesting results, which have a bearing not just on the understanding of Hellenism, but also on the population of Galilee in Hellenistic and Roman times. In response to the question posed at the outset, neither the Phoenicians nor the Itureans were the agents of an active Hellenization process in Galilee, despite the close proximity and varied contacts in the early Hellenistic age. Rather, we need properly to assess the character of the Hasmonean expansion to the north in order to understand the Hellenization of Galilee and the cultural affiliations of its people.

The available evidence, literary and archaeological, points to rather different profiles of the encounter of the east with Hellenism in the early centuries, before the arrival of Rome accentuated the process considerably. In terms of maintenance of a distinctive ethos within the larger cultural framework, the trajectory moves from the Itureans at the bottom of the scale, through the Phoenicians to the Galileans, in respect of resistance by "the little" to "the great tradition." At least in the initial phase of their emergence the Itureans were a dimorphic society, partly settled and partly nomadic, and therefore with a less developed sense of both territory and culture that goes with a strong assertion of identity. Our very lack of knowledge of either their language or belief system is highly indicative of their relatively undeveloped state when they first encountered the Greek way of life. They appear in the pages of history mainly as irritants to the dominant traditions in the region of southern Syria, a destabilizing influence as far as the great powers were concerned. Any incipient sense of their separate identity has virtually vanished from the archaeological record of the region where they are first encountered. It is surely ironic that when they do resurface as a distinctive ethnic force, it is in western Europe, on the Rhine, as defenders of the order that had submerged them in their native ambience.

By contrast the Phoenicians were an old and confident cultural power, exemplified by the existence of independent kingdoms and territories along the littoral that linked the two dominant political forces of the Hellenistic age, Ptolemaic Egypt and Seleucid Syria. Long before the advent of Alexander, they had made the most of their location by becoming masters of the eastern Mediterranean through their seafaring prowess. Their mobility was not enforced by necessity but by inventiveness and a desire to explore the larger world. Consequently, their encounter with Hellenism as a cultural force was not a totally new or threatening experience. It was, rather, an enrichment of their native qualities that made for easy adaptation and translation without being submerged by a superior political or cultural force. While Tyre, Sidon, and Berytus did expand to the interior, their main orientation was toward the west, and in terms of the argument of this paper, it is surely significant that the cult of Melqart/Herakles did not impose itself on the interior, even at Qadesh, as part of an active colonization policy. Otherwise the use of the Tyrian shekel as "the coin of the sanctuary" in Jerusalem would have been unthinkable.

Galilee was to become a Jewish territory under the Hasmoneans, and though this did not preclude the adoption and adaptation of Greek ways in terms of trading, ceramic production, architectural forms, and even language, the extent of the mingling was both selective and limited. The attitude adopted by the advancing Hasmoneans toward the signs of Greek culture in terms of city structures and cultic centers was to establish a pattern of resistance to full participation in the Greek way of life that continued to operate long after the Greeks had been superseded by the Romans as masters of the eastern Mediterranean. Millar is surely correct in emphasizing the importance of a distinctive sacred literature in the establishment and maintenance of this separate identity, in a way that others, not even the Phoenicians, could aspire to. Yet, one must also stress that that literature was itself the product of living and lived memories that continued to be activated through cultic participation in, and active support for the Jerusalem center, even after it ceased to exist in reality. In such a climate it is difficult to see how Galilean cynics might have survived, despite the boast of Meleager, the native of Gadara, the "Attis among the Assyrians," as he proudly, if exaggeratedly, describes his native place, that "Tyre had nurtured him." And Galilee lay between the two cities!

Notes

1. M. Hengel, The "Hellenisation" of Judaea in the First Century after Christ (London: SCM Press, 1989); E. Will and C. Orrieux, Ioudaismos-Hellenismos: Essai sur le judaisme judéen à l'époque hellénistique (Nancy: Presses Universitaires, 1986) 24–33; F. Miller, "The Phoenician Cities: A Case Study of Hellenisation," Proceedings of Cambridge Philological Society 209 (1983) 57–71, esp. 59f.; U. Rappaport, "The Hellenization of the Hasmoneans," in M. Mor, ed., Jewish Assimilation, Acculturation and Accomodation (Studies in Jewish Civilization 2; Lanham/New York/London: University Press of America, 1991) 2–13; T. Rajak, "The Hasmoneans and the Uses of Hellenism," in P. R. Davies and R. White, eds., A Tribute to Geza Vermes: Essays on Jewish History and Literature (JSOTSup 100; Sheffield: Sheffield Academic Press, 1990) 261–80, esp. 262–65.

2. F. Millar, "Empire Community and Culture in the Roman Near East: Greeks, Syrians, Jews and Arabs," JJS 38 (1987) 143–64; idem, "The problem of Hellenistic Syria," in A. Kuhrt and S. Sherwin-White, eds., Hellenism in the East (London: Routledge, 1987) 110–33.

3. F. Millar, The Roman Near East, 31 BC–AD 337 (Cambridge, Mass.: Harvard University Press, 1994).

4. A. Alt, "Galiläische Probleme," in idem, Kleine Schriften des Volkes Israels (3 vols.; Munich: Beck, 1953–64) 2:363–435; G. Bertram, "Der Hellenismus in der Urheimat des Evangeliums," Archiv. Rel. Wiss. 32 (1935) 265–81; W. Bauer, "Jesus der Galiläer," in G. Strecker, ed., Aufsätze und Kleine Schriften (Tübingen: Mohr, 1967) 91–108; A. Oepke, "Das Bevölkerungsproblem Galiläas," Theol.

Literaturblatt, 62 (1941) 201–5; J. Colin, "La Galilée de L'Évangile et les Villes Paiennes de la Palestine," *Ant. Class.* 34 (1965) 183–92. See now also R. Horsley, *Galilee: History, Politics, People* (Valley Forge, Pa.: Trinity Press International, 1995).

   5. Millar, "The Phoenician Cities," 66.

   6. H. Niehr, "JHWH in der Rolle des BAALSHAMEM," in W. Dietrich and M. Klopfenstein, eds., *Ein Gott allein?* (Orbis Biblicus Orientalis 139; Freiburg: Universitätsverlag Freiburg, 1994) 306–24; E. Würthwein, "Zur Opferprobe Elias. 1Reg 18, 21–39," in V. Fritz, K.-F. Pohlman, H.-C. Schmitt, eds., *Prophet und Prophetenbuch: Festschrift für Otto Kaiser zum 65. Geburtstag* (Berlin: de Gruyter, 1989) 277–84; R. D. Barnett, "Ezechiel and Tyre," *Eretz Israel* 9 (1984) 6–13.

   7. E. Bickerman, "Sur une Inscription grecque de Sidon," in *Mélanges Syriens offerts à M.R. Dussaud* (Paris: P. Geuthner, 1939) 91–99.

   8. H. Attridge and R. Oden, *Philo of Byblos, the Phoenician History* (CBQMS 9; Washington: Catholic Biblical Association, 1981) esp. 3–9.

   9. J. Elayi, *Pénétration Grecque en Phenicie sous l'empire Perse* (Nancy: Press Universitaires, 1988).

   10. H. Donner and W. Röllig, *Kanaanäische und Aramäische Inschriften* (2 vols.; Wiesbaden: Harassowitz, 1964) 2:64, no. 47; C. Bonnet, *Melqart: Cultes et Mythes de l'Héracles Tyrien en Mediterranée* (Studia Phoenicia 8; Leuven: Peeters, 1988) 244–47.

   11. L. Jalabert, R. Moutherde, J.-P. Rey-Coquais, eds., *Inscriptions Greques et Latines de la Syrie* (Paris: Librairie Orientaliste Paul Geuthner, 1929–), see VII (1969) 25–27, no. 4001. Hereafter cited as *IGLS*.

   12. J. Teixidor, "L'Interprétation Phénicienne d'Héracles et d'Apollo," *RHR* (1983) 244–55.

   13. E. Lipinski, *Dieux et déesses de l'univers phénicien et punique* (Studia Phoenicia 14; Leuven: Peeters, 1995) 276–88.

   14. Bonnet, *Melqart*, 404–16.

   15. G. Bunnens, "Aspects religieux de l'expansion phénicienne," *Religio Phoenicia* (Studia Phoenicia 4; Leuven: Peeters, 1986) 119–25; H. G. Niemeyer, *Phönizier im Westen: Die Beiträge des Internationalen Symposiums* (Mainz: von Zabern, 1982); J. Elayi, "The Relations between Tyre and Carthage during the Persian Period," *JANES* 13 (1981) 15–29.

   16. E. Schürer, *The History of the Jewish People in the Age of Jesus Christ* (3 vols.; rev. and ed. G. Vermes et al.; Edinburgh: Clark, 1973–87) 2:10.

   17. Horsley, *Galilee*, 41–43.

   18. W. Schottroff, "Die Ituräer," *ZDPV* 98 (1982) 125–47 is the most detailed study of the evidence. See also Schürer, *History*, 1:561–73 for the later history.

   19. M. Hartal, *Northern Golan Heights: The Archaeological Survey as a Source of Regional History* (Qazrin: Israel Department of Antiquities and Museums, 1989) 124–27 (Hebrew); idem, "Kh. Zemel, 1985, 1986," *IEJ* 37 (1987)

270–72; Z. Maoz, "The Golan," *The New Encyclopedia of Archaeological Excavations in the Holy Land* (4 vols.; Jerusalem: The Israel Exploration Society, 1993) 2:535 (henceforth *NEAEHL*); D. Urman, *The Golan: Profile of a Region during the Roman and Byzantine Periods* (BAR International Series 269; Oxford: Biblical Archaeological Society, 1985) 162f.

20. J.-M. Dentzer, *Hauran I. Recherches archeologiques sur la Syrie du sud a l'epoque hellénistique et romaine* (2 parts; Paris: Librairie Orientaliste Paul Geuthner, 1985) 2:399–403.

21. E. Will, "Un vieux problème de la topographie de la Beqa' antique: Chalcis du Liban," *ZDPV* 99 (1983) 141–46; G. Schmitt, "Zum Königreich Chalkis," *ZDPV* 98 (1982) 110–23.

22. Schottroff, "Die Ituräer," 139, n. 68 pointing to *IGLS* 6.2851, which reports a monument to Zenodorus, the son of Lysanias, the tetrarch, there.

23. N. Kokkinos, *The Herodian Dynasty: Origins, Role in Society and Eclipse* (Sheffield: Sheffield Academic Press, 1998) 304–14.

24. See articles by F. Villeneuve, J. Starcky, and M. Barrett-D. Orssaud, dealing respectively with rural economy, Nabatean and Safaitic inscriptions, and ceramics in Dentzer, *Hauran I.*

25. Millar, *Roman Near East,* 274.

26. D. Krencker and W. Zschietzschmann, *Römische Tempel in Syrien* (2 vols.; Berlin: de Gruyter, 1938) 1:101–21.

27. J.-P. Rey-Cocquais, "Des Montagnes au Désert: Baetocécé, le Pagus Augustus de Niha, la Ghouta à l'est de Damas," in E. Frezouls, ed., *Sociétés urbaines, sociétés rurales dans l'Asie Mineure et la Syrie hellénistique et romaines* (Strasbourg: Université des Sciences Humaines de Strasbourg, 1987) 192–216, especially 198–207. See also *IGLS* 6.2935.

28. M. Avi-Yonah, "Syrian Gods at Ptolemais-Akko," *IEJ* 9 (1959) 1–12.

29. M. Avi-Yonah, "Mount Carmel and the god of Baalbek," *IEJ* 2 (1951) 118–24.

30. S. Dar, *Settlements and Cult Sites on Mount Hermon, Israel: Iturean Culture in the Hellenistic and Roman Periods* (BAR International Series 589; Oxford: Tempus Reparatum, 1993). See the review by Z. Uri Ma'oz, *IEJ* 47 (1997) 279–83.

31. S. Dar and N. Kokkinos, "Greek Inscriptions from Senaim on Mount Hermon," *PEQ* 124 (1992) 9–25.

32. E. Lipiński, "El's Abode: Mythological Traditions Related to Mount Hermon and the mountains of Armenia," *Orientalia Lovaniensia* 2 (1971) 13–69. Philo of Byblos (*PE* 1.10.23) attributes the discovery of baetyls to Ouranos, "by devising stones endowed with life." See Attridge and Oden, *Philo of Byblos,* 87, n. 86 for differing views as to the background and derivation of the baetytl as representative of the divine.

33. E. Klostermann, *Eusebius. Das Onomastikon der Biblischen Ortsnamen* (reprint ed., Hildesheim: Olms Verlag, 1966) 20; Ch. Clérmont-Ganneau,

"Le Mont Hermon et son dieu d'après une inscription inédite," *Receuil d'Archaeologie Orientale* 5 (1903) 346–66.

34. H. Seyrig, "Le cult de Soleil en Syrie," *Syria* 48 (1971) 340–72, argues that the cult of the sun in Syria is not the result of any syncratization, as Cumont had argued, but rather was traditional to those who practiced such worship, especially among the Arabs.

35. Dar and Kokkinos, "Greek Inscriptions," 15. The name occurs in a number of inscriptions with slight variations of spelling from Syria/Jordan: Rahle, Jerash, Kalaat-Jendal, Al-Burg.

36. Horsley, *Galilee*, 45 and passim.

37. Alt, "Galiläische Probleme 1: Die Herkunft des Namens Galiläa," *Kleine Schriften*, 3:363–74.

38. A. Alt, "Galiläische Problem 2: Die assyrische Provinz Megiddo und ihr späteres Schicksal, and 5: Die Umgestaltung Galiläas durch die Hasmonäer," *Kleine Schriften*, 2:374–84 and 407–23; Horsley, *Galilee*, 8f.

39. Z. Gal, *Lower Galilee during the Iron Age* (ASORDS 8; Winona Lake, Ind.: Eisenbrauns, 1992); K. Lawson Younger Jr., "The Deportations of the Israelites," *JBL* 117 (1998) 201–27; Horsley, *Galilee*, 290 n. 13.

40. M. Aviam, "Galilee: The Hellenistic to the Byzantine Periods," *NEAEHL*, 2:453–58.

41. Urman, *The Golan: A Profile of a Region.*

42. E. Meyers, J. Strange, D. Groh, "The Meiron Excavation Project: Archaeological Survey in Galilee and Golan, 1976," *BASOR* 230 (1978) 1–24. See, however, D. Adan-Bayewitz, "The Tannaitic List of Walled Cities and the Archaeological-Historical Evidence from Iotapata and Gamala," *Tarbiz* 66 (1997) 449–70, who argues on the basis of the archaeological evidence that the two sites in question correspond to Tannaitic requirements of fortification by gentiles with subsequent transfer to Jews, and wonders whether the same might not also apply to the other sites listed in *m.* ʿArak 9.6, namely, Sepphoris, Gush Halav, Gedor, Hadid, and Ono.

43. M. Aviam, "The Hasmonean House in Galilee," *Idan* 19 (1995) 261–71 (Hebrew); idem, "A Second-First Century BCE Fortress in Eastern Upper Galilee," in D. R. Edwards and C. Thomas McCollough, eds., *Archaeology and the Galilee: Texts and Contexts in the Greco-Roman and Byzantine Periods* (SFSHJ 143; Atlanta: Scholars Press, 1997) 97–105.

44. I discuss this issue in detail in "Behind the Names: Galileans, Samaritans, Ioudaioi," in E. Meyers ed., *Galilee through the Centuries* (Winona Lake, Ind.: Eisenbrauns, 1999) 57–73.

45. Elayi, *Pénétration Greque en Phénicie*, especially the series of maps (177–203) indicating the presence of Greek imports in Phoenicia in the Persian period. A. Lemaire, "Population et territoire de la Palestine à l'epoque Perse," *Transeuphratene* 3 (1990) 33–66.

46. Aviam, "Galilee," *NEAEHL*, 2:453; J. Briend, "L'occupation de la Galilee occidentale à l'epoque Perse," *Transeuphratene* 2 (1990) 110–23.

47. V. Tcherikover, "Palestine under the Ptolemies: A Contribution to the Study of the Zenon Papyri," *Mizraim IV-V* (New York: Stechert, 1937) 9–90, especially 48–51.

48. R. Frankel, "Har Mispe Yamim, 1988/9," *ESI* 9 (1990) 100–102; R. Frankel and R. Ventura, "The Mispe Yamim Bronzes," *BASOR* 311 (1998) 39–56.

49. Rajak, "The Hasmoneans and the Uses of Hellenism," in *A Tribute to Geza Vermes,* 261–80. See also D. Mendels, *The Rise and Fall of Jewish Nationalism* (New York: Doubleday, 1992), especially 81–99 dealing with the tensions between ethnic particularity and universalistic history which were part of the intellectual climate of the early Hellenistic age in which the Jews participated.

50. R. Hanson, *Tyrian Influence in the Upper Galilee* (Cambridge, Mass.: ASOR, 1980) 53, with Meyers' comment on p. 3.

51. J. Raynor and Y. Meshorer, *The Coins of Ancient Meiron* (Winona Lake, Ind.: Eisenbrauns/ASOR, 1988) 88.

52. E. Meyers, "Galilean Regionalism: A Reappraisal," in W. Scott Green, ed., *Studies in Judaism and Its Greco-Roman Contexts* (BJS 32; Atlanta: Scholars Press, 1985) 115–31, especially, 123–25.

53. D. Barag, "Tyrian Currency in Galilee," *INJ* 6/7 (1982/83) 7–13.

54. U. Rappaport, "Phoenicia and Galilee: Economy, Territory and Political Relations," *Studia Phoenicia* 9 (1992) 261–68, especially 263.

55. Horsley, *Galilee,* 162.

56. D. Syon, "The Coins of Gamala: An Interim Report," *INJ* 12 (1992/93) 34–55; S. Gutman, "Gamala," *NEAEHL*, 2:459–63.

57. D. Adan Bayewitz and M. Aviam, "Iotapata, Josephus and the Siege of of 67: Preliminary Report on the 1992–94 Seasons," *JRA* 10 (1997) 131–65, especially 161 and 164f.

58. S. Herbert, ed., *Tel Anafa II, i: The Hellenistic and Roman Pottery* (Ann Arbor, Mich.: Kelsey Museum of the University of Michigan, 1997); Andrea Berlin, "The Plain Wares," especially 1–36, and "From Monarchy to Markets: The Phoenicians in Hellenistic Palestine," *BASOR* 306 (1997) 75–88.

59. David Adan Bayewitz, *Common Pottery in Roman Galilee: A Study of Local Trade* (Bar-Ilan University Press, 1993), especially 51–59 and 235–43.

60. Z. Ilan, "Galilee: Survey of Synagogues," *ESI* 5 (1986/87) 35–37 and "Meroth," *NEAEHL*, 3:1028–31.

61. M. Fischer, A. Ovadiah, and I. Roll, "The Roman Temple at Kadesh," *Tel Aviv* 11 (1984) 147–72, and idem, "The Epigraphic Finds from the Roman Temple at Kadesh," *Tel Aviv* 13 (1986) 60–66.

62. Adan Bayewitz and Aviam, "Iotapata, Josephus and the Siege of 67," 136f. with photograph. See also Urman, *The Golan,* 164 (opposite) with photo-

graph of large shard of a similar jar from Kh. Zemel, with fragmentary Greek inscription, and Hartal, *Northern Golan Heights,* 177, map 7, giving Hellenistic sites in the Golan where this ware was found.

63. S. Freyne, "Bandits in Galilee: A Contribution to the Study of Social Conditions in Galilee," in J. Neusner et al., eds., *The Social World of Formative Christianity and Judaism: Essays in Tribute of Howard Clark Kee* (Philadelphia: Fortress, 1988) 50–69; R. Horsley, "Popular Messianic Movements around the Time of Jesus," *CBQ* 46 (1984) 475–95.

Hellenism
in Unexpected Places

SHAYE J. D. COHEN

In his long account of the Scythians and their customs, Herodotus includes the following wonderful story:[1]

> Scyles, king of Scythia, was not at all content with the Scythian manner of life, and was much more inclined to Greek ways. . . . Having led the Scythian army to the city of the Borysthenites, he would leave his army in the suburb of the city but he himself, entering within the walls and shutting the gates, would remove his Scythian apparel and don Greek clothing. . . . [There he] followed in every way the Greek manner of life and worshipped the gods according to Greek usage. Then having so spent a month or more, he put on Scythian dress and left the city. This he did often; and he built a house in Borysthenes, and married there a local woman.

Alas, Scyles, like many another Herodotean hero, meets a tragic end. His people discover his passion for Greek ways and rebel against him. He is beheaded by his successor. In the last line of the story Herodotus comments, "Thus do the Scythians maintain their ways, and such are the penalties that they impose on those who arrogate foreign customs."[2]

This little story shows the powerful attraction that Greek culture exercised on non-Greek peoples. It also shows the powerful antagonism that it aroused. Scyles tried to be a Greek among Greeks and a Scythian among Scythians, but was unable to play this double game for long. Perhaps if he had been a private citizen his amphoteric behavior might have been tolerated, but he was a king, and a king must represent his people and uphold ancestral customs. To defend their ancestral customs and their national honor, the Scythians had no choice but to kill Scyles.

Attraction and antagonism, the two reactions elicited by Greek culture from the Scythians, are particularly well attested among the Jews of antiquity as a result of their contact with Greek culture. We find Jews who, like Scyles, tried to be both Greek and non-Greek at the same time: a Greek among the Greeks, and a Jew among the Jews. More commonly we find Jews who wanted to be both Greek and Jewish at the same time and in the same place. At the extremes we find Jews who wanted to abandon their Jewishness and simply to be Greek, and we find Jews who were adamantly opposed to all things Greek, and perhaps who sought to kill any of their compatriots who dared to adopt Greek ways.

In this paper I would like to consider three examples drawn from sources or settings that we might have thought would have more in common with the Scythians who slew Scyles than with Scyles himself: the Qumran scrolls, the history of the Jewish war of 66–73 CE, and rabbinic literature. All three were, or at least would seem to have been, reactions to and against the Hellenistic-Roman world, and all three consequently are unexpected places in which to find evidence for Jewish Hellenism. The various scholarly studies of Hellenism at Qumran and the numerous scholarly studies of Hellenism in rabbinic Judaism have not yet clarified the degree or kind of Hellenism we can expect to find in these law-observant, Hebrew-writing, book-focused, ethno-centric communities.[3] How much Hellenism was there in Jewish Palestine,[4] specifically at Qumran, among the revolutionaries, and among the rabbis? Because the answer remains elusive, evidence for Hellenism in these places, as in distant Scythia, still retains an unexpected quality. I freely concede that the examples that I am about to discuss are, in and of themselves, trivial and nonsignificant. Nevertheless, I would like to think that they portend something significant.

Two Lists from Qumran

Among the texts found in Qumran cave 4 are two lists, one a list of false prophets (4Q339) and the other a list of *netinim* (4Q340). Each is fragmentary and difficult to read, but full of interest. Here is the first, as reconstructed and translated by Magen Broshi and Ada Yardeni in *Discoveries in the Judaean Desert:*[5]

4Q339: List of False Prophets
    The false prophets who arose in [Israel]
    Balaam [son of] Beor
    [the] Old Man from Bethel
    [Zede]kiah son of Cha[na]anah
    [Aha]b son of K[ol]iah
    [Zede]kiah son of Ma[a]seiah
    [Shemaiah the Ne]hlemite
    [Hananiah son of Az]ur
    [a prophet from Gib]eon

Here is the second, again as reconstructed and translated by Broshi and Yardeni in *Discoveries in the Judaean Desert:*

4Q340: List of Netinim
    These are the *netin[im]*
    who were designated by [their] n[ames]
    Yitra and *'qw* [
    hmsmrw [
    hrtw
    qwwk To[biah?

These two lists are not part of the same scroll, as a glance at the published photographs will reveal. The hand of 4Q339 (false prophets) is "formal Herodian," while the hand of 4Q340 (*netinim*) is "formal Hasmonaean," to be dated to "the first half of the first century BCE." Nor are the texts part of the same composition: the list of false prophets is in Aramaic, while the list of *netinim* is in Hebrew. The list of false prophets is contained on a single free-standing piece of parchment; it may have had one additional line at the end, now entirely lost, but it is likely that the text as presented above very nearly represents the entire original list. In contrast, the original list of *netinim* may have been very long; it may have run on for columns, we cannot say. The two lists, then, in spite of their similarity in form, are not a unit, and may well differ from each other in setting and purpose.

Many of the works preserved in the Qumran library are sectarian compositions, reflecting an us/them mentality, hostility toward the Jerusalem temple and its personnel, and a rigorism in ritual and legal matters. These tendencies are so marked and so well known that scholars look for them everywhere in the Qumran corpus, even in jejune texts like ours. In the preliminary publication of the list of false prophets, the editors offered no supplement to the last line, whose final three letters alone are extant.[6] Immediately after publication, Alexander Rofé and Elisha Qimron independently suggested that the line be supplemented to read "[Yohanan ben Sim]eon," the Hebrew name for John Hyrcanus, the Hasmonean prince who ruled 135–104 BCE. Josephus, one of his admirers, tells us that John possessed the gift of prophecy and thus combined in himself three of the highest privileges attainable by a mortal: supreme command, high priesthood, and prophecy.[7] According to the restoration of Rofe and Qimron, however, this list will show us that in the eyes of his critics John was a false prophet, the last and presumably the worst in a series of deceivers.[8] Qimron himself apparently changed his mind about this, however, since the editors credit him the restoration "[a prophet from Gib]eon." With this restoration all polemic vanishes and we are left with a list of false prophets mentioned in the Bible.

If the editors have erased the polemic from the first text, they have introduced it to the second, not in their supplementation but in their interpretation. *Netinim,* literally "those who have been given (sc. to the temple)," usually translated "temple-slaves," "temple-servitors," or "temple-servants," appear several times in the historical narratives and genealogical lists of the books of Ezra and Nehemiah.[9] They clearly were an integral part of the Judaean community of that period, no less than the temple gatekeepers and singers. They appear as signatories to the covenant of Nehemiah 10, the "constitution" or "magna carta" of Nehemiah's Jerusalem. However, six hundred years later or so, as we shall see in a moment, the Mishnah groups the *netinim* with the offspring of illicit unions (*mamzerim*) and others of blemished ancestry who cannot legally marry, or be married to, Israelites of good standing. Between Ezra and Nehemiah (middle of the fifth century BCE) and the Mishnah (ca. 200 CE) the social and legal status of the people known as *netinim* declined markedly.

To interpret our list of *netinim,* Broshi and Yardeni make two fundamental assumptions: first, that the precipitous decline in the status of *netinim* had taken effect before our list was composed; second, that real *netinim,* that is, the lineal descendants of the *netinim* known to Ezra and Nehemiah, continued to live in Judaea in the last centuries of the second temple period and in the time of the Mishnah. Relying on these assumptions, Broshi and Yardeni conclude that "it is likely, then, that 4Q340 is a list of blemished people unfit for marriage, a negative genealogical list." Many members of the Qumran community led normal family lives, and this list warns them against marriage with certain people (members?) of improper lineage. This list, then, had a polemical purpose, to defend the genealogical purity of the group.

Elsewhere I hope to demonstrate that both of the assumptions on which this interpretation rests are likely to be wrong, or, at least, not necessarily correct. This list was not social polemic but scholarship. It was meant to collect the names of the *netinim* that are mentioned in the Bible or some other closed group of texts. The fact that we are unable to identify securely any of the names on the Qumran list with any of the *netinim* named in our texts of Ezra and Nehemiah renders this suggestion tentative and uncertain, but I think that this interpretation is simplest and best. Henceforth in my discussion I shall assume that the two Qumran lists belong to the same genre: they are works of scholarship that collect all the available biblical data on a given topic. In the first, some anonymous scholar collected biblical references to individual false prophets; in the second, if my interpretation is correct, some anonymous scholar collected biblical (and nonbiblical?) references to named *netinim*. Scholarship of this sort is Hellenistic, and these two fragmentary lists, one in Hebrew and the other in Aramaic, constitute evidence for the Hellenization of Judaism.

Scholarship begins with lists: the organized collection, classification, and presentation of data. A list is an attempt to make order out of chaos, to take discrete bits of information and to make them useful, to make connections explicit that otherwise are implicit or invisible. An organized thematic list is the result of a scholarly way of thinking. One does not have to be Greek or a student of Aristotle, of course, to create thematic lists or to think in a scholarly way, but it helps.[10] Influenced by Hellenistic culture, the Jews of antiquity looked at the Torah and/or the entire Bible as a book of history akin to Herodotus or Thucydides, as a book of chronology akin to a world chronicle, and as an authoritative text whose elucidation required learned or inspired commentary.[11] Influenced by Hellenistic culture, the Jews of antiquity also considered the Bible to be a source of data to be collected, catalogued, and presented in thematic lists. History, chronology, commentary, and *Listen-*

wissenschaft: four hallmarks of Hellenistic culture and of Judaism in the Greek age.

Scholars of the Hellenistic age drew up lists of everything. In 1904 Hermann Diels published a work that he titled *Laterculi Alexandrini*.[12] The work is preserved in a papyrus of the first century BCE, so it is safe to assume that the scholarship it contains derives from the third and second centuries BCE. The work is a sort of "who's who," a series of short lists giving the most famous or best representatives of twelve categories: lawgivers, painters, sculptors of statues of the gods, sculptors of statues of humans, architects, inventors (literally, mechanics), seven wonders of the world, large islands, highest mountains, greatest rivers, most beautiful springs, and seas. Some of the lists are bare names, others contain a brief statement about the person or object listed. The lists have no connection one with another and amply illustrate the penchant of Hellenistic scholars for classification and list making.[13]

Of particular interest for our purposes are those lists that are bound by "canonical" limits; the data which they collect and classify derive from a fixed, if large, set of books and traditions, namely, the works of Homer and the Greek mythographers. Thus one Greek papyrus contains the following lists of names: the Greek leaders of the expedition against Troy, the suitors of Penelope, the daughters of Danaus, and the Argonauts.[14] Another papyrus contains a list of the people killed by Herakles.[15] The most extensive collection of such lists is found in the *Fabulae* of Hyginus, a Latin writer probably of the second century CE. Based on Greek and occasionally Roman mythology, Hyginus gives dozens of lists, including lists of those who have killed their fathers, those who have killed their mothers, those who have killed their brothers, fathers who have killed their sons, fathers who have killed their daughters, and so on. My three favorites are his lists of those who have eaten their sons at a meal, those who were eaten by dogs, and those who were crushed to death by a boar. This is antiquarian scholarship at a very high (low?) level.[16]

List making of this sort is frequently found in rabbinic lore. One page of *Avot de Rabbi Nathan,* for example, lists all those individuals denoted by scripture as "slaves" (*avadim*), as "youths" (*bahurim*), as "beloved" (*yedidim*), not to mention the seven scriptural synonyms for a lion, a poor person, and a serpent.[17] One passage of the Babylonian Talmud claims that forty-eight male prophets and seven female prophets prophesied for Israel; the seven women are listed (Sarah, Miriam, Deborah, Hannah, Abigail, Huldah, and Esther), although not all of them are described as "prophets" in the Bible. Alas, the forty-eight male prophets are not listed.[18]

Scholarship of this sort also reached Christian circles. Recently, Robert M. Grant and Glen Menzies published a bilingual edition of the *Hypomnestikon* or "Bible Notes" of one Joseph.[19] The work, which was probably compiled in Egypt, represents Greek Christian scholarship of the late fourth or early fifth century CE. The work consists entirely of lists, 167 in number, some of them mere names, others containing names and short explanatory statements. The editors note the striking similarity of the work to the *Laterculi Alexandrini* edited by Diels and the *Fabulae* of Hyginus. Most of the lists derive their data from the Old and/or New Testaments exclusively. There are lists of Hebrews with gentile wives, polygamists, women who corrupted their husbands, women who helped their husbands, men admirable for wisdom, and women admirable for wisdom. Among the lists are two on themes that we have already encountered. Like the Babylonian Talmud, the *Hypomnestikon* contains a list of seven female prophets (Sarah, Rebecca, Miriam, Zipporah, Deborah, Huldah, and Hannah); the list is not the same as the Talmud's but here, too, not all of the women who are listed are described as "prophets" in the Old Testament. Like our Qumran text it contains a list of false prophets. The Qumran list of eight false prophets does not coincide with the Christian list of nine false prophets, although there is some overlap to be sure (Zedekiah son of Chanaanah, four hundred prophets slain by Elijah, Pashhur son of Immer, Hananiah, Shemaiah the Nehlemite, Ahab son of Koliah, Zedekiah son of Maaseiah, Jaazaniah son of Azzur, Pelatiah son of Benaiah). I am not suggesting that the Christian lists somehow derive from the Talmud or from Qumran; the parallel simply illustrates the same Hellenistic scholarly impulse in all three settings.[20]

One final note. The Qumran list of false prophets was written on a free-standing piece of parchment. It was not part of a scroll. Broshi and Yardeni even refer to it as resembling a "card." In Greek such a list on such a card would be known as a *pinax*.[21] We may conjecture that works like that of Hyginus were compiled out of stacks of *pinakes* much like this one; sometimes *pinakes* on related themes were juxtaposed to each other, thus creating strings of thematically related lists, but usually the lists were assembled helter-skelter, one list having little to do with the one that came before it or after it. As far as I have been able to determine, all the Hellenistic lists that are attested papyrologically were written in scrolls; the individual *pinakes* had already been assembled and forgotten by the time our papyrus scrolls were written. The Qumran list is the only known exemplar that retains its original form as an independent *pinax*. Not only is the form of the composition Hellenistic, but so is its presentation on parchment.

In sum: The creation of thematic lists based on data from a closed "canon" of authoritative texts is an expression of Hellenistic textual scholarship. Ever since the nineteenth century, scholars have postulated the influence of Hellenistic scholarship on the textual scholarship of the Jews, especially the rabbis.[22] The Qumran list of false prophets and perhaps also the list of *netinim* provide our earliest evidence for the penetration of this type of scholarship into Jewish circles, both those that wrote in Hebrew and those that wrote in Aramaic.[23]

Rebels against Rome

That the *Jewish War* of Josephus is a good specimen of Jewish Hellenism hardly requires demonstration. Written in fine Greek, filled with verbal echoes of Thucydides and Euripides, enlivened with commonplaces (*topoi*) drawn from Greek historiography, the *Jewish War* is one of the best extant exemplars of Greek historical writing in the Roman Empire. A more complicated question is whether the Jewish war of 66–73 CE—that is, the war itself, its course, its leadership, its ideologies—is a manifestation of Jewish Hellenism. This question is virtually ignored in modern scholarship. I would like to focus here on two points: first, the participation by non-Judaean Jews and non-Jews in the war; second, the possibility that some of the things that the revolutionaries said and did can be explained by appeal to hellenized Judaism.

Josephus, our main and usually our sole informant about the events of the war, is not a promising source for either of these points. His goal is to restrict guilt: only a small number of Jews rebelled, and they represent neither the Jews nor Judaism. The rebels consisted of small bands of impious and despicable hoodlums, who alone are responsible for the war and its catastrophic conclusion. They foisted the war on an unwilling and captive populace. The rebels claimed to be fighting for the temple and for the Jewish laws, but in reality they respected neither. Hence Josephus has every reason to conceal any report about the participation in the war by anyone other than the rebels themselves and the people whom they controlled; he certainly does not want to give the impression that the rebels enjoyed broad support, or that anyone aside from the scum of Judaea fought alongside them. Similarly, Josephus has every reason to deny or conceal any connection between the rebels and any ideology that could endow legitimacy or respectability on them and their actions. But, luckily for us, Josephus is a sloppy thinker and a sloppier writer, so that he often provides evidence against his own theses. He occasionally reveals what he wants to conceal. The *Jewish War* reveals that non-Judaean Jews and non-Jews joined the rebels, and that the rebels said and did things that seem to derive from the thought world of hellenized Judaism. If the rebels were simply Judaean patriots, religious militants, and sectarian millenialists, as they are usually depicted in modern scholarship, these facts are unexpected.

First point: The ranks of the rebels included non-Judaean[24] Jews and non-Jews. In the great speech that Josephus places in the mouth of King Agrippa II at the outbreak of hostilities, the king explains to the revolutionaries that they have no hope of success. Your cause is not just, he explains; if independence is your aim you should have fought the Romans long ago; nations much mightier than you have fallen under Roman dominion. Furthermore, you will have no allies in your struggle. In the civilized world all are Roman. As for your coreligionists across the Euphrates in Adiabene, do not expect them to come to your aid, since the Parthians, fearful of war with Rome, will not permit it.[25] Agrippa's arguments, or should I say Josephus' arguments, are not entirely correct. In particular, the claim that members of the royal family of Adiabene would not join the rebels turned out to be false. Some members did join the rebels and even stayed with them to the bitter end.[26] The revolutionaries were joined also by members of Agrippa's own royal house, namely, Silas the Babylonian and one Magassarus, not to mention Niger the Peraean.[27]

The most surprising, interesting, and important of the non-Judaean Jewish revolutionaries is Simon bar Giora.[28] In the eyes of the Romans, Simon was *the* leader of the revolutionaries; as the enemy general it was he, and only he, who was executed at the conclusion of the triumphal procession in Rome.[29] This generalissimo was the son of a proselyte and a native of Gerasa. Simon's proselyte extraction is implied by his patronymic, "son of Giora," or, as Dio and Tacitus have it, "Bargioras." The Aramaic word *giora* is the equivalent of Hebrew *ger* which, depending on context, means either "proselyte" or "resident alien."[30] Hence the common opinion that he was the son of a proselyte; his father was a gentile who converted to Judaism.[31] Similarly, several talmudic sages were known as "so-and-so son of proselytes" or other similar designations. In one passage Josephus calls Simon *Gerasenos to genos,* that is, a native of Gerasa.[32] If this is the well-known city of the Decapolis, we may conclude that Simon was born in a city no less hellenized than, say, Tarsus, home city of Paul, Samosata, home city of Lucian, or Gadara, home city of a host of Greek writers.[33] What brought a native of a Hellenistic city, the son of a proselyte, to the revolutionary politics of Jerusalem is a mystery. Hans Bietenhard adduces psychological factors, "The fanaticism of Simon bar Giora perhaps can be explained from the psychological state of this renegade shoot, who fundamentally has not freed himself from his old beliefs and thereby works out his inner tension towards the outside with all the more zeal."[34] The zeal of the convert might perhaps be relevant if Simon himself were the convert, but the name "bar Giora" strongly suggests that the father was the convert. Is the zeal of the convert transferred from father to son?[35]

An even greater mystery is the willingness of the revolutionaries of Jerusalem to accept such a one as Simon as their leader. I cannot explain this mystery—nor, as far as I can see, has anyone else. Some scholars have been so puzzled by these two mysteries that they reduce their number. Samuel Krauss once suggested that *giora* was simply a man's name, not the designation for proselyte; Joseph Klausner once suggested that *bar giora* was nothing more than a derogatory nickname. These suggestions fail to convince.[36] More plausible is the suggestion of various scholars that Simon's home town Gerasa is not the hellenized city of the Decapolis but a village in Judaea not far from Jerusalem, mentioned by Josephus only a few paragraphs before his ascription of Gerasene origin to Simon.[37] This suggestion has much to recommend it, and if we accept it, Simon is no longer the urbane cosmopolitan that I have been depicting but just another revolutionary militant from the villages of Judaea. Still, his proselyte origins remain, and I think that a small village in Judaea, mentioned only once or twice in Josephus and nowhere else in antiquity, is an unlikely location for the conversion of a gentile to Judaism. I prefer the traditional identification of Gerasa, but I admit that the matter is uncertain and therefore that my argument is somewhat weakened. Still, if Simon could make himself the leader of the revolutionaries of Jerusalem, in spite of his birth in a Greek city and in spite of his gentile origins, then the revolutionary movement in Jerusalem must have been a variegated and multifarious phenomenon, attracting not only Judaean Jews but Jews of all sorts.

The war in Judaea began with fighting in the Greek cities. Tension between "Greeks" and Jews was clearly a major component in the outbreak of the war.[38] The revolutionaries may have been animated by a desire to purify the land of Israel from gentile contagion, but this desire did not prevent them from allowing gentiles to join them, or at least to associate with them. Josephus attempts to conceal this fact, of course, but occasionally he lets down his guard. Gentiles (*allophyloi*) were admitted by the revolutionaries into the temple to sacrifice, even in the midst of the severest internecine fighting.[39] After the temple had fallen some rebels took refuge in the fortress of Machaerus, where they were supported by the local non-Jewish population.[40] During the siege of Jerusalem the forces of John of Gischala received instruction from "deserters" in the use of Roman military machines that had been seized earlier. Thackeray, in his Loeb translation, suggests that these deserters will have been "from the ranks of the auxiliary (Syrian) forces of the Roman army."[41] This suggestion is entirely possible but is not likely, since Josephus tells us that the Syrian and Arab troops hated the Jews, and that their hatred abetted their ferocity.[42] Thackeray cannot imagine that "real" Roman troops would desert to the Jews, but this possibility seems the likeliest. Why would Roman troops desert to the Jews? Cassius Dio explains:[43]

> Meanwhile, some of the Romans, too, becoming disheartened, as often happens in a protracted siege, and suspecting, furthermore, that the city was really impregnable, as was commonly reported, went over to the other side. The Jews, even though they were short of food, treated these recruits kindly, in order to be able to show that there were deserters to their side also.

The desertions alluded to by Josephus will have taken place earlier in the drama than the desertions described by Dio, but the motivation of the deserters will have been the same throughout: the prospect of improving their fortune (and fortunes) by changing sides. Thus, Dio also tells us, many members of other nations joined the Jews in the revolt of 132–135, what we call the Bar Kokhba war; these soldiers of fortune were animated by a "desire for gain."[44] We are not speaking here of conversion to Judaism; this is not the case of Metilius, the prefect of the Roman cohort in Jerusalem, who, having surrendered to the revolutionaries at the outbreak of the hostilities, promised "to judaize as far as circumcision."[45] The meaning of this striking phrase is not quite clear, but there is no sign that whatever Metilius offered was offered, too, by the deserters who instructed the revolutionaries in the use of the military machines or the deserters who were received in a friendly manner in spite of the famine. We have to reject the notion that every act of support for Jews must be understood in religious terms, as if one cannot befriend Jews or support them without converting to Judaism.[46]

The presence of non-Judaean Jews and non-Jews among the revolutionaries does not, of course, prove that the revolutionaries generally were hellenized or that the uprising is a manifestation of Hellenistic thought. Still, the presence of non-Judaean Jews and non-Jews in the camp of the revolutionaries suggests that the revolutionary movement was much more open to general society than is usually thought

And now to my second point: The attitude of the rebels to the temple in Jerusalem is strikingly similar to the attitude that characterized some segments of Hellenistic Judaism. If other Jews in antiquity said and did what the revolutionaries are said to have said and done, we would not hesitate to call them "hellenized Jews."

One of Josephus' favorite themes in the *Jewish War* is the impiety of the revolutionaries: in great detail and with great relish he tells of their acts of murder, rapine, and pillage. They violate the laws of Judaism and the norms of civilized society. They prohibit the burial of their victims.[47] In one remarkable passage he even accuses some of them of dressing up as women and engaging in homosexuality.[48] The point of all this, of course, is to prove that the revolutionaries deserved to lose and did not represent pious Jews or authentic Judaism.

Part of this theme is the claim that the revolutionaries do not respect the sanctity of the temple. This motif first appears not long after the Zealots take over the temple and convert it into a fortress.[49] They oust the legitimate high priest and substitute an illegitimate one in his place, a man not of high priestly stock and chosen by lot.[50] In the fighting that ensues, the Zealots did not hesitate to use the temple as their base, even if that meant that the injured would stain the sacred pavement with their blood, while the high priestly party, in contrast, thought it unlawful to allow its soldiers into the sacred precincts without prior purification.[51] By these actions the Zealots fulfilled the ancient prophecy that the city would be taken and the temple burnt when "native hands should be the first to defile God's sacred precincts."[52] The adherents of Eleazar ben Simon—in his defense I should note that he may have been a priest[53]—barricaded themselves in the inner precincts of the temple where they were able to use all the sacred things for supplies.[54] John of Gischala in the outer precincts used some of the sacred timber to build towers to aid him in his fight against his rivals.[55] Later in the action, John was able to seize the inner precincts back from Eleazar by having some of his followers, "most of whom were unpurified," sneak in during the Passover bearing concealed weapons.[56] Later, when the city was gripped by famine, John distributed the stores of sacred wine and oil to his troops, and even melted down for his own use some of the gold and silver vessels that had been donated to the temple.[57] John "had unlawful food served at his table and abandoned the established rules of purity of our forefathers"; this accusation may also refer to the misappropriation of temple foodstuffs, or, as I suggested years ago, may refer to the abandonment in general of the Jewish food laws.[58]

Thus the Zealots, Eleazar ben Simon and John of Gischala—all of them violated the sanctity of the temple, either by introducing impure people into the sacred precincts (cf. Paul) or by misappropriating temple property or both. What are we to make of this string of accusations? We have several possibilities.

First of all, we might dismiss most of these claims as Josephus' own exaggerations or inventions, since they constitute an important part of his rhetoric of reversal. At the center of the narrative of the *Jewish War* is the paradox that the revolutionaries, who ostensibly are the ones fighting to protect the temple, in reality are the ones who have attacked it, profaned it, and will destroy it. And the reverse: The Romans ostensibly are the ones attacking the temple but in reality are the ones who defend it, venerate it, and are attempting to preserve it. This argument appears several times in the great speeches of books 5 and 6. Josephus wants to present the revolutionaries not only as sinful but also as disrespectful to Judaism's holiest site. This allows him to claim that the revolutionaries are fighting against the temple, not for it. Hence we could perhaps dismiss all of the Josephan claims of revolutionary disrespect for the temple as Josephan polemic, nothing more.[59]

If, in contrast, we are willing to allow at least some level of veracity or "facticity" to Josephus' claims—and this strikes me as the wiser course, since Josephus frequently exaggerates and engages in polemic but seldom invents whole episodes outright—perhaps we could explain that the worst of these actions will not have been the work of the pious, sincere, and ideologically committed revolutionaries, but of the hoodlums and other lawless types who are always to be found on the periphery of revolutionary groups in times of social stress.[60] Or we might accept Josephus' claim that it was the revolutionaries themselves who acted in this manner, and explain that the revolutionaries were motivated by an eschatological or messianic or gnostic theory which required antinomian behavior in order to precipitate the final crisis of the end time.[61] Or, what I think is likeliest and simplest, the revolutionaries came to the conclusion that sometimes, in order to defend the law, you must break the law. Mattathias the Hasmonean concluded that to defend the Sabbath he had to violate the Sabbath; not all Jews agreed with him, but for the author of 1 Maccabees and for Josephus this was clearly the correct choice. When John partakes of the sacred wine and oil, he is reported to have said: "Those who fought for the temple should be supported by it."[62] He could even have cited the example of David, had he wished; when fleeing Saul, David was given by Ahimelekh the priest some of the sacred bread that had been presented to God. In an emergency even a non-priest can eat of the sacred offerings.[63]

There is yet another possibility. In response to Titus' plea to lay down their arms and save themselves, their city, and their temple, the revolutionaries reply that "they scorned death . . . that they would do the Romans every injury in their power . . . that they, so soon to perish, were unconcerned for their native place, and that the world was a better temple for God than this one. But, they added, it would yet be saved by him who dwelled there. . . ."[64] The only surprising line in this oration, reported in indirect speech by Josephus, is the claim "that the world was a better temple for God than this one."[65] Whence did the revolutionaries derive such a striking idea? Biblical thinkers, too, noted that a building, no matter how grand or how beautiful, was unable to contain God's glory, let alone God himself, but biblical thinkers did not conclude that the temple was somehow dispensable, or, as the revolutionaries said, that "the world was a better temple for God than this one."[66] For this sentiment we have go to the Greeks, namely, the Stoics and the Cynics.[67]

In his *Republic,* Zeno, the founder of Stoicism, forbade the building of temples and statues of the gods; Plutarch formulates the idea thus, "It is a doctrine of Zeno's not to build temples of the Gods; for a temple not worth much is also not sacred, and nothing made by builders or workmen is worth much."[68] Even closer to our Josephan passage is the Cynic formulation, "You ignorant men! Don't you know that God . . . does not have a single enclosure but that the whole world, adorned with animals, plants, and stars, is his temple?"[69] Unless we insist that Josephus (or his literary assistant) has invented this little speech whole-sale—which is, of course, entirely possible, if not likely[70]—we must conclude that the revolutionaries were influenced by Greek thought, or perhaps, a bit more cautiously, that Stoic-Cynic ideas allowed the revolutionaries to adopt an ambivalent attitude toward the temple, especially when its capture by the enemy was imminent and its loss had to be justified.

The argument of the preceding paragraphs is meant to be suggestive, nothing more. Just as scholars for a long time were blinded by the rhetoric of 1 Maccabees and 2 Maccabees and insisted on seeing the Hasmoneans as "anti-Hellenistic," as figures who saved Judaism from Hellenism, so, too, I suggest we should not allow ourselves to be blinded by the rhetoric of Josephus. Modern scholars realize that we must read Josephus through a mirror: if he says that the revolutionaries were impious, it is because they were, and claimed to be, pious; if he says that the revolutionaries profaned the temple, it is because they revered it and ostentatiously fought in its defense; and so on. But neither Josephus, for whom the revolutionaries were impious thugs, nor his modern revisers, for most of whom the revolutionaries were zealous defenders of the Torah, allow for the possibility that at least some of them may have been Greek-speaking and shaped by Hellenistic thought. Neither Josephus, for whom the revolutionaries were anti-social types in the extreme, nor his modern revisers, for most of whom the revolutionaries were ethno-centric, gentile-hating, Jewish sectarians, allow for the possibility that at least some of them may have been open to outsiders, even gentiles. What Josephus and his modern revisers have not allowed, I have tried to suggest.

The Customs of the Persians

My last unexpected place is a rabbinic text. Like the Qumran text, which I discussed above, this text, too, contains no Greek words and would seem on first reading to have no connection with our theme. But it, too, I suggest, is a manifestation of Jewish Hellenism. The text is from the Babylonian Talmud, tractate *Berakhot:*[71]

It has been taught:
R. Aqiva says:
For three things do I like the Medes: when they cut meat, they cut it only upon the table; when they kiss, they kiss only upon the hand; and when they hold counsel, they do so only in the field. . . .

It has been taught:
R. Gamaliel[72] says:
For three things do I like the Persians: they are modest in their eating, modest in the privy, and modest in sexual intercourse.[73]

R. Aqiva admires the Medes, and R. Gamaliel admires the Persians. For both rabbis the first virtuous behavior concerns eating: the Medes cut meat on the table, and the Persians are modest in their eating. Otherwise the two lists have no overlap. R. Aqiva praises habits of eating, greeting,[74] and consorting, while R. Gamaliel praises habits of eating, elimination, and sex.

The paragraph here attributed to R. Aqiva (a sage of the early second century) is attributed to R. Simeon b. Gamaliel (a sage of the mid-second century) in various sources of Israelian provenance.[75] Some of these texts also attribute these laudatory customs not to the Medes but to the Persians or to "the men of the east," rabbinic parlance for "the Jews of Babylonia." I am confident, however, that both of these readings are secondary and that the primary reading is "Medes," as it appears before us on the page of the Babylonian Talmud.[76] (This point is not essential to my argument, since the Babylonian text stands no matter what the parallel readings may have.) The only other interesting variation affects the statement about cutting food with a knife. Several lines before citing R. Aqiva, the Talmud cites Rava, a Babylonian *amora* of the late fourth century:

Rava said to his children:
When you are cutting meat, do not cut it upon your hand. Do not sit upon the bed of an Aramaean woman. Do not pass behind a synagogue when the congregation is praying.
"Do not cut meat upon your hand"[77]—[why did Rava say this?] Some say on account of danger, and some say in order not to spoil the meal.

The Talmud proceeds to discuss Rava's other two dicta, but these do not concern us. Rava's first piece of advice to his children seems to have a clear connection with R. Aqiva's statement about the Medes. R. Aqiva tells us what the Medes do and, by implication, what we ought to do: they cut meat only upon the table. Rava tells his children and, by implication, us, the readers, what we ought *not* to do: do not cut meat upon your hand.[78] Why? The anonymous voice of the Talmud offers two possible explanations: do not cut meat upon your hand either because you may hurt yourself ("danger") or because you may nick yourself and get some blood in the food ("spoil the meal").[79] No matter which explanation we adopt, the Talmud clearly implies that R. Aqiva's advice to cut meat on the table is the proper alternative to the improper practice of cutting meat on the hand. The sources of Israelian provenance that cite this text, however, understand R. Aqiva as speaking in opposition to tearing off pieces by the mouth. The Medes "do not bite (off) with the mouth but cut with the knife."[80] Why the Babylonian and Israelian sources should differ on this minor point, I do not know.

Let us return to our original text. The tradition ascribed to R. Gamaliel appears only here in ancient rabbinic literature.[81] Immediately after citing R. Gamaliel, the Talmud adduces R. Joseph, a Babylonian *amora* of the late fourth century. Unlike R. Gamaliel who praises the Persians, R. Joseph condemns them to hell.

I have summoned my consecrated ones (Isaiah 13:3):
R. Joseph taught:
These (consecrated ones mentioned in the verse) are the Persians who are consecrated and destined for Gehinnom.

Elsewhere, too, R. Joseph rejects R. Gamaliel's favorable estimation of the Persians. Here R. Gamaliel tells us that the Persians are modest at table;[82] elsewhere R. Joseph, in connection with the verse *Then I saw a second, different beast, which was like a bear* (Daniel 7:5), comments, "These are the Persians, who eat and drink like bears, and are coated with flesh like bears, and are hairy like bears, and can never keep still like bears."[83] So, according to R. Joseph, Persians are not modest at table but are gluttonous. Here R. Gamaliel complements the Persians for their modesty in sex; elsewhere R. Joseph criticizes that modesty as improper and intolerable. The rabbis understood Exodus 21:10 to enumerate the three obligations incumbent on a husband vis-à-vis his wife; unfortunately, the three terms used by the verse are obscure and of uncertain reference. The first is *she'er,* which R. Joseph says means "flesh":[84]

> R. Joseph taught:
> *Her flesh* (in Exodus 21:10) means bodily contact, namely, that a husband must not treat his wife in the manner of the Persians who have sex in their clothes.
> This (ruling of R. Joseph) supports (a ruling of) R. Huna, for R. Huna said:
> A husband who says, "I cannot (have sex with my wife) unless I be in my clothes and she in hers," must divorce her and give her also her marriage settlement (*ketubah*).

The behavior that R. Joseph here finds objectionable is presumably the same behavior that R. Gamaliel had found laudatory. Persians maintain their modesty in sex by keeping themselves covered at all times; but, objects R. Joseph, this violates the scriptural requirement of complete bodily contact between husband and wife. The manner of the Persians is not the manner of Israel, and the husband who insists on behaving like the Persians must divorce his wife.

It is striking that the Babylonian Talmud in three separate contexts attributes to R. Joseph comments hostile to the Persians. In his opinion the Persians are destined for hell; they eat and drink like bears; and they are insufferably modest in sex. What provoked R. Joseph's spleen is not known. If the "Persians" in these passages are really the Parthians, as seems likely, we may assume that some contemporary incident, edict, or debate provoked R. Joseph's scorn for the ruling power.[85] In contrast, R. Aqiva and R. Gamaliel have nice things to say about the Medes and the Persians. What prompted these comments, we also do not know; we can only be sure that the comment attributed by the Talmud to R. Aqiva certainly is of Israelian provenance, but there is no way to determine its context. The comment attributed by the Talmud to R. Gamaliel may, for all we know, be a Babylonian pseudepigraph; we have no corroborating sources by which to assess its origin or date. Whether Israelian or Babylonian, second century or fourth, these comments are striking, for they represent something unusual, if not unique, in the rabbinic discourse about the Other.

As a rule the rabbis were not interested in ethnography, in the analysis and appreciation of the ways and mores of other nations.[86] Just as the Bible condemns the ways of the Canaanites, the Egyptians, and the Babylonians, so, too, the rabbis condemn the ways of the Greeks, the Romans, and indeed of all seventy nations. The Nations constitute the Other against which Israel is defined. Israel is sanctified by the Torah and commandments, the Nations are not; Israel has a special relationship with God, the Nations do not. Their worship of the gods is *avodah zarah*, "foreign worship" or "idolatry," and the prohibition for a Jew to aid or abet idolatry in any form severely restricted social and commercial intercourse between Jew and non-Jew in rabbinic law.[87] No cultural relativism here, no appreciation for the ways of the Other or for the truths that their manners might reveal. This is not to deny, of course, that individual gentiles in the rabbis' eyes may have been wise or pious or virtuous; the Bible can cite non-Israelite sages like Job, and the rabbis can cite a non-Jewish sage like Oenomaus of Gadara, but appreciation for exceptional individuals does not offset the denigration of the collectivity of the Nations.[88] In rabbinic discourse the dominant assumption is that we Jews have nothing to learn from the gentiles, because we have the Torah and they do not. R. Joseph's attitude toward the Persians, then, is entirely unexceptional. The Persians, R. Joseph is saying, are no better than any of the other nations; they are characterized by gluttony and priggishness, and like all of the other nations are destined for hell.

An amazing exception to this pattern is the praise of the Persians and Medes that the Babylonian Talmud attributes to R. Aqiva and R. Gamaliel. The authors of these statements clearly imply that the Jews would do well to imitate the ways of these gentiles. Like the Medes, Jews, too, should cut meat only upon the table, should kiss only upon the hand, and should hold counsel only in the field. Like the Persians, Jews, too, should be modest in their eating, in the privy, and in sexual intercourse. What is particularly amazing is that the Persians are attributed the quality of *tzeniut,* "modesty," which otherwise serves as a marker between Jew and gentile. We Jews are modest and self-controlled in all things, especially in all matters connected with food and sex, but gentiles are promiscuous in all things, especially in matters connected with sex. And yet here the Persians are said to be modest just like Israel.[89] Whence such a benign attitude to these nations? Whence the idea that the Jews, too, have what to learn from other nations and their ways? Whence the idea that the Other can yet be a source of wisdom for the Self?

The obvious answer is Greek ethnography. I am not suggesting that the authors of these rabbinic statements read Herodotus, or that Greek ethnographers somehow confirm the accuracy of these remarks about the Persians and the Medes. (As far as I have been able to determine, neither Herodotus nor any other ancient writer confirms these rabbinic reports about the manners of the Persians and Medes.) I am suggesting rather that these statements reflect a Herodotean view of the world. Herodotus was highly interested in the Otherness of the nations that he describes (for example the Scythians with whom I began this lecture), often focusing on their culinary and sexual habits. But Herodotus' tone throughout is so fair and so nonjudgmental that it clearly implies that we Greeks have no right to consider ourselves better than the barbarians, for they, in their own way, are just as good as we are. With reason then, later critics accused Herodotus of being *philobarbaros,* a lover of non-Greeks.[90] Respect and appreciation for the Other form the conceptual basis of Herodotean ethnography, indeed of Greek ethnography in general, but are entirely exceptional within rabbinic writings. As far as I have been able to determine, the explicit appreciation for, and implicit recommendation of, the customs of gentiles are not evident in any other passage of any other ancient Jewish text written in Hebrew or Aramaic, and are uncommon even in Jewish texts written in Greek.[91] How such a perspective reached the rabbis, and why it surfaces only here—I do not know, but the tone and perspective of the passage are undeniably Greek.

Conclusion

In this lecture I have considered three examples of Jewish Hellenism. First, two lists from Qumran provide the earliest evidence for Hellenistic textual scholarship in a Jewish setting. Greek scholars scoured Homer and the mythographers for information on diverse subjects; the data were collected in thematic lists. Jewish scholars did the same with data from the Bible. In both cultural spheres the resulting lists were inconsequential collections of trivia, or, phrased somewhat differently, the lists were manifestations of encyclopedic knowledge and high scholarship. Second, the revolutionaries who fomented the war of 66–73 CE and led it to its catastrophic conclusion included in their number hellenized Jews whose mother tongue was Greek. Even gentiles joined them. When the temple was about to be captured by the Romans, the revolutionaries consoled themselves, at least according to Josephus, with words that come straight out of Stoicism or Cynicism. Third, a passage in the Babylonian Talmud praising the ways of the Medes and the Persians sounds more Herodotean than rabbinic; the rabbis typically condemn gentiles and gentile culture, but in this passage the rabbis observe that in various facets of personal behavior the Medes and the Persians behave properly and set an example for the children of Israel. This appreciation for the ways of the Other is Greek, or at least Greek-like.

The Hellenism that is manifest in each of these examples is unexpected. The Jews of Qumran, like the rabbis after them, formed law-observant, Hebrew-writing, book-focused, ethnocentric communities. In addition, the Jews of Qumran attempted to separate themselves from the rest of the Jews whom they regarded as sinful, from the Jerusalem temple which they regarded as profaned, and from the powers of this world whom they regarded as illegitimate. Rabbinic hostility to outsiders was not nearly as extreme as this, but even so the self-referential character and insularity of rabbinic texts and culture are evident at every turn. The revolutionaries who fought against the hellenized upper classes of Jerusalem, who led the fight against "the Greeks" in the cities round about Judaea, and who were prepared to resist the Romans to the death, would seem to have been unlikely purveyors of Jewish Hellenism. Hence the Hellenism in all three places is unexpected.

Unexpected and yet not unexpected. Hellenism was everywhere in the Hellenistic and Roman near east, so that it should not surprise us anywhere. Hellenism was evident in art and architecture, pottery and clothing, literature and philosophy, scholarship and language, technology and politics. I do not mean to say that the Jews became "just like" everyone else, or that Judaism became just another indistinguishable ingredient in the Hellenistic cultural mix, because in many important respects Jews and Judaism remained distinctive. Judaism fostered its own ethnic specificity, whereas Hellenism was universal, or at least was meant to be; Judaism found truth in God's revelation and not in the humanism of the philosophers; Judaism had its own sacred books, instead of, or in addition to, Homer, Euripides, and Plato; and so on. Through it all, Jews remained Jews, and Judaism remained Judaism, but even in their non-Hellenism they were hellenized.

Notes

1. Herodotus 4.78 (trans. A. D. Godley, Loeb Classical Library, slightly modified).

2. Herodotus 4.79–80.

3. For a convenient recent summary of the ancient evidence and contemporary scholarship, see Lee I. Levine, *Judaism and Hellenism in Antiquity* (Seattle: University of Washington Press, 1998), esp. 20 (on Hellenism at Qumran) and 96–138 (on Hellenism and rabbinic Judaism).

4. I am paraphrasing the title of Saul Lieberman's much-cited article, "How Much Greek in Jewish Palestine?" in *Biblical and Other Studies,* ed. Alexander Altmann (Cambridge, Mass.: Harvard University Press, 1963) 123–141, reprinted in his *Texts and Studies* (New York: Ktav, 1974) 216–34. Otherwise in this essay I avoid the designation "Palestine" and prefer to speak of the land of Israel. To describe something that derives from the land of Israel, I use the adjective "Israelian," a word I have learned from H. L. Ginsberg, *The Israelian Heritage of Judaism* (New York: Jewish Theological Seminary, 1982).

5. Magen Broshi et al., eds., *Discoveries in the Judaean Desert XIX: Qumran Cave 4 XIV Parabiblical Texts, Part 2* (Oxford: Clarendon Press, 1995) 77–79 (4Q339), 81–84 (4Q340), and plate XI (cited below as "Broshi and Yardeni"). The texts are also conveniently available in F. G. Martínez and E. J. C. Tigchelaar, eds., *The Dead Sea Scrolls Study Edition* (Leiden: Brill, 1998) 2:709.

6. Magen Broshi and Ada Yardeni, "On *Netinim* and False Prophets," *Tarbiz* 62 (1992–93) 45–54 (Hebrew).

7. Josephus, *War* 1.68–69; *Ant.* 13.300.

8. Elisha Qimron, "On the list of false prophets from Qumran," *Tarbiz* 63 (1994) 273–75 (Hebrew), cited by Broshi and Yardeni.

9. For a convenient collection and discussion of the evidence, see J. P. Healey, "Netinim," *ABD* 4 (1992) 1085–86.

10. On the lists of the Hebrew Bible, see Ben Scolnic, *Theme and Context of Biblical Lists* (Atlanta: Scholars Press, 1995).

11. History: Shaye J. D. Cohen, "History and Historiography in the *Against Apion* of Josephus," *History and Theory Beiheft 27: Essays in Jewish Historiography* (1988) 1–11. Chronology: B. Z. Wacholder, "Biblical Chronology in the Hellenistic World Chronicles," *HTR* 61 (1968) 451–81; Elias Bickerman, "The Jewish Historian Demetrios," *Studies in Jewish and Christian History* (Leiden: Brill, 1980) 2.347–58. Commentary: M. Horgan, *Pesharim: Qumran Interpretations of Biblical Books* (Washington, D.C.: Catholic Biblical Association, 1979).

12. H. Diels, "Laterculi Alexandrini," *Abhandlungen der könglich preussischen Akademie der Wissenschaften, philosophisch-historische Klasse* (Berlin, 1904) 1–16. On this work see O. Regenbogen, "Pinax," *Pauly-Wissowa Realenzyklopädie* 20 (1951) 1409–1482, esp. 1468–69; Bernhard Hebert, "Attische Gelehrsamkeit in einem alexandrinischen Papyrus?" *Tyche* 1 (1986) 127–31 (a reference I owe to Hermann Harrauer); K. Brodersen, *Reiseführer zu den sieben Weltwundern* (Frankfurt/Leipzig, 1992) (a reference I owe to Monique van Rossum); and Raffaella Cribiore, *Writing, Teachers, and Students in Graeco-Roman Egypt* (American Studies in Papyrology 36; Atlanta: Scholars Press, 1996) 270 no. 380 (a reference I owe to Raffaella Cribiore).

13. Similar to the *Laterculi Alexandrini* is *Oxyrhynchus Papyri* 10.1241.

14. *Oxyrhynchus Papyri* 53.3702.

15. *Oxyrhynchus Papyri* 61.4098; see, too, 4097 and 4099.

16. H. J. Rose, ed., *Hygini Fabulae* (1933; repr. Leiden: Sijthoff, 1967); Regenbogen, "Pinax" 1470–72; C. J. Fordyce, in the *Oxford Classical Dictionary*, s.v. Hyginus, writes that "its absurdities are partly due to the compiler's ignorance of Greek."

17. *Avot de Rabbi Nathan* B 43, pp. 61a-b, ed. Schechter.

18. B. Megillah 14a; Noadiah is omitted probably because she was a false prophet (Nehemiah 6:14). For rabbinic parallels see Eliezer Segal, *The Babylonian Esther Midrash* (BJS 291–293; Atlanta: Scholars Press, 1994) 2.145–46 n. 10 and 2.162.

19. Robert M. Grant and Glen W. Menzies, *Joseph's Bible Notes (Hypomnestikon)* (Atlanta: Scholars Press, 1996).

20. Female prophets: *Hypomnestikon* no. 16 (p. 70–71). False prophets: *Hypomnestikon* no. 18 (pp. 72–73).

21. Regenbogen, "Pinax."

22. See the classic studies of David Daube, "Rabbinic Methods of Interpretation and Hellenistic Rhetoric," *HUCA* 22 (1949) 239–64; Saul Lieberman, *Greek in Jewish Palestine* (New York: Jewish Theological Seminary, 1942); and idem, *Hellenism in Jewish Palestine* (New York: Jewish Theological Seminary of America, 1950).

23. In discussion with me, Prof. John Meier of the University of Notre Dame suggests that Ben Sira's praise of the ancestors of old (Ben Sira 44–50) can also be seen as a thematic list. True, but the rhetorical function of those chapters, which mingle praise, prayer, and "biography" with list-making, is very different from the function of the lists I have described here. Nevertheless, perhaps Ben Sira's historical survey of Israel's *exempla virtutis* was also influenced by Hellenistic models; see Martin Hengel, *Judaism and Hellenism* (London: SCM, 1974) 1:136.

24. I use the term "Judaea" broadly, including Galilee and Idumaea.

25. *War* 2.388–89.

26. *War* 2.520, 6.356

27. *War* 2.520 and 5.474.

28. See Gideon Fuks, "Some Remarks on Simon Bar Giora," *Scripta Classica Israelica* 8–9 (1985–88) 106–19, a useful summary of the ancient evidence and modern discussion.

29. The Romans executed Simon but merely imprisoned John (*War* 6.434 and 7.154). The death of Bargioras is also reported by Dio Cassius 66.7.1 (=M. Stern, *Greek and Latin Authors on Jews and Judaism* no. 430).

30. The word *geiôras* appears twice in the Septuagint (Exod 12:19 and Isa 14:1) and once in Origen's Hexapla (Lev 19:34).

31. At least this is the standard scholarly view; see, for example, Martin Hengel, *The Zealots* (trans. David Smith; Edinburgh: T. & T. Clark, 1989) 374–75; Stern, *Greek and Latin Authors*, 2:59.

32. *War* 4.503. On this construction in Josephus, see Shaye J. D. Cohen, "*Ioudaios to genos* and Related Expressions in Josephus," Fausto Parente and Joseph Sievers, eds., *Josephus and the History of the Greco-Roman Period: Essays in Memory of Morton Smith* (Leiden: Brill, 1994) 23–38.

33. On Gerasa see Emil Schürer, *The History of the Jewish People in the Age of Jesus Christ* (3 vols.; rev. G. Vermes et al.; Edinburgh: T. & T. Clark, 1979) 2:149–55.

34. Hans Bietenhard, "Die syrische Dekapolis von Pompeius bis Traian," *ANRW* 2.8 (1977) 220–61, at 242, "Der Fanatismus von Simon bar Gioras erklärt sich vielleicht aus dem geistig-seelischen Zustand des Renegaten-Sprosses, der im Grunde vom alten Glauben nicht losgekommen ist und darum den innen Zwiespalt gegen aussen mit um so grösseren Eifer ausficht."

35. For whatever it is worth, I also note that Simon had a nephew named Eleazar who fought alongside him (*War* 6.227, perhaps also 4.518)—no sign of any *Zwiespalt* here.

36. For an assessment of these and other suggestions, see Fuks "Some Remarks," 107–10.

37. *War* 4.487. The precise identification and location of this Gerasa are disputed. B. Lifshitz, "Jérusalem sous la domination romaine," *ANRW* 2.8 (1977)

443–89, at 465, says that Simon was "donc un prosélyte, originaire des environs de Sichem (Neápolis) et non pas de Gerasa." Other scholars prefer a site northeast of Jerusalem; see Abraham Schalit, *Namenworterbuch zu Flavius Josephus* (Leiden: Brill, 1968), s.v. Gerasa 2 and Gerasênos 2; Otto Michel and Otto Bauernfeind, *Flavius Josephus De Bello Judaico* (4 vols.; Munich: Kösel Verlag, 1962–1969) 228 n. 150, note on *War* 4.487; Fuks, "Some Remarks," 111–13.

38. U. Rappaport, "Jewish-Pagan Relations and the Revolt against Rome in 66–70 CE," *Tarbiz* 47 (1978) 1–14 (Hebrew) = *Jerusalem Cathedra* 1 (1981) 81–95.

39. *War* 5.15–18, cf. 5.443.

40. *War* 7.191 and 206 clearly imply that the inhabitants of the town were not *Ioudaioi*, in contrast with the revolutionaries in the fortress. Two facets of the narrative of the fall of Machaerus are striking: first, that the revolutionaries separated themselves from the *xenoi* (*War* 7.191); second, that the *xenoi* nonetheless were hostile to the Romans and were regarded by the Romans as enemies. Michel-Bauernfeind, *De Bello Judaico* 2.2:254 n. 96 and 256 n. 101, note on *War* 7.178 and 7.191, explain the former by appeal to the "18 decrees" and the anti-gentile ethos of the revolutionaries, but this explanation is hard to sustain in the light of the second striking point: Why would gentiles support such revolutionaries, and why would such revolutionaries accept the support of gentiles?

41. *War* 5.268, with Thackeray's note ad loc. Thackeray's note is translated into German by Michel-Bauernfeind, *De Bello Judaico* 2.1 261 n. 114.

42. *War* 5.556.

43. Cassius Dio 66.5.4 = Stern, *Greek and Latin Authors* no. 430 (2:374).

44. Stern, *Greek and Latin Authors* no. 440 (2:404).

45. *War* 2.454.

46. On the "judaizing" of Metilius, see Shaye J. D. Cohen, *The Beginnings of Jewishness* (Berkeley: University of California, 1999) 182–84; on the larger point, see *Beginnings of Jewishness,* 140–74.

47. Zealots do not allow burial: 4.380–85; brigands do not allow burial of victims: 5.516–18, 531.

48. *War* 4.556–65.

49. *War* 4.151.

50. *War* 4.152–57.

51. *War* 4.201 and 205.

52. *War* 4.388.

53. If, as is usually assumed, he is the one mentioned in *War* 4.225.

54. *War* 5.8.

55. *War* 5.36.

56. *War* 5.100.

57. *War* 5.565 and 562–63.

58. *War* 7.264; Shaye J. D. Cohen, *Josephus in Galilee and Rome* (Columbia Studies in the Classical Tradition 8; Leiden: Brill, 1979, 88–89 n. 11.

59. Josephus is exaggerating: Hengel, *Zealots*, 15 n. 65, lists *War* 4.559–565 and 5.562ff as typical exaggerations of Josephus.

60. This suggestion is developed by J. Klausner, *History of the Second Temple*, 5.232–34, cited and discussed by Michel-Bauernfeind, *De Bello Judaico* 2.1:233 n. 188, note on *War* 4.561.

61. See discussion in Michel-Bauernfeind 2.1:211–12, an excursus on the libertine behavior of the revolutionaries.

62. *War* 5.564.

63. 1 Sam 21:2–7; cf. the references to David's action in the story about Jesus' disciples in Matt 12:1–8//Mark 2:23–28//Luke 6:1–5 and the principle stated by Paul in 1 Corinthians 9:13. Simon Price reminds me of the debate in Thucydides 4.97–98 regarding the behavior of the Athenians in the temple of Delium. They treated the temple as a fortress, even using the sacred water; in their defense they claimed that "anything done under the constraint of war and danger might reasonably meet with some indulgence, even from the God."

64. *War* 5.458–59.

65. There is some textual uncertainty here, but the basic meaning of the line is the same in all testimonia.

66. Isa 66:1, cf., too, 1 Kings 8:27. The author of Stephen's speech (Acts 7:48–50) has overinterpreted these passages.

67. Michel-Bauernfeind, *De Bello Judaico* 2.1:269 n. 185, note on *War* 5.458, and Hengel, *Zealots*, 307 n. 422, cite the idea, found in various Greek Jewish writers, that the temple is a model of the cosmos; I am not sure of the relevance of that idea here. They do not mention the Stoic-Cynic parallel.

68. A. A. Long and D. N. Sedley, *The Hellenistic Philosophers* (Cambridge: Cambridge University Press 1987) 1.430, no. 67C = I. Von Arnim, *Stoicorum Veterum Fragmenta* no. 264.

69. Letters of Heraclitus 4:2 in A. J. Malherbe, ed., *The Cynic Epistles* (Atlanta: Scholars Press, 1977) 190–91; see further H. Attridge, *First-Century Cynicism in the Epistles of Heraclitus* (Missoula, Mon.: Scholars Press for Harvard Theological Review, 1976) 13–23.

70. Cf. the speech of Eleazar at Masada, certainly an invention of Josephus.

71. *b. Berakhot* 8b; I have modified the translation published by the Soncino press.

72. The Munich manuscript reads: "R. Simeon ben Gamliel."

73. I translate the text of the Munich manuscript; our printed editions read "and modest in something else" which means the same thing.

74. Kissing on the hand, as the commentators explain, applies to greetings; married couples can kiss wherever they want.

75. Texts of Israelian provenance: *Genesis Rabbah* 74.2, pp. 858–59, ed. Theodor-Albeck; *Pesiqta deRav Kahana*, p. 60, ed. Mandelbaum; and *Ecclesiastes Rabbah* 7.23 21a, ed. Vilna. Texts of uncertain provenance but which draw inter

alia on Israelian traditions: *Tanhuma* (*Buber*) *Vayetze* 24 and *Huqqat* 11; *Tanhuma* (*nidpas*) *Huqqat* 6. All of these texts read: "R. Simeon b. Gamaliel."

76. I assume that the reading "men of the east" originates in a desire to avoid praising Medes and/or to make the saying echo more closely the language of the verse (1 Kings 5:10) to which it is juxtaposed.

77. I follow the Munich manuscript.

78. I follow the explanation of R. Samuel Eliezer Edels of Poland (known as the Maharsha, 1555–1631).

79. I follow Rashi's explanation.

80. There are further variants: "they do not bite (off a piece of) bread but they cut it with a knife" (*Pesiqta deRav Kahana*; "bread" *[bepat]* is probably a mistake for "by the mouth" *[bepeh]*); "they do not bite with the mouth but they cut with the knife" (*Ecclesiastes Rabbah*); "they do not bite (off a piece) and eat but they cut (off a piece) and eat" (*Genesis Rabbah,* according to the manuscripts).

81. It also appears in medieval anthologies that cite our text: *Yalqut Isaiah* no. 417; *Hupat Eliyahu Rabbah,* published by H. G. Enelow in his edition of the *Menorat Ha Maor,* vol. 4, p. 463.

82. R. Gamaliel was not the only one to admire the table customs of the Persians; the exilarch did as well (*b. Berakhot* 46b).

83. *b. Megillah* 11a; *Qiddushin* 72a; *Avodah Zarah* 2b.

84. *b. Ketuvot* 48a.

85. I find nothing relevant or helpful in J. Neusner, *History of the Jews in Babylonia.* Moshe Halbertal suggests to me that R. Joseph, in his comment on having sex while clothed, may be polemicizing against a Mazdean ascetic ideology which permitted sexual intercourse only for the sake of procreation. At my presentation of this lecture at Oxford, I was informed of the forthcoming publication of an Achaemenid seal which depicts the copulation of a clothed couple.

86. Sacha Stern, *Jewish Identity in Early Rabbinic Writings* (AGJU 23; Leiden: Brill, 1994) 14, "Rabbinic sources are not ethnographically inclined." For glimmerings of a rabbinic ethnography, see for example *b. Shabbat* 31a (on the physical characteristics of the Babylonians, Tadmoreans, and Africans) and *Qiddushin* 49b ("Ten *kabim* of strength descended to the world; nine were taken by the Persians and one by the rest of the world. Ten *kabim* of witchcraft descended to the world; nine were taken by Egypt and one by the rest of the world. Ten *kabim* of sexual immorality descended to the world; nine were taken by Arabia and one by the rest of the world."), but these passages do not amount to much.

87. Stern, *Jewish Identity,* 27–29.

88. Oenomaus of Gadara: *Genesis Rabbah* 65.20 (p. 734 Theodor-Albeck) with the note of Lieberman, "How much Greek," 129–130 (original pagination).

On righteous gentiles in rabbinic literature, see Lieberman, *Greek in Jewish Palestine*, 68–90.

89. Gentiles as sexually promiscuous: Stern, *Jewish Identity*, 23–26. Praise of Persians is exceptional: Stern, *Jewish Identity*, 6–7 n. 33 and 226–27 n. 175. Self-control as rabbinic ideal: Michael Satlow, "Try to be a Man: The Rabbinic Construction of Masculinity," *HTR* 89 (1996) 19–48.

90. Plutarch, *On the Malice of Herodotus* 12 (857a).

91. Cf. Philo, *Every Good Man Is Free* 74 (Magi and Gymnosophists); Josephus, *War* 7.351–357 (Indians).

ELEVEN

Greeks and Barbarians in Josephus

TESSA RAJAK

An unexpected literary formula makes several appearances in Josephus' writings. The author uses expressions of the type "both Greeks and barbarians" and "neither Greeks nor barbarians" to mean "the entire world." Often this occurs when he wants to ascribe unparalleled horror or magnificence to something by saying that it has never been matched. Thus, for example, the Temple altar was honored "by both Greeks and barbarians" (*War* 5.117); and the mother who consumed her own child during the famine in Jerusalem under siege performed an act previously unrecorded "among Greeks or barbarians" (*War* 6.199). The author's own *Jewish Antiquities* are favorably compared with all those hitherto written by either Greeks or barbarians (1.107). And in the *Antiquities* there are at least six further instances of the use of this formula, spreading across the different parts of that work, while four are to be found in the *Against Apion*. The use of this expression seems to suggest that Josephus has internalized Greek cultural priorities. We cannot but ask where the Jews fit into the Greek/barbarian dichotomy as Josephus invokes it. Are they to be considered Greeks or barbarians? Or could they perhaps even count sometimes as one and sometimes the other? Or, again, it is conceivable that some of the time the Jews were in Josephus' eyes exempt from the categorization as a "third race," foreshadowing an important line of Christian thought. It might be argued that we are dealing with nothing more than the unconsidered use of a cliché; however, Josephus' particular predilection for it does suggest that he would have had some interpretation to offer, had the question been put to him. This makes the matter an intriguing one.

Now if, by the statement that he had directed his first history of the Jewish Revolt τοῖς ἄνω βαρβάροις, "to the barbarians up-country" (*War* 1.3), Josephus meant to include Babylonian Jews as well as other inhabitants of the Parthian empire, then it seems that he was quite comfortable, at the outset of his writing career, with the inclusion of Jews among the barbarians. The position of this statement within a grand programatic prologue is a prominent one, though the context—we may note—is the issue of language: Josephus is talking about those who needed a non-Greek version of his narrative. The *Jewish War* also offers a less flattering instance in Vespasian's address to his troops at Gamala where the commander contrasts Roman experience and organization with the rashness and impetuosity which characterized barbarian fighters and which was the undoing of the Jews (4.45–46). But here the historian's intention may be to reflect, not his own perception, but that of the Roman general.

This classification remains an option in the *Antiquities* (14.187), where the historian speaks of writings by Persians and Macedonians that testify to the recognition of Jewish rights by earlier rulers that are only deposited among the Jews themselves and other barbarians, but not among the Romans. Here the superiority of the barbarian archival system is a source of credit denied to the Romans. We catch, in this association of Jews with the traditions of the east, a foretaste of the argument on the superior value of the Jewish historical record which is central to the author's own last work, *Against Apion*. At the same time, the connection points forward to another strand in Christianity, the later assertive insistence, exemplified especially by the Syrian apologist Tatian, that, for all the pretensions of Greek culture, Christian barbarism was in fact vastly superior to Hellenic superstition.

On the other hand, Jews are unmistakably not barbarians when, in the *Jewish War* (4.239), the high priest Ananus admonishes the Idumaean troops for coming to the assistance of the rebels with an enthusiasm "hardly to be looked for had they come to defend their mother city against barbarians." Rengstorf's concordance to Josephus gives "non-Jew" as a primary meaning of βάρβαρος. While we cannot pursue Josephus' barbarians here, it is appropriate to look at the principal entity on the other side of the equation, by investigating at least some aspects of Josephus' definition of Greeks. For "Greek" and "Greeks" are common terms of description in Josephus' writings, and the first question that arises is what he meant by these terms. What were "Greeks" to him? How were they demarcated from the members of other ethnic, cultural, or political groups?

Perspectives

In a brief survey published recently,[1] I made a number of claims on which I base this further study. A general perspective was proposed as a context for a glance at the ethnic labeling applied by Josephus to pre-70 Palestine. I want to refine and develop that exploration. However, the perspective itself is not wholly uncontentious: some of the assertions I made may well provoke discussion in themselves. So I shall restate the essential points, with some clarification.

1. The ethnic map of late Second Temple Palestine was an untidy patchwork. Within this, it is not easy to say which of the various ethnic identities were at any particular stage functional. It is likely that membership of a distinct group, be it Phoenician, Idumaean, Samaritan, was not readily discernible.[2] Language could not have been the distinguishing factor more than occasionally, with Aramaic still functioning as a *lingua franca*. Still less discernible, it seems, was membership of any broader group. Fergus Millar has now shown us how little justification there is in conceiving the ancient Near East in terms of a common, long-standing Semitic culture. For the ancients, at any rate, there seems to have been little sense of a common past among the peoples of the region, and it is hard to detect significant elements of a shared culture beyond the linguistic inheritance.[3]

2. It is in this context that we have to consider the "Greek" identity label. Who could be regarded as "Greeks" in that patchwork world? Would they have been instantly recognizable? We should now, moreover, look at this issue in the light of Rappaport's judgment that toward the end of the Second Temple period, under the impact of the Roman domination, these separate identities of peoples came to be subsumed in the general understanding under the label "Greek." A rough equivalent to "Greek," it is asserted, was the broad description "Syrian."[4] This interesting interpretation rests primarily on Josephus' own use of ethnic terminology, together with the evidence for contemporary behavior contained in his narratives. This claim about the new importance of the "Greek" identity deserves our attention and I shall return to it.

3. The Jews were thus exposed to a range of influences. But modern scholarship focuses on the Jews' relationship with Greek culture more than on any other. There are various reasons for this emphasis: above all, perhaps, the cause lies in the strong reaction evoked by the force which we call Hellenism, a reaction to be accounted for, in turn, by the fact that Greek culture was the most dynamic of those among which the Jews moved, the one that encroached on others. For the Greek culture of our period was the culture of empire. Indeed, for the Jews, this culture was an instrument of three successive empires to which they fell, the Ptolemaic, the Seleucid, and the Roman.

4. Roman rule in the east used the Greek language, Greek political ideas and Greek literature as its tool. This was particularly true in Palestine because of the power of Herod and the Herodian dynasty, who flaunted themselves as benefactors and Philhellenes around cities of the Roman east and even in front of the Roman emperor.[5] It is of great assistance in running an empire to have a culture to "sell." And having an empire to run is a stimulus to evolving a superior cultural "product." At least as long as foreign rule was not stabilized in Palestine, the symbols of the culture which was its tool would be at times perceived as a threat and a provocation.

5. But there was also a different reality: Greek culture was deeply intertwined with Jewish life from the early Hellenistic period to an extent where contemporaries were not themselves wholly aware of the strands.[6] By Josephus' day, "Greekness" had been an intrinsic part of Judaism for some centuries. No doubt, the Jews of Palestine were well aware that around the Roman empire lived Jews who knew no Hebrew and spoke no Aramaic; they lived their lives, heard their Bible, did their reading (if they did it) in Greek—and who, we should not forget, contributed significantly to the evolving Hellenism of their environments as well as taking from it. In Palestine, Greek was widely spoken by Jews who were often (as Jews have been through the ages) actively multilingual. That there was considerable Hellenization in Palestine as well as in the Diaspora is no longer in doubt: it is the great achievement of Martin Hengel to have demonstrated this, both for the Hellenistic and for the Roman period, even if critics have raised objections on many individual issues.[7]

6. And yet those who dispute with Hengel by stressing the distinctiveness of the Jews, are no less justified.[8] In Palestine, Jewry had its own

rooted social and cultic organization, and the Jews' reaction to foreign rule was first to accentuate their uniqueness and eventually to systematize their own religious tradition.

7. If debate about the Hellenization of the Jews has seemed inconclusive, it is, I suggest, because both sides are right on their own terms and a resolution may therefore be superfluous. In effect, the two sides are talking about different things: Hengel speaks of cultural phenomena—language, tangible ideas. He reminds us of the literary productivity of Jerusalem: "Between the Maccabaean period and its destruction, the extent of its literary production was greater than that of the Jews in Alexandria."[9] Some specific attributions of extensive Greek influence may be open to dispute. How, in the end, do we measure the impact of the Greek conception of *paideia* (in itself highly elusive) on the pessimistic wisdom of Qohelet? Or, again, is there a true parallel between Pythagorean purity regulations (which themselves can only be extrapolated from much later evidence) and those of the Essene community? Nevertheless, the cumulative impact of the data on the pre-Maccabaean period presented in *Judaism and Hellenism* is incontrovertible; and equally so is Hengel's brilliantly focused analysis, in his short later book, of the Greek culture of Jewish Palestine in the era leading up to 70. For the latter period, new archaeological evidence continues to fill out the picture. The alternative viewpoint prioritizes those aspects of Judaism which stand apart, essentially, it might be said, on two grounds: (a) the sense of difference was more significant politically—sparking off both small conflicts and large-scale revolts; (b) historical hindsight lends significance to the uniquely Jewish, since Judaism triumphantly survived through its distinctive form, rabbinism, rather than its more obviously Hellenized manifestations. Neither of these points undermines Hengel's argument.

8. Given that identities are social constructions and depend on subjective criteria as well as objective, perceptions justifiably play a central role in analysis. Recent work in anthropology helps us to grasp this basic point: cultures are read as expressions of symbolic identity, relational and shifting with context.[10] In such interpretations, ethnic boundaries are attitudinal, and significant symbols are vital to them.[11] Attitudes to others can be exposed through the human voice, through action, or through visual representation.[12] Tension between groups may, but does not have to, be involved in such boundary-drawing.

9. A question that arises therefore is just how far a Jewish-Greek dichotomy will actually have mattered to the diverse local inhabitants in

their day-to-day interactions, outside those rare historic episodes when a sharp polarization emerged—and those episodes might not occur even once in a lifetime. While there is good reason to view the distinctions as activated only intermittently, this is not to say that, in the group memory, the rare occasions of tension may have loomed as large as the links; for those moments when Jews saw themselves as diametrically opposed to what Greeks stood for, in the broadest sense, were indeed defining moments.[13] At such moments, physical violence often accompanied ideological conflict. Not only the most important but also the most formative of such experiences was the revolt of the Maccabees in the 160s BCE, which in retrospect was seen as having been provoked specifically by the promotion of a Greek lifestyle in Jerusalem by the Jewish high priest Jason, followed by his supplanter, Menelaus, and backed by the Seleucid-Greek imperial government. It is worth pointing out, however, that this division does not justify the modern tendency to describe as "Hellenizers" those unreconciled members of the Jewish establishment who held out against the Maccabees in Jerusalem's Akra fortress after the rededication of the altar. The Maccabaean literature does not define their identity.

10. Thus, by the late Second Temple period, symbolic opposition with Hellenism was indubitably a part of the way in which the Jews of Palestine constructed their own identity. It was helpful to see the Greeks as different from themselves in particular respects. And we can find in literature reflections of the symbols of those contrasting identities, suggesting that to distinguish between Jews and Greeks was a commonplace in Second Temple Jewish society. To Paul this was a primary division in society: salvation is for "the Jew first, but the Greek also" (Rom 1:16). It is also worth noting that in this same passage, speaking to the Christian community of Rome about his message to the world, Paul draws on the formula which we have seen coming so readily to Josephus' lips, pointing to both Greeks and barbarians as its recipients (Rom 1:14) and qualifies that dichotomy with the designations "wise" on the one hand and "simple" on the other, suggesting that the contrast is mainly a matter of education. However, the Greek-Jewish distinction is the more central one for Paul's thought, and it is precisely because this distinction comes so naturally that he can claim that faith abolishes, along with other differences between person and person, the gap between Greek and Jew.[14] The implication is that this pair of opposites, whether taken as ethnic, linguistic, religious, social, or all of these, represented familiar

identity markers in Paul's world. And it is of course from the Jerusalem scenes in Acts that comes the unique evidence for a split between the group known as "Hellenists" and the group known as "Hebraists" in the earliest church (6:1), mirroring, we are told, a division in Judaism itself. This evidence is supplemented by a later statement that Saul in Jerusalem debates exclusively with the Hellenists (9:9).

11. It is worth recalling that in the post-70 era the emphasis was to change quite dramatically. Many of the Palestinian Amoraim would be overtly relaxed about Hellenism, while 'idol-worshipper" was to become the main identity-forming label, the obvious antithesis to "Jewish." Other components of Hellenism, such as use of the Greek language and of Greek visual iconography, became less of a threat, as, perhaps, did the Roman government itself.[15]

At that stage the idolatry which, after all, was always a very significant part of what Jews did not like in the Greek cultural package, stood out more sharply than earlier from the rest of the distinctive features of the Greek way of life. For the Second Temple period, the challenge for us is to assess what made up that consciousness which the Jews of Palestine held, of standing apart both from Greeks and from many things Greek, at the same time as they had happily assimilated some of the enemy's habits.

Ethnic Identities in Josephus

The writings of Josephus have special value as both representative of and witness to attitudes current in the Palestine of the later Second Temple period. Any description of first-century Palestine which does not allocate a prominent place to Josephus' perceptions misses a golden opportunity. Josephus wrote his historical works in Greek, outside Palestine, after 70 CE. But he was born, around 37, a member of the Jerusalem priestly aristocracy, and educated in the city, as well as with desert sects. In the early part of the Jewish revolt, he operated as a leader in upper and lower Galilee and in the Golan area. Where the population of Palestine figures in his writings, we would expect to find both knowledge and at least the elements of a Palestinian perception—however distorted by hindsight and muffled by the cloak of a Greek writer. A native provincial voice of this kind is a unique phenomenon in ancient literature, and we should make the most of it. Moreover, in contrast to the writings of the New Testament, where there is of course also valuable evidence to be found, in Josephus we are dealing with a known author and man of action, of definable background and experience in the region (even if we come to learn of this from his own mouth), and a more or less established chronology.

Since we are here concerned with Palestine, in the forefront of consideration among Josephus' writings comes, naturally, the *Jewish War*. Though this first work is already, in the form in which we have it, a book written in Greek, for Greeks and Romans as well as Jews, the *War*, produced in the decade after the fall of Jerusalem, is necessarily formed by Josephus' home experience. The *Life*, written so much later but covering a portion of the same ground, has an occasional role to play.

It is worth putting a number of direct questions to Josephus' text. We might ask how the historian himself chose to describe the Jews in relation to other peoples and cultures in the region. We might contrast this usage with the operation of other relevant identity tags in Josephus. And, in particular, we will want to know which groups and individuals are Greeks for Josephus. Do Greeks differ in any way from Syrians? Do the Greeks of Palestine have anything to do with the Greeks of culture? In other words, are those living Greeks in any sense representatives of a superior, perhaps threatening culture? Finally, is there a marked shift between the *Jewish War* and the later writings in their approaches to Greeks and to Hellenism?

Jews and Other "Semites"

It is logical to start with the way in which Josephus speaks of his own people, for whom his usual term is the ambiguous Ἰουδαῖοι, "Judaeans," a label which may also have a simple geographical connotation. The biblical people of Israel are, by contrast, generally called Ἑβραῖοι, "Hebrews."[16] Josephus believes that the Jews acquired the name Ἰουδαῖοι when they returned from Babylon, and he offers the explanation that Judah was the first tribe to resettle Palestine (*Ant.* 11.173, with no mention of Benjamin). For Josephus, the Jews are an ἔθνος or, even more often, a γένος, to which affiliation in differing degrees is possible by conversion.[17] The criterion for Jewishness is not primarily linguistic, since for the most part the Jews spoke Aramaic in Palestine, sharing a language long widespread through the region; Hebrew was adopted in limited circles, for specific ideological purposes.[18] Josephus' distinction between Jews and Samaritans is notably sharp, probably in part at least because of the brutal conquest of Samaria by the Hasmonean John Hyrcanus. The differentiation from the Idumaeans is also surprisingly clear, considering that this people underwent a relatively peaceful conversion at the hands of the Hasmoneans. For Josephus they are at best "half-Jews" (*Ant.* 14.403), though they identify enough with Judaism to fight tenaciously on the rebel side in the great revolt.[19] The boundaries of what may count as Jewish do thus appear relatively non-negotiable.

The various "Semitic" identities generally figure in the narrative in sharp opposition to the Jews. But this is not universal. Thus, Josephus seems to have been the first to enunciate a distinct conception of an Arab ethnic identity, developing a line of descent from Hagar, through Ishmael, and Ishmael's eldest son Nabaiotes, for the circumcized Ishmaelites whom he identifies exclusively with the Nabataeans. A certain supposed affinity between the Arab people in general, or perhaps the Nabataeans in particular, and the Jews would seem to be implied in this reconstruction.[20]

Greeks in the *Jewish War*

When Josephus deploys the label "Greek" in his narrative history, this does usually form part of an implicit "them" and "us" dichotomy, in which Greeks are "them," as we might expect. But there may be exceptions, as we shall see.

The use of the term "Greeks" as a general description of non-Jews figures regularly in Josephus. The mercenaries of King Alexander Jannaeus, actually, we are told, Pisidians and Cilicians, are also simply called "Greeks" (*War* 1.94). Foreign oil is also Greek oil (*Life* 94).

Furthermore, in a number of violent episodes surrounding the Jewish Revolt, Greeks and Jews are presented as natural antagonists within a city. Perhaps the most striking instance is the quarrel between Jews and Greeks in Caesarea, which Josephus regards as the trigger of revolt. This revolved around the question of whether the city was a Greek one with a Greek constitution, or a city for Jews. Cultic divergences caused mutual suspicion, too, with Greek mockery of practice in the city's synagogue inflaming the situation.

Greeks and Syrians in Josephus

As we have already seen, it is unexpectedly hard to establish the difference between the element in the population of Palestine described as "Greek" and that spoken of as "Syrian." Syrian identity seems to be a relatively new and arbitrary phenomenon. It may well reflect the Roman provincial division and thus may be regarded as a consequence of Rome's disruption of the area. For Jews, "Syrian" was a convenient description, and in its use by our author it might indeed at first sight seem to be interchangeable with "Greek."[21]

A distinction may, however, be suggested and it is a potentially important one. Greeks, I would propose, are regularly urban, citizens of some polis, while Syrians tend to be rural, or at least to be people living in villages and towns without either formal constitutions or official Roman standing. The cities in and around Palestine are often described as "Greek" by Josephus, and their inhabitants straightforwardly as "Greeks." There was a real difference in organization and functioning between proper Greek cities and other settlements, as Josephus was well aware. The language in which the public business of the cities was transacted will have been Greek. This gap between the two kinds of entity may help to explain a remarkable shift in the account in the *War* of the flare-up in Caesarea which precipitated the revolt in 66 CE. Josephus states that the Jews who lived there took up arms against the Syrians, with each party claiming control of the city, and the Jews insisting that Herod had established the foundation with them in mind (*War* 2.266). It may be suggested, therefore, that, at the opening of the account, the opponents are not designated "Greeks," because the point at issue for the Jews (with whom Josephus sympathizes) is precisely that this was no Greek city. Yet the self-designation of the non-Jews, consonant with their claims to a foundation equipped with statues and temples—that is to say, with the appurtenances of a *polis*—is precisely as Greeks, and thus they do get to be so characterized when Josephus, in the next sentence, sets out their side of the argument. We then learn (268) that these Greeks are supported by local troops, recruited by the Romans in the province of Syria, another reason why the collective term for the opposition as a whole can appropriately be "Syrian."

Later, the villagers around Caesarea, attacked by parties of Jews after the troubles in the city, are described as "Syrians" (*War* 2.458). But the neighboring cities listed by Josephus are not included in the Syrian zone. After that, however, the massacre which follows the disaster in Caesarea is referred to as a massacre of Jews by Syrians (*War* 2.461ff.). This is the same collectivity of which the writer had talked earlier. But there is also an additional factor: the perspective is now that of events across an entire region, or perhaps even the breadth of the province, specified by Josephus as ὅλην τὴν Συρίαν, "the whole of Syria" (*War* 2.462). So under "Syrians" he means to include all those who inhabited Syria. It is consonant with this that, still in the same context, when Josephus enlarges upon the massacre of their Jewish population perpetrated by the people of the Greek city of Scythopolis, the term "Syrians" is not applied to them, and instead they are carefully designated "Scythopolitans."

Later, the inhabitants of Trachonitis, in the kingdom of Agrippa II, are explained as a mixture of Jews and Syrians (*War* 3.57). This was a region of villages. Elsewhere, troops fighting for the Romans, when not called simply "Roman," can be admitted as Syrian (*War* 4.38). Deserting Jerusalemites who have swallowed gold coins before escaping the siege are ripped open by the Arabs among the Syrians on the other side (5.549ff.).

Thus, in a formal sense, Syrians in the *Jewish War* appear to be those who live in the province of Syria, of which the cities, with their own territories, were, according to Roman arrangements, strictly not a part. Arguably, for Josephus this was the term's principal connotation. To this may be added what later became a crucial defining mark, that of language. The use of Aramaic, in Greek called the language of the Syrians, distinguished the people who could be called "Syrians."[22] In the *Antiquities* (8.154), discussing the different names for the desert town of Palmyra, Josephus contrasts the usage of the Greeks with that of the Syrians, who use the name Tadmor. It follows, however, that if, in Josephus' world, Greeks are simply the citizens of the cities, then we remain sadly ignorant about the real profile of those thus described. There is little doubt, as has been said, that the cities will have had Greek-style public institutions, at least of a rudimentary kind.[23] Moreover, if Syrians were speakers of Aramaic, Greeks were supposed to speak Greek. Yet even then, Greek need not have been the principal spoken language in the new or revamped polis foundations during the early stages of the Roman presence in the region. It is impossible for us to ascertain how sharp a distinction existed between the kinds of lives lived by the average inhabitants of the two types of towns, those that were officially Greek as against those that were not Greek but Syrian. There are allusions in Josephus' later autobiographical sketch to the communal conflicts of 66 in Galilee and Syria which parallel his comments in the *Jewish War*. The later references deploy the ethnic terminology in a manner quite compatible with its use in the earlier work, as here interpreted. Thus, the massacres which followed the defeat of Cestius Gallus are located in Syria (i.e., throughout the province) and perpetrated by Syrians (*Life* 25). The non-Jewish inhabitants of Scythopolis are once again referred to as "Scythopolitans" (26). It is at first sight puzzling to read of the "Syrians" of Caesarea encouraging the ambitions of Agrippa II's overseer Varus (52). Yet it might be suggested if the enthusiasts in question are subjects of the king, they might not be Greek citizens of a polis, but rather residents of territory where the royal writ ran. The designation "Greeks" make its only appearance in Josephus' *Life* in connection with Tiberias when the Greek inhabitants (κατοικοῦντες) of the city are apparently all annihilated by the Jewish pro-revolt party (*Life* 67). The city had been founded by Herod Antipas for Jewish immigrants, but we do not know how power was shared in the sixties.

Jews and Gentiles in Josephus

It is perhaps surprising to find the resonant Jew-Gentile polarity playing a part in Josephus' thinking, given his own continuing role as intermediary between the two groups and his avowed purpose of reconciling them (*Ant.* 16.175). There is a depiction of the hostile crowd as made up of *allophuloi*, "other peoples," or "foreigners," figures in the historian's description of the Alexandrian troubles under the emperors Caligula and Claudius (*War* 2.488): this may be explained as no more than a convenient shorthand way of taking both Greeks and Egyptians into account. At Scythopolis, in 66 CE, the same lineup of the Jewish element against the foreign is envisaged, although this was the city where the Jews had lived in amity with their neighbors, where they had supported them against the revolutionaries until this very trust had brought about their downfall (*War* 2.466). Olive oil not produced by Jews, as well as being called "Greek oil," is described as foreign, ἀλλόφυλον (*Ant.* 12.199), or, which comes to the same thing, as not supplied by ὁμόφυλοι (compatriots, *War* 2.259), thus indicating its unsuitability for Jewish use. If Goodman is right, the basis of this practice was not any *halakhah* (legal ruling) of any kind, but, in the first instance, instinctive revulsion.[24] On the other hand, when Josephus castigates the revolutionaries during the siege of Jerusalem, in a bitter speech which he puts into his own mouth, he paradoxically contrasts foreign respect for the Temple with the Jews' desecration of their own shrine (6.102). Further examples of this ironic contrast might be cited.

So non-Jews are "the other," and the expectation is that they will be hostile. Yet that polarity does not come as readily to Josephus' lips as we might expect—not as readily, indeed, as the less predictable Greek/barbarian dichotomy. Nor, it may be pointed out, do we find any verbal expression of separatism in Josephus comparable with that enunciated in 2 Maccabees, where the extraordinary term ἀλλοφυλισμός, is conjured up to describe the process of adopting foreign habits and then put side by side with the author's more long-lived and famous coinage, Ἑλληνισμός.[25] Indeed, Josephus can even go so far as to stand his normal use of the term ἀλλόφυλος on its head. In his preface to the *Jewish War* (1.16), he happily describes himself as an ἀλλόφυλός, a foreigner, addressing Greeks and Romans, thus demonstrating that the concept did not in itself carry the strong negative implications for him that the terms "gentile" or *goy* have done for Jews in many situations.[26]

Greeks by Culture

There is an unexpected and intemperate attack on Greek historians in the preface to the *Jewish War* (1.13), where Josephus promotes his own history by denigrating its predecessors. Latter-day Greeks are not to be compared with the ancients. The Greek writers, described as "native-by-birth" (γνήσιοι, 1.16) are castigated as liars, voluble in the lawcourts but silent when expected to bring forth facts. These are the negative terms in which Roman stereotypes of the Greek character were often expressed.[27] Yet the posture is a remarkable one for an author whose desired readership around the Roman Empire (1.3) is said to consist of Greeks along with "those Romans who were not involved" (1.6). For all these aspirations, he at this moment wholly detaches himself by his contemptuous critique from the Greek cultural scene of his day. But the classical historians are explicitly excluded from the strictures and by implication accorded respect (1.14).

Yet it seems that, on at least one occasion in the *War*, Greeks are "us" to Josephus. Thus, those writers who came before Josephus, here unnamed, who according to him translated Jewish writings into Greek, are simply called Greeks (1.17). Yet here he can only be referring to the Hellenistic-Jewish authors whose work was based on the Greek Bible, writers such as those whom he himself, many years later, identified in a similar assertion in *Against Apion* (1.218). Not only were these writers manifestly Jews, but it is extremely hard to believe that Josephus, even at an early stage in his career, was so ignorant as to believe otherwise. There are, however, obvious apologetic considerations. The shift made it possible to claim that Greek writers had in the past taken an interest in Jewish tradition. Moreover, it could be advantageous in writing history designed for Greek readers to identify Jews with Greeks, just as it was the purpose of the first-century Greek historian Dionysius of Halicarnassus, who wrote at Rome, to prove that the Romans were Greek by origin. And there is more. The passage shows that Josephus is able to deploy a linguistic and cultural rather than an ethnic definition of what is Greek. In terms of such a construction, Greekness, far from being alien to Judaism, can be something in which Jews shared. In any interpretation of Josephus' ability to speak in this way, the important fact of the existence of a large class of Jews, among them many of his readers, whose only language was Greek should not be overlooked.[28]

In other words, at the time of writing of the *Jewish War*, Josephus was on the way to forming a conception of a Greek culture as something distinct from the people who were contemporary Greeks, or would-be Greeks. Some of this culture's modern manifestations were to him derisory, but its scope went well beyond its inadequate native exponents of historiography to a linguistic world which might in theory include Jews.

In the later works, this awareness emerges more distinctly. Thus, Josephus ascribes the distinctive attribute of Greek *paideia*, which he takes as self-explanatory for his readers, to a number of individuals, including the Jewish writer Justus of Tiberias.[29] More telling, perhaps, is the well-known passage in which Josephus chooses, in the peroration to his *Antiquities*, to recount the rigorous training in Greek prose and poetry through which he had put himself as preparation for writing, mentioning that such skills were a rarity in the world from which he came, even if not wholly unknown (*Ant.* 20.263–64). Returning to the dichotomy with which we opened, we now see how Jews could perfectly well have been classed among the Hellenes, even if they were more readily incorporated on the barbarian side.

Summary: Josephus' Perspectives on Greeks and Their Culture

The following significant points emerge from this exploration.

1. It appears that in relation to pre-70 Palestine, Greeks were for Josephus usually those who lived in cities with Greek-style constitutions, the rest of the non-Jews (and non-Romans) in the vicinity being Syrians, inhabitants of the Roman province of Syria.
2. At this stage Josephus' conceptualization of the Jew/Greek dichotomy overlaps with the less prominent Jew/Gentile dichotomy.
3. Greeks and the Greek lifestyle seem to have been rather distant from Jews in Josephus' representation of the scene in Jewish Palestine.
4. Josephus, at any rate, at the time of writing of the *War*, did not have a coherent conception of any broader Greek identity. So it seems that this was not something he had brought with him out of Judaea or, for that matter, out of Galilee.
5. We can, nonetheless, observe at this stage the beginnings of the writer's awareness of the cultural power of Hellenism.
6. What perhaps had been a latent interest could flourish in Josephus' personal circumstances after he took up residence in the Diaspora. His later writing career shows an ever-increasing awareness of the cultural significance of addressing a Greek audience and of the challenge posed by Greek culture. The aims of his later writings—that Greeks should respect and admire Jews and be drawn to Judaism—suggest that he was concerned not just with peaceful communal coexistence but with cultural claims. The terms in which he promotes Judaism there leave us in no doubt that he is at this stage more conscious of the attractions in the Greek tradition.

Explaining the Evidence of Josephus

From Josephus we derive the impression that, while Greeks were often enemies, the Jewish society of Palestine in the late Second Temple period was less concerned, either positively or negatively, about the attractions of Greek culture than that same society had been at the dawn of Hellenism. One reason for this may lie precisely in the bad relations between Greeks and Jews in the cities of the region: those so-called Greeks (some of them so designated only since Pompey's conquest) may have put Hellenism itself out of play. And yet to see that there is no simple connection between intergroup relationships and the broader process of cultural appropriation, we have only to think of Philo's Alexandria, where hostility between Jews and Greeks did not deter Jews like Philo himself from profound immersion in Greek thought.

Another, perhaps more important, reason for the weakening of the threat posed by Hellenism may be put forward: In Jewish Judaea there was in reality relatively little opportunity to sense the impact of Greek culture as a world-dominant force. Until the destruction of the Temple, a way of life centered, quite simply, on the practices of Judaism, held the stage in the immediate environment. That Greek culture was an instrument of empire under the Romans was at this stage a quite remote fact to many of Rome's subjects. Late Second Temple Jerusalem was a cosmopolitan milieu containing a spectrum of humanity, as Hengel has brilliantly shown: the prevailing style in the Jewish establishment appears to have been one of detachment from Greek institutions and ideas, even if use of the Greek language for external and even internal communication will already have been a fact of life and even if close relations with the Roman government were a necessity. That the Greek-educated Agrippa II and his more outward-looking circle were at some distance from this Temple-based establishment is clearly shown by the divergent courses the two groups took during the revolt, with Agrippa supplying troops to the Romans. Significantly, in the pages of Josephus, we meet no Jewish Hellenizers from the post-Hasmonean period; only, it may be pointed out, the exact opposite—the pagan Judaizers of the cities of Syria who were resented as an alien element by their fellow-citizens (*War* 2.463). But that is to enter a new discussion.

As for the riddle in Josephus' adoption of the Greek-barbarian cliché, there is no real solution, but we can now perhaps understand a little better what Josephus is up to. When he wrote the *Jewish War,* he saw no disgrace in the Jews being classed as barbarians. In the later works, the overt barbarian identification has fallen away. By linguistic criteria, certain Jews could count as Greeks, an assimilation which could be used in the apologetic argumentation of *Antiquities* and *Against*

Apion. On the whole, however, ambiguity reigns there, and the possibility that the Jews were conceived as a third force, outside the distinction, cannot be excluded. This uncertainty suited the historian rather well and may even have given him pleasure.

Notes

1. T. Rajak, "The Location of Cultures in First Century Palestine: The Evidence of Josephus," in R. Bauckham, ed., *The Book of Acts in Its First Century Setting,* vol.4: *Palestinian Setting* (Grand Rapids, Mich.: Eerdmans, 1995) 1–14.

2. For a painstaking endeavor to locate a distinct Phoenician element in western Idumaea in the Herodian period, see N. Kokkinos, *The Herodian Dynasty: Origins, Role in Society and Eclipse* (Journal for the Study of the Pseudepigrapha Supplement Series 30; Sheffield: Sheffield Academic Press, 1998) chap. 3.

3. F. Millar, *The Roman Near East 31 BC–AD 337* (Cambridge, Mass.: Harvard University Press, 1993).

4. Uriel Rappaport, "Les juifs et leurs voisins à l'époque perse, hellénistique et romaine," *Annales: Histoire, Sciences Sociales* 5 (1996) 955–74.

5. On the novelty Herod's pathbreaking benefactions, see now Millar, *The Roman Near East 31 BC–AD 337,* 353–56.

6. E. J. Bickerman, *The Jews in the Greek Age* (Cambridge, Mass.: Harvard University Press, 1988).

7. M. Hengel, *Judaism and Hellenism* (2 vols.; Philadelphia: Fortress, 1974); idem, *The "Hellenization" of Judaea in the First Century after Christ* (London: SCM, 1989). Critique in L. H. Feldman, "Hengel's *Judaism and Hellenism* in Retrospect," *JBL* 96 (1977) 371–82.

8. Especially F. Millar, "The Background to the Maccabean Revolution: Reflections on Martin Hengel's *Judaism and Hellenism,*" *JJS* 29 (1978) 1–21.

9. Hengel, *"Hellenization,"* 29.

10. U. Östergard, "What is National and Ethnic Identity?" P. Bilde, T. Engberg-Pedersen, L. Hannestad, and J. Zahle, eds., *Ethnicity in Hellenistic Egypt* (Aarhus: Aarhus University Press, 1992) 32; B. Anderson, *Imagined Communities: Reflections on the Origins and Spread of Nationalism* (London: Verso Editions, 1983) 15.

11. On the interaction of subjective ethnicity with social reality, see now S. Jones, "Identities in Practice: Towards an Archaeological Perspective on Jewish Identity in Antiquity," S. Jones and S. Pearce, eds., *Jewish Local Pa-*

triotism and Self-Identification in the Greco-Roman Period (Sheffield: Sheffield Academic Press, 1998) 29–49.

12. F. Barth, ed., *Ethnic Groups and Boundaries: The Social Organization of Cultural Difference* (London: Allen and Unwin, 1969) 9.

13. See T. Rajak, "The Hasmoneans and the Uses of Hellenism," P. R. Davies and R. T. White, eds., *A Tribute to Geza Vermes: Essays on Jewish and Christian History and Literature* (JSOTSup 100 (Sheffield: JSOT Press, 1990) 261–80.

14. Rom 10:11–12; Gal 3:28; cf. Col 3:11, where barbarians and Scythians also figure by way of contrast with Greeks.

15. For the spectrum of rabbinic attitudes, see now the assessment by L. I. Levine, *Judaism and Hellenism: Conflict or Confluence* (Seattle: University of Washington Press, 1998) chap. 3.

16. However, in his invective against the revolutionaries (*War* 5.443), conceived on a large historical canvas, Josephus writes of their dragging down "the whole of the Hebrew race." On the terminology, see P. Spilsbury, *The Image of the Jew in Flavius Josephus' Paraphrase of the Bible* (TSAJ 69; Tübingen: J. C. B. Mohr [Paul Siebeck], 1998) 12–14.

17. S. J. D. Cohen, "Religion, Ethnicity and 'Hellenism' in the Emergence of Jewish Identity in Maccabaean Palestine," in P. Bilde, T. Engberg-Pedersen, L. Hannestad and J. Zahle, eds., *Religion and Religious Practice in the Seleucid Kingdom* (Aarhus: Aarhus University Press, 1990) 204–23.

18. S. Schwartz, "Language, Power and Identity in Ancient Palestine," *Past and Present* 148 (1995).

19. On the conversion of the Idumaeans, see A. Kasher, *Jews, Idumaeans and Ancient Arabs* (TSAJ 18; Tübingen: J. C. B. Mohr [Paul Siebeck], 1988) 44–78; Cohen, "Religion, Ethnicity and 'Hellenism' in the Emergence of Jewish Identity in Maccabaean Palestine," 212–21; Kokkinos, *The Herodian Dynasty*. On Idumaean status in Jewish eyes and the Idumaean part in the revolt, M. Goodman, *The Ruling Class of Judaea: The Origins of the Jewish Revolt against Rome* A.D. 66–70 (Cambridge: Cambridge University Press, 1987) 222–23.

20. F. Millar, "Hagar, Ishmael, Josephus and the Origins of Islam," *JJS* 24 (1993) 233–45. More fully on Arab identity, Millar, "The Background to the Maccabean Revolution," 387–407.

21. See Rappaport, "Les juifs et leurs voisins à l'époque perse, hellénistique et romaine."

22. See Millar, *The Roman Near East*, 507.

23. A. H. M. Jones, *The Greek City* (Oxford: Clarendon, 1940) 170–91.

24. M. Goodman, "Kosher Olive Oil in Antiquity," *Ethnic Groups and Boundaries*, 227–45.

25. On *allophulismos*, see Hengel, *The "Hellenization" of Judaea in the First Century after Christ*, 22.

26. On Jewish separation from gentiles in the rewritten bible of Josephus' *Antiquities,* see Spilsbury, *The Image of the Jew in Flavius Josephus' Paraphrase of the Bible.*

27. See A. Wardman, *Rome's Debt to Greece* (London: P. Elek, 1976) 1–13.

28. My reading of these difficult passages is close to that suggested for the *Against Apion* passage by B. Z. Wacholder, *Eupolemus: A Study of Judaeo-Greek Literature* (Monographs of the Hebrew Union College 3; New York: Hebrew Union College, 1974) 3. Other interpretations have been offered. I owe my awareness of the complications to Professor D. S. Schwartz (who has a different solution).

29. Josephus, *Ant.* 19.213; *Life* 40, 336–59; *Ag. Apion* 1.73.

TWELVE

Judaism between Jerusalem and Alexandria

GREGORY E. STERLING

The first occurrence of the term "Judaism" ('Ιουδαϊσμός) appears in the preface of 2 Maccabees. In a list of the basic contents the epitomizer of Jason of Cyrene mentions "the epiphanies from heaven that occurred for those who fought valiantly and zealously on behalf of Judaism (ὑπὲρ τοῦ Ἰουδαϊσμοῦ)."[1] The same author also gave us the first attestation of the noun "Hellenization" or "Hellenism" (Ἑλληνισμός) in the extended sense of Greek culture; previously it had meant to speak correct Greek. In his summary critique of the Jewish high priest Jason, the epitomizer says: "There was such an extreme of Hellenization (ἀκμή τις Ἑλληνισμοῦ) and advance of foreign ways because of the surpassing depravity of the impious and false priest Jason that the priests were no longer interested in their duties at the altar...."[2] What is striking about these neologisms is that the epitomizer has used them in opposition: Judaism represents the ancestral ways of the Jews; Hellenism represents the unlawful lifestyle of the Hellenes.[3]

The tension between Judaism and Hellenism developed in 2 Maccabees has become the occasion for an extended debate in modern scholarship. For most of this century it was common for students of Second Temple Judaism and early Christianity to distinguish between Palestinian and Hellenistic Judaism. The most important representative of this view in the English-speaking world was George Foot Moore, who spoke of the "not inconsiderable" gulf between Aramaic-speaking and Greek-speaking Jews. He considered the former the normative forerunner of the rabbis and the latter an aberrant form of Judaism that eventually disappeared. He wrote: "The history of Greek-speaking Jewry in these centuries is exceedingly obscure; but in the end the triumph of normative Judaism as it had been developed in the schools of Palestine and Babylonia seems to have been complete. . . ."[4] In recent decades Moore's gulf has been filled. The chief excavator is Martin Hengel, who wrote: "From about the middle of the third century BC *all Judaism* must really be designated *'Hellenistic Judaism'* in the strict sense."[5] Hengel filled the gulf by arguing that Palestinian Judaism had been as thoroughly hellenized as the Diaspora. In my opinion Hengel has made his case. This does not, however, mean that Jews in Judaea inculturated Hellenism in the same way that Jews in the Diaspora did nor that all Diaspora communities did so in the same ways or to the same degree.[6] While all Jews were hellenized, the specifics of their Hellenization varied markedly. There were several variables that controlled the extent of Hellenization. The most important of these was the community to which an individual Jew belonged and its situation within the larger Graeco-Roman world.[7]

I propose to test this hypothesis by comparing two Jewish communities from c. 175 BCE–135 CE: Jerusalem and Alexandria.[8] I have selected these communities for two reasons. First, they are two of the most important communities in Second Temple Judaism: Jerusalem is the most important community within Judaea and Alexandria is one of the—if not the—most significant communities in the Diaspora. Second, we have enough information about the two communities to permit a comparison.[9] While the selections seem obvious, the process of comparing them is not without difficulties. One of the most obvious is that Judaism and Hellenism are complex concepts. We should not assume that either was clearly defined or uniform in antiquity.[10] I will offer stipulative definitions to clarify my own understanding. I offer these as modern constructs designed to assist analysis, not as definitions that specific individuals or groups in antiquity would espouse. They represent minimal standards that are flexible enough to incorporate a wide range of variations. By Judaism I mean the ethnic-religious identity of the Jews whose ancestral traditions required some distinctive religious and social practices. By Hellenism I mean the post-Alexander culture of the Greeks that was based in cities and cultivated in specific educational and social practices. Next we must ask how to measure the inculturation of the latter by the former. We can not use modern social science methods, since they require more quantifiable data than we have. We therefore must work inductively with the data that we have. I propose to do so under three headings: the political-social situations of the communities, the linguistic practices of the communities, and the social-religious practices of the communities.[11] These are not exhaustive categories, but they will supply us with enough information to form a comparison in general terms.

The Political-Social Situations

The first criterion helps us to understand the external constraints each community had to face as it forged its own identity as a subgroup within the larger world. I will examine this under three subheadings.

The Political Situation of the City

The political state of each city changed several times during this period. Jerusalem had a constant and a variable political factor: the constant was the presence of the high priest and the high priestly families; the variable was the presence or absence of a distinct political ruler. At the outset of the second century BCE Jerusalem passed from Ptolemaic to Seleucid control when the Seleucids finally wrestled Palestine away from the Lagids in the fifth Syrian War at the battle of Paneion.[12] The Syrians, however, found their prize hard to hold: the Hasmoneans won independence for nearly a century.[13] When the Hasmoneans fought among themselves for control of the throne in the first century BCE, Pompey settled the matter by incorporating Judaea into the newly fashioned Roman province of Syria.[14] Eventually the Romans found it expedient to appoint either a client king or a prefect/procurator to rule Judaea.[15] In the case of the latter, the seat of foreign government was Caesarea, not Jerusalem. This means that throughout this period, Jerusalem was either the capital of an independent Jewish state or the capital of a subject Jewish state. It was, however, always a Jewish city—unless it was briefly constituted as a Greek πόλις under Antiochus IV Epiphanes[16]—and always the recognized center of Judaism.

The situation was quite different in Alexandria. Alexandria was founded as a Greek city by Alexander the Great.[17] It served first as the capital of the Ptolemaic empire and then of Roman administration in Egypt. The Jewish community constituted a distinct minority within this Greek city. Ancient sources indicate that there were three main groups within the city: Polybius says there were Egyptians, mercenaries, and

Alexandrians;[18] Josephus says there were Greeks, Jews, and Egyptians.[19] The two lists are roughly the same: Polybius' mercenaries must have included Jews. According to Josephus, Ptolemy VI Philometor (180–145 BCE) appointed two Jews as generals over his army: Onias and Dositheus.[20] This is hardly surprising, given the history of Jews in Egypt: they had served the Persians in this capacity in Elephantine at an earlier date.[21] This means that the Jewish community had to deal with both Greeks and Egyptians.

Sometime prior to the middle of the second century BCE the Alexandrian Jewish community organized itself into a πολίτευμα.[22] While the specific nature of this political unit is a matter of debate, it is clear that the Jews enjoyed the right of self-governance.[23] Strabo says that they had an ethnarch "who manages the nation and adjudicates lawsuits and deals with contracts and ordinances as if he were the ruler of an independent state."[24] When the Romans took over Alexandria, they left the Jewish community intact. Augustus made only two notable modifications: he imposed a poll tax[25] and created a Jewish senate to govern Jewish affairs c. 10–12 CE.[26]

The Jews were not, however, content to remain an isolated unit with the larger *polis*. Families such as Philo's whose brother, Gaius Julius Alexander, and nephew, Tiberius Julius Alexander, served in official capacities, must have been citizens of the Alexandrian *polis* and of Rome. They were, however, only representative of the upper strata of the Alexandrian Jewish community. The riots that took place and the embassies to Caligula and Claudius brought the issue of Jewish relations with the Greeks to a head. It appears that the second and later Jewish delegation sent by the Alexandrian Jewish community to Claudius pressed for Jews to be accorded equal rights with Alexandrians.[27] Claudius demurred and only gave them the right to observe their ancestral traditions.[28] While he did not revoke the citizenship of those who already had it, he closed the possibility of extending citizenship to the families of Jews who were not already citizens by excluding them from the gymnasium and—by extension—the ephebate.

Complicating Jewish relations with the Greeks and Romans were their relations with the Egyptians. Initially, the Jews had the upper hand. From the battle of Raphia to the death of Philometor (217–145 BCE) Jewish fortunes flourished as they supported the Ptolemies against the rising threat of Egyptian nationals.[29] From the death of Philometor to the annexation by Rome the situation changed. The Ptolemaic regime was marked by internal strife. Jewish fortunes rose and ebbed as they backed the successful or unsuccessful claimant among the Ptolemies. The Jewish community often backed one claimant and the Alexandrians another. Egyptian nationals found such splits an opportunity to express their contempt for the Jews.[30] Although many must have thought that the entrance of Rome would have solved the problem by stabilizing the situation, it only exacerbated it. Each group appealed to the Romans, who permitted the sectional rivalries to flourish. Josephus captured the reality of life during the final century of Ptolemaic rule and the early century and a half of Roman rule when he wrote: "There was always discord in Alexandria between the Jews and the native residents."[31]

There are thus significant political differences between the two communities. Jerusalem was a Jewish city; Alexandria was a Greek city. Jews in Jerusalem were either independent or semi-independent. While they had to relate to Greeks and Romans in distant locales, they completely dominated Jerusalem. Alexandrian Jews were semi-independent; however, their situation was complicated by the fact that they were a minority group who had to cope with at least two other groups: the ruling Greeks and the native Egyptians. Since the Greeks controlled the city, members of the Jewish community sought access to citizenship in the Greek *polis*. The heterogeneity of the Alexandrian situation thus played a decisive role in the Alexandrian Jewish community's stance toward Hellenism.

Population

We now need to turn to the relative sizes of the populations. Estimates of ancient populations are notoriously difficult since we generally lack reliable census information. Nevertheless, I think that we can gain a general impression. According to Pseudo-Hecataeus, there were 120,000 residents in Jerusalem.[32] At a later date Josephus puts the number much higher: he claims that there were 3,000,000 in Jerusalem at the Feast of Unleavened Bread in 65 CE and that during the siege of Jerusalem in 70 CE 1,100,000 perished. He explains what even he realized were extremely high numbers by stating that the population had temporarily risen to 2,700,000 as a result of Passover.[33] Tacitus is more realistic when he says that 600,000 were besieged.[34] These ancient numbers and those of modern scholars who follow them are inflated in my judgment.[35] On *a priori* grounds it is not likely that Jerusalem rivaled the largest cities in the eastern half of the Roman Empire. Ancient census information and statements indicate that Alexandria had a free population of 300,000 (first century BCE), Antioch on the Orontes of 250,000 (first century BCE), Pergamum of 140,000 (second century CE), Ephesus of approximately the same number as Pergamum, and Apamea in Syria of 117,000 (6/7 CE). Rome, the largest city in the empire, had an estimated population of 1,000,000.[36] Jerusalem's population must have been considerably lower. Two recent studies based on different criteria have reached similar conclusions about the size of Jerusalem's population: Magen Broshi working with size and density estimates and John Wilkinson working with size and available water supply estimates place the population in the first century BCE around 35,000 and around 70,000–80,000 at the time of the First Jewish Revolt.[37] The strength of these numbers is that they meet numerous criteria. I will therefore use 75,000 as a working estimate for the population of Jerusalem c. 70 CE. While there were some non-Jews among this number, they were a minority: Jerusalem was Jewish.

As we have already seen, Alexandria had a different complexion. We are fortunate to have a census to calculate the total population. Diodorus Siculus claims that a first-century BCE census indicated a free population of 300,000.[38] Based on this figure, P. M. Fraser calculated the total population at 1,000,000 at the time of Strabo and 1,500,000 at the time of Josephus, a little over a century later.[39] More recently Diana Delia has reduced the total to 500,000–600,000.[40] Assuming the higher of Delia's lower numbers we may conservatively place the population at c. 600,000. How large was the Jewish population? Philo estimates the number of Jews in Egypt to have been 1,000,000.[41] A textually problematic fragment in the *Acts of the Alexandrian Martyrs* refers to 180,000 after a reference to 173 elders.[42] This coincides with Philo's statements about the size of the Jewish community in Alexandria. In speaking of the five districts of the city he says: "Two of these are called Jewish because most of the Jews reside in them; however, not a few Jews also live scattered about in the other (parts)."[43] It is therefore possible that the Jewish community numbered about 180,000.

The numbers that we have reached suggest that both Jewish communities were large. The Alexandrian community was probably more than twice the size of the Jerusalem community. While Jerusalem had a symbolic importance that went beyond its size, the magnitude of the Alexandrian community gave it a political importance that could not be ignored.

Revolts

The importance of both communities in the larger world made them the focal points of Jewish interactions with larger political powers. Ultimately this proved disastrous for both communities. We begin with the relations each community had with the successors of Alexander. As is well known, the Jerusalem community successfully revolted against their Syrian masters. The Alexandrian community, on the other hand, enjoyed relatively good relations with the Ptolemies. What is the difference? We cannot reduce these two responses *tout court* to different postures toward Hellenism, since there is no indication that Palestinian Jews ever contemplated revolting against the Ptolemies in the third century BCE. Further, when the Hasmoneans established themselves, they acculturated to Hellenism. These factors suggest that something more was at stake. What set off the crisis in 167 BCE was the attempt to eliminate Judaism.

It would be simplistic, however, to leave matters at this. The nationalistic spark that ignited the Maccabean revolt refused to fade: it simmered until it exploded in the First and Second Jewish Revolts. However, the circumstances were now different: Rome had entered the picture. The wars for independence were fought against Rome, not Hellenistic states. Hellenism was not therefore one of the direct causes.[44] It was, however, an indirect cause in my opinion. One of Rome's policies and certainly that of the first client king, Herod the Great, was to build Hellenistic cities in Palestine.[45] For this reason it is difficult to disassociate Hellenism from Rome in Palestine. Josephus hints at this when he begins his account of the revolt with a summary of the Hellenistic period.[46] For Josephus the struggle that began with Antiochus IV Epiphanes ended with the destruction of Jerusalem by the Romans. While the centrality of the temple in both the Maccabean revolt and the First Jewish War underscores the role of religion (see below), it is impossible to divorce the cult from political and cultural independence in these confrontations.

The situation in Alexandria was much longer in coming. When the First Revolt in Palestine failed, a number of Sicarii migrated to Egypt, where they attempted to continue their campaign. The leaders of the Jewish senate in Alexandria convened a session and persuaded the people to hand the revolutionaries over to the Romans.[47] Why? Perhaps they were realists: they had witnessed the anger of the 3rd and 22nd legions firsthand in 66, when a scuffle between Egyptians and Jews developed into a full riot;[48] they also knew the fate of Jerusalem. Perhaps they were not yet willing to surrender the long-established policy of collaboration. Or perhaps both factors shaped their judgment. It is telling that they were successful where their Jerusalem counterparts had not been. Their success was, however, short-lived. In 115 civil strife between Greeks and Jews in Egypt erupted in war. When the Romans sided with the Greeks the Alexandrian Jewish community was decimated.[49]

Why did the Alexandrian Jewish community revolt? As is the case in Judaea the causes are complex. The entrance of Rome is one of the contributing factors.[50] In particular, Rome exacerbated the problem by assigning greater importance to Alexandrian citizenship and then banning the Jewish population from it. Two of the most important privileges the Romans granted citizens of Alexandria were exemption from the poll tax and the possibility of becoming Roman citizens. Other privileges which may or may not be carryovers from the Ptolemaic period include restrictions in the forms of punishment (a flat implement rather than a whip) and the exemption of landed property in Alexandria from taxation.[51] Privileges such as these made Alexandrian citizenship valuable and, consequently, gave those who held it high social status. When Claudius closed the doors of the gymnasium to Jews, he cut off their access to citizenship, its privileges, and its status. The result was predictable: Jewish nationalism began to rise. At least three works from this period use past conflicts as a means of reintrenching Jewish values in the present: *Jannes and Jambres* uses Moses' confrontations with the Egyptian magicians, 3 Maccabees uses Ptolemy IV Philopator (222/221–204 BCE), and the Wisdom of Solomon uses the events of ancient Israel. *Sibylline Oracle* 3.46–96 is more direct: it pronounces doom on Rome. Such anti-Roman sentiment is tied to Hellenism: Rome cut off the right of the Jews to enter this world and its privileges, a position that Jews had enjoyed under the Ptolemies. When the community realized that it had been permanently cut off, it responded violently. The destruction of the Alexandrian Jewish community left a bitter taste in the mouths of those who lived in the shadow of the once great community. It is not surprising that the literary work that we have after the revolt is a bitter critique of Hellenism.[52] The great Alexandrian effort to create a symbiosis between Hellenism and Judaism was over.

At first glance it appears that the Jerusalem and Alexandrian communities had the same ultimate reaction to Hellenism. I would, however, suggest a different interpretation. While the causes of the First Jewish Revolt in Palestine are complex, Hellenism lay in the background. The Alexandrian Jewish community, on the other hand, only revolted when it was excluded from the privileged world of the Greeks in Alexandria. The reason is simple: they lost their political power when they lost their right of full entry into Hellenism. Thus, resistance to Hellenism fueled nationalism in Jerusalem, while exclusion from Hellenism fueled nationalism in Alexandria.

The Linguistic Situations

The second criterion represents the extent to which each community *acculturated* to its larger environment while maintaining its own social boundaries. The most effective way to assess this is to examine the writings of each community.

The Evidence

I have attempted to summarize my findings in a series of charts. The first chart (see Appendix for charts) lists texts that were likely either composed or translated in Jerusalem. It is extremely difficult to situate ancient texts which typically provide little or no help in identifying their *Sitz im Leben*. We are left to use the few hints that we have. For example, should we place Philo the Epic Poet's Περὶ Ἱεροσόλυμα in Jerusalem or Alexandria? If we emphasize the fact that he describes Jerusalem, we will place him there. If we situate him among Hellenistic epic poets, we will locate him in Alexandria. It is, of course, possible that he wrote in a different locale yet.[53] We can only make a tentative decision.[54] Similar ambiguities exist for many other works, e.g., was the Tobiad Romance (Josephus, *Ant.* 12.154–236) written in Jerusalem, Transjordan, or Egypt? I would prefer to situate it in Transjordan with the subject it celebrates, but recognize this is tentative at best. We will probably never reach a level of confident judgment for many of these texts. For this reason I do not expect unanimity with my judgments about all of the texts that I have listed. I have marked my own doubts with a question mark and serious reservations with a double question mark. I suggest that these texts represent the range of material that came from Jerusalem.[55] The second chart lists the Jewish inscriptions written in Greek that we have from Jerusalem and that are not on ossuaries.[56] While the prohibition for non-Jews to enter the temple is not directed to Jews, I have included it because it presumes the presence of Greek-speakers in Jerusalem. The third chart sets out the inscriptions on ossuaries that have come from Jerusalem.[57] I have designated the languages with the following sigla: J=Jewish script; G=Greek script; B=bilingual (Jewish and Greek).[58] The fourth presents the Greek manuscripts that have been unearthed in the Judaean desert.[59] I have not included material that dates after 135 CE, e.g., the large number of Byzantine papyri at Khirbet Mird, or material that is known to be non-Jewish. I have included the Judaean wilderness material because it demonstrates the extent of Greek within the heartland of Judaism. My rationale is a modification of the argument *a minore ad majus:* if there was this much Greek in the place where we would least expect it, we should not be surprised when we encounter a significant presence of Greek in Jerusalem. I have made the same effort for Alexandria that I have for Jerusalem.[60] The fifth chart lists the literary works that I place in Alexandria. It is, of course, subject to the same reservations as chart 1.[61] The sixth chart lists the nonliterary documents that relate to the Alexandrian Jewish community.[62] I have made an attempt to provide a comprehensive list of all the known material. This does not mean that it represents the actual output of these communities. Much of what we have is due to the vagaries of chance. For example, even though the Alexandrian community was more than double the size of the Jerusalem community, we have far more epitaphs in the Jerusalem ossuary inscriptions than we have from inscriptions in Alexandria. Again, we know that we only have approximately two-thirds of the Philonic corpus.[63] We have nothing from the other Jewish exegetes to whom Philo frequently alludes.[64]

Analysis

With these stipulations in mind we need to ask what we can make of the evidence that we have. First, it is clear that both communities knew and used Greek. However, the extent to which they used it differed. The evidence above suggests that Greek was an important secondary language in Jerusalem; Aramaic probably continued to be the main language.[65] This is evident from the literary output and the ossuaries. The literary output in Judaea during these years was considerably greater than the Greek works that we have listed as anyone familiar with the pseudepigrapha and Dead Sea Scrolls knows. The ossuaries confirm this impression: there is a higher percentage of Semitic than Greek inscriptions. Of the 186 inscriptions there are 118 Semitic inscriptions (63%), 57 Greek inscriptions (31%), and 11 bilingual inscriptions (6%). If we factor the bilingual inscriptions into the totals, the Jewish script is used in 69 percent of the inscriptions and the Greek in 36 percent. The same results obtain if we consider the number of tombs where the inscriptions were found. There were inscriptions in at least 63 tombs (possibly more): 49 or 78 percent of these contained Semitic inscriptions, 29 or 46 percent contained Greek inscriptions, and 8 or 13 percent contained bilingual inscriptions. Some of the tombs that use Greek are from Diaspora Jews who came to Jerusalem.[66] This cannot be true, however, of all the Greek inscriptions: there are too many. The most reasonable explanation is that the common residents of Jerusalem used Greek from Herod the Great to the end of the First Revolt.[67] By "used" I mean that they had functional abilities in Greek, not sophisticated literary skills. The Greek of the ossuaries is not impressive from a literary perspective. Many residents probably knew enough to carry on a conversation or conduct a business transaction. At least the legal documents from the second century CE in the various caves of the Judaean wilderness suggest this.

The situation was different in Alexandria. Here the evidence is almost entirely Greek. There are only a handful of Semitic inscriptions.[68] While these could indicate the presence of pockets of Semitic-speaking communities in Alexandria,[69] it is more likely that they reflect periodic migrations of Jews from Judaea.[70] Several factors lead me to this judgment. First, the inscriptions jump from the third century BCE to the second century CE without any intervening evidence. Second and decisively, all the literature that we have from Alexandria is in Greek; we do not have a single known work composed in a Semitic language. Third, the preface to Ben-Sira and the colophon of Esther presume that Greek was the norm for Alexandrian Jews, since if Semitic languages were common there would not have been a need for a Greek translation. Fourth, the veneration of the LXX by Pseudo-Aristeas, Philo, and the festival in its honor suggest that the populace used a Greek translation for their scriptures rather than the Hebrew text.[71] Fifth, Philo of

Alexandria does not appear to know any Semitic language, a strange phenomenon for someone in his position if there were significant groups of Semitic-speaking members of the Alexandrian community.[72] These factors lead me to believe that while Aramaic was spoken in Alexandria, it did not play the same role here that Greek did in Jerusalem. For all practical purposes, the Alexandrian Jewish community was a Greek-speaking community. However, they did more than speak in it; they composed in it extensively. If our extant literature is any indication of relative material in antiquity, the Alexandrian Jewish community produced far more Greek literature than did Jerusalem. Even if my placements of some of the texts are incorrect, it would be difficult to create a plausible list for Greek works composed in Jerusalem that would rival the list for Alexandria.[73] While some of the literature is typical of the same level of Greek attested in the literature produced in Jerusalem, other works attest highly refined Greek sensibilities.

Summary
    It therefore appears that Greek was the second language for many Jerusalem Jews, but the sole and primary language for Jews in Alexandria. The use of Aramaic seems to have been a point of pride for some first-century Jews; at least Saul of Tarsus thought that being a "Hebrew of the Hebrews" was worthy of inclusion in a credentials list.[74] Conversely, no one seems to have thought that the use of the Greek language compromised Judaism. It is worth noting that Bar-Kokhba carried on correspondence in Greek, even if the Greek letters were written by members of his staff.[75] The use of Greek was therefore a matter of acculturation not assimilation.

The Social-Religious Practices

    The third criterion explores the issue of assimilation by asking how far communities integrated into the larger culture. The question is complicated by the fact that communities with populations as large as those of Jerusalem and Alexandria did not have single views. There are, however, some identifiable features that we can note. I will focus on several that are attested at the end of the first century BCE and beginning of the first century CE.
    While Jerusalem was a Jewish city, it did have a number of the standard institutions of a Greek city. Jason actually tried to provide most—

if not all—of the typical features, including a gymnasium.[76] The next time that we hear about the presence of such institutions is in connection with the building program of Herod the Great. It is not entirely wrong to say that Herod accomplished architecturally what Jason set out to do: he made Jerusalem a Greco-Roman city. We should recall the common aphorism Josephus reports about Herod: "He had more affinity with the Greeks than with the Jews."[77] Josephus confirms this opinion when he tells us that Herod's projects were not entirely in keeping with Jewish traditions. He wrote: "He went beyond the ancestral customs even more and corrupted the long-established way of life which was inviolable with foreign practices." He then explains: "For in the first place he established pentennial athletic games for Caesar, built a theater in Jerusalem, and again a great amphitheater in the plain. Both were conspicuous for their extravagance but foreign to Jewish custom. For the use of these and the display of such spectacles are not traditional."[78] Elsewhere he tells us that Herod built a hippodrome.[79]

Several items strike me about these statements. First, Josephus suggests that Herod introduced new practices through these games and structures and that these were contrary to Jewish tradition.[80] This suggests that Jason's Hellenistic city had disappeared. Second, the historian tells us that Herod built a theater,[81] amphitheater, and hippodrome. He thus made Jerusalem into a Greco-Roman city.[82] We do not know the specific nature of these or who attended them. Since they are part of Herod's larger building program, we should assume that they were parallel to the structures that he built elsewhere and that the general populace made use of them (see below). If this assumption is valid, then the theater and amphitheater had distinctively Roman architectural features while the hippodrome followed a Hellenistic model.[83] Third, Josephus does not mention a gymnasium. On three occasions he does mention the ξυστόν, a noun that typically denotes either the open air space for exercising in a gymnasium or the covered colonnade of a gymnasium where winter exercises took place.[84] It was probably the site of Jason's earlier gymnasium.[85] Was this still functioning as a gymnasium[86] or had it been converted into an area for public assemblies?[87] It served as the stage for Herod Agrippa II's famous address to the Jerusalem populace on the eve of the revolt.[88] This and the absence of any reference to a gymnasium in Josephus suggests that it had become a place for public assemblies and ceased to function as a gymnasium. Why? Although we can only speculate, I suggest that a gymnasium and

ephebate such as Jason is said to have established would have been unacceptable for Jerusalem Jews. Herod was not adverse to such himself:
he built gymnasia in Tripolis, Damascus, Ptolemais, and endowed a
gymnasiarch in Cos.[89] These, however, were far from Jerusalem. Herod
neither rebuilt Jason's old gymnasium nor a new one because his
Jewish subjects had different scruples than he did.[90] Fourth, this difference in conscience is unquestionably true in regard to the cult. The
sharpest reaction to Herod's building program was a response to the
trophies which the Jews thought were a subterfuge for the introduction
of images. According to Josephus a group protested: "If everything else
is endurable, the images of human beings in the city is not."[91] Herod
summoned a group of leaders to the theater and asked them what they
thought the trophies were. When they replied "images of human beings," he stripped their ornamentation so that they could see the wood.
When they did, they all had a good laugh and dropped their opposition. This suggests that while some found the games and structures
problematic, the majority only drew the line when Jewish monotheism
was directly threatened. Herod knew this. It is why the designs were
geometric: there were no images of any sort. The temple was sacro-
sanct: no foreign cult or image could encroach without provoking a
severe reaction. The only time Herod dared to violate this was when
he foolishly set up the golden eagle over the great gate; the reaction was
predictable.[92] Jewish sensitivity on this point extended beyond the
temple. It prohibited the presence of any pagan cult within the city. In
his narration of the crisis provoked by Pilate when he brought the
Roman standards into the city, Josephus says: The laws "do not permit
any image to be set up in the city."[93] Jerusalem Jews therefore might
go to the theater or hippodrome, but they could not attend a gymnasium, pass through the ephebate there, or have anything to do with a
pagan cult.

The standards were different in Alexandria. This is not surprising
since Alexandria was itself a Greek city which had all the requisite institutions. First, the Alexandrians did not apparently have the same
reservations about Greek cultural activities as some of their Jerusalem
counterparts. Philo specifically mentions watching wrestling, boxing,
foot racing contests, and chariot races.[94] On at least two occasions he
mentions the reactions of audiences in the theater. Once he noted how
a song had radically different effects on various members of the audi-

ence.[95] On another occasion he witnessed an audience burst into a spontaneous standing ovation at a production of a Euripidean play.[96] Nor is he the only Alexandrian Jew to comment on the theater. One of the sages in *The Letter of Aristeas* suggested to the king that his idea of relaxation was "to observe whatever is performed with decorum."[97] We should also recall that we have extensive fragments of one Jewish playwright, Ezekiel the tragedian. It is difficult to believe that Alexandrian Jews had serious reservations about the theater. At least there are no statements similar to that of Josephus claiming that these activities were contrary to Jewish customs. Second, the Alexandrian Jews frequented gymnasia. In a statement about parental upbringing of children, Philo says that progenitors provide for both the body and the mind of the children: "They benefit the body through the training of the gymnasium and the trainer for both vigor and good health as well as for condition and fluid movement with grace and propriety."[98] This statement presumes that it was a normal course of affairs for Jewish families in Alexandria, at least for wealthy Jewish families, to send their children to the gymnasium. We have at least one example of this, Helenos, son of Tryphon, who protested the enforcement of the poll tax since he had received a Greek education.[99] Third, the place where Alexandrian Jews drew the line over the cult was different than it was in Jerusalem. All agreed that participation in a pagan cult was unacceptable.[100] Philo goes so far as to recommend the death penalty for such activity.[101] His refusal to cross this line was apparently widespread.[102] Apion used Jewish refusal as a powerful argument against the community's claim that they were citizens. He asked: "Why, then, if they are citizens, do they not worship the same gods whom the Alexandrians worship?"[103] Caligula threw this in the face of the Jewish embassy when he said: "These things may be true, you have sacrificed, but to another even if on my behalf. What good is that?"[104] The most the Alexandrian Jewish community could have said to such charges was that they respected the gods of others. So the LXX renders Exod 22:27 with a plural: "You will not curse gods."[105] It is here where the line is different. Greek institutions in Jerusalem were shorn of pagan cults, Greek institutions in Alexandria were not. Alexandrian Jews who lived away from the Jerusalem temple were apparently able to make a distinction between cultural institutions and their cultic associations that Jerusalem Jews could not.

Conclusions

We may now return to our initial hypothesis. Our overview of the evidence confirms Hengel's argument that Judaea was hellenized. At the same time, it also makes it clear that Jews living in different communities related to Hellenism in different ways. The political and demographic situation of each community had an enormous impact on how Jews within each community integrated into the larger culture. Language does not appear to have been much of an issue. This was a simple matter of acculturation not assimilation. There were also some distinctively Hellenic activities in which members of both communities participated, e.g., attendance at the hippodrome or theater. Although even here there were apparently different comfort zones. Other activities brought sharply different responses: residents of Jerusalem appear to have opposed the most significant Greek institution, the gymnasium; residents of Alexandria, on the other hand, apparently not only thought that it was acceptable to attend, but actually pressed for the right to do so. Both communities refused to participate in pagan cults, but the Alexandrians made sure that their copies of the Torah protected the local cults, an assurance they needed since they could not extricate themselves from association with them.

How did the two communities relate to each other? We have seen that there is some evidence for migration to Alexandria. We also know that Alexandrians made their way to Jerusalem, at least Philo made a pilgrimage.[106] His brother and Nicanor also helped to adorn the temple.[107] There were apparently relatively good relations between the two communities. The experience of being a Jew in each was, however, different. The difference was—to a significant degree—a result of how each community responded to Hellenism.[108]

Appendix

CHART 1.   Graeco-Jewish Literature in Jerusalem

Second Century BCE

LXX	Esther
Historiography	Eupolemus, Περὶ τῶν ἐν τῇ Ἰουδαίᾳ βασιλέων
	2 Maccabees (?)
Epic	Philo the Epic Poet, Περὶ Ἱεροσόλυμα (??)
Romance	The Alexander Romance (Josephus, Ant. 11.304–5,
	313–47)

First Century CE

LXX	Ruth, Song of Songs, Lamentations
	Some Psalms (?)
Biography	*Lives of the Prophets* (?)

Second Century CE

LXX	Ecclesiastes (?)
Translation	Aquila (?)

CHART 2.   Inscriptions in Jerusalem

Date	Contents	Locale/Name
First Century BCE	Proverb	Jason's Tomb
First Century BCE	Donation	Temple
First Century CE	Prohibition of Entering Temple	Temple
First Century CE	Synagogue Inscription	Theodotus Inscription

CHART 3.   Ossuaries in Jerusalem

Location	Tomb	Language(s)			Catalogue Nos.
		J	G	B	
Abu Tor	a	1	2		50, 51, 80
	c	1			125
Ammunition Hill		1			293
Arnona		1			192
French Hill	b	1			354
	d	1			370
	g	1		2	559, 560, 561
	k	1			603
Giv'at Hamivtar	a	5			200, 217, 218, 220, 222
	f	1			403
	g	4	2		411, 413, 414, 428, 430, 444
Giv'at Mordecai		1			501
Hizmeh		1			38
Kefar Sha'ul		1			651
Kidron Valley	a	1	7		95, 97, 98, 99, 100, 101, 102, 104
	b	1			57
	c	2	2		84, 85, 86, 87
	d	12		1	12, 13, 15, 16, 17, 18, 20, 21, 22, 23, 24, 26, 27
	e	1	2		53, 54, 55
	f	6	1		61, 62, 63, 64, 66, 67, 68
	g	2	1		107, 108, 110
Meqor Hayim		1			351
Mount of Offense	a	1			117
	c			2	88, 89
Mount of Olives		1	1	1	31, 32, 35
Mount Scopus (E slope)	d	1			435
	e	2			455, 456
	f		1	1	643, 648
	i	2			694, 696
	j	1			421
	k	1			468
	l	1			469
Mount Scopus (S slope)	a	4	3		475, 477, 478, 483, 488, 490, 592

CHART 3. *(continued)*

Location	Tomb	Language(s) J	G	B	Catalogue Nos.
Mount Scopus (W slope)	a	2	3		1, 3, 5, 8, 11
	b	3	1		41, 42, 44, 45
	e		2		319, 322
	g	1	1		380, 383
	h	2			390, 396
	j	5	1	2	570, 581, 572, 573, 576, 579, 582, 584
	m	1			893
		1			856
	n	1		1	121, 122
Qatamon		1			191
Qiryat Shemu'el			1		142
Ramat Eshkol	a	3			226, 227, 228
	b	2			342, 344
	c		3		404, 405, 406
	e		1		565
	f		2		567, 568
Romena	a		1		137
	b		1		179
Sanhedriyah		1	2		141, 700, 751
Sanhedriya-Mahanayim		2			150, 151
Schneller's Syrian Orphanage			1	1	135, 139
Shemu'el Hanavi St.			1		202
Silwan			2		236, 239
Talbiyeh		1			152
Talbiyeh (S slope)		8			70, 71, 72, 73, 74, 75, 76, 77
Talpiyot			2		113, 114
East Talpiyot		9	2		701, 702, 703, 704, 705, 706, 716, 717, 718, 725, 730
Valley of the Cross	b		3		330, 332, 333
Zikhron Mohse		2			82, 83
Jerusalem		12	5		132, 198, 243, 254, 256, 257, 258, 259, 266, 270, 286, 287, 288, 310, 461, 820, 868
TOTALS		118	57	11	=186

CHART 4.   Greek Manuscripts in the Judaean Desert

Number	Official Name	Date (Century)	Contents
Masada			
Mas 739	pap Literary Text? gr	Before 74 CE	
Mas 740	pap Documents ? gr	25–35 CE	
Mas 741	pap letter of Abakantos to Judas gr	Before 74 CE	
Mas 743	Wooden Tablet gr	Before 74 CE	
Mas 744	pap List of Names? gr	Before 74 CE	
Mas 745	pap Letter gr	Before 74 CE	
Mas 746	pap Letter(s) gr	Before 74 CE	
Mas 747	pap Frag. gr	Before 74 CE	
Mas 749	pap Frags. lat or gr	Before 74 CE	
Mas 772	ostr gr	Before 74 CE	
Mas 773	ostr gr	Before 74 CE	
Mas 774	ostr gr	Before 74 CE	
Mas 775	ostr gr	Before 74 CE	
Mas 776	ostr gr	Before 74 CE	
Mas 777	ostr gr	Before 74 CE	
Mas 778	ostr gr	Before 74 CE	
Mas 779	ostr gr	Before 74 CE	
Mas 780	ostr gr	Before 74 CE	
Mas 781	ostr gr	Before 74 CE	
Mas 782	ostr gr	Before 74 CE	
Mas 783	ostr gr	Before 74 CE	
Mas 784	ostr gr	Before 74 CE	
Mas 785	ostr gr	Before 74 CE	
Mas 786	ostr gr	Before 74 CE	
Mas 787	ostr gr	Before 74 CE	
Mas 788	ostr gr	Before 74 CE	
Mas 789	ostr gr	Before 74 CE	
Mas 790	ostr gr	Before 74 CE	
Mas 791	ostr gr	Before 74 CE	
Mas 792	ostr gr	Before 74 CE	

CHART 4. *(continued)*

Number	Official Name	Date (Century)	Contents
Mishmar, Ghweir, Nar			
1Mish 2	pap List of Personal Names (recto) gr	132–35 CE	Bar Kokhba F.
1Mish 8	ostr unclassified gr		
Gwheir?1	pap cursive frag. gr		
Nar 1	pap frag. gr		
Nar 3	skin frag. gr		
Murabbaʿat			
Mur 89	Account of Money gr		
Mur 90	Account of Cereals and Vegetables gr		
Mur 91	Account of Cereals and Vegetables gr		
Mur 92	Account of Cereal gr		
Mur 93	Account? gr		
Mur 94	Resume of Accounts gr		
Mur 95	List of Personal Names gr		
Mur 96	Account of Cereals gr		
Mur 97	Account of Cereals gr		
Mur 98	Accounts? gr		
Mur 99	Accounts? gr		
Mur 100	Accounts? gr		
Mur 101	Accounts? gr		
Mur 102	Accounts? gr		
Mur 103	List of Personal Names gr		
Mur 104	Corners and Edges of Leather gr		
Mur 105	Corners and Edges of Leather gr		
Mur 106	Corners and Edges of Leather gr		
Mur 107	Corners and Edges of Leather gr		
Mur 108	pap Philosophical Text gr		
Mur 109	pap Literary Text gr		
Mur 110	pap Literary Text gr		
Mur 111	pap Literary Text gr		

CHART 4. *(continued)*

Number	Official Name	Date (Century)	Contents
Murabbaʿat (continued)			
Mur 112	pap Literary Text gr		
Mur 113	pap Proceedings of Lawsuit gr	100–50 CE	
Mur 114	pap Recognition of Debt gr	171 CE (?)	
Mur 115	pap Remarriage Contract gr	124 CE	
Mur 116	pap Marriage Contract gr		
Mur 117	pap Extracts from Official Ordinances gr	150–200 CE	
Mur 118	pap Account gr		
Mur 119	pap Account gr		
Mur 120	pap Account gr		
Mur 121	pap Account gr		
Mur 122	pap Account gr		
Mur 123	pap Account gr		
Mur 124	pap Account gr		
Mur 125	pap Account gr		
Mur 126	pap Literary or Notorial Writing gr		
Mur 127	pap Literary or Notorial Writing gr		
Mur 128	pap Literary or Notorial Writing gr		
Mur 129	pap Literary or Notorial Writing gr		
Mur 130	pap Literary or Notorial Writing gr		
Mur 131	pap Literary or Notorial Writing gr		
Mur 132	pap Literary or Notorial Writing gr		
Mur 133	pap Cursive Text gr		
Mur 134	pap Cursive Text gr		
Mur 135	pap Cursive Text gr		
Mur 136	pap Cursive Text gr		
Mur 137	pap Cursive Text gr		
Mur 138	pap Cursive Text gr		
Mur 139	pap Cursive Text gr		
Mur 140	pap Cursive Text gr		
Mur 141	pap Cursive Text gr		

CHART 4. *(continued)*

Number	Official Name	Date (Century)	Contents
Mur 142	pap Cursive Text gr		
Mur 143	pap Cursive Text gr		
Mur 144	pap Cursive Text gr		
Mur 145	pap Cursive Text gr		
Mur 146	pap Cursive Text gr		
Mur 147	pap Cursive Text gr		
Mur 148	pap Cursive Text gr		
Mur 149	pap Cursive Text gr		
Mur 150	pap Cursive Text gr		
Mur 151	pap Cursive Text gr		
Mur 152	pap Cursive Text gr		
Mur 153	pap Cursive Text gr		
Mur 154	pap Cursive Text gr		
Mur 155	pap Document gr		
Mur 157	Magical Text gr		
Mur 164	Document in Shorthand gr		
Mur 164a	Document in Shorthand gr		
Mur 164b	Document in Shorthand gr		
Mur 165	ostr gr		
Mur 166	ostr gr		
Mur 167	ostr gr		

Qumran

Number	Official Name	Date (Century)	Contents
4Q119	LXXLev[a]	2nd–1st BCE	
4Q120	papLXXLev[b]	1st BCE	
4Q121	LXXNum	1st BCE–1st CE	
4Q122	LXXDeut	2nd BCE	
4Q126	Unidentified Text gr	1st BCE–1st CE	
4Q127	pap paraExodus gr	1st BCE–1st CE	
4Q350	Account gr (=verso of 460)		
4Q361	Unidentified Fragment gr (opistograph?)		
7Q 1	papLXXExod	100 BCE	Exod 28:4–7
7Q 2	papEpJer gr	100 BCE	Vv. 43–44
7Q 3	pap Biblical Text? Gr	100 BCE	
7Q 4+12+14	pap Enoch gr	100 BCE	1 Enoch 103:3–4
7Q 5	pap Biblical Text? Gr	50 BCE–50 CE	
7Q 6	pap unclassified frags. gr		
7Q 7	pap unclassified frags. gr		
7Q 8	pap Enoch gr	100 BCE (?)	1 Enoch 103:7–8

CHART 4. *(continued)*

Number	Official Name	Date (Century)	Contents
Qumran (continued)			
7Q 9	pap unclassified frags. gr		
7Q 10	pap unclassified frags. gr		
7Q 11	pap Enoch gr	100 BCE (?)	1 Enoch 100:12 (?)
7Q 13	pap Enoch gr	100 BCE (?)	1 Enoch 103:15 (?)
7Q 15	pap unclassified frags. gr		
7Q 16	pap unclassified frags. gr		
7Q 17	pap unclassified frags. gr		
7Q 18	pap unclassified frags. gr		
7Q 19	pap Imprint gr		
Sdeir, Ḥever, Seiyal			
Sdeir 3	Unidentified Text A gr		
Sdeir 4	Unidentified Text B gr		
5/6Ḥev 5	pap Deposit gr	110 CE	Babatha
5/6Ḥev 11	pap Loan on Hypothec gr	124 CE	Babatha
5/6Ḥev 12	pap Extract from Council Minutes gr	124 CE	Babatha
5/6Ḥev 13	pap Petition to Governor gr	124 CE	Babatha
5/6Ḥev 14	pap Summons gr	125 CE	Babatha
5/6Ḥev 15	pap Deposition gr	125 CE	Babatha
5/6Ḥev 16	pap Registration of Land gr	127 CE	Babatha
5/6Ḥev 17	pap Deposit gr	128 CE	Babatha
5/6Ḥev 18	pap Marriage Contract gr	128 CE	Babatha
5/6Ḥev 19	pap Deed of Gift gr	128 CE	Babatha
5/6Ḥev 20	pap Concession of Rights gr	130 CE	Babatha
5/6Ḥev 21	pap Purchase of a Date Crop gr	130 CE	Babatha
5/6Ḥev 22	pap Sale of a Date Crop gr	130 CE	Babatha
5/6Ḥev 23	pap Summons gr	130 CE	Babatha
5/6Ḥev 24	pap Deposition gr	130 CE	Babatha
5/6Ḥev 25	pap Summons, Countersum. gr	131 CE	Babatha
5/6Ḥev 26	pap Summons and Reply gr	131 CE	Babatha
5/6Ḥev 27	pap Receipt gr	132 CE	Babatha
5/6Ḥev 28	pap Judiciary Rule gr	124–25 CE	Babatha
5/6Ḥev 29	pap Judiciary Rule gr	124–25 CE	Babatha
5/6Ḥev 30	pap Judiciary Rule gr	124–25 CE	Babatha
5/6Ḥev 31	pap Contract? gr	110 CE (?)	Babatha

CHART 4. *(continued)*

Number	Official Name	Date (Century)	Contents
5/6Ḥev 32	pap Contract? gr	?	Babatha
5/6Ḥev 32a	pap Contract? gr	?	Babatha
5/6Ḥev 33	Petition gr	125 CE (?)	Babatha
5/6Ḥev 34	pap Petition gr	131 CE	Babatha
5/6Ḥev 35	pap Summons? gr	132 CE (?)	Babatha
5/6Ḥev 37	pap Marriage Contract gr	131 CE	Babatha
5/6Ḥev 52	pap Letter gr	132–35 CE	Bar Kokhba L.
5/6Ḥev 59	pap Letter gr	132–35 CE	Bar Kokhba L.
5/6Ḥev 64	pap Frag. gr	132–35 CE	
8Ḥev 1	8HevXII gr	1st BCE–1st CE	Minor Prophets
8Ḥev 4	pap Unidentified Text gr		
XḤev/Se 60	pap Tax (or Rent) Receipt from Mahoza gr	125 CE	Salome Komaïse
XḤev/Se 61	pap Conclusion to a Land Declaration gr	127 CE	Salome Komaïse
XḤev/Se 62	pap Land Declaration gr	127 CE	Salome Komaïse
XḤev/Se 63	pap Deed of Renunciation of Claims gr	127 CE	Salome Komaïse
XḤev/Se 64	pap Deed of Gift gr	129 CE	Salome Komaïse
XḤev/Se 65	pap Marriage Contract gr	131 CE	Salome Komaïse
XḤev/Se 66	pap Loan with Hypothec gr	99 or 109 CE	
XḤev/Se 67	pap Text Mentioning Timber gr	127/128 CE (?)	
XḤev/Se 68	pap Text Mentioning a Guardian gr	2nd century CE	
XḤev/Se 69	pap Cancelled Marriage Contract gr	130 CE	
XḤev/Se 70	pap Unidentified Fragment A gr	?	
XḤev/Se 71	pap Unidentified Fragment B gr	?	

CHART 4. *(continued)*

Number	Official Name	Date (Century)	Contents
Sdeir, Hever, Seiyal (continued)			
XHev/Se 72	pap Unidentified Fragment C gr	?	
XHev/Se 73	pap End of a Document gr	106/107 or 109 CE	
XHev/Se 74–139	pap Unidentified Fragments gr		
XHev/Se 140–69	pap Unidentified Fragments gr		
Hev/Se ? 1–12	pap unidentified Fragments gr		
Hev/Se ? 13–14	pap Unidentified Fragments gr		
Hev/Se ? 15–23	pap Unidentified Fragments gr		
Hev/Se ? 24–35	pap Unidentified Fragments gr		
Hev/Se ? 36–57	pap Unidentified Fragments gr		
34 Se 4	pap List of Names and Ages gr	132–35 CE	Bar Kokhba F.
34 Se 5	Account gr	132–35 CE	Bar Kokhba F.

CHART 5. Graeco-Jewish Literature in Alexandria

Third Century BCE	
LXX	Pentateuch, Some Prophets?, Some Psalms?
Historiography	Demetrius, Περὶ τῶν ἐν τῇ Ἰουδαίᾳ βασιλέων

Second Century BCE	
LXX	Prophets, Some Writings, Some Apocryphal/Deuterocanonical Works
Historiography	Artapanus, Περὶ Ἰουδαίων (?)
	Aristeas, Περὶ Ἰουδαίων (??)

CHART 5. *(continued)*

Philosophical	Pseudo-Orphic Fragments (Cited in Aristobulus)
	Aristobulus
Gnomology	Gnomologion of Pseudo-Greek Epic Poets (Cited in
	Aristobulus)
Epistle	*Epistle of Aristeas*
Epic	Philo the Epic Poet, Περὶ Ἱεροσόλυμα (??)
Drama	Ezekiel, Ἐξαγωγή

First Century BCE

LXX	Writings, Some Apocryphal/Deuterocanonical Works
Expansion of LXX	*Joseph and Aseneth* (or first century CE ?)
Testament	*Testament of Job* (or first century CE)
Epic	Sosates (?)

First Century CE (30 BCE–70 CE)

LXX	Some Apocryphal/Deuterocanonical Works
Historiography	3 Maccabees (LXX)
	Pseudo-Hecataeus, Κατ᾽ Ἄβραμον καὶ τοὺς
	Αἰγυπτίους
Expansion of LXX	*Jannes and Jambres* (?)
Philosophical	Wisdom of Solomon (LXX)
	Philo of Alexandria
Gnomologies	Gnomologion of Dramatic Verses (Cited in Pseudo-
	Hecataeus)
	Pseudo-Phocylides
Poetry	*Sibylline Oracle* 11

Between the Wars (70 CE–117 CE)

LXX	Some Apocryphal/Deuterocanonical Works
Expansions of LXX	*History of Joseph* (??)
Oracular Poetry	*Sibylline Oracle* 3.1–96 (?)
Testaments	*Testament of Abraham* (?)
	Testament of Isaac (??)
	Testament of Jacob (??)
Homilies	Pseudo-Philo, *De Jona*
	Idem, De Sampsone
	Idem, De Jona (Fragment from another homily on
	Jonah by a different homilist)

Post War (117–200 CE)

Apology	Pseudo-Clement, Clement and Apion (*Hom.* 4–6)

CHART 6.   Non-Literary Jewish Texts from or Dealing with Alexandria

Inscriptions from Alexandria

Function	*Date*	*Inscriptions (JIGRE)*
Epitaphs	3rd Century BCE	3, 6, 7, 8
	2nd Century BCE	10
	1st Century BCE (Ptolemaic)	1, 2, 11, 12
Votive	Late Roman	15, 16, 17, 19 (cf. also
(Synagogues)		127–28)
Proseuche	2nd Century BCE	9
	1st Century BCE	13 (Honorific)
Honorific	1st Century BCE (Ptolemaic)	14?
	2nd Century CE	18
Dedication	1st Century CE	20
Painted Stucco	3rd Century BCE	4, 5 (and 3 above)
Amphora	2nd Century CE	21

Inscriptions concerning Alexandrian Jews

Function	*Date*	*Locale*	*Inscriptions (JIGRE)*
Ossuary	1st Century CE	Jerusalem	153
Epitaph	2nd–4th Centuries CE	Jaffa	148, 150
	?	Tiberias	151
	Late	Greece	143, 144
	5th Century CE	Milan	142

Papyri

Date	*Contents*	*Papyri (CPJ)*
3rd Century BCE	Dositheus, son of Drimylus	127 a–e
1st Century BCE	συγχωρήσεις ('Agreements')	142–49
(Roman)		
	'*Boule* Papyrus'	150
	Petition of Helenus	151
1st Century CE	Warning about Jewish money lenders	152
	Letter of Claudius	153
	Tiberius Julius Alexander	418 a–f
	Marcus Julius Alexander	419 a–e
	Gaius Julius Alexander	420
2nd Century CE	Revolt in Alexandria	435
	Revolt in Egypt	436–50

Notes

1. 2 Macc 2:21. Cf. also 8:1; 14:38 (*bis*); 4 Macc 4:26.
2. 2 Macc 4:13–14. Other Jewish sources do not use the term. Philo of Alexandria does use ἀφελληνίζω (*Legat.* 147). For a discussion of the basic concept by a Greek writer see Strabo 14.2.28 who uses it to mean the correct way to speak Greek.
3. Cf. the use of Ἑλληνικός in the same contrast in 2 Macc 4:10, 15; 6:9; 11:24; 4 Macc 8:8; 13:2.
4. G. F. Moore, *Judaism* (*In the First Centuries of the Christian Era: The Age of the Tannaim*) (2 vols.; Cambridge, Mass.: Harvard University Press, 1927) 1:109–10. For the relationship between Alexandria and Palestine see pp. 107–8.
5. M. Hengel, *Judaism and Hellenism: Studies in their Encounter in Palestine during the Early Hellenistic Period* (2 vols.; Philadelphia: Fortress, 1974) 1:104, cf. also 105; idem, *Jews, Greeks and Barbarians: Aspects of the Hellenization of Judaism in the Pre-Christian Period* (Philadelphia: Fortress, 1980); idem, *The Hellenization of Judaea in the First Century after Christ* (London: SCM, 1990). For a compact review of the evidence see E. Schürer, *The History of the Jewish People in the Age of Jesus Christ* (3 vols.; revised by G. Vermes, F. Millar, and M. Black; Edinburgh: T. & T. Clark, 1973–86) 2:52–80.
6. Hengel, *The Hellenization of Judaea*, 11, recognizes this.
7. Hengel, *The Hellenism of Judaea*, 55–56, suggests that the level of education is one of the most important factors. I agree, but think that the educational possibilities were determined by the community.
8. On Jerusalem see J. Jeremias, *Jerusalem in the Time of Jesus: An Investigation into Economic and Social Conditions during the New Testament Period* (Philadelphia: Fortress, 1969); B. Lifshitz, "Jérusalem sous la domination romaine," *ANRW* 2.8 (1977) 444–89; and M. Hengel, "Jerusalem als jüdische und hellenistische Stadt," in idem, *Judaica, Hellenistica et Christiana. Kleine Schriften II* (WUNT 109; Tübingen: Mohr, 1999) 115–56. On Alexandria see P. M. Fraser, *Ptolemaic Alexandria* (3 vols.; Oxford: Clarendon, 1972); D. Delia, *Alexandrian Citizenship during the Roman Principate* (American Classical Studies 23; Atlanta: Scholars Press, 1991); G. E. Sterling, "'Thus are Israel': Jewish Self-Definition in Alexandria," *SPhA* 7 (1995) 1–18; D. Sly, *Philo's Alexandria* (London/New York: Routledge, 1996); and C. Haas, *Alexandria in Late Antiquity: Topography and Social Conflict* (Baltimore: Johns Hopkins University Press, 1997).
9. The only other possibilities are Antioch (in Syria) and Rome. If the comparison were expanded from cities to regions it would be possible to include Judaea, Galilee, Perea, Egypt, Syria, Asia Minor, and Italy.

10. Some of the more helpful discussions of the terms include Hengel, *Judaism and Hellenism*, 1:2–3; idem, *Jews, Greeks and Barbarians*, 49–82; L. L. Grabbe, *Judaism from Cyrus to Hadrian* (2 vols.; Minneapolis: Fortress, 1992) 1:147–70; and J. M. G. Barclay, *Jews in the Mediterranean Diaspora: From Alexander to Trajan* (*323 BCE–117 CE*) (Edinburgh: T. & T. Clark, 1996) 88–91.

11. I have followed the categories worked out by Barclay, *Jews in the Mediterranean Diaspora*, 92–98, for numbers two and three.

12. Josephus, *Ant.* 12.129–34.

13. 1 Macc; 2 Macc; Josephus, *War* 1.31–119; *Ant.* 12.235–13.432.

14. Josephus, *War* 1.120–58; *Ant.* 14.4–79.

15. On Herod the Great's appointment see Josephus, *War* 1.282–85; *Ant.* 14.381–85. On Herod's sons see *War* 1.665–69; 2.93–100; *Ant.* 17.188–89, 317–20. On the incorporation of Judaea as a Roman province see Josephus, *War* 2.117; *Ant.* 17.355. Herod Agrippa I became king, interrupting the reign of prefects/procurators (Josephus, *War* 2.214–17; *Ant.* 18.224–39).

16. On the issue of whether Jerusalem was a πόλις see V. A. Tcherikover, "Was Jerusalem a Polis?" *IEJ* 14 (1964) 61–78.

17. On Alexandria as a Greek city see A. H. M. Jones, *Cities of the Eastern Roman Provinces* (Oxford: Clarendon Press, 1937) 296–350, esp. 303–6, and idem, *The Greek City from Alexander to Justinian* (Oxford: Clarendon Press, 1940).

18. Polybius 34 F 14 (Strabo 17.1.12).

19. Josephus, *Ag. Apion* 2.68–72. For a similar tripartite division of humanity see Philo, *Spec.* 2.165–66; Josephus, *Ant.* 4.12; 16.177. Cf. also Rom 1:14–16; Col 3:11.

20. Josephus, *Ag. Apion* 2.49–52.

21. For details see B. Porten, *Archives from Elephantine: The Life of an Ancient Jewish Military Colony* (Berkeley/Los Angeles: University of California Press, 1968).

22. The evidence is a disputed text in *Ep. Arist.* 310.

23. For details and bibliography see Sterling, "'Thus Are Israel,'" 11–12.

24. Strabo in Josephus, *Ant.* 14.117 (*GLAJJ* XLII.105). Cf. also Philo, *Flacc.* 74; Josephus, *Ant.* 19.283.

25. *CPJ* 150 ll. 1–6 and *CPJ* 151. For details see V. Tcherikover, "Syntaxis and Laographia," *Journal of Juristic Papyrology* 4 (1950) 179–209.

26. Philo, *Flacc.* 74, 77, 80; Josephus, *War* 7.412. Josephus' statement that Augustus did not suspend the appointment of ethnarchs in *Ant.* 19.283 is either incorrect or indicates that the ethnarch's authority was curtailed.

27. Claudius' letter does not specify the privileges that this second delegation requested, only that they exceeded "more than they previously had." Since they previously had the right to observe their ancestral traditions, the additional demands must go beyond this. Tcherikover, *The Jews in Egypt in the Hellenistic-Roman Age in the Light of the Papyri* (Jerusalem: Hebrew University,

1945) 154–205 (18–26 in English summary), and idem, *CPJ* 2:50–53, argued this was citizenship in the *polis*. Kasher, *The Jews in Hellenistic and Roman Egypt: The Struggle for Equal Rights* (Texte und Studien zum antiken Judentum 7; Tübingen: J. C. B. Mohr [Paul Siebeck], 1985) 322–23, suggested it was the right to open Alexandria to more Jews. The fact that Claudius prohibited the Jews from obtaining the prerequisites of citizenship leads me to think they wanted equal rights as citizens.

28. *CPJ* 153, esp. ll. 87–93.

29. E.g., the appointment of Onias and Dositheus as generals over the army noted above (Josephus, *Ag. Apion* 2.49–52).

30. E.g., the Jews backed Ptolemy VII Philopater Neos rather than Ptolemy VIII Euergetes II who was nicknamed Physcon (Josephus, *Ant.* 13.284–87; *Ag. Apion* 2.50–52; cf. also *Ag. Apion* 2.53–55 and 3 Macc 3:1–6:29). Another struggle took place over Cleopatra III's (116–101 BCE) sons: Ptolemy Alexander I (c. 140–87 BCE) whom the Jews supported and Ptolemy IX Soter (Lathyrus) (87–81 BCE) whom the Alexandrians supported (Porphyry in Eusebius, *Chron.* 1 p. 165 [*GLAJJ* CXXVIII.457a] and Iordanis, *Rom.* 81, cited by Tcherikover, *CPJ* 1:25 n. 630). During this period anti-Jewish sentiment became more and more pronounced.

31. Josephus, *War* 2.487.

32. Pseudo-Hecataeus in Josephus, *Ag. Apion* 1.197.

33. Josephus, *War* 2.280 and 6.420–27.

34. Tacitus, *Hist.* 5.13.3.

35. E.g., A. Byatt, "Josephus and Population Numbers in First Century Palestine," *PEQ* 105 (1973) 51–60, estimates the permanent population was 220,000 which swelled to 1,000,000 at major feasts.

36. Cf. R. P. Duncan Jones, "Population (Roman World)," *OCD* (1970) 863–64 and M. H. Crawford, "Population, Roman," *OCD* (1996) 1223. On Alexandria see below and D. W. Rathbone, "Alexandria," *OCD* (1996) 62. On Antioch see A. H. M. Jones, H. Seyrig, W. Liebeschuetz, and S. Sherwin-White, "Antioch," *OCD* (1996) 107. Carthage was about the same size as Alexandria.

37. M. Broshi, "La population de l'ancienne Jerusalem," *RB* 82 (1975) 5–14, 76 BCE: 32,000; 4 CE: 38,500; 66 CE: 82,500; J. Wilkinson, "Ancient Jerusalem: Its Water Supply and Population," *PEQ* 106 (1974) 33–51, Herod the Great (early): 36,280; Herod the Great (late): 70,398; Herod Agrippa I: 76,130. It is worth pointing out that this is similar to Jeremias' earlier estimate of 55,000 at the time of Jesus in *Jerusalem in the Time of Jesus*, 83 n. 24. He later lowered this to 25,000–30,000 (p. 84).

38. Diodorus Siculus 17.52.6. Strabo 16.2.5 estimates that Alexandria and Antioch of Syria are roughly the same size. Dio Chrysostom 32.47 reduces all argument with the simple hyperbole that it is the most populous city of all. Cf. also 29, 35, 37, 41, 87, 94.

39. Fraser, *Ptolemaic Alexandria*, 2:171–72 n. 358. M. Rostovtzeff, *The Social and Economic History of the Hellenistic World* (3 vols.; Oxford: Clarendon, 1941) 2:1138–39, also puts the total population at c. 1,000,000. Diodorus Siculus puts Egypt's total population at 7,000,000 (1.31.8). A century later, Josephus gives 7,500,000 as the total population of Egypt outside of Alexandria (*War* 2.385).

40. D. Delia, "The Population of Roman Alexandria," 275–92, esp. 284, 288, 290. She is followed by R. S. Bagnall and B. W. Frier, *The Demography of Roman Egypt* (Cambridge Studies in Population, Economy and Society in Past Time 23; Cambridge: Cambridge University, 1994), 54.

41. Philo, *Flacc.* 43.

42. Delia, "The Population of Roman Alexandria," 286–88, pointed this out and argued that it referred to the Jewish community. It is, of course, possible that the number refers to the Alexandrian senate, e.g., M. A. H. El-Abbadi, "The *Gerousia* in Roman Egypt," *JEA* 50 (1964) 115, and A. K. Bowman and D. Rathbone, "Cities and Administration in Roman Egypt," *JRS* 82 (1992) 115.

43. Philo, *Flacc.* 55. The explanatory clause can also be rendered: "because the Jews are the principal residents in them." Cf. also *Legat.* 132, 350; Josephus, *War* 2.487–98.

44. On the causes of the first Jewish revolt see M. Goodman, "The First Jewish Revolt: Social Conflict and the Problem of Debt," *JJS* 33 (1982) 417–26, and idem, *The Ruling Class of Judaea: The Origins of Jewish Revolt against Rome AD 66–70* (New York/Cambridge: Cambridge University Press, 1987).

45. See the overview of F. Millar, *The Roman Near East 31 BC–AD 337* (Cambridge, Mass.: Harvard University Press, 1993) 353–59.

46. Josephus, *War* 1–2.

47. Josephus, *War* 7.407–19.

48. Josephus, *War* 2.487–98.

49. For details see A. Fuks, "Aspects of the Jewish Revolts in AD 115–117," *JRS* 51 (1961) 98–104.

50. It is now common to speak of the Romanization of Egypt. For recent work see N. Lewis, "'Greco-Roman Egypt': Fact or Fiction?" *Proceedings of the XII International Congress on Papyrology*, American Studies on Papyrology 7 (1970) 3–14, and idem, "The Romanity of Roman Egypt: A growing consensus," *Atti XVII Congr. Int. Pap.* (1984) 3:1077–84.

51. For details with bibliography see Bowman and Rathbone, "Cities and Administration in Roman Egypt," 115–16, esp. 116.

52. W. F. Adler, "Apion's 'Encomium on Adultery': A Jewish Satire of Greek Paideia in the Pseudo-Clementine *Homilies*," *HUCA* 64 (1993) 15–49.

53. For details see C. F. Holladay, *Fragments from Hellenistic Jewish Authors* (SBLTT; 5 vols.; Scholars Press, 1983–) 2:209–10.

54. I have used the following criteria: ancient *testimonia* (Esther [the colophon], Eupolemus [1 Macc 8:17]); distinctive concerns of Jerusalem (the

Alexander Romance [the meeting between the high priest and Alexander]; 2 Macc [the liberation of the temple]; *Lives of the Prophets* [familiarity with Jerusalem, e.g., 1:1, 9–10 {however, the life of Jeremiah probably came from Egypt}, and a bilingual Hebrew-Greek environment evidenced in the use of scripture]; and distinctive translation techniques (the *megilloth* and Psalms).

55. There are a number of other possibilities. For example, a number of other books of the LXX are debated. Second century BCE: 1 Esdras, Judith, 1 Macc. First century BCE: Pss of Sol, Dan. These are dubious. For details see G. Dorival, M. Harl, and O. Munnich, *La Bible Grecque des Septante: Du judaïsme hellénistique au christianisme ancien* (Initiations au christianisme ancien; Paris: Cerf, 1988) 83–125. One of the problems that has not received sufficient attention with respect to the Palestinian provenance of the LXX is that Philo of Alexandria knows a number of the works which are often situated there, e.g., the Psalter, which he cites fifty times, and Ecclesiastes, which he cites twice (*Spec.* 1.288, 295). Two other works which might belong in Palestine are the *Testament of Solomon* and the *Apocalypse of Adam*. However, these are probably both Christian compositions. The *Apocalypse of Adam* probably stems from the Archontics, an early Gnostic sect which was Christian. See C. W. Hedrick, *The Apocalypse of Adam: A Literary and Source Analysis* (SBLDS 46; Chico, Calif.: Scholars Press, 1980) 209–15. On the Archontics see H. Ch. Puech, "Archontiker," *RAC* 1 (1950) 633–43. Another work that should be mentioned as a possible composition is the *Prayer of Joseph*. For other attempts to situate Jewish documents written in Greek in Palestine see B. Z. Wacholder, *Eupolemus: A Study of Judaeo-Greek Literature* (Monographs of the Hebrew Union College 3; Cincinnati/New York/Los Angeles/Jerusalem: Hebrew Union College, 1974) 259–306, and Hengel, *The Hellenism of Judaea*, 25.

56. On Jason's tomb see L. Y. Rahmani, "Jason's Tomb," *IEJ* 17 (1967) 61–100, and P. Benoit, "L'inscription grecque du tombeau de Jason," *IEJ* 17 (1967) 112–13. The inscription reads: εὐφραίνεστε οἱ ζῶντες| [τ]ὸ δὲ (λοι)πὸ[ν. . .] πεῖν ὅμα φα[γεῖν]. On the donation see B. Isaak, "A Donation for Herod's Temple in Jerusalem," *IEJ* 33 (1983) 86–92. The inscription is from a Paris, son of Akeson, who was living in Rhodes and donated pavement in the temple (in the southern court?). For the temple inscription see *CIJ* 1400 and *OGIS* 598. There are actually two examples (see also *SEG* 8.169). The contents are well known. Cf. also Philo, *Legat.* 212; Josephus, *War* 5.192; *Ant.* 15.417; and Acts 21:27. The Theodotus inscription can be found in *CIJ* 1404 and *SEG* 8.170. There is another inscription from the second century BCE which was apparently an oath by the soldiers in the garrison in the Akra. See S. Applebaum, "A Fragment of a New Hellenistic Inscription from the Old City of Jerusalem," *Jerusalem in the Second Temple Period: Abraham Schalit Memorial Volume* (ed. A. Oppenheimer, U. Rappaport, and M. Stern; Library of the History of the Yishuv in Eretz-Israel; Jerusalem: Ministry of Defense, 1980) 47–60 (Hebrew) and *SEG* 30 (1980) 1695.

57. I have used the catalogue of L. Y. Rahmani, *A Catalogue of Jewish Ossuaries* (*in the Collections of the State of Israel*) (Jerusalem: The Israel Antiquities Authority/The Israel Academy of Sciences and Humanities, 1994) which is hereafter abbreviated *CJO*. Rahmani has a useful Table of Tomb Groups (pp. 304–7) which unfortunately has a number of errors and omissions. The most important earlier collection is *CIJ* 1210–1387. There may be other evidence for the use of Greek in Jerusalem from elsewhere. For example, R. Hachlili, "The Goliath Family in Jericho: Funerary Inscriptions from a First Century AD Jewish Monumental Tomb," *BASOR* 235 (1979) 31–66, has suggested that the 17 Greek, 15 Jewish, and 3 bilingual inscriptions on the ossuaries in this tomb are from a priestly family that resided in Jericho (p. 62). For the ossuaries see E. M. Meyers, *Jewish Ossuaries: Reburial and Rebirth* (Biblica et Orientalia 24; Rome: Biblical Institute, 1971). On the inscriptions see P. W. van der Horst, *Ancient Jewish Epitaphs: An introductory survey of a millennium of Jewish funerary epigraphy* (*300 BCE–700 CE*) (Contributions to Biblical Exegesis and Theology 2; Kampen: Kok Pharos, 1991).

58. 579 is a bilingual inscription of Jewish script and Palmyrene.

59. The most helpful comprehensive list is E. Tov, "Appendix III: A List of the Texts from the Judaean Desert," in *The Dead Sea Scrolls after Fifty Years* (P. W. Flint and J. VanderKam, eds.; 2 vols.; Leiden: E. J. Brill, 1999) 2:669–717. This updates the earlier list in E. Tov, *Companion Volume to the Dead Sea Scrolls Microfiche Edition* (second edition; Leiden: E. J. Brill, 1995). Tov includes 4Q349 Sale of Property? gr in his list, but the editors have now canceled the publication of the fragment. See also the list of papyri in H. M. Cotton, W. E. H. Cockle, and F. G. B. Millar, "The Papyri of the Roman Near East: A Survey," *JRS* 85 (1995) 214–35, esp. 226–35. The Masada material is in H. M. Cotton and J. Geiger, *Masada II: The Yigael Yadin Excavation 1963–65* (*Final Reports*). *The Latin and Greek Documents* (Jerusalem: Israel Exploration Society, 1989). The material from Mishmar, Gweir, and Nar is available in S. J. Pfann et al., *Qumran Cave 4 XXVI; Cryptic Texts and Miscellanea, Part I* (DJD 36; Oxford: Clarendon, 2000). The Murabba'at material is in P. Benoit, J. T. Milik, and R. de Vaux, *Les Grottes de Murabba'at* (DJD 2; Oxford: Clarendon, 1961). The Qumran material is in P. Skehan, E. Ulrich, and J. E. Sanderson, *Qumran Cave 4. IV: Paleo-Hebrew and Greek Biblical Manuscripts* (DJD 9; Oxford: Clarendon, 1992); M. Baillet, J. T. Milik, and R. de Vaux, *Les "petites grottes" de Qumran: Exploration de la falaise, les grottes 2Q, 3Q, 5Q, 7Q à 10Q, le rouleau de cuivre* (DJD 3; 2 vols.; Oxford: Clarendon, 1962); E. Puech, "Notes sur les fragments grecs du manuscrit 7Q4=1 Hénoch 103 et 105," *RB* 103 (1996) 592–600; E. A. Muro, "The Greek Fragments of Enoch from Qumran Cave 7 (*7Q4, 7Q8, & 7Q12=7QEngr=Enoch 103:3–4, 7–8*) *Revue de Qumrân* 70 (1997) 307–12; and E. Puech, "Sept fragments grecs de la *Lettre d'Hénoch* (*1 Hén* 100, 103 et 105) dans la grotte 7 de Qumrân

(=7QHéngr)," *Revue de Qumrân* 70 (1997) 313–23, for the identifications of some of the fragments in cave 7. The Sdeir, Hever, Seiyal material is in N. Lewis, *The Documents from the Bar Kokhba Period in the Cave of Letters* (*Greek Papyri*) (JDS 2; Jerusalem: Israel Exploration Society, 1989); E. Tov, *The Greek Minor Prophets Scroll from Naḥal Ḥever: 8 HevXII gr* (DJD 8; Oxford: Clarendon, 1990); and H. M. Cotton and A. Yardeni, *Aramaic, Hebrew and Greek Documentary Texts from Naḥal Ḥever and Other Sites: With an Appendix Containing Alleged Qumran Texts* (*The Seiyâl Collection*) (DJD 27; Oxford: Clarendon, 1997). I am indebted to my colleague James VanderKam for assistance in collecting this information.

60. I published this earlier in "Jewish Self-Definition in Alexandria," 2–8, where I offered a brief rationale for my placement of these documents.

61. I have used the following criteria for situating these works in Alexandria: ancient testimonia (e.g., the LXX=Torah [*Ep. Arist.*; Sir, Prologue; Philo, *Mos.* 2.25–44]; Aristobulus [2 Macc 1:10]; Sosates [*Excerpta Latina Barbari* in C. Frick, ed., *Chronica Minora* {Leipzig: B. G. Teubner, 1892} 278 ll. 24–29 cited with a discussion in S. J. D. Cohen, "Sosates the Jewish Homer," *HTR* 74 {1981} 391–96; and Philo of Alexandria [Josephus, *AJ* 18.257–60]); distinctive Alexandrian concerns (Pseudo-Phocylides 102, a prohibition against human dissection which was practiced only in Alexandria; *T. Job* which has striking similarities to the Therapeutae; 3 Macc 2:28, 30, which I understand to refer to the struggle in Alexandria under Rome; and *Sib. Or.* 11.219–20, 233–35 [panegyric on Alexandria and her founding]); the literary character of the work (Demetrius, who is the first Jewish author to use the LXX and whose work is a Jewish parallel to Eratosthenes in Alexandria; Ezekiel the Tragedian, who knew the tragedies of Euripides and Aeschylus well enough to incorporate their techniques; and Philo the Epic Poet, who knew Greek epic poetry); the geographical setting of the work (Artapanus, *Ep. Arist.*, Ezekiel, Joseph, and Aseneth, 3 Macc, Wis, *Jannes and Jambres*, *Sib. Or.* 11, *H. Jos.*, *Sib. Or.* 3.1–96, are all set in or deal almost exclusively with Egypt; *Ep. Arist.* and 3 Macc concentrate on Alexandria specifically; the tract preserved in Pseudo-Clement uses an Alexandrian, Apion, as the major figure); the textual transmission of the work (Pseudo-Orphica is cited in Aristobulus; Gnomologion of Pseudo-Epic Greek Poets is cited in Aristobulus; Aristobulus is preserved by Eusebius, who drew from the library which Origen brought to Caesaerea from Alexandria; Pseudo-Hecataeus is cited by Clement of Alexandria, the Gnomologion of Dramatic Verses from which Pseudo-Hecataeus drew his citation from Sophocles was known in Alexandria, if my placement of Pseudo-Hecataeus is correct; *Jannes and Jambres* is mentioned first by Origen [*Comm on Matt* 27:9 {although see 2 Tim 3:8}]); and strong thematic connections (Aristeas explicitly builds on the LXX text of Job; *Sib. Or.* 3.1–45 is very similar to Philo; 3.75–92, shares a common assessment of Cleopatra with 11.243–60).

62. The standard collection of inscriptions is W. Horbury and D. Noy, *Jewish Inscriptions of Graeco-Roman Egypt: With an Index of the Jewish Inscriptions of Egypt and Cyrenaica* (Cambridge: Cambridge University Press, 1992), which I have abbreviated *JIGRE*. The papyri are in V. A. Tcherikover, A. Fuks, M. Stern, and D. M. Lewis, *Corpus Papyrorum Judaicarum* (3 vols.; Cambridge, Mass.: Harvard University Press, 1957–64), which I have abbreviated *CPJ*.

63. On the transmission of the Philonic corpus see D. T. Runia, *Philo in Early Christian Literature: A Survey* (CRINT 2.3.3; Assen/Minneapolis: Van Gorcum/Fortress, 1993) 16–31.

64. On these see M. J. Schroyer, "Alexandrian Jewish Literalists," *JBL* 55 (1936) 261–84; D. M. Hay, "Philo's References to Other Allegorists," *SPhilo* 6 (1979–1980) 41–75; idem, "References to Other Exegetes," in *Both Literal and Allegorical: Studies in Philo of Alexandria's* Questions and Answers on Genesis and Exodus (ed. D. M. Hay; BJS 232; Atlanta: Scholars Press, 1991) 81–97.

65. A great deal has been written about the languages in Palestine. Some of the more important recent treatments include J. Fitzmyer, "The Languages of Palestine in the First Century A.D.," *CBQ* 32 (1970) 501–31; S. Safrai and M. Stern, *The Jewish People in the First Century: Historical Geography, Political History, Social, Cultural and Religious Life and Institutions* (CRINT 1.2; Assen: Van Gorcum/Philadelphia: Fortress, 1987) 1007–64; and J. Barr, "Hebrew, Aramaic and Greek in the Hellenistic Age," in *The Cambridge History of Judaism* (eds. W. D. Davies and L. Finkelstein; Cambridge: Cambridge University Press, 1989) 2:79–114.

66. E.g., Kidron Valley, Tomb a, probably represents a family from Cyrene. See N. Avigad, "A Depository of Inscribed Ossuaries in the Kidron Valley," *IEJ* 12 (1962) 1–12. She thinks that this Cyrenean family came to Jerusalem and was part of the Cyrenean community in Jerusalem that is attested in the NT (Acts 6:9; Mark 15:21).

67. *Contra* Schürer, *The History of the Jewish People*, 2:74–80. Some of the most important works that concur with this general assessment include S. Lieberman, *Hellenism in Jewish Palestine: Studies in the Literary Transmission of Palestine in the I Century BCE–IV Century CE* (New York: Jewish Theological Seminary of America, 1962[2]); idem, *Greek in Jewish Palestine: Studies in the Life and Manners of Jewish Palestine in the II–IV Centuries C.E.* (New York: Philipp Feldheim, 2d ed. 1965); and J. N. Sevenster, *Do You Know Greek? How Much Greek Could the First Jewish Christians Have Known?* (NovTSup 19; Leiden: E. J. Brill, 1968).

68. *JIRGE* nos. 3, 4, 5 (third century BCE); 15, 17 (bilingual from the second century ce). Cf. also nos. 118 (Al-Minya), 119 (Antinopolis), and 133 (?) which all date from the second century CE and later.

69. Cf. also Philo, *Flacc.* 39, where the populace knows the Aramaic word *mar*. This does not, however, establish the presence of Aramaic-speaking Jews

in Alexandria any more than the use of *Maranatha* in 1 Cor 16:22 proves that the Corinthians spoke Aramaic. Cf. also Acts 21:37–38 which could mean that the author assumes Aramaic was spoken in Egypt.

70. So also W. Horbury, "Jewish Inscriptions and Jewish Literature in Egypt, with Special Reference to Ecclesiasticus," in J. W. van Henten and P. W. van der Horst, eds., *Studies in Jewish Epigraphy* (AGJU 21; Leiden: E. J. Brill, 1994) 12–21. Cf. also Barr, "Hebrew, Aramaic and Greek in the Hellenistic Age," 101–2.

71. *Ep. Arist.* esp. 307–11; Philo, *Mos.* 2.25–44. On the feast see Philo, *Mos.* 2.41–43.

72. The point is disputed, but the evidence is against his knowledge of Hebrew in my judgment. See V. Nikiprowetzky, *Le commentaire de l'écriture chez Philon d'Alexandrie* (ALGHJ 11; Leiden: E. J. Brill, 1977).

73. *Contra* Hengel, *The Hellenization of Judaea,* 29.

74. Phil 3:5 in the credentials list in vv. 4–6.

75. On these letters see Y. Yadin, *Bar-Kokhba: The Rediscovery of the Legendary Hero of the Second Jewish Revolt against Rome* (New York: Random House, 1971) 130–32. Letters associated with Bar-Kokhba have been found at Naḥal Ḥever (5/6Hev 52 pap Letter gr and 5/6Hev 53 pap Letter gr [see Y. Yadin, "Expedition D," *IEJ* 11 (1961) 36–51, esp. 42–44, 50]) and at Nahal Mishmar (1 Mish 2 [see B. Lifshitz, "The Greek Documents from Nahal Seelim and Nahal Mishmar," *IEJ* 11 (1961) 53–62]), and at Seiyal (34 Se 4; 34 Se 5). Y. Yadin thought that some of the letters at Masada also belonged to Bar Kokhba (Y. Yadin, "The Excavation of Masada—1963/64: Preliminary Report," *IEJ* 15 [1965] 1–120, esp. 110).

76. 1 Macc 1:14–15; 2 Macc 4:9–17.

77. Josephus, *Ant.* 19.329; cf. 328–31.

78. Josephus, *Ant.* 15.267–79, esp. 267 and 268.

79. Josephus, *War* 2.44; *Ant.* 17.255. He built an amphitheater in Jericho (*War* 1.667).

80. He makes this point repeatedly. Cf. Josephus, *Ant.* 15.267, 268, 274, 275.

81. The theater has not been found, although we *may* have two "theater tickets". For bibliography see A. Segal, *Theatres in Roman Palestine and Provinica Arabia* (Mnemosyne Supplements 140; Leiden: E. J. Brill, 1995) 4 n. 6.

82. On the prerequisites of what a city should have, see the comments of Pausanias 10.4.1, who lists government offices, a gymnasium, a theater, an agora, and a fountain.

83. For details see D. W. Roller, *The Building Program of Herod the Great* (Berkeley: University of California Press, 1998) 90–94, 117–18.

84. Josephus, *War* 2.344; 5.144; 6.325.

85. 2 Macc 4:9.

86. So E. S. Gruen, *Heritage and Hellenism: The Reinvention of Jewish Tradition* (Hellenistic Culture and Society 30; Berkeley: University of California Press, 1998) 31. Cf. also Roller, *The Building Program of Herod the Great,* 178.

87. So G. Cornfeld, *Josephus, The Jewish War: Newly translated with extensive commentary and archaeological background illustrations* (Grand Rapids, Mich.: Zondervan, 1982) *in loco* (2.344; 5.144).

88. Cf. also Josephus, *War* 1.143 (where it is not named) and 6.325.

89. Josephus, *War* 1.422–23. Cf. *Ant.* 12.241; 16:314.

90. So also Roller, *The Building Program of Herod the Great,* 117: "Gymnasia were the most common Herodian athletic constructions, but they seem to have been built only in Syria. Although a gymnasium had been built in Jerusalem as early as the second century BC, such a construction was still seen as a conspicuous example of excessive hellenization, something Herod would have sought to avoid. But he constructed gymnasia in the more appropriate environmnet of the hellenized cities of Syria. . . ."

91. Josephus, *Ant.* 15.278

92. Josephus, *Ant.* 17.149–67.

93. Josephus, *War* 2.170. Cf. 169–74. On paganism in Judaea see Safrai and Stern, *The Jewish People in the First Century,* 1.2:1065–1100.

94. On wrestling and boxing see *Agr.* 113–14; *Prob.* 26, 110; on races see *Agr.* 115; on chariot races see *Prov.* 2.58.

95. Philo, *Ebr.* 177.

96. Philo, *Prob.* 141. The play was Euripides' *Auge.* Cf. also the reference in *Anim.* 23.

97. *Ep. Arist.* 284. There is a textual problem here. The mss read πλίζε-ται, which the editors have responsibly replaced with παίζεται.

98. Philo, *Spec. Laws* 2.230.

99. *CPJ* 151.

100. On this question see P. Borgen, "'Yes,' 'No,' 'How Far?': The Participation of Jews and Christians in Pagan Cults," in T. Engberg-Pedersen, *Paul in His Hellenistic Context* (Minneapolis: Fortress, 1995) 30–59.

101. Philo, *Spec.* 1.315–16. On the death penalty in Philo see T. Seland, *Establishment Violence in Philo and Luke: A Study of Non-Conformity to the Torah and Jewish Vigilante Reactions* (Biblical Interpretation Series 15; Leiden: E. J. Brill, 1995).

102. For exceptions see Dositheos (*CPJ* 127a-e; 3 Macc 1:3); 3 Macc 2:31–32; and Tiberius Julius Alexander.

103. In Josephus, *Ag. Apion* 2.65. Cf. also *Ant.* 12.126 where the residents of Asia Minor demanded that "if the Jews were of the same status they would have to worship the same gods."

104. Philo, *Legat.* 357.

105. On this text see P. W. van der Horst, "'Thou shalt not revile the gods': The LXX Translation of Ex 22:28 (27), Its Background and Influence," *SPhA* 5 (1993) 1–8.

106. Philo, *Prov.* 2.64. On Philo's view of pilgrimages to Jerusalem see Y. Amir, "Philo's Version of the Pilgrimage to Jerusalem," *Jerusalem in the Second Temple Period*, 154–65.

107. On Alexander see Josephus, *War* 2.201–5. On Nicanor see *CIJ* 1256 or *OGIS* 599.

108. I want to thank the participants in the conference for their comments, especially Martin Goodman who offered a formal response.

Epilogue

MARTIN GOODMAN

The papers in this volume demonstrate the impressive consensus achieved over the past twenty-five years among scholars of very different backgrounds in the light of the evidence and arguments presented in Martin Hengel's magisterial *Judaism and Hellenism*. No one now would want to deny that many Jews in Palestine were acculturated to some aspects of Greek language, art, commerce, philosophy, and literature by the end of the third century BCE. The questions which remain and which have dominated the conference papers do not challenge this consensus, but they are no less important. Major issues are still unresolved. Which sort of Jews imbibed Greek culture more than others? How much Greek culture did they absorb? To what extent can variations be traced between places and over time? Above all, how much difference did Hellenism make to the life and religion of any Jew?

If these questions still await answers, it is only in part because they have not often enough been asked in the past, for the search for solutions is inherently difficult. None of the answers can be found simply through the collection and analysis of empirical evidence, and in this field, in which a claim that Judaism was or was not hellenized in antiquity can often mask a contemporary theological stance, reliance by scholars on instinct as a guide to interpretation is particularly dangerous.

Thus, for instance, it has seemed obvious to some that Jews living as a minority in Diaspora communities were more likely to imbibe the surrounding culture than those in the homeland, but on reflection it is evident that an embattled minority might in theory have rejected Greek mores more vigorously than the relaxed community in the land of Israel, where cosmopolitan culture was brought to Jerusalem by pious pilgrims whose use of Greek self-evidently did not impede their devotion to Judaism. So, too, many have thought that Greek Judaism must have faded away after c. 100 CE because no Graeco-Jewish literature survives from later antiquity to match the writings from before that time, but again it is evident on reflection that the survival of Jewish writings in Greek from the Second Temple period was almost entirely brought about by the interests of early Christians in preserving their works for religious purposes and that since a plethora of Jewish inscriptions survives from the late Roman period it is implausible, to say the least, that Jewish Greek literature died out entirely. It is simply a sad fact that neither Christians (who after the first century had their own literature) nor rabbinic Jews (who operated in Hebrew and Aramaic) had any interest in writing down what Greek Jews wrote.

Such examples simply demonstrate how easy it is to jump to probably erroneous conclusions in this difficult field. Far-reaching claims may be based on little more than a circular argument. So, for instance, a contrast between the alleged deep Hellenization of Alexandrian Jewry and the more superficial Hellenization of Jerusalem sounds plausible enough, but it is not reinforced by enumerating the literary works ascribed to each city by modern scholars, since those ascriptions are themselves often based on the original contrast: thus the works of Demetrius the Chronographer, Philo the Epic Poet and Ezekiel the Tragedian are frequently ascribed to Alexandria primarily because of their Greek nature, but all of them might have originated in Jerusalem, as might the Wisdom of Solomon and the Jewish fragments which purport to have been composed by Orpheus and various epic poets. Here again some headway is possible by taking the issue of transmission into account, since the Alexandrian Jewish writings evidently aroused the interest, in later centuries, of Alexandrian Christians such as Clement, who was devoted to Philo and displayed an encyclopedic knowledge of literature of diverse kinds, whereas the Jerusalem traditions were mostly preserved by the rabbis and thus only in Hebrew and Aramaic.

Scholars may with due caution prove able to avoid at least the more vicious forms of circularity, but only by seeking more recondite and precisely placed and dated evidence, and the great advances of recent years in the publication and analysis of inscriptions are thus much to be welcomed. However, the significance of this evidence, too, may be judged differently in each case. Thus, not much can be learned about Jewish use of the Greek language from the fact that the warning inscriptions set up in the Temple were in Greek, since these inscriptions were specifically aimed at gentiles. By contrast, rather more could be made of the significance of the occasional inscriptions in which a full text in one language coexists with a brief text in another, suggesting that one of the languages used is not, or may not be, fully understood by all those to whom the inscription is addressed and that one of the languages used is essentially only symbolic. Perhaps the most striking aspect of Jewish culture in early Roman Palestine is the apparent insouciance with which Greek is used alongside Hebrew and Aramaic: all efforts to find a regular pattern to explain particular language choices have so far proved inconclusive.

The apparent unselfconsciousness of Jewish appropriation of Greek cultural forms, according to much of the evidence, contrasts to Jewish attitudes to Roman culture from the time of Herod, a subject still too little studied despite the obvious impact of Rome on Jews and Judaism in this period. The city of Jerusalem was transformed by Herod and by Agrippa I as much along Roman as Greek lines, but when the city was finally taken altogether out of Jewish hands by Hadrian it was as the Roman colony of Aelia Capitolina, in which presumably the language of administration was, at least at the beginning, Latin rather than Greek.

The Roman destruction of the Temple in 70 CE promoted an image of Rome in rabbinic literature as the hereditary enemy Edom. Greek rulers of the Hellenistic period suffered similar abuse in earlier Jewish literature, but there is curiously little evidence, despite numerous comments about Greeks themselves, that any Jews saw Greek culture—that is, Hellenization—as any sort of threat to Jewish society after the rhetoric surrounding the Maccabean revolt. And, as has long been noted, the Hasmonaeans themselves, who based their right to rule on their opposition to Hellenism during the revolt, rapidly become Hellenophiles.

All of which may suggest that in the end the Hellenization of the land of Israel in the late Second Temple period may have had less effect on Judaism than we commonly assume, precisely because it was so ubiquitous. The Greek language could be so thoroughly adopted by some Jews that it became a Jewish language itself, as it must have seemed for those gentiles who converted to Judaism in one of the Greek-speaking Jewish communities in the Latin West of the Roman Empire: for them, the Jewish sacred book was the Septuagint. The most remarkable feature of Jewish linguistic history in this period is not so much the adoption of Greek by Jews as their failure to make greater use of the national language, Hebrew, which still carried immense symbolic significance (as shown by its use on the coinage issued by the rebels in the First Revolt) and was still apparently available for colloquial use if the evidence of the secular documents from the Judaean Desert can be taken as representative. That the issue is far more than the attraction of Greek is clear from the spread of Aramaic at the expense of Hebrew; it is curious that no claims are generally made about the impact of Aramaic on Jewish culture comparable to the claims so often made about Hellenization.

It may well be that the triumph of Martin Hengel's thesis will in a way mark the end of the longstanding question to which he addressed himself. The Maccabean revolt was acclaimed by the victors as a victory for Judaism against Hellenism. For later Jews, such as the supremely hellenized Philo, such rhetoric was nonsensical. For him Hellenism was simply the normal mode of discourse in the modern age, and the notion that Jews might wish to fight against it would have been as bizarre as to suggest to an orthodox American Jew today that religious devotion might be prejudiced by the use of the English language and a computer. In the end it was precisely the triumph of Hellenism that deprived it of its sting.

Contributors

SHAYE J. D. COHEN

Shaye J. D. Cohen is the Samuel Ungerleider Professor of Judaic Studies and Professor of Religious Studies at Brown University. He is the author of *Josephus in Galilee and Rome: His Vita and Development as a Historian* (1979), *From the Maccabees to the Mishnah* (1987), *The Beginnings of Jewishness* (1999), editor of *The Jewish Family in Antiquity* (1993), *Studies in the Cult of Yahweh by Morton Smith* (1996), *The Synoptic Problem in Rabbinic Literature* (2000), co-editor of *Ancient Studies in Memory of Elias Bickerman* (1987), *The State of Jewish Studies* (1989), *Diasporas in Antiquity* (1993), and author of numerous articles on the history of Judaism, rabbinic law, Josephus, Judaism and Hellenism, and early Christianity. He is currently working on a study of circumcision and gender in Judaism.

JOHN J. COLLINS

John J. Collins is Holmes Professor of Old Testament Criticism and Interpretation at Yale Divinity School. He previously taught at the University of Chicago and the University of Notre Dame. He has served as editor of the *Journal of Biblical Literature* and as president of the Catholic Biblical Association. He is currently vice-president of the Society of Biblical Literature. His books include *Daniel* (1993); *The Scepter and the Star* (1995); *Jewish Wisdom in the Hellenistic Age* (1997); *Apocalypticism in the Dead Sea Scrolls* (1997); *The Apocalyptic Imagination* (2nd ed., 1998); and *Between Athens and Jerusalem* (2nd ed.; 1999). He is co-editor of the three-volume *Encyclopedia of Apoca-*

lypticism (with B. McGinn and S. Stein; 1998) and of *Religion in the Dead Sea Scrolls* (with R. Kugler; 2000).

ROBERT DORAN

Robert Doran is Professor of Religion at Amherst College. He is author of *Temple Propaganda: The Purpose and Character of 2 Maccabees* (1981), *The Lives of Simeon Stylites* (1992) and *The Birth of a Worldview: Early Christianity in Its Jewish and Pagan Context* (1995).

SEAN FREYNE

Sean Freyne is currently Professor of Theology at Trinity College, Dublin. He has also taught in the USA and Australia. His scholarly publications include *Galilee from Alexander the Great to Hadrian* (1980, reprint 1998); *Galilee, Jesus and the Gospels: Literary Approaches and Historical Investigations* (1988) and most recently *Galilee and the Gospel: Collected Essays* (2000). He is a member of the Royal Irish Academy and a Trustee of the Chester Beatty Library, Dublin, and has served on the editorial board of *Concilium: An International Journal of Theology* since 1990.

MARTIN GOODMAN

Martin Goodman is Professor of Jewish Studies at Oxford University, a Fellow of Wolfson College, and a Fellow of the Oxford Centre of Hebrew and Jewish Studies. He is the author of *The Ruling Class of Judaea* (1987), *Mission and Conversion: Proselytizing in the Religious History of the Roman Empire* (1994), and other books on Jewish and Roman history.

ERICH S. GRUEN

Erich S. Gruen is Gladys Rehard Wood Professor of History and Classics at the University of California, Berkeley. His publications include *The Last Generation of the Roman Republic* (1974), *The Hellenistic World and the Coming of Rome* (1984), *Studies in Greek Culture and Roman Policy* (1990), *Culture and National Identity in Republican Rome* (1992) and *Heritage and Hellenism: The Reinvention of Jewish Tradition* (1998). He is completing a book on the Jewish Diaspora in the Greco-Roman period.

MARTIN HENGEL

Martin Hengel is Professor Emeritus of New Testament and Ancient Judaism at the University of Tübingen, where he also directed the Institute for Ancient Judaism and Hellenistic Religion. He has written voluminously on the New Testament and Ancient Judaism. Books directly relevant to this volume include *Judaism and Hellenism: Studies in Their Encounter in Palestine during the Early Hellenistic Period* (1974), *Jews, Greeks and Barbarians: Aspects of the Hellenization of Judaism in the Pre-Christian Period* (1980), *The Hellenization of Judaea in the First Century after Christ* (1989), *Die Septuaginta zwischen Judentum and Christentum* (1994), *Judaica et Hellenistica: Kleine Schriften I* (1996) and *Judaica, Hellenistica et Christiana: Kleine Schriften II* (1998).

JAN WILLEM VAN HENTEN

Jan Willem van Henten holds the chair in New Testament and Hellenistic Jewish Literature at the University of Amsterdam. He is director of the Netherlands School for Advanced Studies in Theology and Religion (NOSTER). His publications include *Die Entstehung der jüdischen Martyrologie* (editor, with B. A. G. M. Dehandschutter and H. J. W. van der Klaauw, 1989), *Studies in Early Jewish Epigraphy* (editor with P. W. van der Horst, 1994) and *The Maccabean Martyrs as Saviours of the Jewish People: A Study of 2 and 4 Maccabees* (1997).

PIETER W. VAN DER HORST

Pieter W. van der Horst is Professor of New Testament Exegesis, Early Christian Literature, and the Jewish and Hellenistic World of Early Christianity at the University of Utrecht. He is a member of the Royal Academy of Arts and Sciences in the Netherlands. He has published widely on early Christianity, ancient Judaism, and Hellenistic philosophy and religion, including *The Sentences of Pseudo-Phocylides* (1978), *Chaeremon: Egyptian Priest and Stoic Philosopher* (1984; 2nd ed. 1987), *Essays on the Jewish World of Early Christianity* (1990), *Ancient Jewish Epitaphs* (1991), *Hellenism, Judaism, Christianity: Essays on Their Interaction* (1994; 2nd ed. 1998), *Mozes, Plato, Jesus: Studies over the wereld van het vroege christendom* (2000) and *Jewish Hellenism and Related Studies* (2001).

EDGAR KRENTZ

Edgar Krentz is Christ Seminary in Exile–Seminex Professor of New Testament Emeritus at the Lutheran School of Theology at Chicago. He is author of *Galatians: Augsburg New Testament Commentary* (1985), and *The Historical-Critical Method: Guides to Biblical Scholarship* (1975) and numerous articles and book chapters.

TESSA RAJAK

Tessa Rajak is Reader in Classics at Reading University in England. Her publications include *Josephus: The Historian and His Society* (1983), and *Jews among Pagans and Christians in the Roman Empire* (1992) and *The Jewish Dialogue with Greece and Rome: Studies in Cultural and Social Interaction* (2000).

GREGORY E. STERLING

Gregory E. Sterling is Professor of New Testament and Christian Origins at the University of Notre Dame. He is author of *Historiography and Self-Definition: Josephos, Luke-Acts and Apologetic Historiography* (1992). He is the co-editor of the *Studia Philonica Annual* and the general editor of the Philo of Alexandria commentary series. He is currently working on *The Jewish Plato: Philo of Alexandria, Greek-Speaking Judaism, and Christian Origins*.

JAMES C. VANDERKAM

James C. VanderKam is John A. O'Brien Professor of Hebrew Scriptures at the University of Notre Dame. His books include *The Book of Jubilees: A Critical Text* (1989); *The Dead Sea Scrolls Today* (1994); *Enoch: A Man for All Generations* (1995); *From Revelation to Canon: Studies in the Hebrew Bible and Second Temple Literature* (1999) and *An Introduction to Early Judaism* (2000). He is co-editor of *The Dead Sea Scrolls after Fifty Years* (with P. W. Flint, 1999) and of *The Encyclopedia of the Dead Sea Scrolls* (with L. H. Schiffman, 2000). He has served as consulting editor for several volumes in the series *Discoveries in the Judaean Desert*.

Index of
Ancient Authors
and Texts

PAPYROLOGICAL AND INSCRIPTIONAL SOURCES

Index of
Modern Authors